MW01626789

Samuel Rosenberg

SAMUEL
ROSENBERG

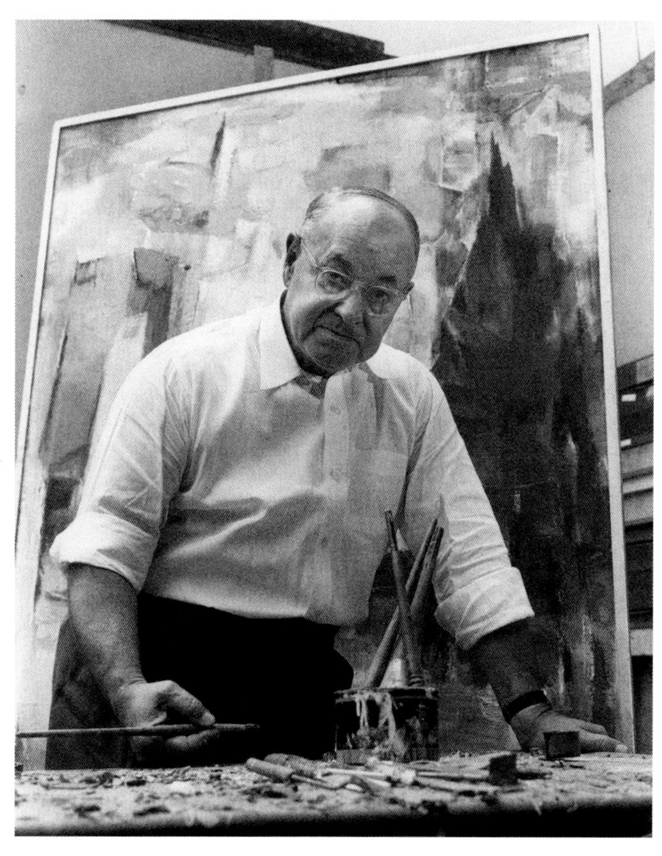

Portrait of a Painter

Barbara L. Jones

UNIVERSITY OF PITTSBURGH PRESS
in cooperation with CARNEGIE MUSEUM OF ART

Published by University of Pittsburgh Press, Pittsburgh, Pa., 15260

Manufactured in the United States of America
Printed on acid-free paper
10 9 8 7 6 5 4 3 2 1
ISBN 0-8229-4213-5

PUBLISHED IN COOPERATION WITH CARNEGIE MUSEUM OF ART, THROUGH THE BEAL PUBLICATIONS FUND.

This book is made possible with support from the Rockwell Foundation and PPG Industries Foundation.

Photo credits: Black and white reproductions—figures 2–5, 7–10, 14–18, 20–27, 29, 34, 38–39, 46–47: Richard A. Stoner, Latrobe, Pa.; figure 32: Peter S. Jacobs, Montclair, N.J. Color plates—All color plates, except where listed below: Richard A. Stoner, Latrobe, Pa.; plates 8, 13: David M. Peters, Vienna, Austria; plate 9: Thomas DuBrock, Houston, Tex.; plate 26: Graphic Color Service, Inc., Fairfield, Maine; plate 31: Kim Harrington Photography, Emeryville, Ca.; plate 40: Dean A. Beasom, Springfield, Va.; plate 58: Booth Studio, Sarasota, Fla.; plate 68: Robert Fogt Photography, St. Paul, Minn. Photograph for figure 19 is from the Kingsley Association Collection, 70:5, Archives Services Center, University of Pittsburgh. Photographs for figures 40, 41, 43–45, and 48–49 are courtesy of Arline Rosenberg (Mrs. Murray).

CONTENTS

FOREWORD

From its inception in the late nineteenth century, Carnegie Museum of Art has understood its obligation to the communities of artists living in western Pennsylvania. Not only are they among the principal beneficiaries of its once annual, now triennial, Carnegie International exhibition, but their work also distinguishes the museum's collections. On both of these counts, Samuel Rosenberg was an exemplary Pittsburgh-based artist, deeply informed about contemporary art by Carnegie Internationals and by the paintings and sculpture collected by the museum from this venerable series. Rosenberg's own work is also richly represented in the museum's collection. His changes and constancies as an artist are well documented in the many paintings and drawings owned here; more transitory was his immense influence. Thus, Carnegie Museum of Art is especially pleased to have supported the research and publication of this catalog. We are grateful to the Westmoreland Museum of American Art and its director, Judith O'Toole, and curator, Barbara L. Jones, for realizing and presenting the survey exhibition this book amplifies. Barbara Jones willingly accepted our invitation to author this monograph and has provided an insightful and accurate study of Rosenberg as an artist and a teacher. Her diligence in researching his life and artistic contributions along with her successful efforts in locating students and collectors of Rosenberg have combined to provide this important study. Just as creativity lies at the heart of both our museums, the stories of singularly creative people like Samuel Rosenberg are central to our region's identity and worth.

Richard Armstrong

THE HENRY J. HEINZ II DIRECTOR,

CARNEGIE MUSEUM OF ART

PREFACE

For his in-depth research, which laid the foundation for this publication, and his unfaltering commitment to his father's enduring legacy as an artist, this book is dedicated to the memory of Murray Z. Rosenberg.

The idea for this book was a collaboration between Carnegie Museum of Art, the Westmoreland Museum of American Art, and University of Pittsburgh Press, and was conceived in complement to an exhibition of Samuel Rosenberg's work presented at the Westmoreland Museum of American Art in Greensburg, Pennsylvania, from June 29 to October 19, 2003. This publication is the culmination of four years of research on the artistic development of Samuel Rosenberg. The essay chronicles Rosenberg's life experiences and artistic vision, while the accompanying sidebars provide in-depth information on the context of the place and time in which Rosenberg lived and worked. The biography is a quick reference guide to the chronology of the artist's life, as well as exhibitions, awards, and memberships. Throughout the book, figures and plates are captioned with title, year, size, and media. All of the reproduced works can be cross-referenced to the catalog in the back of the book.

My gratitude, first and foremost, goes to Libbie Rosenberg, without whose tireless efforts to maintain a record of her husband's achievements this publication would not have been possible. Second, I would like to acknowledge Sam and Libbie's only son, Murray. While his desire to see his father's work published as a catalogue raisonné in conjunction with a retrospective exhibition has not materialized exactly as he envisioned it, I hope that he would be pleased with the results. I feel that Murray has been with me, looking over my shoulder, nearly every step of the way. His prior efforts on behalf of his father have been a tremendous help to me, allowing me time to pursue my research on the paintings without having to recreate the artist's biography. My sincerest gratitude goes to Arline Rosenberg, Murray's wife, who sadly had to assume responsibility for the project following his death in 1996, and has indeed risen to the challenge. She has been not only supportive of every aspect of this project, but generously opened her home and the family archive in Asheville, North Carolina, for my study purposes. She trusted me from the first day we met to create the kind of in-depth publication that Murray would have accomplished, had he been given more time. Arline and I have attained a closeness that has brought me even closer to Murray and Sam, both of whom I wish I could have known.

I am especially grateful to Richard Armstrong, director of Carnegie Museum of Art, for selecting me for this project, for his confidence in me as an art historian, for his recognition of Sam's artistic abilities, and for the museum's financial support to make this publication a reality, and Maureen Rolla, assistant director, for her patient oversight throughout this lengthy process. My thanks also to Cynthia Miller director of the University of Pittsburgh Press, whose collaboration on this project will provide a broader public access to Rosenberg's work. Thanks also to Deborah Meade, Ann Walston, Dennis Lloyd, and the rest of the staff at the University of Pittsburgh Press for their contributions to this project. I would particularly like to thank Judith O'Toole, director and CEO of the Westmoreland Museum of American Art, for recognizing the need to be an art historian as well as a curator and for her ongoing support through every phase of this project. My appreciation, too, to the Westmoreland Museum of American Art Board of Trustees for their continued support.

I am indebted to Ruth Westerman, the artist's niece, whose assistance has been invaluable to this project from the very beginning. I am grateful to her for creating the momentum on which this project has progressed. Her efforts in the organization of two previous exhibitions and a symposium on Sam's work have not only contributed to the public's awareness of the artist, but have assisted in perpetuating Sam's legacy in Pittsburgh. I appreciate her and Dr. Walter Jacob for suggesting the idea of a publication to Richard Armstrong.

My continued thanks to Joel and Dorothy Rosenberg, Sam's grandson and granddaughter-in-law, who opened their home in Asheville so that I could have access to so many of Sam's paintings, and to Sue Rosenberg Wieser, Sam's granddaughter in Vienna, for her willingness to share his paintings with a larger audience and for her kind words.

My thanks to Sam Berkovitz of Concept Art Gallery for his ongoing assistance and support; to Richard Stoner, whose expert photography ensures that Sam's paintings are reproduced as close to reality as possible; to the photographers I enlisted outside the state to do the same: Kim

Harrington, California; Robert Fogt, Minnesota; Dean Beasom, Virginia; Thomas DuBrock, Texas; Booth Studio, Florida; Peter Jacobs, New Jersey; David M. Peters, Vienna, Austria; and Peter Lunder, for his assistance with photography in Maine. I also want to extend my thanks to the four contributors to this publication: Barbara Burstin, Eric Davin, Laurence Glasco, and Bennard Perlman, whose essays have helped to place Rosenberg's art in a broader context.

This ambitious project would not have been possible without the assistance of so many individuals in both the public and private sectors. To all of them who were willing to share their time and information on the artist and his work with me, I would like to express my sincere appreciation. Each one has contributed to this ongoing art historical investigation: Lulu Lippincott, Linda Batis, Heather Domencic, and Allison Revello at Carnegie Museum of Art; Susan Melnick, Steve Dell, and staff of the Senator John Heinz Regional History Center Archives; Jennie Bedford and Adrien Finley of the Carnegie Mellon University Archives; Patricia Duck and her staff at the University of Pittsburgh Greensburg Campus Millstein Library; Ray Anne Lockard, Marcia Rostek, and staff of the Frick Fine Arts Library, University of Pittsburgh; Josie Piller and David Wilkins, University of Pittsburgh Art Collection; Irma Smith, Archivist, Chatham College; Susan Seese, Somerset Historical Society; Rob Ruck, history department, University of Pittsburgh; Miriam Meislik and other staff at the University of Pittsburgh Archives; Kathy Logan, Cathy Tack, and reference staff in the music and art department, social sciences department, and Pennsylvania room of the Carnegie Library; Museum of Modern Art and Whitney Museum of Art reference libraries; the Archives of American Art and the United States Holocaust Memorial Museum Library; Rebecca Davis, registrar, Butler Institute of American Art; Frank Bolden; Father Carmen D'Amico, St. Benedict the Moor Church; Rabbi Sara Rae Perman, Congregation Emanuel Israel; Toni Hulse, registrar, William Benton Museum of Art; Hildy Cummings; Rachel Berget, Chancellor Mark Nordenberg, Maxine Bruhns, Ron Bellisario, and Gee Chin, University of Pittsburgh; Leslie Golomb-Hartman, Jewish Community Center of Greater Pittsburgh; Hy Richman; Ann Fortescue, Director of Education, Historical Society of Western Pennsylvania; Laura McGee, Pittsburgh Board of Education; Carol Murray, registrar, Baltimore Museum of Art; Jim and Ann Loney; Allen Samovich; Elaine, Richard, and Jay Avner; Linda Bringman; Florence Schneider; William Warner; Brooke Zimmerman; Sara Berlin; Ellen Rabin; Barbara Bailey, Anne Molloy, and Martha Berg, Rodef Shalom Congregation; Carin Mincemoyer, Associated Artists of Pittsburgh; Elvira Peake; Aline Cunningham; Phyllis Weinkle, Temple Sinai; Jo Beth Ravitz; Barbara Lissfelt; Wade Shehady; Rick Nedley; Jennifer McCay; and Rochelle Solomon.

My ongoing appreciation to the staff of the Westmoreland Museum of American Art, especially to Doug Evans; Regina Narad, Judy Ross, Susan Nemet, and Amy Baldonieri.

My sincere thanks to all of Rosenberg's students who took the time to respond to my questionnaire about their former teacher (see list of students in note 3 to the essay). They each added their own important dimension to that significant part of the artist's life and career. I will miss those near weekly letters from David Schnabel that were filled with such detailed descriptions of Sam and his teaching style. My special thanks also to Hugh Fitzgerald, Dale Stein, Constantine Kermes, Bennard Perlman, Randolph Chalfant, Eleanor Fax, Jane Haskell, Chellie Blumenfeld, Aaronel deRoy Gruber, and Philip Pearlstein, who provided much more than they were asked.

Most importantly, I would like to express my gratitude to all of the private collectors listed in the catalog for their willingness to share their time and allowing me access to their Rosenberg paintings. They made this project an exciting one.

My appreciation to my family, who did not see much of me over the past four years, and to my friends, who listened to my endless ramblings on this subject. And finally, to David Ludwig, who endured the many phases of this project, my heartfelt thanks for his continued support of my career, but most of all, for just being here with me.

SAMUEL ROSENBERG · *A Life in Art*

Whenever the name Samuel Rosenberg is mentioned in Pittsburgh, it is met every time with the same response, "Oh, Sam, he was a wonderful man . . . and a great painter." Being a wonderful human being, it seems, was ingrained in Rosenberg's personality, which made the people he came in contact with—friends, students, colleagues, and patrons—not only like him, but also love him.

Over the years, Rosenberg has been referred to as "painter laureate," "dean of Pittsburgh painters," "a human sort of artist," "father of Pittsburgh painting," and "painter of light," among other such flattering titles, and in his day he was considered one of the city's finest painters. Today, Rosenberg's legacy as both an artist and an inspirational teacher endures. His paintings, especially those with Pittsburgh subjects, are especially sought after, while his mature work of abstract and nonobjective paintings of the 1950s, 1960s, and 1970s are becoming increasingly popular. That fact would especially please Rosenberg today, because he felt that, with the late work, he was finally coming into his own artistically.

Unfortunately, no taped interviews with Rosenberg remain to confirm, in his own words, his ideas and philosophy about art.[1] There are written records, however, including contemporary newspaper articles, periodicals, exhibition brochures, and catalogues, as well as two interviews with the artist's wife, Libbie, in 1983.[2] Art critics Penelope Redd and Dorothy Kantner of the *Pittsburgh Sun-Telegraph;* Douglas Naylor of the *Pittsburgh Press;* Jeanette Jena of the *Pittsburgh Post-Gazette,* and other contemporary critics of the city's newspapers followed Rosenberg's work and his artistic progress closely, reviewing nearly all the exhibitions he participated in, as well as his lectures in Pittsburgh and elsewhere. They frequently interviewed him to learn more about his work, and these interviews with Rosenberg provide insight into the artist's philosophy and thoughts about his own work, his teaching, and the work of other artists. Rosenberg's thoughts about his own work are also discernable in his letters to his son, Murray, and recollections from friends, patrons, and students who were willing to share personal experiences and memories of Rosenberg.[3]

Rosenberg's painting and teaching career spanned nearly six decades of the twentieth century. He worked through fifty volatile years in the development of American art, through the depression era, which was followed by economic and cultural prosperity, through decades that were once again fraught with wars, dissent, and disillusionment. From 1915 to 1972, he created over five hundred paintings, over four hundred preparatory sketches and drawings, and over one hundred collages. In the three-quarters of a century that he lived, Rosenberg experienced major life-altering events—the Great Depression, World War II, the atomic bombings of Hiroshima and Nagasaki, Japan, the Jewish struggle for independence in Israel, war in Korea and Vietnam. Artistically as well, in the United States alone, he witnessed dramatic stylistic changes, from Ashcan School realism and early abstraction, to regionalism, social realism, surrealism, abstract expressionism, color field, pop, op, and minimalism, all in one lifetime. In response, his style shifted rather dramatically through the years, in his search, he said, to find his own personal style, his own artistic path. Rosenberg never remained static in his exploration and through continual experimentation he kept both himself and his work fresh and current. His work, in fact, follows the history of American art, from his early portraits, through his socially conscious subjects of the 1930s, his allegorical abstractions of the 1940s, and, finally, to his own personal form of abstract expressionism. Rosenberg had no trademark, nor one recognizable style, yet his approach to painting was always the same. The effects of light and color were the common denominators that bridge his work together. His work can be divided into the following four periods, with frequent overlapping or transitional episodes within each: 1915–1930, portraits (and a few still lifes); 1930–1942, Pittsburgh's urban landscape and the American Scene; 1942–1952, allegory to abstraction; and 1949–1972, abstract expressionism.

Over three hundred paintings sold during the artist's lifetime, thanks in large part to his wife, Libbie, who was his art dealer, stenographer, organizer, record keeper, and cook. Libbie sought out appropriate homes for Rosenberg's work when the couple needed additional income. Both Sam and Libbie were fond of his work and were often reluctant to sell the paintings. Those paintings that they wanted to keep close they gave to family members so Rosenberg could visit the work at the same time he visited the relatives.

Libbie Rosenberg's contribution to her husband's development as an artist cannot be underestimated. She was his constant companion for nearly fifty years and his staunchest supporter. She created two comprehensive scrapbooks that contained, in chronological order, newspaper clippings, magazine articles, newsletters, and any other published information on Rosenberg and his work from 1921 to 1958. These volumes are not only vital records of the critical reception of Rosenberg's work, but they also serve as an overview of the Pittsburgh art scene through the many years that Rosenberg was active in the city. She prepared an index of all of Rosenberg's paintings that included an exhibition history for each work; she annotated all of his drawings that were left in her possession when he died; kept records of the sale of his paintings that documented to whom each was sold and the sale price. While her husband was described as shy, reticent, unobtrusive, and gentle, she, on the other hand, was described as assertive, outspoken, possessive, passionate, and dominant. It was necessary for Libbie to possess all of these traits in order to handle every situation that arose. She relieved Rosenberg of these responsibilities so that he could devote all his free time and energy to painting.

For nearly sixty years, Samuel Rosenberg devoted his life to his art and his teaching and through both he disseminated a wealth of knowledge and understanding. His family was important to him, but art was this man's life. He taught for over forty years just so he could have summers off to paint while earning enough money to support his family. Whether spending the summer in New York, Pennsylvania, Maine, Arizona, California, Mexico, or Europe, Rosenberg never ended a day without making, looking at, or talking about art. Always the teacher, his lengthy, detailed letters home to his son, Murray, from California or Venice, read like an introduction to an art history class. His surroundings, the light and color of the natural world, were the subjects he incorporated into his work. His paintings are filled with his images of the visible world, his emotions, and his imagination. From his early portraits, commissioned and otherwise, through his social realist studies of Pittsburgh's Hill District where he grew up, to his allegorical subjects and universal themes of suffering, and finally, to his enigmatic abstract expressionist canvases of light and color, Rosenberg's growth as an artist was a slow and steady, ever-evolving progression.

Born in Philadelphia in 1896, the fifth of six children, Rosenberg showed

Agricultural societies in southern Italy, as well as central and eastern Europe, were undergoing great turmoil in the late 1800s as the ongoing industrialization of these societies pushed peasant peoples off their lands. Mechanization required fewer agricultural workers and was most effective on large-scale farms, so there was increasing pressure to consolidate small farms into large commercial holdings. The result was the displacement of vast numbers of farm laborers. While the factory cities of Europe swallowed many of these people, they could not take them all. Industrial America's need for workers at that time therefore coincided with these people's need for gainful employment.

America thus witnessed the greatest wave of immigration up to that point in its history, as these "New Immigrants" flooded into the country. One million European immigrants per year poured into America for six of the nine years between 1905 and 1914; up to three-quarters were from southern and eastern Europe, while only 14 percent came from northern Europe. In one year, 1907, nearly 188,000 of these New Immigrants listed Pittsburgh as their final destination. By 1910, 80 percent of Pittsburgh's foreign-born residents were New Immigrants from Italy, the Austro-Hungarian Empire, and the Russian Empire (which then included much of Poland). Shortly thereafter, more than a quarter of Pittsburgh's inhabitants were foreign born. By some estimates, these Pittsburghers represented as many as seventy nationalities. In this, Pittsburgh was typical of the entire industrial American northeast. As late as 1940, such immigrants and their children accounted for more than half the population of twenty large American cities, including two-thirds of the population of Cleveland, three-fourths of New York City, and three-fifths of Newark, N.J.

Because of their origins, these former peasants—from the most underdeveloped areas of southern and eastern Europe—shared certain deeply embedded social and psychological traits. They came from a background in which there was very little wealth, health, or security of any kind. Disaster could strike at any moment. Economic advancement, let alone wealth, was considered unachievable. In such circumstances, economic security was the overriding goal of life.

Thus, rather than personal advancement, these immigrants mainly sought secure employment. The highest compliment one could pay a man was to call him a "good worker," one who worked stolidly and steadily, year after year. "Good worker" Slavs gravitated especially toward work in the steel mills, as these were considered secure jobs. Thus, these immigrants quickly filled the lower echelons of the American industrial workforce, rapidly transforming its demographic composition. By the time of the great failed steel strike of 1919, the majority of America's—and Pittsburgh's—industrial workers were these New Immigrants. Once Slavs got jobs in the mills, they clung to them tenaciously.

Much of this "work ethic" was successfully passed on from Pittsburgh's first-generation Slavic immigrants to their children, with many sons following their fathers not only into the mills, but into the same jobs within the mills—where they remained for life. Thus, thousands of young Slavic boys started work in the glass factories on Pittsburgh's South Side as a prelude to lifetime adult jobs in the nearby J & L steel mill, both of which adult relatives obtained for them. And, once the sons got a steady job, they were as reluctant as their fathers to change positions.

This "work ethic" of Pittsburgh-area immigrants persisted for generations. Kristin Kovacic grew up in the Pittsburgh neighborhood of Carrick. She saw the same steady dependability in her parents. In an op-ed piece for the March 24, 1999 *Pittsburgh Post-Gazette*, she wrote, "We are all (with some much-maligned exceptions) excellent employees," she said. "We stay at jobs for lifetimes. . . . Dependable, our word. . . . Staying put was a value. A steady paycheck the definition of ambition."

Workplace stability was complemented by another aspect of Slavic peasant life which, when transplanted to America, contributed to remarkable neighborhood stability. The prevailing family structure among Slavic immigrants was that of a communal family organized around the patriarch, or oldest male. It was expected that sons and their families would remain within the homes of their fathers, contributing to the family finances. Meanwhile, daughters would leave upon marriage to join the communal families of their husbands. Both the perpetuation of this peasant family structure and the peasant worldview of economic scarcity—which necessitated a dogged pursuit of security in the same lifelong jobs—contributed to the enduring cohesion of ethnic enclaves in Pittsburgh. These ethnic enclaves did not exist in their coherent form before 1920. They did not exist long after 1960. Far from being a basic, ongoing fact of American history, they were instead a mere forty-year phenomenon. But it is out of such strong communities, not out of atomized or transient communities, that political protest comes. These were the strongholds from which ethnic workers transformed American society and politics in the 1930s.

ERIC LEIF DAVIN

an interest in art from a very early age. His father, Solomon, had emigrated to Philadelphia from Vienna around 1890, where he had presumably met his new wife, Anna Dickstein Turetsky, who had come from Minsk. Solomon had three children from a previous marriage and had another three with Anna. The family moved to Erie, Pennsylvania when Rosenberg was two years old. In Erie, Solomon was an expert tailor of fine women's fashions, and years later, Rosenberg could still recall the decorative painted sign that used to hang over the door to his father's shop.

When Rosenberg was eleven, the family moved south to Pittsburgh where they lived at 256 North Craig Street at Centre Avenue in Oakland, which, according to Rosenberg, was much like living in the country then. When the Rosenbergs arrived in Pittsburgh, the city was a booming industrial center, commonly referred to as "steel town," "the smoky city," and "hell with the lid off," among other epithets. What began as a frontier village in 1800 had grown into an internationally recognized industrial giant. Just three years after Rosenberg found himself in Pittsburgh, the popula-

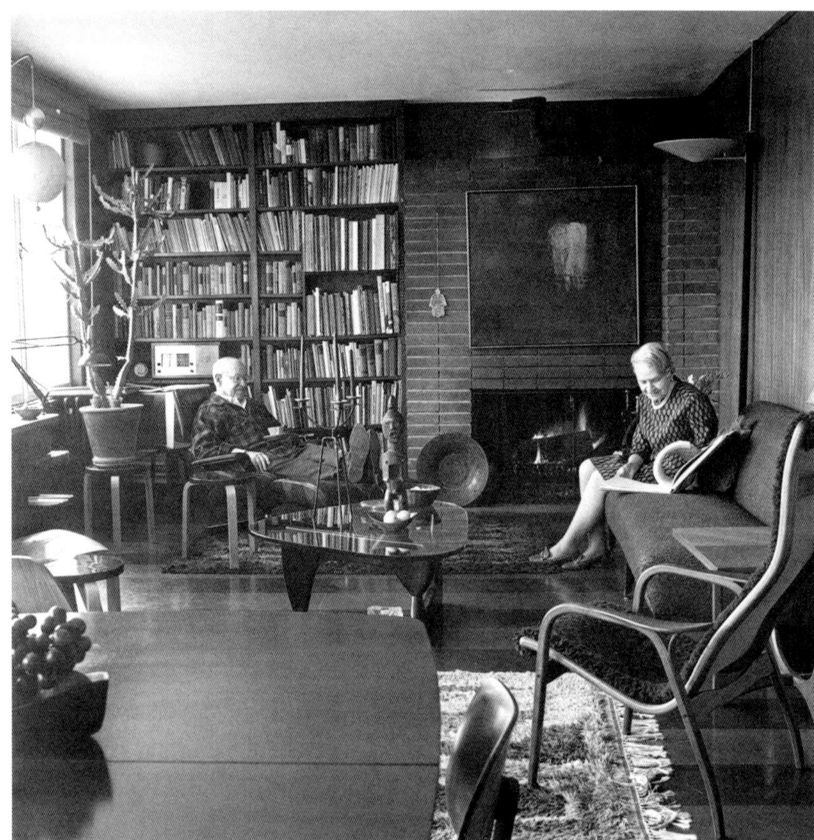

FIG. 1.
Sam and Libbie in their living room with Sam's painting *Horizon No. 2*, 1962, hanging over the fireplace, 2721 Mount Royal Road, Pittsburgh, c. 1955.

tion reached more than half a million people. The city smelled bad, and it was noisy, polluted, and full of activity; it was an environment in which he and many others would find artistic inspiration. Years later, Rosenberg would say, "You can hate and like Pittsburgh at the same time. It is not the most pleasant place in the world, for the atmosphere here is not particularly clean. But from an artist's standpoint, I contend that it is one of the most interesting cities in the United States."[4]

In 1912 the family moved from Oakland to 213 Dinwiddie Street in the Lower Hill District, where Rosenberg would live until 1918. According to the Pittsburgh city directories, Rosenberg lived at several different addresses in the Hill District between 1918 and 1924, the year he and his wife of two years moved to 340 Coltart Street in Oakland. Sam and Libbie would remain at Coltart Street for the next twenty-eight years. In 1952, they made their final move to the first and only home they owned at 2721 Mount Royal Road in Squirrel Hill.

Throughout his artistic development, Rosenberg resisted conforming to a single signature style. After years of experimentation, his own style

In 1907, when eleven-year-old Samuel Rosenberg arrived in Pittsburgh with his family from Erie, Pennsylvania, the Jewish community was well established. It had been founded in the 1840s by a group of Jews who had emigrated from German lands to America. They had soon been joined by small groups of Jews arriving from England, the Netherlands, the German part of Poland, and Lithuania, so by 1880, their numbers had grown to about 2000. By 1907 they had achieved solid middle-class status and were living in upscale neighborhoods in the process of moving from Allegheny City, (now the north shore of Pittsburgh) to the East End of Pittsburgh. While they could not compete financially in the same leagues with the likes of Carnegie, Mellon, and Frick, Jews were integrated into the economic and political landscape of the city. A. Leo Weil was head of the reform-minded Voters League, intent on attacking political corruption in the city; Enoch Rauh, a prominent clothing manufacturer, was soon to be appointed to the first nine-member city council and be reelected thereafter until his death in 1919; his wife, Bertha, head of the local chapter of the National Council of Jewish Women and involved in a myriad of social reform causes, was to become the first woman ever appointed to a mayor's cabinet in Pennsylvania; Enoch's brother Marcus was to head the Chamber of Commerce; Marcus Aaron became president of the city school board; Joseph Stadtfeld was a prominent attorney; and Josiah Cohen was a judge on the Court of Common Pleas. Jewish merchants led by the Kaufmann brothers were well known. Barney Dreyfuss, who had taken over the Pittsburgh Pirates in 1899, won the Pirates' first world championship in 1909. That same year he opened Forbes Field, which critics labeled "Dreyfuss's Folly" because it was seen as too big, too fancy, and too far from downtown Pittsburgh.

But there also was another, distinctly different, Jewish community in 1907. It was composed of eastern European Jews who had come to America after 1881, fleeing persecution, pogroms, and poverty. Between 1880 and 1930, out of more than twenty-five million immigrants who came to the United States, two and a half million were Jews. The majority of Jews stayed in New York City, constituting one-fourth of that city's population in the opening rounds of the twentieth century. Pittsburgh saw its Jewish population escalate dramatically, as well. By 1907 it was estimated at 25,000, by 1913 at 35,000, and by 1930 about 50,000 (its peak) out of a city population of nearly 670,000 people. These newcomers were different from the older, established German Jewish community in a whole host of ways. They were poor; they spoke Yiddish; they were unAmericanized; they were often either Orthodox in their Jewish observance, Socialists, and/or Zionists. Any and all of this was totally unpalatable to the Reform, assimilated German Jews. Their differences were highlighted by their geographical separation—"the Hill" being the primary residence for the incoming rush of Eastern Europeans.

BARBARA BURSTIN

Many think of the Hill District as Pittsburgh's version of New York's Harlem, but, in fact, the two differed significantly in their origin and evolution. Harlem began in the 1870s as an exclusive development for wealthy whites, while the Hill was settled in the 1820s by both blacks and whites. Blacks were attracted by the district's location just east of downtown and the availability of cheap land on which to build. Whites—mainly businessmen and professionals—were attracted by the easy commute to work and the ample green spaces offered by the district's farms, orchards, and woodlands.

Harlem shifted rapidly from an elite white to an impoverished black neighborhood in the early 1900s, when the area's speculative real-estate bubble burst and desperate landlords scrambled to find tenants for their overbuilt properties. The Hill, on the other hand, evolved from a primarily native-born district in the 1820s to one of foreign-born laborers in the 1850s. Irish and German immigrants, fleeing famines and hard times at home, poured into the area and drove many of the native-born elite away. But the departure of the native-born elite occurred more gradually than in Harlem; as late as 1887, Pittsburgh's directory of

emerged in his mature work of the late 1950s and early 1960s, when he finally, as he said, "came into his own." He carried through in a methodical development from one artistic stage to the next and continuity in his method and approach was a constant. The importance of the edge of the canvas, balance, color harmony, and working on the composition as a whole was his mantra, both to himself, and to his students. Despite the diversity of his subject matter, through the years his paintings share a consistency in painterly style and purpose, attempting to convey his feelings and the effects of light through his application of paint. The common thread that ties all Rosenberg's work together throughout his career is the artist's emphasis on light. It can be seen in the chiaroscuro of his early portraits, in the light and shadow of his genre paintings of Pittsburgh's urban landscape, and most predominantly in his later abstractions. Light as the sole subject of his painting, however, did not take precedence until the early 1950s, when Rosenberg began his experiments with light and color exclusively in his search for a universal, and perhaps spiritual, truth.

When other artists were leaving Pittsburgh, and traveling to Paris or New York, Rosenberg made the conscious decision to remain at home.

Education and Formative Years

Rosenberg's mother recognized his artistic abilities at an early age and sent him, at age twelve, to his first art classes at the Columbian Council School, the upper class, the Blue Book, still contained the names of 114 Hill residents.

From the 1880s until the outbreak of World War I, the district's Irish and Germans were, in turn, displaced by other newcomers, primarily Jews and Italians. A trickle of Jews had come from Germany and Lithuania around mid-century, settling in the downtown area. But in the 1870s and 1880s, a massive wave of Jews escaping persecution began arriving from eastern Europe—primarily Russia, Poland, and Romania—and settling in the southern part of the Lower Hill between Wylie and Fifth Avenues. Italian immigrants came soon afterwards, sometimes settling among the Jews but also establishing a colony north of Wylie Avenue around lower Webster and Bedford Avenues. Smaller groups of other nationalities also settled in the Hill. Syrians, Armenians, Lebanese, and Greeks clustered around the Italians on lower Bedford and Webster Avenues; Irish moved up from downtown and, with the Scots-Irish, settled around Tunnel and Congress Streets and Webster and Fifth Avenues; Chinese merchants were represented throughout the district.

LAURENCE GLASCO

predecessor of the Irene Kaufmann Settlement, in the Hill District. While studying there, Rosenberg won first prize for best drawing and was awarded a small box of oil paints. Shortly thereafter, he won a scholarship to study art with Jacob R. Coblens, a Pittsburgh artist who had studied in Paris. A close childhood friend of Rosenberg's, William Wolfson, remembered Rosenberg as "a master," at the age of fourteen, "because even then he was already painting in oils, original things, not copies. He had a cellar full of them, on canvas and cardboard. They were mostly portraits . . ."[5] Coblens privately tutored young Rosenberg from 1908 until Coblens moved to New York City in 1911. Later in his life, Rosenberg would recall, "Coblens was an important influence. He made me aware of the Old Masters, Velázquez, Rembrandt, Hals, El Greco, Botticelli, and (taught me) to respect the past and thus become well-grounded in art."[6] Rosenberg would subsequently incorporate Coblens' art historical method of teaching with his own students.

Even after Coblens had moved to New York City, his influence on the young Rosenberg continued for a number of years. In one of his letters, Coblens referred Rosenberg to the book *The Techniques of Painting* by C. Moreau-Vauthier, which introduced him to the painting techniques used by artists of the Renaissance. Those techniques would play a significant part in his own art as well as in his teaching. He also sent him books on Velázquez and Holbein to study. Rosenberg would send drawings to his mentor and Coblens would mail them back with his critique. Rosenberg considered

Not long after Rosenberg's arrival in Pittsburgh, he enrolled in art classes at an institution that by that time was already a major center in the life of immigrant Jews. More than fourteen hundred children and adults were participating in the various activities of what was soon to become known as the Irene Kaufmann Settlement at 1835 Centre Avenue. The school and settlement, originally started in the late 1890s by the German Jewish women of Pittsburgh's chapter of the National Council of Jewish Women, was bursting at its seams. Accordingly, a number of the women approached Henry Kaufmann, one of the four brothers who founded the landmark Kaufmann's Department Store, to help them. He donated $150,000 to these women to construct a new building for the facility and provide an additional $40,000 endowment fund. The new building would henceforth be named in memory of his daughter, Irene, who had just died.

The settlement provided a whole variety of health services, clubs, activities and classes. Its free adult evening classes in English and citizenship, begun in 1899, were the first in the city. Indeed, free evening classes for immigrants of any stripe did not begin in the Pittsburgh public schools until 1906, after a concerted campaign by the women of the NCJW to bring this about. The vital efforts of the IKS to promote better health in the community were under the watchful eye of the legendary nurse, Anna B. Heldman, who was to have a street in the Hill named after her.

BARBARA BURSTIN

this experience his "correspondence school." Rosenberg visited Coblens in New York in 1913 and together they made the rounds of the art galleries and museums, including the Metropolitan Museum of Art. Rosenberg always referred enthusiastically to this time he spent with Coblens in the New York museums, where he could study firsthand the works of art by artists he admired. This was a tremendous learning experience and a method he would continue to use throughout his career. In a letter from 1911, Coblens wrote to Rosenberg, "Keep yourself in shape and don't wear yourself out by over work or study. Keep cool, but I do not mean not to be enthusiastic. Some fellows, you know, are living roman candles. They make a lot of sparks and sputter out." In another letter of 1911, Coblens encouraged Rosenberg to continue in his studies and advised his student to "Draw! Draw! Draw! And construct solidly, as if you were modeling in clay. I have come to the conclusion," he wrote, "that this is the best foundation . . . of course you should sketch too—and train your memory. I mean to draw from memory."[7]

Rosenberg attended elementary school at the Osceola School in Pittsburgh but quit at age fourteen after only the eighth grade. He was presented with a decision by one of his teachers to either come to school or make art, and naturally, he chose the latter course. In those years, it was a luxury to complete a full twelve years of school and Rosenberg, like many other boys his age, was expected to earn a living to contribute to the family's income. In doing so, his early 'artistic' career found him doing a variety of odd jobs in machine shops, for Westinghouse, as a porter in a movie theater, and painting billboards for the decorator G. G. O'Brien.[8] Rosenberg studied painting for a short time with Pittsburgh artist Arthur Watson Sparks at the Carnegie Institute of Technology (hereafter Carnegie Tech) between 1915 and 1916. Sparks found Rosenberg peering in the windows of the art school and invited him in to join the class. Rosenberg, however, had been exposed to his teacher years earlier, while still in grammar school, in an art class taught by Sparks where Rosenberg made drawings from plaster casts.

Thanks to his older brother Harry, who had married into wealth, Rosenberg was able to continue his art education at the National Academy of Design (NAD) in New York for one year in 1917, where he studied with the academic painter, Douglas Volk. His friend, William Wolfson, attended the NAD at the same time and they roamed around New York together and visited the city's art museums and galleries, as he had done with Coblens. He said he only saw Volk once in the two semesters he was there. To escape the overcrowded classes of the NAD, he and Wolfson attended lectures at the Art Students League. Rosenberg's most vivid memory of that year in New York was hearing George Bellows's lecture at the Art Students League on the visual memory technique. In later years, Rosenberg would express his pleasure that Bellows, a well-respected artist, had validated a method he had discovered for himself while sketching at the Highland Park Zoo. He said the animals wouldn't pose, so it taught him to work fast and from memory. "What Bellows talked about," he said, "I was already doing at the zoo." He took his sketches back to the studio, where he would complete more finished drawings. No drawings or paintings exist however of any animals from these early zoo exercises. This technique has a subconscious aspect to it, some familiar sight, image, or aspect of a person, may appear years after it has passed. According to Rosenberg "Some years after I painted *Israel* (plate 53), an imaginary portrait of a patriarch, I examined it to learn I'd painted the eyes of my father." *Israel* was painted in 1945, nine years after his father's death. This was a method that Coblens advocated in his letters, as well. While at the NAD, Rosenberg received an Honorable Mention for one of his still-life drawings.[9]

Portraiture: 1920s

Rosenberg began his career painting portraits, and it is clear in his early work that his teachers were the seventeenth-century Spanish master Diego Velázquez, and the Dutch masters Rembrandt van Rijn and Frans Hals. Rosenberg's dynamic portraits reveal not only the activity of the painter's hand, multiple color layers and texture, but the personality of the sitter as well. His use of egg tempera, distempera, and glazing techniques reference the painting techniques of the Old Masters of the Renaissance; his color brilliance, the Venetian masters Titian and Tintoretto. With the exception of a brief experiment with acrylic paint, Rosenberg always made his paint the old-fashioned way, by mixing his own colors from a recipe of dry pigment, linseed oil, and damar varnish.

Between 1915 and 1930, Rosenberg painted nearly one hundred portraits. In addition to commissioned works, his family, colleagues, fellow artists, and friends were his subjects (figure 2). His earliest known portrait dates from 1915. Entitled *Woman in Green No. 1 (Green and Gold)* (figure 3), Rosenberg's first full-length portrait of an unidentified woman reveals the skilled hand of the nineteen-year-old artist.

In 1915, Patrick J. Byrne, Rosenberg's neighbor on Dinwiddie Street, commissioned him to paint nine members of his family (figure 4). Rosenberg utilized these portraits, he said, as educational exercises to practice his portrait style and become more proficient at it. Indeed, his proficiency paid off, as he would become a professional portrait painter, completing commissions for judges, industrialists, civic leaders, ministers, rabbis, priests, and deans of universities throughout the city. For his portraits, Rosenberg utilized his visual memory training, first creating sketches from life of his sitters, and then completing the portraits from memory in his studio (figure 5).[10] Because he couldn't always afford a model, Rosenberg painted self-portraits as well as family members (Libbie, his father, sisters, and his father-in-law), fellow artists, students, and, as previously mentioned, he also made sketches at the Highland Park Zoo. At least five self-portraits of the artist are known to exist. The earliest, from 1918, won first prize in the Associated Artists of Pittsburgh annual exhibition held at the Carnegie Institute (now Carnegie Museum of Art) in 1920. This award was not Rosenberg's first from the organization nor certainly his last. Rosenberg became a member of the Associated Artists of Pittsburgh (AAP) in 1916, just six years after the group was founded. He participated in his first AAP exhibition that year and continued to exhibit with them annually, with the exception of 1958 and 1959, until 1967. He won his first award in 1917, second

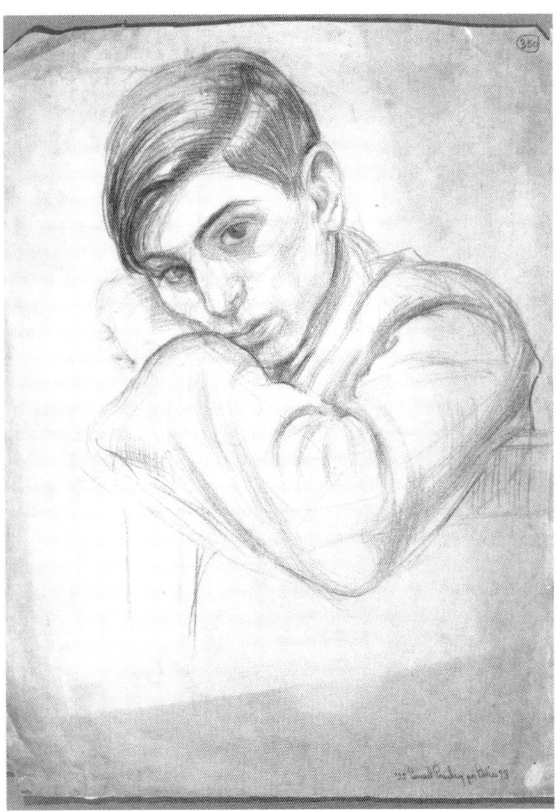

FIG. 2. *Portrait of Milton Weiss,* 1922. Pencil on paper, 17 x 13″.

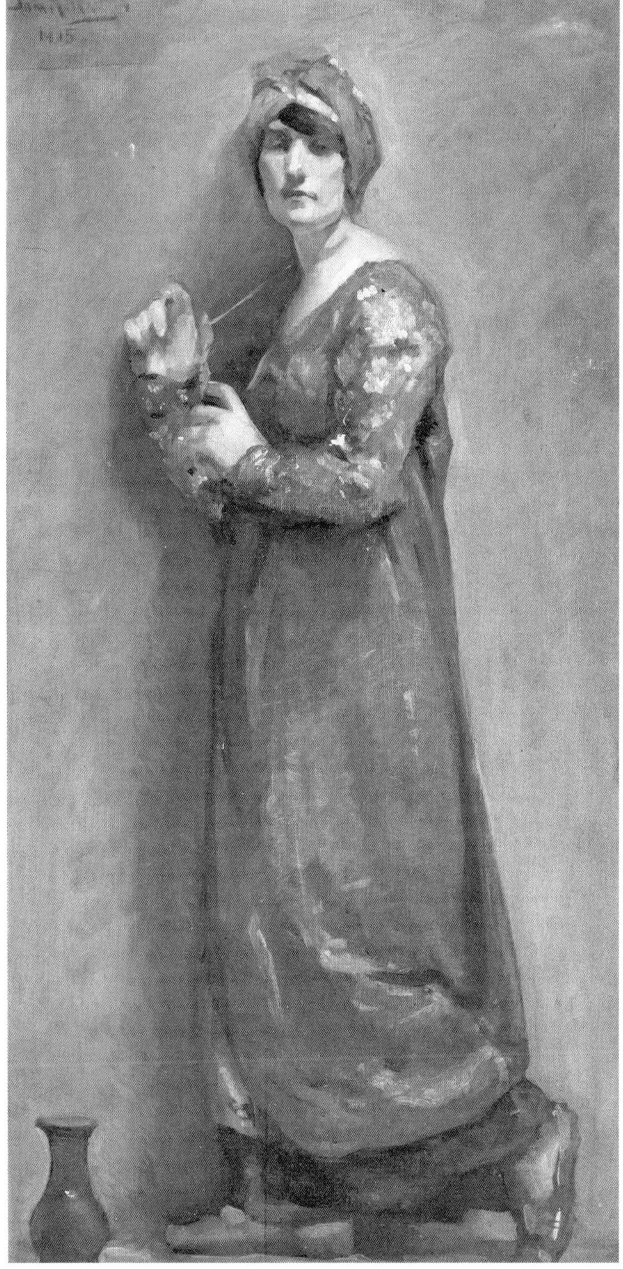

FIG. 3. *Woman in Green No. 1 (Green and Gold),* 1915. Oil on canvas, 36 x 18″.

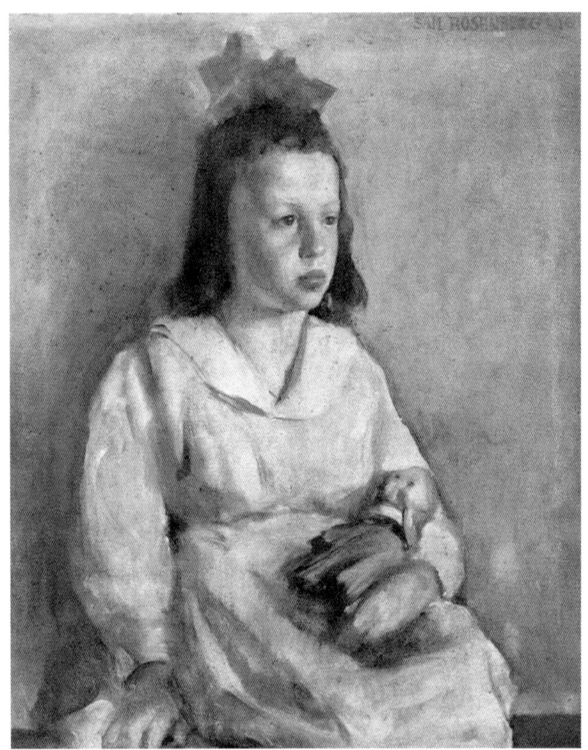

FIG. 4. *Portrait of Eleanor Byrne with Doll,* 1916. Oil on canvas, 27 x 22″.

FIG. 5. *Portrait of a Young Girl,* 1929. Pencil on paper, 8 x 5″.

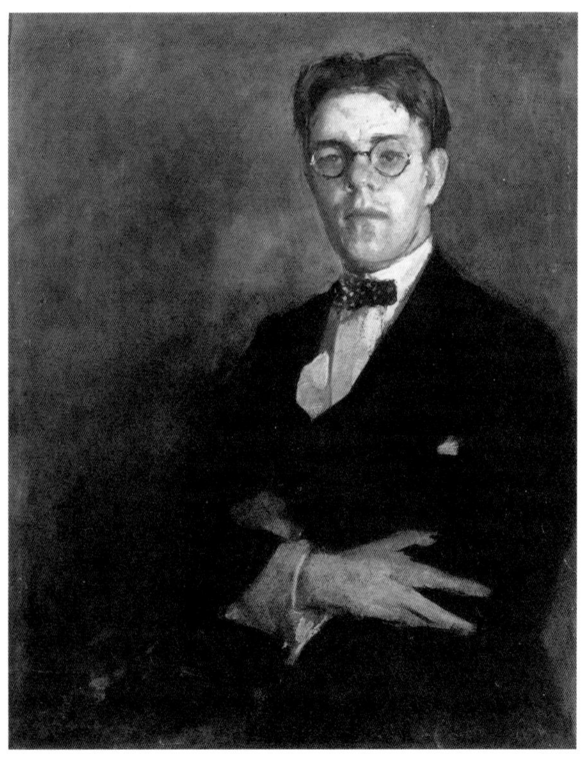

FIG. 6. *Man with a Red Nose,* 1916. Oil on canvas, 30 x 25″.

honor for his portrait *Man with a Red Nose* (figure 6), and subsequently won every prize the association offered during the fifty-one years he was a member (a complete list of Rosenberg's awards is available in the biography in this book).

In this *Self-Portrait* of 1918, as in his four others, Rosenberg presents himself as a confident artist, staring out at the viewer with a self-assurance that would be revealed in his art throughout his career.[11] This essentially monochromatic painting of the artist set before a dark wall and darkened doorway was an experiment in light and shadow. Illuminated by a single light source situated in front of him, Rosenberg incorporated a formal convention of painting, revealing the influence of the Spanish and Dutch Masters that he would draw on for his commissioned portraits as well. A year later, in the more complex arrangement of *Self-Portrait by a Window* of 1919 (figure 7), Rosenberg included a partially drawn shade over a window, one of two light sources illuminating the sitter. The pattern of the plant and the upholstered chair are the only two objects to breach the minimalist geometry of the composition. His translucent painter's smock, which reads as white, is actually comprised of an array of colors reflecting the light in the room as well as the artist's shirt underneath. It too appears to be an experimental exploration of shape, form, and color. In 1921, a year before his marriage, Rosenberg painted a more mature, three-quarter-length *Self-Portrait,* with pipe in his mouth, clean-shaven, and dressed in a suit, tie, and white shirt, an attire that would become his trademark. Over the next seven years, Rosenberg painted two more self-portraits (plate 3), culminating in his *Self-Portrait in Sweater* of 1928 (plate 9). In this painting, the artist sits in the midst of a simplified imaginary landscape, a few years older and a bit heavier (partially due to the bulky sweater he wears), in the act of painting *en plein air.* This painting seems unusual, as Rosenberg did not often paint canvases out-of-doors but made sketches instead, which he then took back to the studio to complete. Through the artist's eyes we see his intense study of his own reflection in the act of painting himself in a vivid russet-colored sweater.

Other portraits of family members are most telling, and reveal a man who was intimately attached to his subjects. Rosenberg married Libbie Levin (1898–1987), a native of Toledo, Ohio, in 1922, and subsequently utilized her modeling services in at least five known portraits that spanned a twenty-three-year period between 1925 and 1948. One of the first portraits Rosenberg painted of Libbie in 1925 (figure 8) reveals both the influence of the Spanish master and the art of Japan on his work. Dressed in a kimono-style robe, Libbie is seated, holding a portrait of Pope Innocent X by

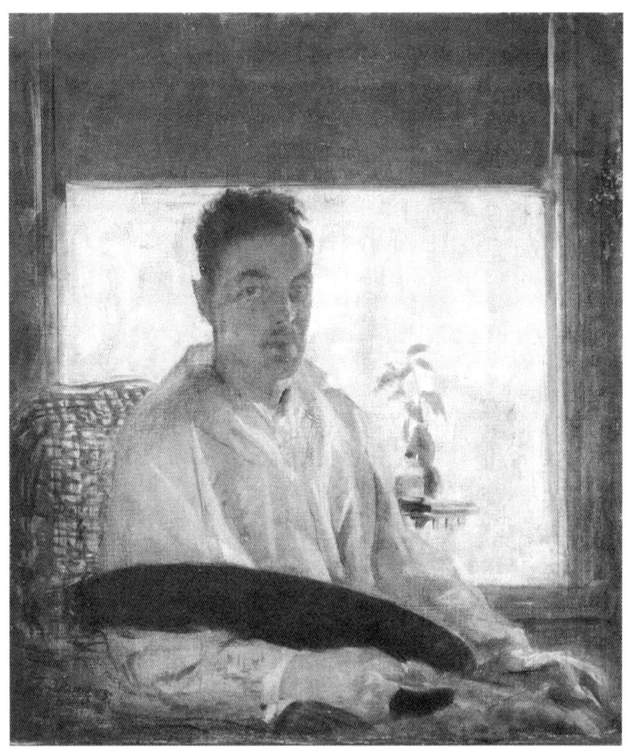

FIG. 7. *Self-Portrait by a Window,* 1919.
Oil on canvas, 18 x 16″.

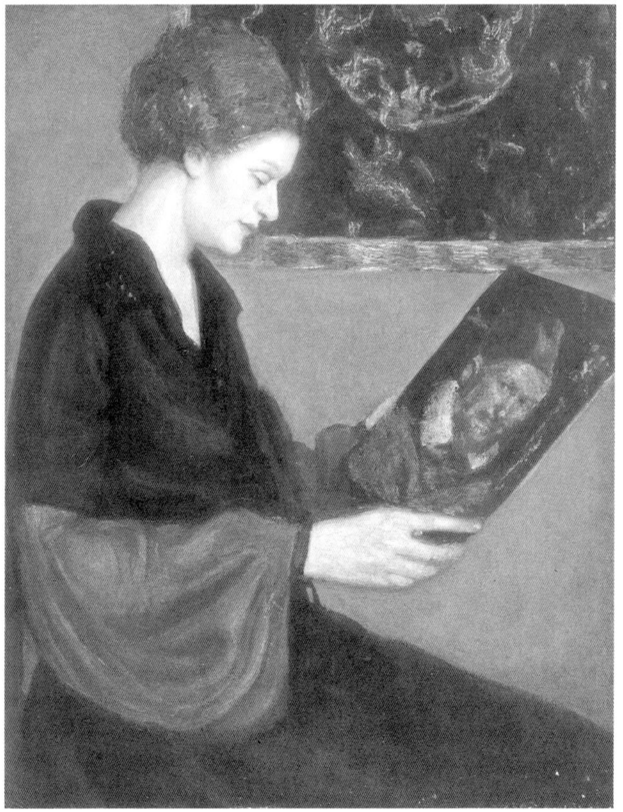

FIG. 8. *Portrait of Libbie with Velázquez,* 1925.
Oil on canvas, 28 x 22″.

Velázquez. A Japanese tapestry hangs behind her on the wall. This portrait within a portrait pays homage to two dissimilar sources of inspiration. Rosenberg retained a lifelong admiration for the Spanish master Velázquez, who, Rosenberg said "kept learning as long as he lived." Rosenberg said he "studied him so much that once I did a self-portrait and, according to Coblens, gave myself a Hapsburg Jaw."[12] In addition, Rosenberg said he was "always fascinated by the Japanese because Japanese artists retained a two-dimensional effect by eliminating shadows and attained a sense of space by overlapping planes." Coblens gave Rosenberg several Japanese prints, which initiated his study of their planar techniques.

Portrait of Libbie in White Sweater of 1926 (plate 6) is another comprehensive study in white, and the myriad colors that comprise it. Situated before a window that looks out to a barely visible landscape, Libbie sits in a Windsor-style chair, her hand in her sweater pocket, staring out at the viewer. In this endearing portrait, Rosenberg captures a quiet moment with his wife, an integral part of his creative energies. This painting was made during the summer in Somerset County, where they spent their vacation that year, following the birth of their only child, Murray.[13]

In 1930, we see an amusing side of both the artist and his wife. In *Vacation Days No. 1* (plate 11), Rosenberg catches Libbie in a light-hearted and relaxed pose, dressed in shorts and sleeveless shirt, with one leg slung up over the arm of the chair. As if a photograph, he captures a moment in time, complete with a portrait of himself, dressed only in shorts, reflected in the full-length mirror. It is an interior view of John Varney's cottage, their summer rental in Woodstock, New York, that year. The painting, with its emphasis on pattern, color, flattened planes, and interior and exterior view (Murray, age five, playing in the lawn), recalls the work of Henri Matisse, especially his *Red Studio.* Rosenberg revered Matisse for his achievements in modern art. A tattered copy of a letter from Matisse to Henry Clifford that was passed around the art department faculty at Carnegie Tech remained in Rosenberg's possession all his life.[14] It was Matisse who Rosenberg frequently spoke about and quoted, to his family, fellow artists and to his students, with regard to his own use of color in his painting as well as his continual references to nature.

Of the five portraits that Rosenberg made of Libbie, the painting entitled *Meditation (Libbie)* of 1932 (plate 16) is without a doubt his most sensitive. Once again, with a monochromatic palette and simplified composition, he achieved a remarkable painting that fully suggests its title. As Libbie rests in her chair, the painting captures the subtlety of her beauty and physical characteristics, her hair, the curve of her forehead, her cheekbones, her hands, one bent holding her head while the other rests on the arm of the chair. It is an exercise in curvilinear forms: the roundness of the chair, the decorative rippled edge of her sweater, and the suggestion of the soft curves of her body underneath.

Rosenberg painted the largest number of portraits of his only son Murray between 1926 and 1941, depicting his son from age one to sixteen. Born in 1925, Murray literally grew up on canvas before Rosenberg's eyes. In both portraits made in 1926, *Portrait of Murray in Red Hat* (plate 7) and *First Halloween* (plate 8), Murray is shown in the act of drawing and painting respectively (revealing a genetic talent that would cause conflict in his choice of careers later in his life). In the former, wearing a brilliant red cap, the bright-eyed one-year-old child sits in his high chair making marks on a piece of paper with a pencil, and in the latter, dressed in his Halloween costume, he sits painting, on the decorative floor of their Coltart Street home.[15] In five out of the eight portraits and numerous drawings that he made of his son, Rosenberg shows Murray either drawing or painting. A reporter for the *Pittsburgh Sun-Telegraph* published a photograph of Murray with the caption that read, "following in his father's brushstrokes."[16] In other images of his son, Rosenberg captures him reading at age seven; playing the clarinet at age eight; and finally, by age sixteen, in front of a drawing board with a work in progress, pointing over his shoulder to a music stand behind. Here Rosenberg reveals young Murray's two passions: art and music, which coincided with his parents' love for both. In the end, however, Murray would pursue neither career. Although he continued to paint throughout his life, he would choose medicine instead, receiving his medical degree from Yale University in 1949. In only one painting does Rosenberg reveal Murray to be a regular kid who played sports. In *Vacation Days No. 2* (figure 9), dressed in overalls, his baseball cap turned sideways on his head and his bat in hand, an eight-year-old Murray prepares to play the game. This telling portrait reveals that the child actually played sports and did not draw, paint, read, or play music all the time, as the other seven portraits of him seem to suggest.

Other family members turn up in Rosenberg's work over the years, including Libbie's father, Joseph Levin (plate 42), who Rosenberg sketched frequently and painted at least four times. Joseph, holding his grandson, is reproduced in an etching in one of Rosenberg's few experiments with the printmaking medium (figure 10). Cantor of the Tree of Life congregation for over forty years, Joseph lived with Sam and Libbie for several years after Mrs. Levin died. Rosenberg painted three identical portraits of his own father Solomon (plate 15), one for each of his sisters; the first in 1932 for

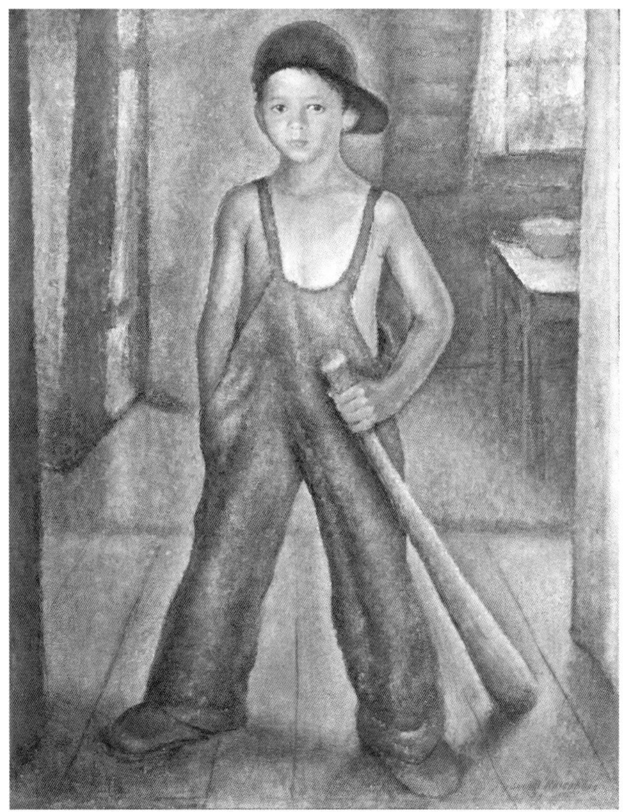

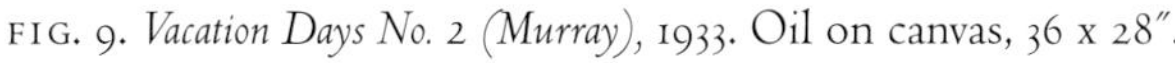

FIG. 9. *Vacation Days No. 2 (Murray)*, 1933. Oil on canvas, 36 x 28″.

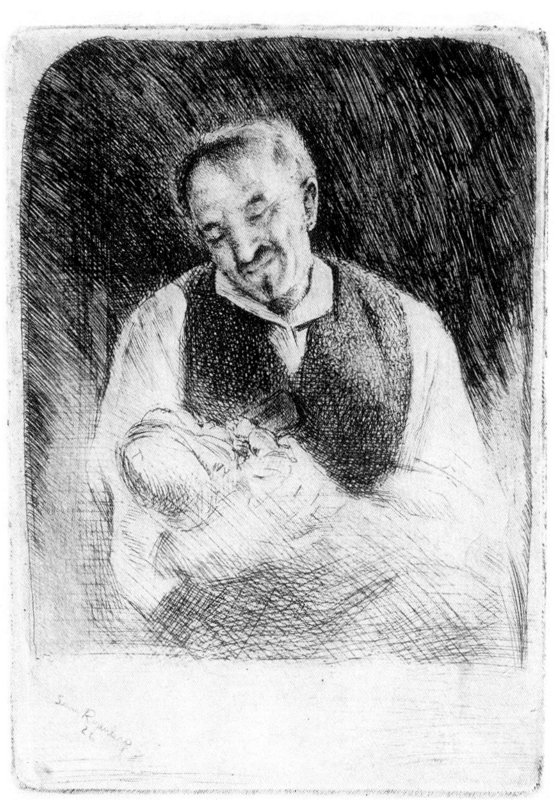

FIG. 10. *Gramps and Grandson (Joseph Levin)*, 1926. Etching, 10 x 7″

Lena, and the other two in 1937 for Sally and Rhea, the year after Solomon died. He painted a double portrait of his parents, but only one portrait of his mother Anna is known to exist. *Portrait of Rhea,* of 1917, reveals a sensitive portrait of his younger sibling at age twelve. The quality of the light in this painting and his use of subtle color combinations imply the tenderness that the artist felt for his sister.

Libbie's family continued to be represented in such portraits as *Coming Home from School* (plate 28) of 1936, which depicts Ruth Levy (now Westerman). Ruth is Rosenberg's niece, the daughter of Libbie's middle sister Belle, whose family lived downstairs from Sam and Libbie on Coltart Street. In this portrait, Rosenberg caught her just as she was arriving home from school on a winter day, dressed in Murray's leggings and jacket, her lunch bag still in her hand.[17] Rosenberg made portraits of Libbie's three other nieces, Mildred, Sara, and Bernice, as well.

In contrast to his commissioned work, Rosenberg was able to be much more fluid and free with his expression in his portraits of friends and family. Two of his portraits, *Around the Corner (Derelict)* of 1928 (figure 11), and

My Friend Twiggs of 1931 (figure 12), reflect Rosenberg's recurrent stylistic investigation into cubism, the avant-garde European movement that was initiated by Picasso and Braque in France around 1907. In the former, a homeless man sits in the midst of a pile of junk; a corked bottle evident in a crate next to him. While the suit that the man is wearing is simplistically rendered, he has taken the care to represent in detail the overall sadness in this unidentified man's face and the age in his hands. The background is comprised of an abstract array of planes that are defined more by light and shadow than by line. In the latter portrait, made three years later, Rosenberg continues his experimentation with this new method of depicting form and space and carries the cubist vocabulary into the portrait of his friend and Carnegie Tech faculty colleague Russell Twiggs. Now the entire composition—face, hands, and suit—possesses an angularity that synthesizes the sitter with the background, which is made up of all hard edges and right angles. The color palette that Rosenberg utilized for these compositions is unknown as the artist destroyed both paintings in 1965 because of irreparable damage. Rosenberg won Second Honor for *Around the Corner* in the Associated Artists of Pittsburgh Twenty-ninth Annual Exhibition in 1929. In his painting *The Gold Gown* of 1930 (plate 12), Rosenberg merges a portrait of an unidentified young girl with the Fox Chapel landscape that surrounds her.

Rosenberg captured the stoic character as well as the gentle nature of his friend and fellow artist in his *Portrait of Christian J. Walter* (plate 2), painted the year before Walter became president of the Associated Artists of Pittsburgh, a position he would hold for sixteen years. Christian J. Walter was as popular an artist in Pittsburgh as Rosenberg was in his day, and "So little you would have had to shake the sheets to find him in bed," as Mary Shaw Marohnic jokingly recalled with regard to his physical stature. "Christ (as he was known) Walter was a powerful, kindly force for good in the history of the Associated Artists. He cut through politics and brought feuding factions together. He loved Pittsburgh and Pittsburgh artists, and believed that 'no other place has the wealth of material that can be found here at home.'"[18]

Rosenberg maintained an interest in portraiture all his life. During the late 1940s, Rosenberg continued to make portraits of his family—Murray, Libbie, and Libbie's father Joseph—but his work became more allegorical and his figures less and less identifiable. Late in his life, Rosenberg painted portraits of his grandchildren Joel (1962), and Sue (1965), and, in 1970, two years before his death, Rosenberg and Murray painted simultaneous portraits of Sue. He also made a detailed pencil drawing of Joel in 1971, prior to Joel's marriage the following year.

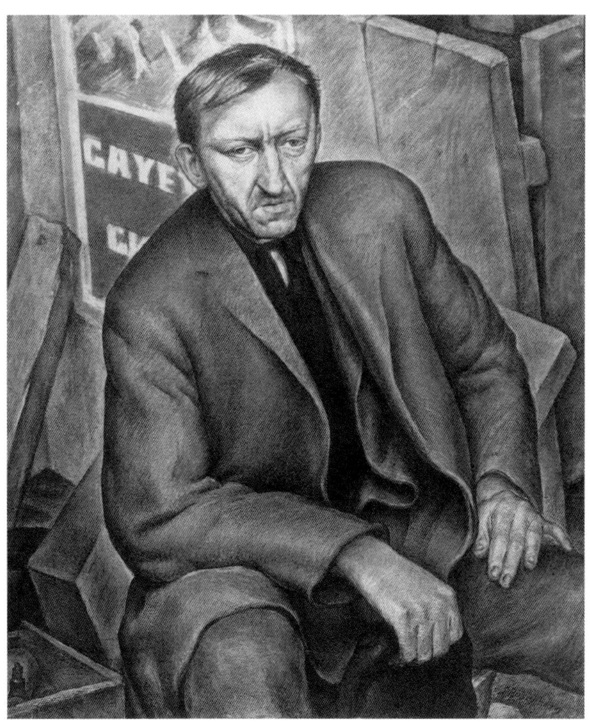

FIG. 11. *Around the Corner (Derelict),* 1928. Oil on canvas, 36 x 30″.

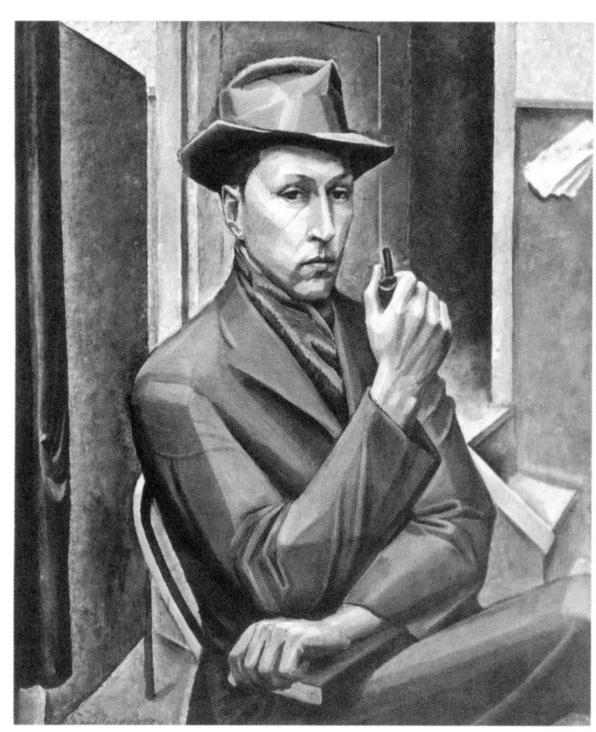

FIG. 12. *My Friend Twiggs,* 1931. Oil on canvas, 40 x 33″.

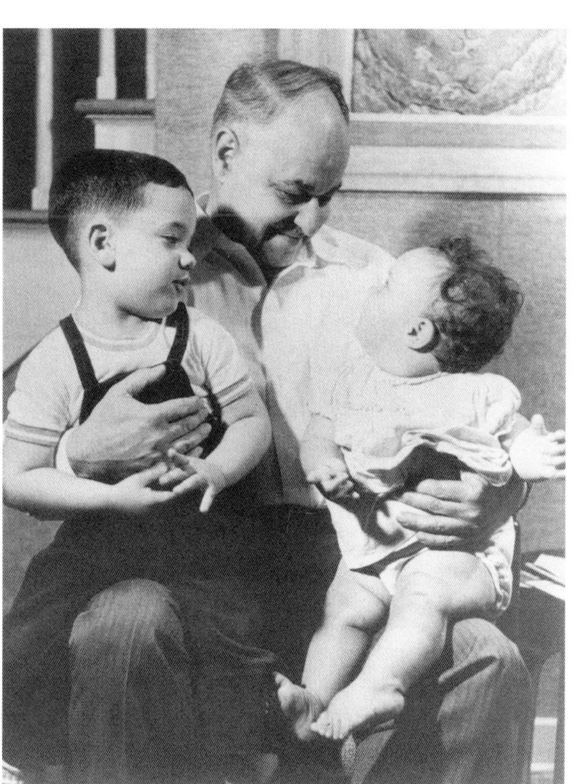

FIG. 13. Sam with his grandchildren Joel and Sue in New Haven, Conn., on Sue's first birthday, November 21, 1954.

Rosenberg gave up commissioned portraits in the early 1940s, saying, "I quit portraits because I felt I couldn't be free enough to paint what I wanted." At no time did portrait commissions provide Rosenberg with more than a welcome supplement to the modest income he derived from teaching, as he charged only 250 to 500 dollars for a commissioned portrait.[19] More importantly, this kind of portraiture was too confining for the artist; it tied him too much to convention, and to his studio. It was the sitter's insistence on a definite likeness that limited him. He acknowledged that he never liked the reaction he got from his sitters when they saw their finished portrait for the first time. He also said he found portraits "too easy."[20] "My first important step," he said, "was getting out of the studio." According to his family, it was a decision he never regretted. Rosenberg gave up formal commissions to concentrate on the surrounding urban landscape subjects of Pittsburgh, particularly the Hill District where he had lived in the 1920s. He left the studio to sketch the markets, factories, and neighborhood life of this and other poorer sections of the city.

Pittsburgh's Urban Landscape and the American Scene: 1930s

> So far as creating a personal style is concerned, artists can do that when they are old. I'd like to leave a record of things I've seen and felt in Pittsburgh. Some of my pictures would be a protest against the kind of a place we live in.

Rosenberg made this straightforward statement, which he would often repeat, to Douglas Naylor, art editor of the *Pittsburgh Press,* during an interview in 1935.[21] Indeed, Rosenberg succeeded in what he set out to do and left an expansive record of the things he'd seen and felt in Pittsburgh. The poignancy of his socially conscious subjects have become still more powerful in recent years because many of the paintings and drawings that Rosenberg left behind are the only records that remain of some sections of Pittsburgh prior to the "urban renewal" of the Lower Hill District.

Rosenberg explained his reasons for choosing the Hill District as his subject to Naylor:

> The Hill District is the spot I know best in Pittsburgh. Although I was born in Philadelphia, I lived for many years on Dinwiddie Street. I founded the art school at the Irene Kaufmann Settlement and taught there for eleven years. . . . So many people who live in Pittsburgh don't realize how much art possibilities there are here. . . . Artists are stimulated by form, and in Pittsburgh you have the forms of the hills,

> of the mills, and rivers. Other cities, in comparison, are deadening and monotonous in appearance. . . . I can't understand why so many artists in Pittsburgh are not wanting to paint this sort of thing. They keep sitting in their studios, waiting for an inspiration. The habit is deadening.[22]

In a later statement he added, "Pittsburgh artists have enough material to keep them painting for the rest of their lives, because the hills, rivers, and valleys relieve the monotony so often associated with industrial centers."[23]

Rosenberg reacted to the art of his times, creating his own brand of urban realism. When other artists were gravitating to the major metropolitan areas to pursue their artistic careers, Rosenberg was content to remain in Pittsburgh and paint the city as he knew it. He did not fully understand the appeal of looking elsewhere for subjects when people were surrounded by myriad subjects in their own backyards.[24]

> Yes, I know there are artists in town who sneer at Pittsburgh, who want to go to Venice and paint canals. But the artist who dislikes the town should, in my opinion, stay here and put his hate into pictures of the Pittsburgh scene. In doing so, he would have something to say. . . . Some great artists have hated social conditions and the environment in which they lived. An example was Daumier. The vehemence these artists have injected into their work has made it very much alive. The only value to be found in a work of art emerges from the personality of the artist and grows out of the emotions experienced in creating it. A painter must have something to say, he must absorb life![25]

Rosenberg's attitude was perfectly in keeping during this period with the nation's turning its attention to itself, and with the call put out by art critics and leaders in the field for a truly "American art." Thomas Craven, the leading voice in this movement, encouraged artists to seek out subjects from their own lives, environments, and experiences in America to use as a basis for their art, rather than looking to Europe for inspiration. This was a widespread attitude, promoted in all the publications and periodicals of the day.

Rosenberg, with other artists of his generation, helped to tell the story of the development of American art, and in a way, assisted in laying the foundation for generations to come. Rosenberg had two artistic choices when he began painting portraits in earnest in the 1920s. He could either take the abstract route, like Max Weber, Stuart Davis, and Alfred Maurer, who responded to the avant-garde movements in Europe, or a realist approach. He chose the latter course, not because he could not relate to the abstract concepts of pure form and color comprising a painting, but because he would take a more methodical artistic approach to his own development. He would arrive at his own personal form of abstract expressionism some decades later.

Earlier in the twentieth century, Robert Henri (1865–1929), had strongly urged his students to study their own environment. Henri was the leader of both "the Eight," a group of painters who exhibited together and represented opposition to the traditional aesthetics of the National Academy, and the related Ashcan School of painters, so named because of their unromantic representation of the seamier side of the urban landscape in which they lived. "Painting," Henri said, "is the expression of ideas in their permanent form. It is the giving of evidence. It is the study of our lives, our environment. The American who is useful as an artist is one who studies his own life and records his experiences; in this way he gives evidence. If a man has something to say he will find a way to say it." In his lectures, Henri advised his students, "If you want to be a historical painter, let your history be of your own time, of what you can get to know personally—of manners and customs within your own experience."[26] The ideology espoused by Henri, and his attitude about life and subject matter, was not lost on Rosenberg, who shared the elder artist's belief that art should express the spirit of its time and the spirit of its people. Indeed, throughout the decade of the 1930s, Rosenberg documented the twentieth-century urban life of Pittsburgh in much the same way as Ashcan School painters John Sloan and George Bellows documented Philadelphia and New York, and some of Rosenberg's subjects reflect that same gritty realism. In such paintings as *Sunshine on Tustin Street,* bright sunlight warms the grimy industrial street while dark shadows haunt this unglamorous area underneath the Brady Street Bridge (later replaced by the Birmingham Bridge) in Pittsburgh. One spot of red on the woman standing in the doorway is the only color to be found in this drab urban landscape. *Sunday Morning* of 1937 (figure 14; plate 30) depicts the weekly routine of churchgoers on Kirkpatrick Street in Soho. High above the same bridge, the all-black congregation leaves the morning worship service. The organization of the painting emphasizes the way in which the population of the Hill District was segregated from the city, although the place was very much a part of Pittsburgh's topography. Across the Monongahela River, the South Side is shrouded in smoke from the steel mills that dominated its banks.

Rosenberg's paintings of the 1930s reflect the socioeconomic conditions

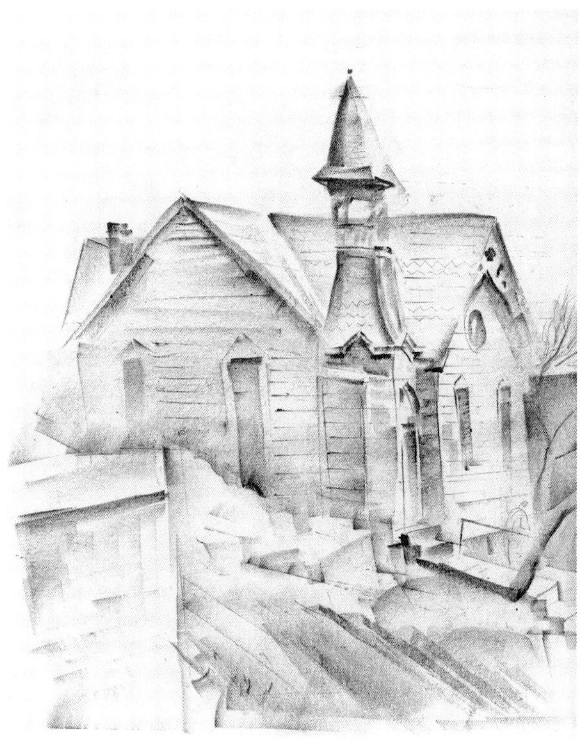

FIG. 14. *Sunday Morning* (preparatory study), c. 1937. Pencil on paper, 10 x 8″.

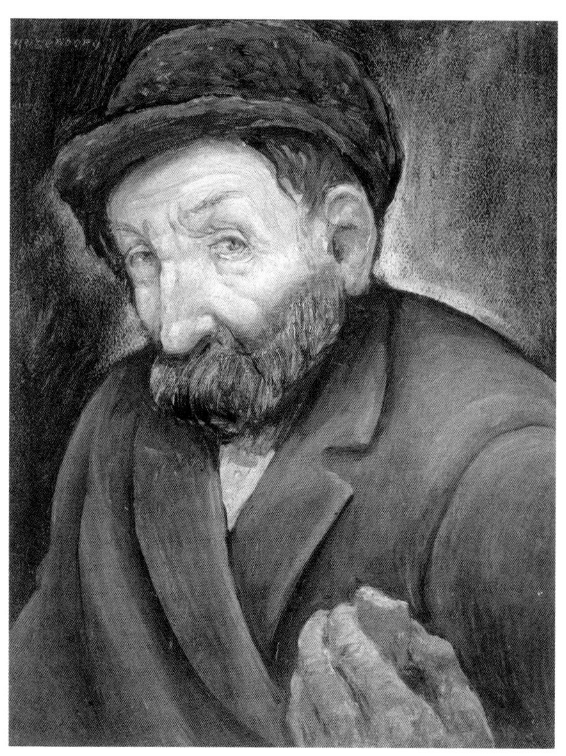

FIG. 15. *Breadwinner (Bearded Man)*, 1931. Oil on board, 20 x 16″.

of a particular neighborhood of Pittsburgh, specifically, the low-income environs of the Lower, Middle, and Upper Hill District, and should be understood within the sociopolitical context of the time. Slum clearances, unemployment, displacement of poor families, and evictions show up in the artist's work of this period. During the Great Depression, Pittsburgh was not unlike so many other large cities in the United States, once vital and thriving, but caught in the mire of unemployment and hard times. Life was dark and pessimism reigned. The entire city suffered, but the neighborhoods that already lived in poverty prior to the stock market crash of 1929 existed in even more dismal circumstances. Because of the predominance of the steel industry in Pittsburgh, the city was slower to feel the impact of the downturn in the economy and even slower to come back from it. Unemployment rose steadily, wages declined dramatically for those who were able to keep their jobs, product prices fell because of the lack of demand, and according to Stefan Lorant, whose 1964 book *Pittsburgh: The Story of An American City* chronicled the city's history, "The crazy, carefree days of the twenties had run their course; they were gone forever." Lorant chose twelve

Blacks had been among the Hill's earliest residents, but until the 1880s, their numbers remained small. The reason was jobs, since in Pittsburgh—as in other northern cities—industrialists hired blacks almost exclusively as temporary strikebreakers. Throughout the nineteenth century, the best jobs blacks could get were in personal service as waiters, barbers, Pullman porters, butlers, and maids. Nonetheless, Pittsburgh's booming economy created so many job opportunities—notably hauling and carting, day labor, and personal service—that blacks were increasingly attracted to the city. Between 1880 and 1910, these migrants, coming primarily from Virginia and the upper south, contributed to a black population that grew from 3,890 to 25,623, some 10,754 of whom settled in the Hill District.

The black presence in the Hill increased even more dramatically with the outbreak of World War I. The war cut off European immigration and created a labor shortage so severe that industrialists recruited black laborers from the south. This touched off a migratory wave that boosted Pittsburgh's black population from twenty-five thousand to over fifty thousand between 1910 and 1930.

Some twenty thousand black newcomers moved to mill towns lining the banks of the Monongahela River, where they worked for one of the Carnegie Steel complexes. Another thirty-five thousand came to Pittsburgh itself, settling mainly in the Hill District, a fairly long walk to jobs at the J & L mills in south Oakland. Those who migrated to the Hill—already overflowing with European immigrants—took lodging wherever they could, often in alleys and side streets and apartments in back of homes in predominantly Jewish neighborhoods of the Third Ward. By the 1920s, black newcomers began settling in the Fifth Ward, termed the Middle Hill, which lay farther east of the principal Jewish settlement, and soon had a higher proportion of blacks than the Third Ward.

In the time-honored American pattern of ethnic succession, as blacks were moving into the Hill, whites were moving out—Jews to Oakland and Squirrel Hill, Italians to Oakland and Bloomfield. As a result, between 1910 and 1940, the number of whites in the Hill dropped from 40,213 to 20,346, while the number of blacks grew from 10,754 to 31,839. The Hill District changed from 21 percent African American in 1910 to 43 percent in the 1920s, 47 percent in the 1930s, and 61 percent in the 1940s (Wolfe, "The Changing Pattern of Residence").

LAURENCE GLASCO

reproductions of Rosenberg's paintings to visually represent what life was like in Pittsburgh during the depression.[27]

Pittsburghers experienced a veritable economic roller-coaster ride during the depression—an up and down cycle of economic slumps that would continue for years. It wasn't a constant situation, as there were brief glimmers of financial prosperity throughout the decade. The depression, however, held its grip on Pittsburgh for over ten years, and Rosenberg's paintings of that period reveal the effect it had on the city and illustrate the environment he experienced and chose to paint. When asked during an interview how the depression impacted Pittsburgh artists, Rosenberg replied that "art is natural feeling, and that in such difficult years people [artists] find it more necessary than ever to create art as a medium through which they may pour out their emotions."[28] The artist, in these troubled times, Rosenberg thought, should make the most of his talent "living to the utmost and experiencing in paint all his impressions and reactions to the world he lives in."[29]

In the late fall of 1929, however, you would hardly know that the stock market had crashed. Pittsburgh's steel industries were operating at near full capacity, and the city seemed immune to the situation. Newspaper headlines reported prohibition news, social events, the Ohio River celebration, the World Series, and gangster activity in Chicago. The fiftieth anniversary of Thomas Edison's invention of the light bulb received more attention than the financial calamity that would grip the nation. "The New York Stock Exchange seemed far away from the furnaces and mills that fired Pittsburgh's economy." Unemployment was not a problem, as industry reported a record payroll of 328 million dollars that year. The financial analysts in the Pittsburgh newspapers were optimistic and reported that the market would come back. The downturn in the stock market was said to be just a "healthy reaction, nothing alarming."[30]

By March of 1930, however, the impact of what had occurred in October of the previous year had reached Pittsburgh: fifteen hundred men were standing in a breadline at Grant Street and Second Avenue. In a small painting of the *Yoder Hotel, Forbes Street* (plate 13) of 1930, Rosenberg presents a haunting scene of a group of homeless or transient men loitering in front of the building, waiting for free food and shelter. A clear economic indicator of the impact of the depression on Pittsburgh is the number of families on Allegheny County's relief rolls. By February of 1931, 6,345 families had been given aid by the various relief agencies in Allegheny County.[31] In that same month, the Allegheny County Emergency Association, an umbrella organization to which all other relief agencies reported, was created to deal with the unemployed. It was Edgar J. Kaufmann's plan to give relief to the unemployed based on work and not dole. His plan put a premium on work and looked toward a stabilization of employment as a means of relief. Laborers were assigned to road crews to repair highways and city streets.[32] *Greater Pittsburgh*, however, reported that the city's businesses had fared better than those in many other cities. Pittsburgh seemed to have escaped the worst of the slump; its building industry and retail sales were not as low as in eastern cities, and its unemployment was only down 11.9 per-

By the 1930s, the city of Pittsburgh and the Steel Valley in which it is located had, like Pennsylvania and the nation, been dominated by Republicans since the antebellum period. Nationally, only two Democrats, Grover Cleveland and Woodrow Wilson, had been elected to the White House since the Civil War—and Wilson had only won in 1912 because William Howard Taft and Theodore Roosevelt split the Republican majority. The picture was just as bleak for Democrats at the congressional level. In the eighteen elections between 1894 and 1930, for instance, the Republicans won the majority in the House of Representatives fifteen times.

The Pennsylvania Democratic Party had also been excluded from power since before the Civil War. Indeed, before 1936, the Democrats had not won Pennsylvania in a presidential election since 1852 and before 1932 the city of Pittsburgh had not been won by a Democratic presidential candidate since 1856. Before the election of Democrat George Earle as governor in 1934, the last Democratic governor had been Robert Pattison, elected in 1883 and again in 1890 only because of splits in the Republican Party. The last time the Democrats controlled either house in the state legislature had been in 1870 and, because of this, then sent the only Democrat to the U.S. Senate from Pennsylvania ever to serve before the 1930s. After the political realignment of the 1890s, the Democratic Party became even more marginalized, as Pennsylvania was converted into a solidly one-party state. For example, of the eighty statewide contests held from 1894 through 1931, a Democrat won only once.

What was true of the state at large was also true of the city of Pittsburgh. In the seventy-seven years between 1856 and 1933, only one Democrat—attorney George W. Guthrie, elected for a single term in 1905 at the head of a reform fusion ticket—served as mayor of the city. During the same seventy-seven years, the Democrats did not elect a single city councilor, local judge, or any other municipal candidate. Only because the law mandated that one of the three Allegheny County Commissioner seats be reserved for the minority

cent compared to declines of 19 percent in Cleveland, 14.9 percent in Philadelphia, 23 percent in Cincinnati, and 25 percent in Buffalo.[33]

In 1931, San Francisco ordered 72,000 tons of fabricated steel from Pittsburgh's mills for construction of the Golden Gate Bridge. By October, seven thousand unemployed workers returned to the mills to produce 125,000 tons of steel plates for New York's Radio City Music Hall.[34] The upturn in industrial activity generated optimism about the business trend, but Father James R. Cox, pastor of Old St. Patrick's Church in the Strip District, was not so optimistic. He had recently made a European tour and said that Pittsburgh was "facing the worst winter in the history of the world." His church was feeding eighteen hundred people a day, and a shantytown of homeless men had sprung up on Pennsylvania Railroad party and there be a space reserved for the minority judge of elections did any Democrat ever make it into any office of any kind in the region. By 1929, Allegheny County, in which Pittsburgh is located, claimed 169,000 registered Republican voters and only 5,200 registered Democrats, virtually all in Pittsburgh itself. Likewise, in the small steel towns clustered tightly around Pittsburgh, hardly a Democrat was to be found.

Meanwhile, the state's dominant Republican Party drew much of its support and leadership from western Pennsylvania. The chairman of the state Republican Party, for instance, William Larimer Mellon, elected in 1926, hailed from Pittsburgh, where his family presided over the city's economic and political life. Further, Pittsburgh's Andrew W. Mellon was Hoover's Secretary of the Treasury.

The Democratic Party, then, especially in the small steel towns of western Pennsylvania, was a hollow shell with a miniscule constituency and no influence. What prevailed in Pittsburgh and Pennsylvania was part of a larger political pattern of Republican-corporation rule which had come to dominate the country around the turn of the century.

But, with the presidential election of 1932, that began to change in Pittsburgh. While the rest of the state, for the time being, remained firmly Republican, Pittsburgh Democrats began a "Long March" through electoral offices, conquering them one by one as their terms came up. At the end of this "Long March," in 1935, Pittsburgh became a Democratic bastion, as it has remained up to the present. No Republican presidential or mayoral candidate has carried the city since then, nor has a Republican been elected to any municipal office since 1932. Indeed, Republican Pennsylvania became a competitive two-party state because of the enduring Democratic dominance of Pittsburgh and surrounding Allegheny County which began at this time. Even as late as 2000, registered Democratic voters continued to outnumber registered Republicans in Allegheny County by a margin of two to one.

ERIC LEIF DAVIN

property adjacent to the church rectory.[35] The downturn in steel exports was the major cause of the economic slump in Pittsburgh. Before the depression, in 1929, foreign markets had bought two hundred million dollars' worth of steel from the tri-state area. In 1932, that number dropped to twenty million.[36] *Second Avenue* of 1932 (plate 18), formerly titled *Man-Made Desert* and then *Street by the Mill,* reinforces the impact that the slowdown of steel production had on inhabitants of the city. Instead of a large group of men crowding the sidewalk on their way to or from work, two lone men walk along the deserted route. Jones and Laughlin Steel Company is located on the other side of the imposing stone wall, but the minimal amount of smoke in the environment is an indication that the mill is not working at capacity. Rosenberg made this painting in the winter of 1932,

What happened in Pittsburgh in the 1930s is part of the larger story of what happened in America at that time. By 1940, virtually every major American city was producing huge Democratic electoral majorities, even though some, like Pittsburgh, had been dominated by powerful Republican political machines just a decade earlier. This almost inconceivable political transformation was a political aberration unique in American history, never seen before or since, not just because it was the last major political realignment this country has experienced, but also because it was based upon class politics.

This did not happen just because of the "Hard Times" of the Great Depression. Indeed, far from making the working class stronger, hard times before and since have often had a crippling effect on union strength and working-class interests in general. Thus, to understand why the urban ethnic working class voted as it did in the 1930s, we have to look at the social environment that formed the political identities of the families, communities, fraternal, and labor organizations to which these voters belonged. When we do this, we find that the class-based political realignment of the 1930s was made possible by a combination of social factors which became characteristic of large American cities, especially in the northeast, from about the beginning of World War I to the coming of the New Deal, approximately 1914–1932. Foremost among them was simply *stability*. But stability was just the essential beginning. The entire constellation of factors included:

1) Long-term job stability for blue-collar workers;

2) Long-term neighborhood stability in blue-collar neighborhoods;

3) The consequent growth of a dense social network centered around churches, extended families, and voluntary societies; and, consequent upon the preceding,

4) The evolution of a working-class identity which transcended, but did not replace, ethnic identities.

when industry was again laying off workers and Father Cox led his famous march of fifteen thousand of Pittsburgh's unemployed on Washington, D.C. The compositional devices that Rosenberg used in this painting—the deserted cobblestone street curving back toward the wall, the telephone poles bending to the right—all direct the viewer's attention to the single men and the wall that divides them from their work. Penelope Redd, in her review of the AAP annual exhibition for the *Pittsburgh Sun-Telegraph*, wrote that Rosenberg "expresses through the abstract elements of visual art, certain facts that are heightened only slightly to point out with Daumier-like intensity, the bitter truth." The original title Rosenberg gave to the painting substantiates the mood he was trying to convey.[37] This painting was included in the annual American Paintings and Sculptures exhibition at the Art Institute of Chicago in 1940. A second painting of the same subject,

Thus, by the 1930s, urban working-class populations witnessed increasing economic and geographic stability, increasing institutional strength, as well as a muting of ethnic divisions among the American-born children of the New Immigrants. These social changes meshed with an inclusive "American rights" ideology—which came to be embodied in the Democratic Party—to eventually foster cross-ethnic working-class consciousness and solidarity.

Part of the phenomenon of the class-conscious political realignment in the 1930s was an intersecting phenomenon, the urban and ethnic demographic revolution. As the 1920 U.S. Census graphically revealed, America finally became an urban nation in the twenties, as the majority of its population for the first time was to be found in the cities. This trend helps us understand why "labor's millions" were "on the march" by the 1930s.

Not only did America's cities continue to mushroom in the 1920s, this urban population was also primarily an ethnic population. However, this population was a patchwork quilt of ethnicities, which may have been a major contributing reason for the perceived lack of "class consciousness" in America during this period. The American working class was constantly being remade over and over as new waves of immigrants entered the workforce, bringing with them their "alien" customs, beliefs, and values. This constant demographic churning brought to the fore ethnocultural differences and issues, making them—prohibition, blue laws, religion, etc.—the cleavage lines of American politics. Further, alien workers were thrown into conflict not only with the "natives," but also with other alien workers transplanted to an alien land. It was difficult for them to even speak to each other. As for them uniting in common cause, it was just as likely they would finish the Tower of Babel as find common grounds for united political action.

ERIC LEIF DAVIN

entitled *Second Avenue No. 2* and made six years later, reveals a scene totally devoid of human activity, but reveals, just beyond the end of the stone wall, a modicum of industrial activity. The somber colors used in both paintings convey the grim conditions of the period.

The harsh reality of the depression years is seen in the monochromatic composition entitled *Greenfield Hill,* formerly known as *Gazzam's Hill,* of 1932 (plate 14). Two exhausted men, their shoulders sagging, walk together along a cobblestone street, on a dreary, gray day in Pittsburgh. The barren landscape and bleak neighborhood of simple, clapboard houses comprise the background of the painting. The curvilinear structure of the composition suggests that these men, resigned to their circumstances, will continuously walk around and around the neighborhood, as if on a treadmill that won't stop. Variations in pattern emphasize this sense of movement, and the artist has even curved the telephone poles at the right to heighten this sensation of the endless cycle. Rosenberg's figures convey the nomadic wandering of a large percentage of the U.S. population from city to city during the depression years; his gray/brown palette captures the dismal mood of the times. When the artist saw a subject that moved him, he would make a record of it immediately, and use his sketches later for one or more paintings. The two sketches he made for this painting were done on the spot, as was his custom, and then the final painting was quickly executed back in his studio at Carnegie Tech (figure 16). He said this was one of the fastest paintings he ever made. While others typically took him from one week to one year to finish, this one was completed in one afternoon. It was a mood that needed to be captured in the moment. The title of the painting was changed twenty-five years later to *Greenfield Hill,* at the suggestion of art critic Dorothy Kantner, who told Sam and Libbie that the area depicted was inaccurately designated. It remains curious to me that the painting was exhibited for the first twenty-five years of its existence with its title of *Gazzam's Hill,* and then so effortlessly changed at the suggestion of one person. Rosenberg was still living when the title was changed, but perhaps he no longer remembered where he had painted the scene and was content to go along with the new attribution. The fact that the majority of Rosenberg's subjects were of Soho and the Hill District in the 1930s leads me to believe that the original title is the more accurate one.[38] In addition, no other paintings or sketches exist that indicate that the artist spent any time painting on the other side of the city in the environs of Greenfield Hill. *Gazzam's Hill* was exhibited on a national scale for three years after it was painted. The Museum of Modern Art in New York selected the painting for inclusion in its 1933 exhibition, Painting and Sculpture from Sixteen American Cities; it was shown at the Corcoran Gallery of Art, Washington, D.C., in 1934; at the Pennsylvania Academy of the Fine Arts in Philadelphia in 1935; and in the Associated Artists of Pittsburgh Twenty-fifth Annual Exhibition the same year. After it had been exhibited at the Museum of Modern Art, the painting was reproduced as the cover illustration for a 1934 issue of *New York Herald Tribune Books.* The book it was used to illustrate, *A College Girl in the Pennsylvania Mines,* recounts the story of Lauren Gilfillan who, at age twenty-two, spent weeks in a Pennsylvania mining town and wrote about her experiences with the miners' families there.[39]

Speaking about the painting, Rosenberg said, "One of the distinctive spots here is Soho and Gazzam's Hill. The hill itself is located in the Soho district. In my paintings of this neighborhood, I have tried to show the changing moods of the Pittsburgh atmosphere, and how it affects the ap-

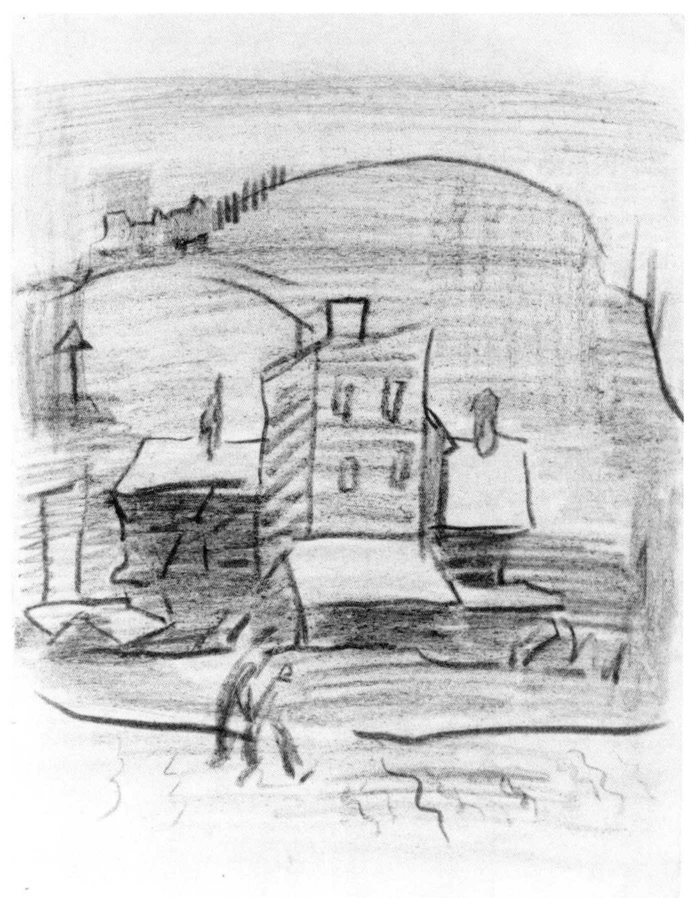

FIG. 16. *Greenfield Hill* (preparatory study), 1932. Crayon on paper, 10$\frac{3}{16}$ x 7$\frac{15}{16}$".

pearance of the hills. The dusty film that envelops Pittsburgh softens the edges of everything, a contrast, for example, to the sharpness of the landscape along the New England coast."[40]

In *Soho* of 1934 (plate 22), Rosenberg details the less than desirable living conditions in the lower part of the Soho District. Adjacent to the Hill District, and comprising part of the Fourth Ward, Soho was one of Pittsburgh's poorest sections. In his stark portrayal, Rosenberg effectively expresses the harsh reality of this poverty-stricken neighborhood. The surrounding piles of dirt suggest the difficult task that the woman, seen sweeping her steps, faces in her attempts to keep her property clean. Of this painting, Penelope Redd wrote:

> Samuel Rosenberg has the best of the Pittsburgh paintings in *Soho.* The stark reality of the approximate spot is the nucleus of his pictorial idea. Jaunty shacks and barren hills are taken as they appear to the eye of the passerby. Rosenberg, however, has transmuted the hard material facts of existence into the poetry of life within us all.

He has performed this ever-recurring miracle of art through the infusion of rhythm in form and color and through his own style of painting. While *Soho* is Pittsburgh, it is likewise any spot on earth where laughter and joy may be gleaned from barren soil.[41]

In his painting *Eviction* of 1935 (plate 24), Rosenberg illustrated a scene he witnessed on Forbes Street in the Soho district during the height of the depression. Caught in the moment of being dispossessed from their home, a couple stands disconsolate in the doorway, while their household belongings are piled in the snow. Many landlords would not rent to families on relief during the depression years, and if they found out a tenant was dependent on relief, they would force them out. The Allegheny County Relief Board acted as a mediating agency to prevent the evictions of needy families, often paying the landlord's bills to allow them to stay.[42] When discussing the painting Rosenberg said: "Plenty of things like that are happening all the time. They are representative of life of our time. And they are things an artist of today should look at, instead of copying from other artists."

In preparation for the painting, Rosenberg created numerous studies of the actual scene as it occurred in January 1935, and these can be seen as something of a stylistic experiment (figure 18). Composed in a much more abstract, cubist vocabulary than the final painting, one of his drawings emphatically translates the movement of the men as they remove the family's belongings from the house (figure 17). In a second drawing, Rosenberg concentrates on the powerful body language of the couple, their bowed heads, and the mother protectively holding one child while sheltering another behind her skirts, reinforcing their shame and despair. In both drawings, the suggestion of movement, simplification of form, and compressed space reveal Rosenberg's intermittent stylistic investigation into futurism and cubism. (Rosenberg's experimentation with cubism continued briefly in 1935 in his painting *Sideshow* (plate 26), and he would reinvestigate this style in his work of the early 1950s.) The subdued colors Rosenberg utilized in the final version of *Eviction* reinforce the pathos he felt about the situation. He said that he passed by the same spot three days later, and the family's belongings were still there.[43] Jeanette Jena wrote that the painting was "more dramatic for its sense of form and color than for the story of Exodus it tells."[44] In an interview he gave years later, Rosenberg told a reporter from the *Pittsburgh Courier* that his main interest in choosing a subject was the appeal of the individual. "I paint from my heart, from the things in life which touch me and which must in turn touch and impress

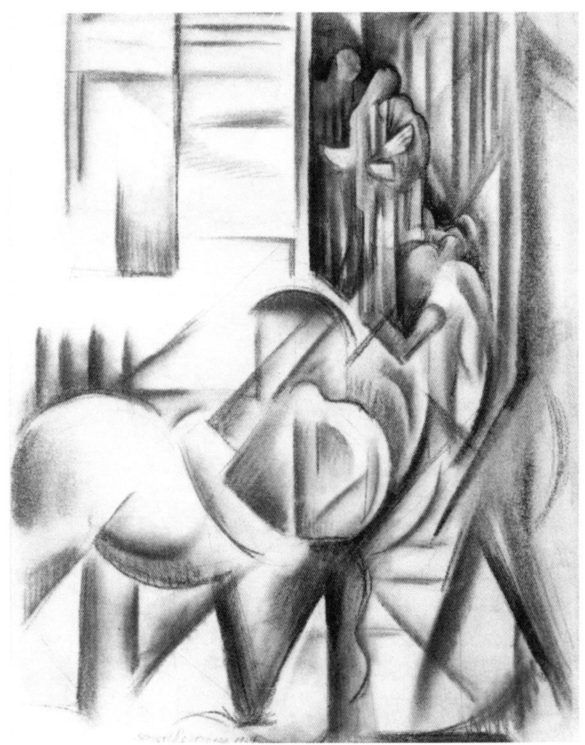

FIG. 17. *Eviction* (preparatory study), 1934. Conte crayon on paper, 23 x 19″.

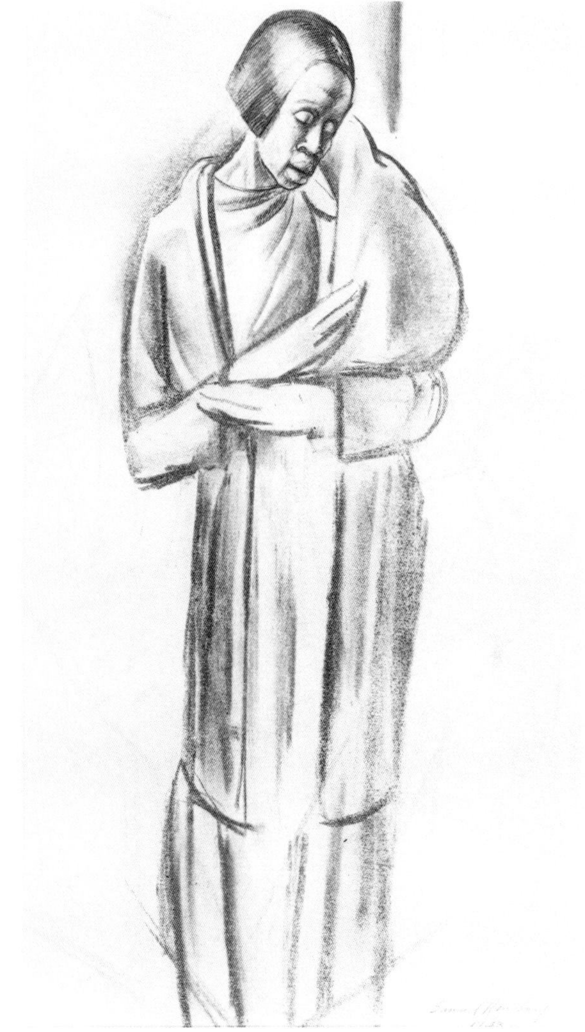

FIG. 18. *Eviction* (preparatory study), 1933. Conte crayon on paper, 20 x 12″.

others."[45] In 1965, Ralph Brem said of *Eviction,* "It's a picture that is completely timeless. It fits today as well as it fit in 1935, and the days that went before and those that come after tomorrow."[46]

In these paintings, and others that Rosenberg created during the 1930s, people that figure into his compositions are clearly subordinated to their surroundings. "To me," Rosenberg said, "Soho seems to typify Pittsburgh in topography and atmosphere, while the people seem to be an integral part of their particular environment. You couldn't say that about East Liberty, for example, a flat section that might be found duplicated in any city."[47]

Each neighborhood in Pittsburgh—Squirrel Hill, East End, Oakland,

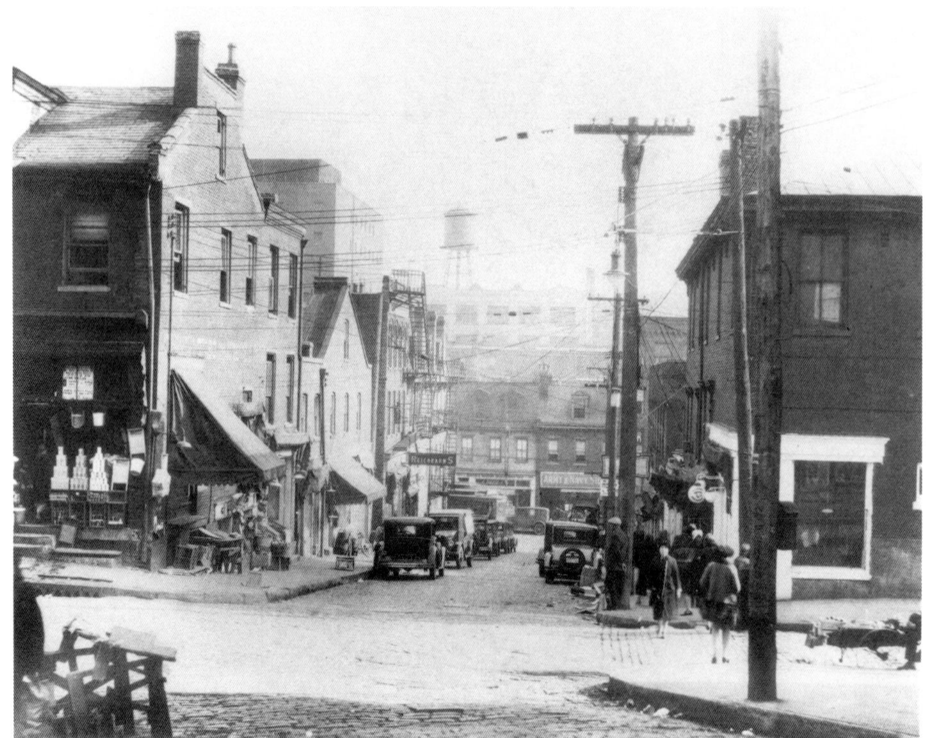

FIG. 19.
Hill District: Logan Alley and Our Way, 1929.

Highland Park, Shadyside—had its own personality and character, and the Hill District was no exception. In 1932, in an article in *Greater Pittsburgh*, Edward Power wrote that the area was "picturesque" and "crammed with romance."[48] The "picturesque" Hill District stretches for two miles east of the Golden Triangle, and is sandwiched in between the Strip District and Oakland. So-named because of its hilly terrain and literal location on a hill, the Hill District overlooks both the Monongahela River to the south and the Allegheny River to the north. Its population has shifted throughout the years, but the Hill District has always been a multiethnic, multiracial neighborhood. The once-vibrant Hill District was initially comprised of three sections differentiated as the Lower, Middle, and Upper Hills. Today the Hill retains only two of its original sections, the Middle and Upper Hill. In the days that Rosenberg roamed the streets there in search of subjects to paint, the neighborhood was a vital place and Rosenberg recorded that vitality in his depictions of the busy markets, street rallies, churchgoers, businesses, etc. But he also exposed the darker side of the neighborhood. While Sam and Libbie did not consider themselves poor in the 1930s, they could relate to the conditions of the people he depicted in his paintings. When they were first married in 1922, before Rosenberg began teaching at Carnegie Tech, the couple experienced difficult times. In the 1930s, when Rosenberg returned to paint the neighborhoods in the Hill District where he had lived early in his career, he became something of a voyeur, detached from his subjects physically, while still very much attached to them emotionally.

For a quiet person, Rosenberg had much to say about the Hill over the years. In 1935, he said: "There is enough material here to keep all the artists of Pittsburgh going for the rest of their lives. Many of the artists who come here to serve on juries for the International Exhibition have told me they are anxious to come back and paint Pittsburgh. Life is constantly changing, so an artist must do so too. The drama of life keeps churning constantly on the Hill. Even the houses have taken on the character of the people who built them and live in them."[49] In *Webster Avenue House* of 1932 (plate 17), located in the Lower Hill District, Rosenberg was not only attempting to recreate the house on the hill, but to express, as he put it, "certain movements." The pictorial tension, created by the opposing movements of the man walking in one direction while the house leans in the opposite direction, is not what the artist had in mind when he painted the house, nor is it why he chose this particular subject. He chose it to paint because he thought the house had a character all its own. "To me, houses take on the human quality of the people who build them, or who live in them. This is particularly true of the older houses of Pittsburgh. In these paintings I am recording architectural ornaments devised by the homeowners who built them, and which reveal their taste. The fancy ornaments represent the end of a period, which began with Victorian bustles and corsets. These houses will seem incredible to people of the future. I noticed one example the other day in Oakland. Fragments of colored bottles were put in the cement on the façade for ornament. It does not conform to the principles of fine art, but to me the house is important as a record of a passing period. It seems that every one who built a house in that period owned a jig saw that was used in making ornamentation. This personal architecture is to be seen along the top of the false second front and around the porches. The painting of Webster Avenue House is a leftover of this period. At one time it was an aristocratic neighborhood. The house was amusing to me because of its long porch. I was far below it, and while gazing up it took on an impression of going forward."[50] His painting *Retaining Wall—Webster Avenue* also describes the ongoing decaying condition of this neighborhood. "You will find, too," Rosenberg said, "that the people of the Hill District are ingrained in their environment. They are a part of the

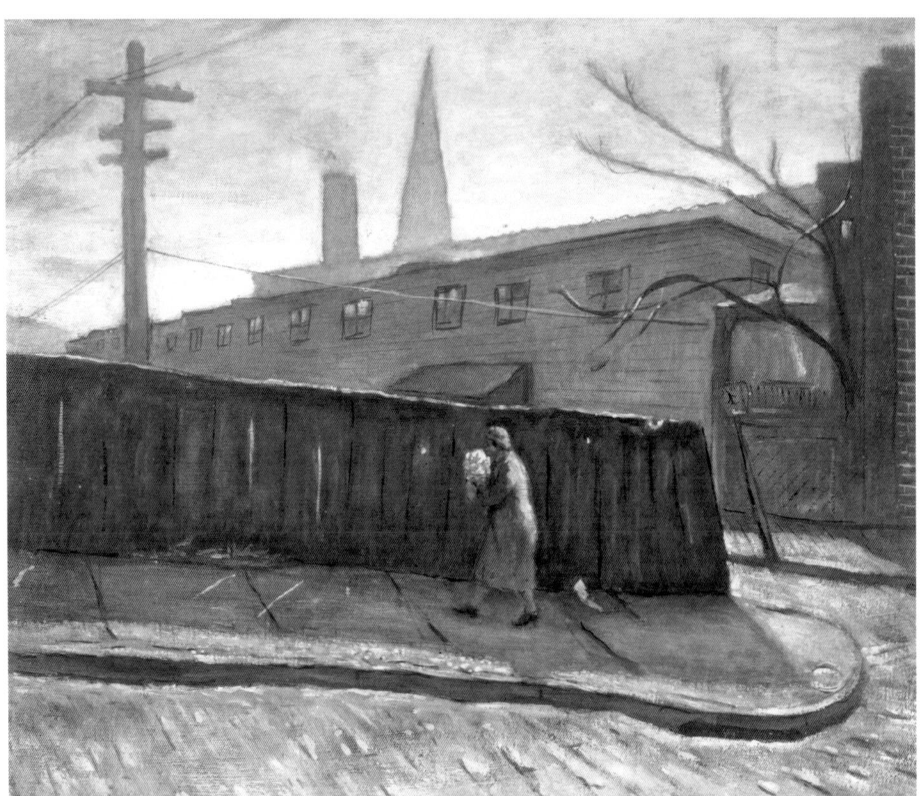

FIG. 20. *Dusk* [*Atwood Street Corner*, 1939 with *Dusk*, 1943, verso]. Oil on masonite, 20 x 24″.

very earth of the Hill. Some of their shanties are plastered on the hillsides, looking as if the wind would blow them off. Such sights are an important part of the distinctive Pittsburgh scene."[51]

At the beginning of the twentieth century, the population of the Lower Hill was made up of immigrants from central and eastern Europe, and the people and culture were primarily Jewish.[52] During the years that Rosenberg lived there, the first two decades of the twentieth century, the population shifted to a diverse blend of eastern European Jews, Italians, and African Americans. During that time, Jewish families continued to migrate to the Lower Hill because of the low rents there, but as Jewish families became more affluent, they moved into the Upper Hill and to other parts of the city, (Squirrel Hill, East End, and Oakland). They were replaced by Italian immigrants and African Americans from the south, who migrated to Pittsburgh to find work in the mills. By the time Rosenberg returned to the Hill District to paint in the 1930s, the population was predominantly African American, but the multiethnic mix still existed. Jewish markets and depressed African American neighborhoods were the principal subjects of his paintings in that decade. He did not satirize Jewish or

It was during the period of racial transition between World War I and the 1950s that the Hill experienced its creative heyday. The vitality of that era is well captured in the PBS video "Wylie Avenue Days," although the video pays little attention to the presence of Jews and Italians. Racial and ethnic mingling, especially among blacks and Jews, created an unrivaled social dynamic. The two lived near one another, typically in racial clusters, but with considerable overlap. The 1920 census shows that one-third of blacks in the Hill had a white neighbor—typically Jewish—who lived not more than five houses away. Children went to school together—the Pittsburgh schools had been desegregated in the 1870s—and an Urban League investigation in the 1920s found little or no interracial fighting among the pupils. Herman Gordon, whose family's shoe store at Centre and Kirkpatrick catered to both blacks and whites, recalls playing with black kids in the neighborhood. Thelma Lovett, a black resident born and raised in the Hill, recalls shopping among people of different racial and ethnic backgrounds along Logan Street, buying groceries, poultry, and dry goods at the Jewish shops while conversing with friends and neighbors.

People got along reasonably well. Johnny Butera, of Italian descent, grew up (and still lives) in the same duplex on Bedford Avenue as the family of playwright August Wilson. Wilson's sister, Linda Jean Kittle-Conroy, recalls growing up in the 1940s in an apartment located behind Jewish-owned Siger's market, which was next door to the Butera family's shoe and watch repair shop. Down the street lived Syrians, Greeks, Italians, other blacks, and Jews, such as the family of Dr. Goldblum, the neighborhood's physician. Butera and Kittle-Conroy agree that neighbors seldom socialized across racial lines, but were friendly with one another and could be counted on in a pinch. Race relations in the Hill were not utopian, but neither the Hill nor Pittsburgh in general suffered the kinds of white-inspired race riots that disfigured New York, Philadelphia, Detroit, Chicago, and a host of other American cities during the 1920s, '30s, and '40s.

Despite the racial ambivalence of some Jews, others worked to improve race relations. Frank Bolden, reporter and city editor for the black-owned *Pittsburgh Courier*, notes that in the 1930s, blacks and Jews in the Hill formed a political coalition which helped both communities, and which secured the election of the city's first black to the state legislature, Homer Brown. In the 1940s, the Irene Kaufmann Center, established to serve the Hill's Jewish population, opened its outstanding facilities to black groups, and a few years later, as its Jewish clientele continued to decline, donated its magnificent building to the black community (Hopkins, "Some Factors in the Discontinuance," 3).

LAURENCE GLASCO

African American life, but depicted people honestly in the circumstances in which they lived and worked.

The *Pittsburgh Courier* (now the *New Pittsburgh Courier*) established itself as an African American newspaper in the Hill in 1910 and remains in business today on the South Side. Charles "Teenie" Harris, an African American photographer employed by the *Courier* for over forty years, documented the vibrancy of the Hill District in his powerful narrative photographs in much the same way that Rosenberg recorded the life of the neighborhoods in his paintings during the same time period. The Hill District functioned much like a city within a city during those years, a necessity brought on by the racial discrimination toward its inhabitants. Because the primarily African American residents were not allowed to shop in the stores downtown, eat in the city's restaurants, or enter the city's theaters, they established their own thriving commercial district, which continued to prosper until the late 1960s. In the 1930s, the intersection of Wylie and Fullerton Avenues became known as the "Crossroads of the World" because of all the famous jazz musicians who passed through the Hill. According to Franklin Toker, "The neighborhood accommodated a diversity unparalleled by any other . . . and it was the cradle for two groups who lived there for generations: Pittsburgh's blacks, and its Jews.[53]

The Hill District (the area Gilbert Love said "might well be named Relief Ridge"), Soho, and the North Side were the hardest-hit sections of Pittsburgh during the depression. Of the 22,140 total population of the Lower Hill, 18,200 persons, or 82 percent, were dependent on direct relief. In the remainder of the Hill, the percentage was just over half. In Soho, 53 percent of the population required relief, on the North Side, 61 percent did; these statistics contrast dramatically with those in other parts of the city, such as 2 percent in Squirrel Hill, 1 percent in Dormont, and 0.5 percent in Mt. Lebanon. About half of Allegheny County's relief-WPA population was crowded into an area within a three-mile radius of the Golden Triangle.[54] Not even the heavily industrial communities of Homestead, McKeesport, Sharpsburg, and McKees Rocks were hit as hard by the depression as the Hill District. As mentioned above, the unemployment situation in Pittsburgh was ongoing and severe. The economic cycle in Pittsburgh took another dramatic downturn in 1934, and in September of that year, 160,000 to 170,000 persons were reported unemployed in this area. "Allegheny County Relief Cases Nearing 70,000" was the *Pittsburgh Post-Gazette*'s headline on September 15. And despite the recovery programs taking place, unemployment continually increased.

In 1936, the *Bulletin Index* headline declared: "Recovery: Pittsburgh Leads

Contrary to myth, the majority of immigrants came, not to stay, but with the intent to work for a short while, build up a financial stake, and return home with their savings. Indeed, over one-third of all immigrants returned to their homelands to stay. For certain ethnic groups, the percentage was higher. Half of all Italians, Hungarians, and Slovaks, 40 percent of Greeks, and 35 percent of Poles returned home. These high rates of return continued until the turmoil of World War I ended the two-way flow.

After the war, however, ethnic communities settled into a pattern of stability as immigrants increasingly decided to stay in America, while the flood of new arrivals from Europe ceased. Not only were economic collapse and revolution devastating Europe, but America was becoming more attractive. Captains of industry began to realize how much they had lost due to high rates of workforce turnover and they began to raise wages and institute various packages of "corporate welfare" benefits in order to create a stable workforce.

More importantly, however, the decades-long battle to restrict immigration finally succeeded in turning off the European faucet. In 1924, the Republican-dominated Congress passed the National Origins [Johnson] Act. This greatly restricted further European immigration by establishing a maximum quota of only 150,000 immigrants per year, and most of them had to come from northern and western Europe. Without continued injections of foreign culture, both the cities and the workforce grew more "Americanized" as the children of the New Immigrants grew up and joined the world of urban work. Thus was established the pattern which persisted for decades. New Immigrant workers settled into what became relatively secure and stable jobs, providing the stock for the stable neighborhoods that began to cluster around the factories where they worked.

A durable and intimate overlap of work, family, and neighborhood was not only one of the most significant aspects of life in the urban ethnic enclave, but was also of paramount importance for the creation of working class solidarity—because "class" solidarity also meant ethnic, neighborhood, and, more importantly, *family* solidarity. To express class solidarity with your fellow workers meant expressing solidarity with your father, your uncles, your brothers, and your fellow Poles or *paesani* with whom you worked. It was hard to say where one kind of solidarity left off and another began.

An overlap of identities strengthened New Immigrant loyalties to each other. In Pittsburgh, and even more especially in the surrounding mill towns, workers lived together, labored together, looked like each other, and married each other. All of these common life experiences helped create a sense of trans-ethnic community. This period of evolving stabilization, from about 1914 to about 1932, therefore laid the foundation for the 1930–1960 pattern of occupational and neighborhood stability, which, in turn, was the basis of class politics.

However, this ethnic pattern was in the process of transition during the 1920s and 1930s as, essentially, "aliens" became "Americans"; the children of the New Immigrants grew up and joined the world of urban work. Born and raised in America, and so citizens by birth, these children of the immigrants spoke English and increasingly, regardless of ethnic background, thought of themselves as "Americans" rather than as strangers in a strange land. They immersed themselves in the culture and values of the society in which they came of age, and mobilized into the electoral arena as their parents had not. This new generation not only shifted the demographic gravitational pull decisively away from the countryside, they completed the political power shift that had likewise been underway from country to city.

This political power shift also changed the longtime content of American politics, changing it into a class-based politics. Overwhelmingly, these children of immigrants worked in the same type of blue-collar jobs. Industrialization was a homogenizing influence because it created a central place of work where most of one's fellow workers, regardless of ethnicity, were laboring under the same conditions. Even as early as 1910, for example, one-third of all manufacturing workers in Pittsburgh labored in open-hearth furnaces and rolling mills. The same was true of the outlying industrial communities of Allegheny County. Lydia Nemanich, age seventy-six in 1999, recalled of life in coal mining town of Morgan, "Everybody was a miner. It was just a way of life" (Ostendorf, "Women Mine Memories," 1). As ethnic differences between the workers declined over time, it became increasingly easy to see what they had in common: class. Ethnicity, therefore, began to combine with an emerging working-class consciousness. By the 1930s, this pervasive ethnic working-class consciousness was widespread in America and dominated the Pittsburgh region's ethnic working-class neighborhoods.

These workers were not exact replicas of Old World workers transplanted to the New. America had transformed them into a combination of the two, with newly emerging characteristics coexisting with remnants of the old. For example, along with an enduring ethnic "family" ethos, these ethnic communities had also become imbued with the ethos of American democracy (which was denied to them by the Republican-corporate alliance) and hungered for it for decades before they were able to gain it in the thirties. In the case of the depression-era Steel Valley, family loyalties, ethnic loyalties, workplace loyalties, and political loyalties went hand-in-hand. The mutualistic ethos of family solidarity (reinforced by the "family economy" where everyone had to work together if the family were to survive) and neighborhood solidarity had mutated into an identification with others who were not of one's family, neighborhood, or ethnicity—indeed, were strangers—but were fellow workers with whom one nevertheless felt a sense of solidarity.

In retrospect, it is easy to see why ethnic class consciousness was so powerful in the working class at this time. When the working class was overwhelmingly white, southern and eastern European Orthodox-Catholic, attended the same churches and fraternal lodges, lived in tight-knit and kin-related urban ethnic villages where everybody was just like everybody else, and engaged in similar industrial occupations with a few, easily identifiable, capitalist enemies thought to be oppressing all equally—it was easy to see what you had in common. It was easy to feel and act upon class solidarity with your fellow workers, who also happened to be your kin and neighbors. The habits, life, and culture of the ethnic village thus became the social basis of class politics in depression-era America. This class politics found expression not only in labor unions (especially the Congress of Industrial Organizations, the CIO, with its ethos of egalitarianism and class solidarity regardless of ethnicity), but also in the Democratic

Party, which began making explicit appeals to the workers' emerging ethos of ethnic class consciousness.

Thus, with the decline of salient ethnocultural conflict and with the economic crisis of the depression, class politics, always present but usually submerged by ethnocultural tensions, became the primary fault line of American political life for the first time. By the early 1930s, the Steel Valley's workers, regardless of ethnic background, tended to think the same way and, in the voting booth, voted the same way. Murals of Roosevelt were on the walls of their fraternal and union halls and Roosevelt was on their minds on Election Day. In conjunction with other major industrial cities of the Northeast and Midwest, the Pittsburgh region emerged as a crucial component of the "New Deal coalition," and the forces which transformed the American political universe in the 1930s were particularly acute in the Steel Valley.

ERIC LEIF DAVIN

the Nation to Prosperity." And perhaps Rosenberg recognized that optimistic viewpoint when he painted *The Sun Shines in Pittsburgh* (figure 21; plate 29) that year. In this painting, Rosenberg presents a fragment of the Upper Hill looking toward the Gulf Building downtown, perhaps part of the area once known as Coal Hill. Sunlight permeates the scene, revealing that, indeed, the sun did shine in Pittsburgh. A man selling baskets of coal sits to the right while an African American child with a gleeful expression on her face absorbs the rays, perhaps a faint sign of optimism. In the majority of his Pittsburgh scenes, however, Rosenberg depicted the city during the winter or early spring months when there were neither leaves on the trees nor sun in the sky. His bleak imagery reinforced the effect that the depression had on the city and its inhabitants. Only a year after the hopeful headlines, steel industries were hit hard again and 35,000 workers lost their jobs. Relief administration offices that had been closed—due to the belief that the depression was over—were now reopened. Pittsburgh was in the midst of a second depression, this time called a "recession." The *Pittsburgh Sun-Telegraph* reported on December 6, 1937, that industrial layoffs affected 65,000 men in the steel and soft coal industries. Pennsylvania had 2,546,000 registered workers in 1938 and more eligible for unemployment than any other state in the union. The numbers of people receiving relief in Allegheny County tell the story: from 1935 to 1936, the numbers had dropped from 326,000 to 197,000, but by 1938, the number had risen back up to 320,000. This means that in 1938, 23 percent of the total population of the county reported receiving relief. The second half of the "economic hurri-

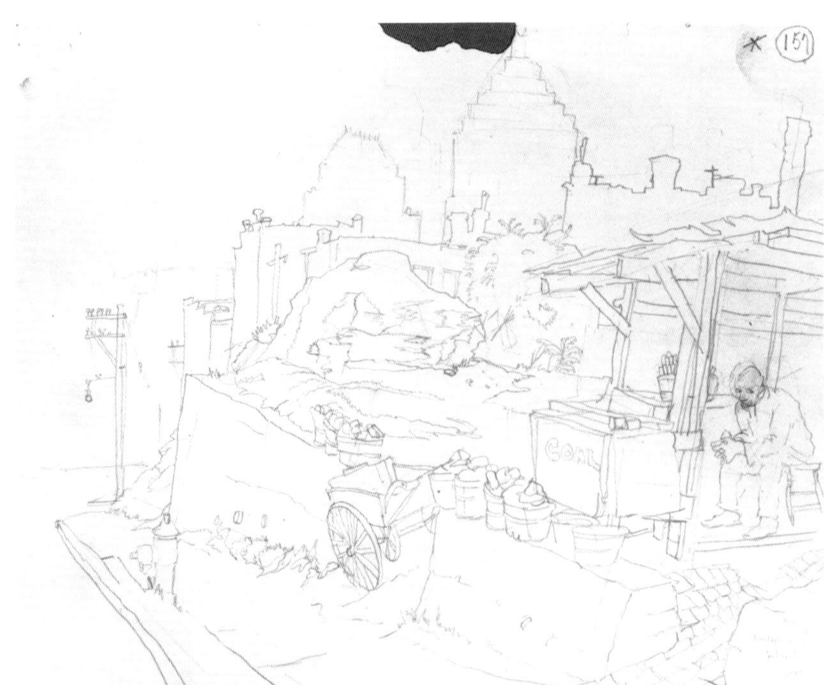

FIG. 21. *Wood for Sale* (preparatory study for *The Sun Shines in Pittsburgh,* 1936). Pencil on paper, 8 13/16 x 10 1/8".

cane," as Gilbert Love referred to the recession of 1937 and 1938, affected families in Pittsburgh who had been able to "weather" the first half of the depression. In the second half of the decade, their savings were exhausted, and they too found it necessary to apply for relief. Some came very near starvation before they did so.[55]

Rosenberg shows his compassion for two members of the community in *Rest* (figure 22; plate 33) of 1938. With his use of diminished color and line, he stresses the weariness of this couple in their ongoing struggle to support their family during the depression. In another painting of 1938, *Fifth Avenue Garden,* Rosenberg documents the thrift gardens, planted with seeds provided by the relief board, that helped lower the fund's budget during the summer months. In his painting entitled *Job Lists* of the same year (plate 36), Rosenberg portrays over a dozen unemployed men poring over the few available jobs posted on bulletin boards outside the Irene Kaufmann Settlement. As is typical of Rosenberg's depictions of people, this painting does not present enough details to identify anyone. All the figures become anonymous participants in the economic crisis, which was not alleviated until well after the end of World War II.

Rosenberg's paintings document many specific locales within the Hill District. The intersection of Logan and Clark Streets was once considered the heart of the Hill (both were eliminated during the Lower Hill redevel-

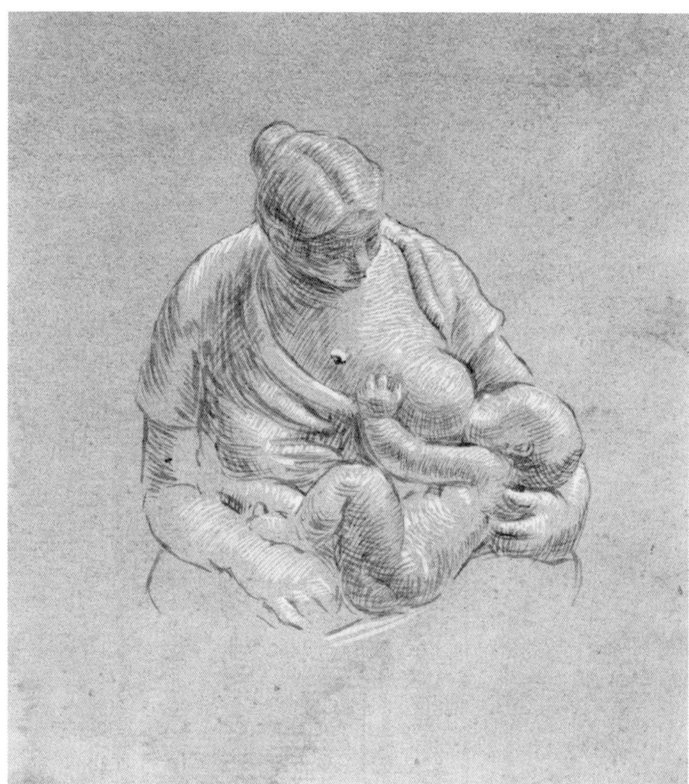

FIG. 22. *Rest* (preparatory study), c. 1938. Ink on card, 15 x 10″.

opment in 1951). The narrow streets were crowded and noisy with pushcart peddlers hawking their wares; customers buying from fruit, vegetable, and fish markets that spilled out onto the sidewalks; kosher shops, bakeries, delicatessens and secondhand clothing stores. Rosenberg revealed the unique character of that area in such paintings as *Orange Seller,* 1933; *Fruit Market,* 1937; *Fruit and Logan Street,* 1938; and *Fruit Market* (oil sketch), 1938. In *Fruit Market* of 1937 (figure 23; plate 31), Rosenberg depicts the disparity between the abundance of the fruit and vegetables available in the market and the people who could not afford to buy any of it. On the left side of the painting, a bright light illuminates the interior and exterior of the corner market, its proprietor, the fruits and vegetables, a man struggling to enter with a full bushel basket, and one lone buyer outside. In the shadows on the right, a group of men warm themselves, their backs turned to the market, their anonymous faces illuminated by the light of the bonfire in the street. The blue haze of the fire's smoke drifts toward the market and unites the two disparate groups. It is a disturbing image, and one that demonstrates the haves and the have-nots during the depression years. The rays of sunlight beyond the men in the street may point to the prosperity that was to come by 1939.

The heart of the Hill's business district for both Jews and blacks was Wylie Avenue, a long street which began at a church—John Wesley A.M.E. Zion on Herron Avenue—and ended at a jail—the Allegheny County Courthouse and Jail downtown on Grant Street. In between—as well as on Centre Avenue, Logan Street, and Fullerton Street—flourished a plethora of black, Jewish, and Italian businesses. Lillian Allen, longtime black beautician, recalls the community's pride in having such stores:

> The Hill was an entity of its own. At one time it boasted five movie theaters. . . . On Sundays, there was a line waiting to eat at [Nesbit's] or take home Nesbit's delicious pies. Around the corner on Centre Avenue was the plant of Robert L. Vann's *Pittsburgh Courier*, our weekly newspaper. . . . Also on Centre Avenue was the Elmore Theater. . . . Back then the Hill was very proud of the New Granada and Roosevelt Theaters, where uniformed ushers seated you, like downtown. . . . On Fullerton Street was the Rhumba that showed old movies. . . . The building had a nightclub in the basement called the Bamboola. The club was the haunt of the nightlife people. . . . The Halloween night party at The Bamboola was a time when the lesbians and the gays could come out of the closet. . . . Among the popular places to go was William Stanley's bar on Fullerton and Wylie. . . . The Crawford Grill [was] a place to relax over a drink and enjoy good food and jazz. . . . Fireman's Department Store on Centre Avenue filled the needs of the average family and Gordon's Shoes fitted the feet of all sizes and types. Johnson's Studios and Lee's Florist were represented at most weddings, funerals, and banquets.

Jazz was a major source of the Hill's liveliness. Pittsburgh nourished musicians of national fame, such as Lena Horne, Billy Strayhorn, Kenny Clarke, Art Blakey, Earl "Fatha" Hines, Roy Eldridge, and Mary Lou Williams. Blacks and whites from all over the city flocked to hear jazz at numerous venues in the Hill, notably the Humming Bird, the Leader House, Derby Dad's, the Harlem Show Bar, the Washington Club, the Ritz, the Bamboola, upstairs over Crawford Grill #1, the Harlem Casino, the Flamingo, the Hurricane, Stanley's Lounge, the Musician's Club, the Sawdust Trail, the Fullerton Inn, the Paradise Inn, and the Bailey Hotel. The Hill also boasted one of the best baseball teams of the Negro Leagues, the Crawfords, and the largest-circulation black newspaper in the country, the *Pittsburgh Courier.*

But the signs of vitality in music, sports, and business masked serious problems. Blacks entered the industrial workforce at the bottom, and discrimination and steady contraction of the city's industrial base kept them there. Living conditions had long been deplorable in the Hill, and only got worse as the housing stock continued to age. The Hill remained the city's most densely inhabited district, and overcrowding and poor sanitation helped push tuberculosis and other deadly diseases to scandalous levels. Conditions that were miserable during the "roaring twenties" became truly intolerable during the Great Depression, as indicated in an unpublished typescript put together by the federally-sponsored antipoverty program of the depression era, the WPA:

> The Hill is the symbol of the worst that a fiercely industrial city like Pittsburgh can do to human beings. Its dominant note is squalor. Narrow streets are lined with tawdry houses, dingy red, their scarred doorways and tottering porches often reached by crumbling wooden steps. Roofs sag. Walls lean. Window frames are rotted and patched. Chimneys are cracked and gaping with holes ("The Negro in Pittsburgh," unpublished WPA typescript, 1940).

LAURENCE GLASCO

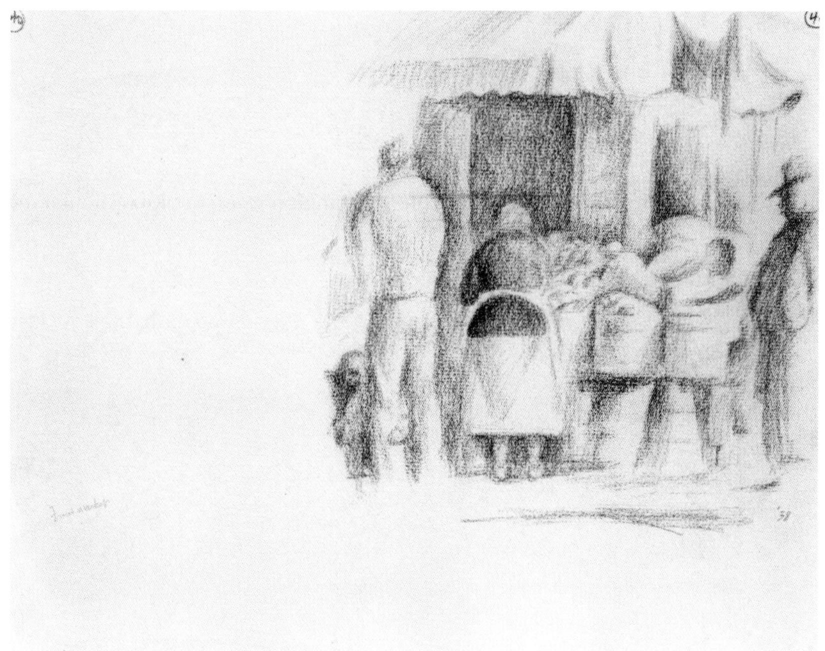

FIG. 23. *Fruit Market*, c. 1937. Charcoal on paper, 9½ x 12⅜″.

Fruit and Logan Street (plate 35) of the following year presents a more positive image of the same proprietor operating a more prosperous business and may also reflect the artist's optimism about the economic improvement that was to come. The market is active in its pyramidal structure. At the peak stands a black man being handed a piece of fruit. The young boy in the foreground is the artist's son, posing with an orange in his hand. This painting reveals the demographics of the Hill as they existed when Rosenberg painted there: primarily Jewish and African American. Rosenberg directs the viewer's eye through his very systematically arranged triangular composition, from Murray's twisted body, to the arm of the black man handing over a piece of fruit, to another man accepting, to the Jewish proprietor, and down to the man in conversation with a potential buyer. All of the activity is caught in the center of the triangle, and the entire composition works toward that end. This painting was shown in the 1938 Carnegie International exhibition at the Carnegie Institute and was reviewed by four art critics for the three daily newspapers. Dorothy Kantner, writing for the *Pittsburgh Sun-Telegraph*, thought the painting carried a "faint biblical strain" that added "drama to an everyday scene."[56] *Pittsburgh Press* contributor, Elmer Stephan, Director of Art Education for Pittsburgh Public Schools, wrote under the headline "Art Everyday" that Rosenberg "finds beauty in the commonplace things all about us. By subordination of minor parts, by use of beautiful color harmonies, and by an emphasis on the center of interest, he has here produced a fine rendering of the Pittsburgh scene."[57] For the *Pittsburgh Post-Gazette,* Jeanette Jena commented that Rosenberg "holds in suspension a moment from everyday life, until we savor all its richness. The market, the people, the fruit, the cobblestones, the old man who dominates the center of the canvas, all flow into a rhythmic pattern, which is Rosenberg's ample style. There is nothing sparse or anaemic about this artist. His opalescent color, never quite realistic, is like a rich juice in which his world is bathed."[58] In the same paper, three days prior, Charles Danver wrote his colorful review of the painting under the headline "Street of Babel":

> Venturesome strangers who delight in elbowing their way along the teeming sidewalks of narrow little Logan Street, in the heart of the Hill District, will look forward to seeing artist Samuel Rosenberg's offering in the International exhibition. It's a lively representation of the Italian fruit market at Logan and Clark Streets. Of all Pittsburgh byways, this throbbing Old-World-ish artery, which begins at Bedford and stumbles and twists down into Fifth, is perhaps the most cosmopolitan and colorful. All races mingle here, and a half dozen tongues may be heard above the endless bedlam of street noises, bellowing offers of bargains, bickering, brawling. Italian, Syrian and colored housewives people the sidewalks in front of the cluttered shops, which display half their wares inside and half out in the open. There are misty-eyed Jewish patriarchs with long, flowing beards; an occasional Chinese bargain hunter, and even tawny-skinned Mexicans. 'Street of Babel,' indeed. Something of all this is caught in Mr. Rosenberg's painting, although the composition is of only one market front. The street itself has a fascination for him, he admits, and he found it most inspiring on Sunday mornings last summer, when he drove there and, sitting in his car, made sketches for this picture.[59]

This was Rosenberg's preferred method for creating his paintings. Throughout his career, he made hundreds of sketches, quickly executed on the spot, to represent the characters that he wished to use later in his paintings. Figure studies of individual mannerisms, gestures, body language, and body parts comprise the majority of his sketches that provided the artist with a sound basis for subsequent works. One of the artist's students said in praise, "When you see a Rosenberg stocking, you know that there's a leg in it."[60] Rosenberg himself explained: "When I go to the Hill District I come home with my head full of paintings: the rivers, the people, the houses perched at precarious angles on the hills, the whole covered with the smell of the steel mills making opalescent lights and transparent

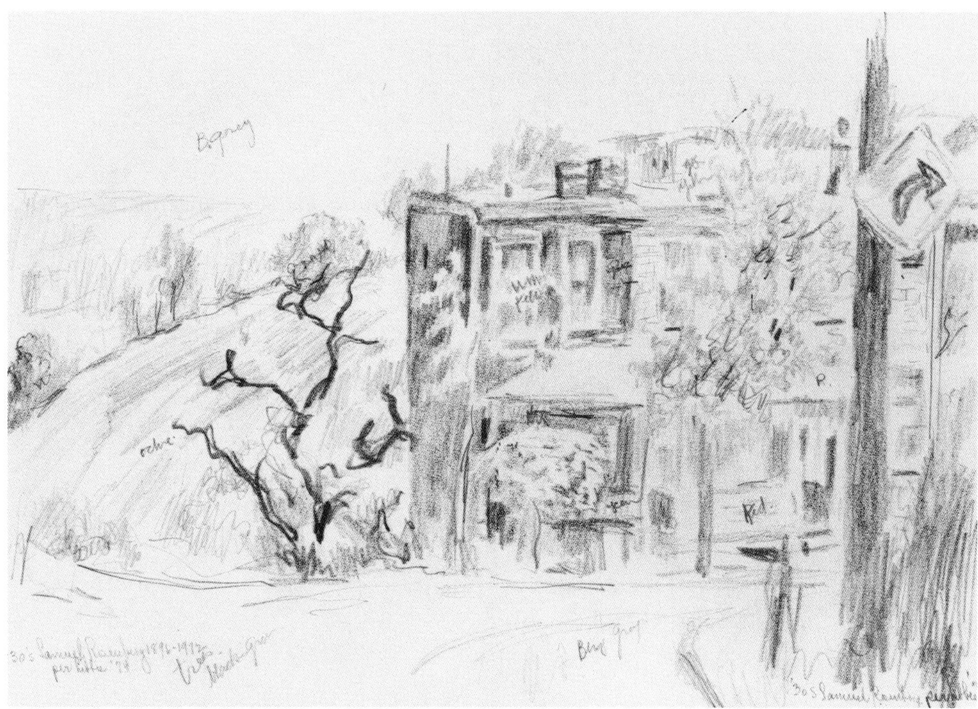

FIG. 24.
Hill District,
c. 1930–39.
Pencil on
paper,
$7\frac{7}{8}$ x $11\frac{1}{8}$″.

blacks, laying color over color, letting each one play its part in the final mood."[61]

Fruit and Logan Street is one of Rosenberg's earliest experiments in composition and texture. He painted it with a combination of egg tempera underpainting and overpainting with glazes. The white ground of the canvas shines through the overpainting and, combined with his transparent glazes, makes the colors appear to glow. Rosenberg used this painting to illustrate an article he wrote entitled "Painting with Egg Tempera" for the September 1940 issue of *Art Instruction* magazine. When it was exhibited at the Carnegie International that year, *Fruit and Logan Street* was ranked number twelve in popular appeal for the Public's Choice award.

In his Hill District works, Rosenberg painted what he saw; not with a photographic exactness, but with an artistic license that freed him to alter the facts to suit his compositional purposes. He did not try to please, as he had in his commissioned portraits; instead he painted what he "saw and felt." As Danver indicated, Rosenberg captured the entire flavor of the many markets that populated Logan Street all in one painting.

Rosenberg saw the beauty in the ramshackle architectural structures, the cobblestone streets, the fish, fruit, and vegetable markets, pushcarts, peddlers, and retail shops in the Hill District. In *Monday Morning,* formerly known as *After the Night Shift,* of 1935 (plate 25), Rosenberg depicts the backyards of a typical set of tenement houses in the Hill. The man of the house, home after working all night, has fallen asleep leaning against the outhouse while his wife is bent over a washbasin, doing the laundry, presumably carrying on a conversation with the woman on the porch above. A preschool-aged child sits in the doorway. This scene was a common sight in the Hill District. Out of a total of 12,341 dwellings in the Third and Fifth Wards, 32.7 percent of them had no hot water, 12.7 percent had no indoor toilet facilities and 82.6 percent were without any furnace-type heating. These figures substantiate the disparity that existed between neighborhoods in the city.[62] Reflecting these circumstances, Rosenberg's other paintings of the time show similar scenes, especially *Monday Morning No. 1,* 1935 (figure 25); *Near Herron Hill,* 1934; *Autumn in Pittsburgh,* 1936; *Doorways, Soho Street,* 1938; and *Mid-Morning Conversation,* 1939 (plates 21, 27, 34, 37).

Rosenberg also used these paintings as a form of social protest. As early as the 1920s, Sidney Teller, director of the Irene Kaufmann Settlement, mounted a campaign to rid the Hill neighborhood of slum properties, and many were demolished at that time. In the 1930s, many tenement houses similar to the one depicted in *Soho* were razed to make way for public housing projects Bedford Dwellings and Terrace Village I and II. Bedford Dwellings, in the Hill District, was actually the first federally funded housing project in Pittsburgh, but it does not seem to appear in any of Rosenberg's paintings. Constructed at a cost of fourteen million dollars, the subsidized housing project of Terrace Village, which does appear in several of Rosenberg's paintings, was the second-largest federal housing project in the United States.[63] It was the city housing authority's second and third most extensive slum-clearance and low-cost housing project. Terrace Village was constructed on the former sites of Gazzam's, Goat, and Ruch's hills. This housing project was one of Mayor David L. Lawrence's significant redevelopment efforts, and President Franklin D. Roosevelt came here himself to dedicate the complex in 1940. An area of twenty-eight acres was cut down from fifty to seventy-five feet and the debris from those hills was used to fill in the deep valley below. This earthmoving unfortunately separated Terrace Village, located in the Middle Hill, from the Lower Hill and from Oakland, and it was seen as an enclave unto itself. In *Hill Street Scene,* 1936, Rosenberg shows the future sites of Terrace Village I and II, completed in 1940 and 1941 respectively. In *Roof Over Their Heads,* 1940 (plate 40), and *Evening Promenade,* 1941 (plate 41), Rosenberg includes the completed housing project off in the distance. The separation of the two areas—and the alienation of the hilltop housing from the rest of the neighborhood below—is emphatically implied, as is the contrast between old and the new,

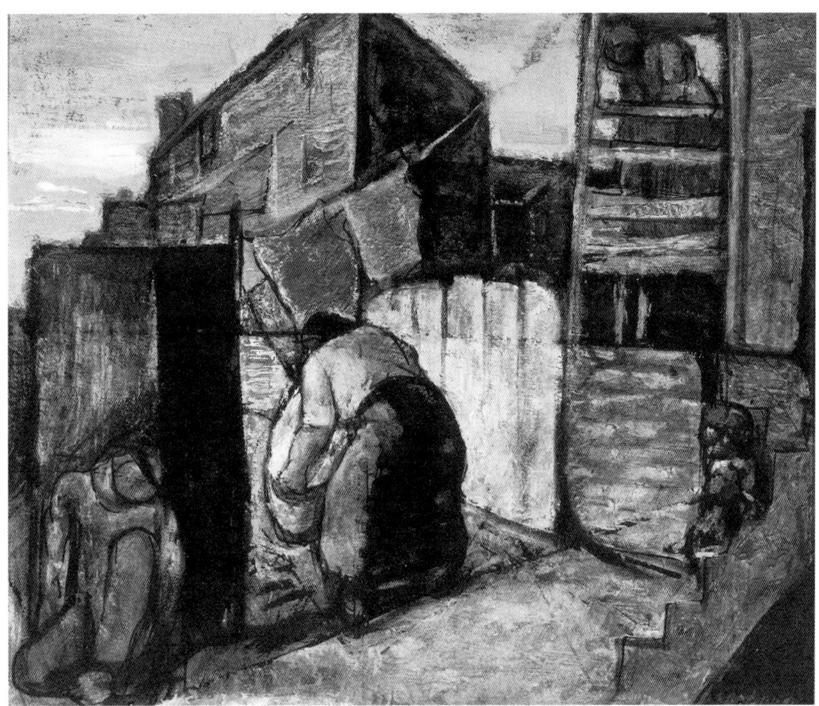

FIG. 25. *Monday Morning No. 1*, 1935. Oil on canvas, 20 x 23″.

historic and modern. The differences are striking: second empire, mansard-roofed architecture versus sleek, modern, rectangular boxes. Rosenberg created a pencil sketch for *Roof Over Their Heads* as well as a full-color oil/pastel preparatory study that shows Terrace Village before completion (figure 26). The building was located at the corner of Jumonville Street and Fifth Avenue. While Rosenberg was driving on Fifth Avenue during a heavy rainstorm, a flash of lightning lit up the top floors of the corner house. He pulled over and sketched the scene on the spot in pencil and then, back at his studio, made a colorful study of it in pastel. The following day he returned to the street corner, set up an easel, oil paints, and masonite, and made the final painting. This is one of the few paintings that Rosenberg is known to have created *en plein air.* The *New York World-Telegram* noted this painting, among others, in its review of the Carnegie Institute's exhibition Painting in the United States, in which it was shown.[64] In both of these paintings, the artist powerfully presents the transformation of the neighborhood, showing what it was, and what it would become. Rosenberg also chronicled other construction projects that occurred as part of Pittsburgh's redevelopment, such as *Bigelow Boulevard Under Construction* (figure 27; plate 39), the heavily traveled roadway, begun in 1936, that was completed with a new concrete surface in 1939. Moreover, Rosenberg anticipated that these changes were just the beginning; the face of the neighborhood would alter

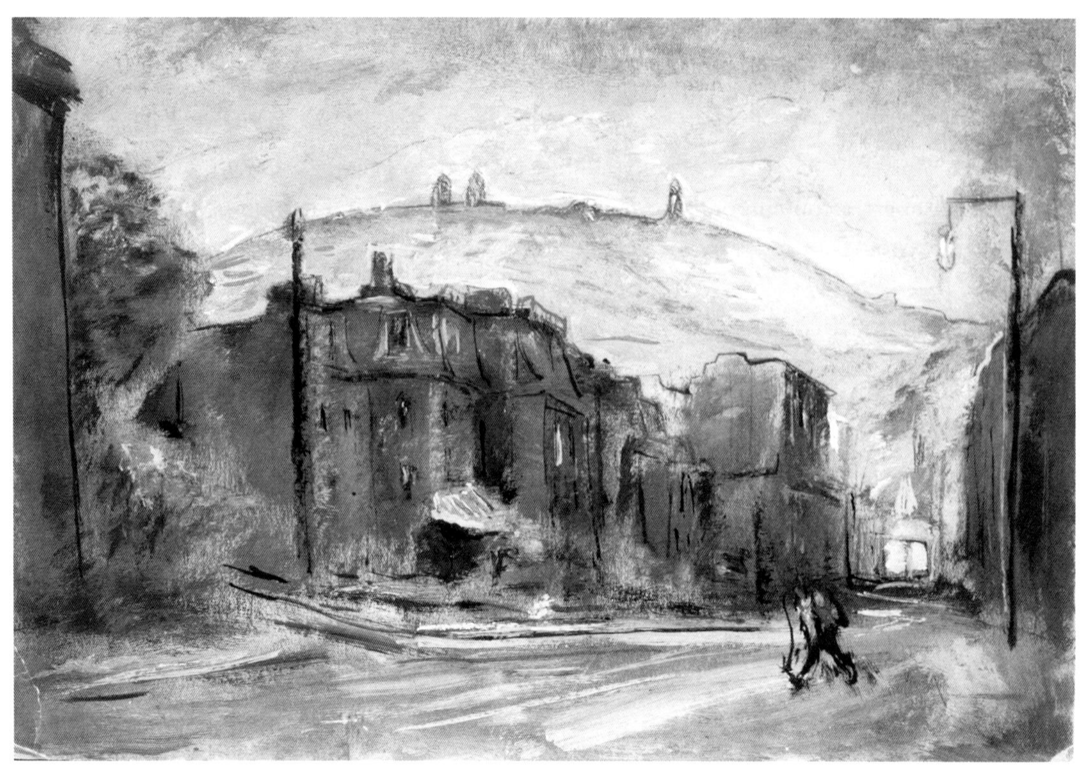

FIG. 26. *Roof Over Their Heads* (preparatory study), 1940. Pastel, oil, and ink on paper, 10 x 15″.

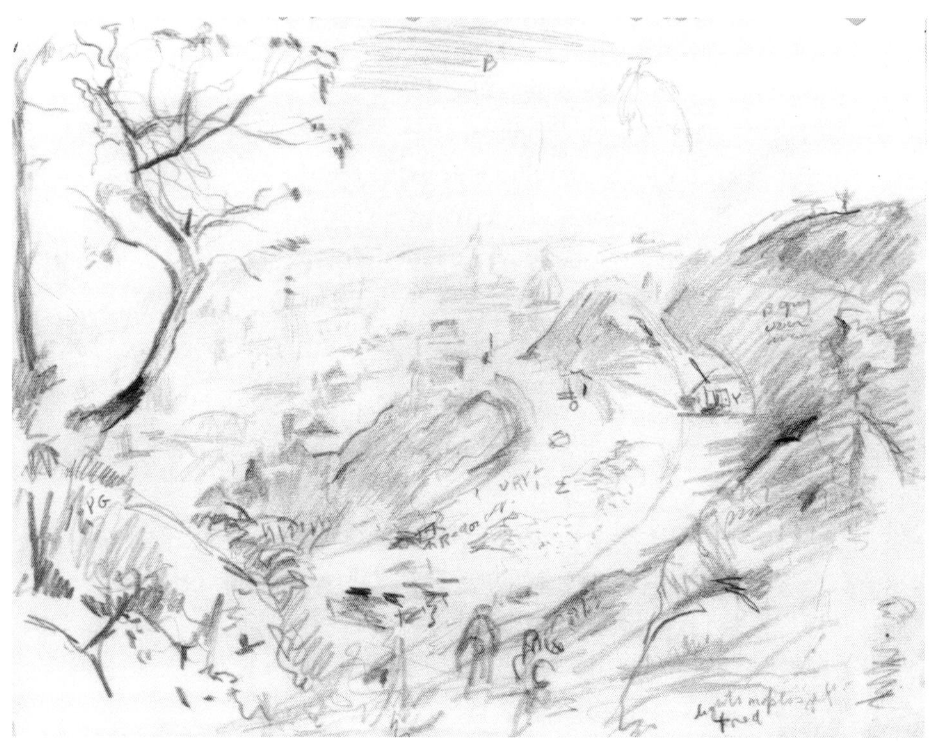

FIG. 27. *Bigelow Boulevard Under Construction,* c. 1940. Pencil and colored pencil on paper, 10 x 12″.

again in less than ten years with the construction of the new Civic Arena complex.[65]

In all of Rosenberg's paintings that include Terrace Village, he emphasizes its disconnection from the human interaction taking place below. Virginia Cuthbert, a contemporary of Rosenberg's who worked in Pittsburgh from 1931 to 1941, also captured the sense of displacement. In her painting *Slum Clearance on Ruch's Hill* of 1937 (figure 28), she depicts construction workers and heavy equipment in the process of tearing down the tenement houses while former inhabitants stand by with their children and watch the destruction.

"What a man knows best," Rosenberg said in 1935, "that he can most easily reproduce on his canvases."[66] Both the content and subject matter of Rosenberg's paintings of the 1930s ally him with a group of artists known collectively as American Scene painters. These realist painters sought to embody the American experience by portraying everyday life. Subdivided essentially into two camps, some gravitated to the rural environment for inspiration, and became known as American regionalists; others turned to urban living for their subject matter, and were called social realists. Regardless of how they responded, artists of the American Scene were tied together by an emotional unity on a national scale. From region to region, artists of the decade found stability in everyday life of the present and the vernacular experience. The collective dialogue of these painters was heard loud and clear and proved instrumental in creating, for a brief time anyway, a truly national art. According to Matthew Baigell, "The American Scene was a movement of hope and optimism, of self-recognition and self-glorification—a movement that looked to the future as well as to the past. Complex and contradictory, it represented the fervent wish that America had artistically come of age and that it would now create an art expressive of its own traditions and aspirations."[67]

Art, specifically American art containing recognizable subject matter, came to be appreciated more and more by the viewing public and art critics alike. The Whitney Museum of American Art opened on Eighth Street in Greenwich Village in 1931. The first museum in the country exclusively dedicated to American art, the Whitney held the first of its ongoing biennial exhibitions the following year. To provide an overview of contemporary art that was being made in America, more than one hundred and fifty painters were invited to exhibit a broad range of subjects, from realism, which dominated the display, to surrealism and abstraction. Rosenberg was invited to submit his painting *God's Chillun* (plate 23) to the 1934 biennial.

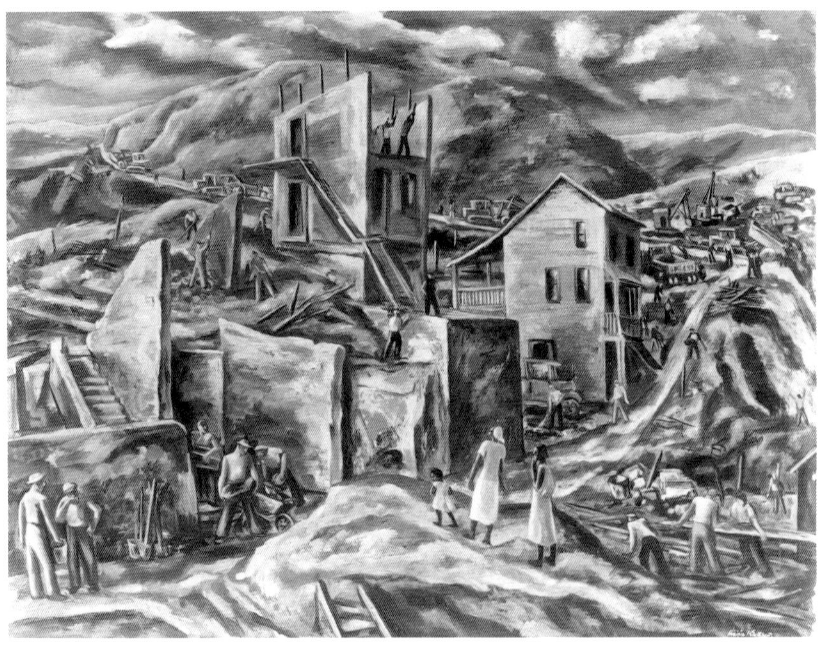

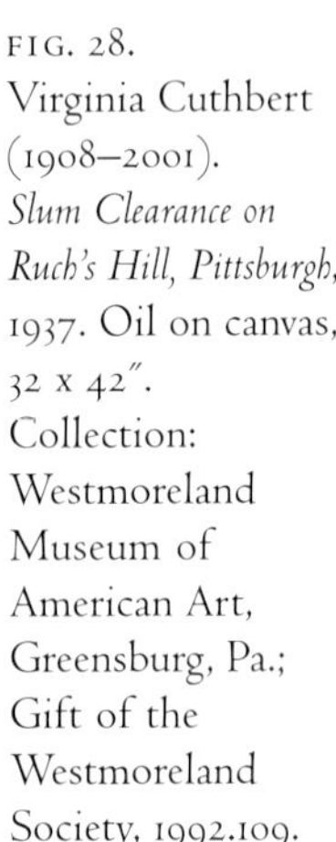
FIG. 28.
Virginia Cuthbert (1908–2001). *Slum Clearance on Ruch's Hill, Pittsburgh,* 1937. Oil on canvas, 32 x 42″. Collection: Westmoreland Museum of American Art, Greensburg, Pa.; Gift of the Westmoreland Society, 1992.109.

Three of his fellow Pittsburghers, Roy Hilton, Alexander Kostellow, and John Kane, also shared in this exhibition's spotlight. Of that exhibition, a writer for the *American Magazine of Art* reported that "the artists, for the most part, are showing a lively response to the life they see," and concluded that "the exhibition, as a whole, gives a most encouraging demonstration that despite hard times our artists are far from downhearted." Royal Cortissoz, art critic for the *New York Herald Tribune,* wrote that the exhibition was symbolic of "the mood now prevailing in American art. It is the mood of men interested in the human things around them, realistic, but at once sympathetic and objective." A conflicting review came from Jane Schwartz for *Art News* in which she claimed it was an exhibition "in which each painter fairly shouts for recognition and the result is a fierce chaos of disharmonies." Rosenberg's painting was reproduced in the exhibition catalog. *God's Chillun* represents a scene on Crawford Street in the Hill District where a spiritual revival or rally is commencing on the cobblestone street. You can almost hear the sound of the gospel music emanating from the mouths of the participants in the parade. Rosenberg has situated himself in front of the large group, representing the congestion of the crowd as far as the eye can see. Displaying swords, epaulets, and top hats, the people are more likely members of an African American Masonic lodge or other brotherhood. The Holy Trinity Church (now St. Benedict the Moor) looms behind the participants on the right, who might also be members of the all-black congregation of St. Benedict the Moor that was formerly located on Heldman Street, just three blocks away. Together with *Portrait* and *Monday Morning, God's Chillun* won the Carnegie Prize for the best group of oil paintings in the Associated Artists of Pittsburgh Twenty-fifth Annual Exhibition of 1935. On February 9, 1935, a *Pittsburgh Post-Gazette* critic wrote that the painting was "riotous and bubbling with the ecstasy of a street corner revival, with a canvas crowded with rhythmic figures which seem themselves the visual embodiment of hallelujah!"[68] Rosenberg was again invited to participate in the Whitney's third biennial, in 1936, with his painting *Watermelon Market* (plate 19).

In addition to the Whitney's 1934 biennial, Rosenberg was represented that year in the Museum of Modern Art's exhibition entitled Paintings and Sculpture from Sixteen American Cities. With this show, MoMA recognized the importance of regional art throughout the country. An anonymous juror from each city was asked to send the best representatives to the exhibit, which totaled one hundred paintings and twenty sculptures. As well as Rosenberg, Pittsburgh's representatives included Alexander Kostellow, Roy Hilton, Everett Warner, and John Kane. In the foreword to the catalog for the exhibition, excerpts from the letter of invitation to those who selected the paintings and sculpture outlined the purpose of the exhibition: "During recent years New York has assumed a role in the American art world of greater importance, many feel, than its achievement deserves. Most of the currents which flow from Europe to America pass through New York and radiate from there throughout the country. This traffic has been too often a one-way affair. We feel that an effort should be made to restore a more even balance of trade. To do this in a concrete way we are proposing that instead of our sending you an exhibition you should send us one." In his review of the exhibition, Edward Alden Jewell called attention to the unfamiliar artists in the exhibition, and though he did not mention Rosenberg by name, he noted that "These talents that are new to us here are especially welcome, since they serve to broaden our knowledge of what is being done in other—often distant—parts of the country."[69] Two years later, MoMA organized the exhibition New Horizons in American Art, for which Holger Cahill, Director of the Federal Art Project of the Works Progress Administration (WPA), wrote the catalog.[70]

Periodicals of the day such as *Art Digest, Magazine of Art,* and *Art News* helped to disseminate the ideas of the American Scene artists. The triumvirate of leading Regionalist painters, Thomas Hart Benton, Grant Wood, and John Steuart Curry, were outspoken in their beliefs about American art. In 1932, Benton declared that "no American art can come to those who do not live an American life, who do not have an American psychology, and who cannot find in America justification of their lives." In the previous decade, he had traveled across America, making portraits of the diverse areas of the country that would culminate in his famous murals of the 1930s. On Christmas Eve, 1934, a significant event occurred in support of Regionalism: Benton's *Self-Portrait* was reproduced on the front cover of *Time* magazine. The issue profiled the major figures of the Regionalist movement—Benton, Wood, Curry, Charles Burchfield, and Reginald Marsh—and the regional characteristics of cities such as Chicago, Detroit, Boston, and Taos. Wood proclaimed that each section of the land had a personality of its own and recommended the common-sense utilization of those natural materials that the artist knew best. Curry thought the American landscape "the most fruitful and genuine medium of a national expression." Reginald Marsh, who documented New York's raucous urban landscape, made the comment, "well-bred people are no fun to paint."[71] He was a student of John Sloan and, like his teacher, prowled the streets of New York in search of his subjects in burlesque theaters and other nocturnal entertainment hotspots. Like Rosenberg, Marsh utilized tempera paint in his work, harkening back to the painting techniques used by painters of the Italian Renaissance.

According to Oliver Larkin, "the artists of the American Scene had discovered one truth: that healthy art springs from its own soil and is nourished by its own climate. There was another truth: that the deeper art penetrates, the closer it comes not to what makes people different but to what they have in common."[72]

Edward Alden Jewell, art critic for the *New York Times,* asked the question: "Have we an American art?" and Thomas Craven, though extreme in his promotion of American art and artists, answered that we did, in the form of the three Regionalists, Benton, Wood, and Curry. The end of the decade brought further public attention to the new American art. In 1939, the San Francisco Golden Gate Exposition in the Palace of Fine Arts exhibited four hundred works of art gathered from every region in the country. Rosenberg, the only artist to represent the city of Pittsburgh, was invited to exhibit his painting *Man-Made Desert* (plate 18). The exhibition proved, in Larkin's words, that "the history of native art could not be written in terms of the eastern seaboard. . . . If any common denominator emerged, it was a fresh consciousness of the American environment and a greater emphasis on factual content than on form."[73] By contrast, the New York World's Fair of the same year promoted the theme The World of Tomorrow, and used as its symbols the abstract forms of the Trylon and Perisphere. The Fair's art exhibition, American Art Today, consisted of 1,214 works of painting, sculpture, and graphic art. Styles ranged from regionalism to abstraction; subjects from social content to surrealism. Rosenberg was represented with his Hill District painting *Fruit and Logan Street* of 1938 (plate 35).

These comprehensive exhibitions of contemporary American art continued throughout the decade. The Metropolitan Museum in New York held Life in America in 1939; the Art Institute of Chicago continued their annual American Painting and Sculpture exhibitions, and the Carnegie Institute mounted its first extensive Survey of American Painting in 1940.

As Rosenberg's inclusion in the aforementioned exhibits shows, Pittsburgh's artists were no strangers to the new aesthetic. Wilfred Readio, Rosenberg's faculty colleague at Carnegie Tech and head of the Department of Painting and Design from 1939–1955, called in *Carnegie Magazine* for a broader definition of the arts—stained glass, wrought iron, carved wood, jewelry, ceramics, and textiles. These materials, he argued, have a "close relation to many phases of everyday life."[74] Later in the decade, Douglas Naylor made the rounds of Pittsburgh artists' studios to learn how they were looking at life. In his second of a series of articles that carried the headline "Art for Life's Sake," he wrote, "The old saying of 'art for art's sake' is being supplanted in Pittsburgh by the more alluring call of art for life's sake."[75]

By 1939, Pittsburgh was emerging from its recent economic slump. Steel industries were operating at 88 percent of capacity, the highest figure since April of 1937. Newspaper headlines announced "Steel Mills Hum at Boom Tempo to Meet Demand" and "Black Skies Take District out of the Red Once More—And Nobody's Blue." Continuing his reports on the effects of the depression on the city, Gilbert Love wrote, "Pillars of smoke by day and pillars of fire by night over the Pittsburgh industrial area are leading this district and the nation out of the wilderness of Recession and into the promised land of Better Times."[76] In such paintings as *The Dance*, 1939 (figure 29; plate 38), Rosenberg reflects the hope of prosperity and an easing of the restrictions and hardships of the depression. Rosenberg utilized his tempera/oil glazing method to achieve an overall color vibrancy. The dynamic composition depicts a boisterous good time being had by all the participants.

Everything, however, was about to change again. Both Rosenberg's immediate surroundings and the artistic environment in which he had been working would undergo dramatic transformations at the end of the decade.

At first, the 1940s appeared to be a turning point that would lead to the Hill's revitalization. The war brought jobs and paychecks to demoralized residents, and the federal government became directly involved in helping to solve the district's housing problems. In 1940, President Roosevelt visited Pittsburgh and dedicated Terrace Village, the nation's second-largest housing project, with 2,653 units that stretched from the southern Hill to Oakland. Also that year, the government opened Bedford Dwellings, located on Bedford Avenue in the northern Hill. Public housing projects later came to represent the worst of living conditions—segregated, dilapidated centers of drugs, crime, family disorganization, and despair—but in that era they were sources of pride and hope, consciously housing blacks and whites in almost equal numbers, and setting strict standards for residents' comportment.

The 1940s may have seemed promising, but the 1950s sounded the death knell for the Hill as a viable community. First, as postwar prosperity enabled increasing numbers of whites to leave for other neighborhoods and the suburbs, the district became ever more segregated. A combination of job contraction and continuing racial discrimination kept blacks in the Hill, and increasingly confined to public housing.

In addition, local government inflicted the greatest damage the Hill District had ever experienced when, in 1956, it condemned the Lower Hill. The district's commercial heart was reduced to rubble in order to make way for the Civic Arena. This decision eliminated over four hundred businesses, most of which were owned by Jewish and Italian proprietors, and displaced some eight thousand residents, most of whom were black. The only buildings remaining were Epiphany Church on Centre Avenue and the small Beth Hamedrash Hagodol Synagogue on Colwell Street.

What the city hoped for was a vibrant cultural district on the edge of downtown that would help change Pittsburgh's "smoky city" image and stop the out-migration of its middle class. What it got was a domed arena, a couple of luxury buildings, and the enduring mistrust of its black residents. In 1968, the riots that followed the assassination of Martin Luther King Jr. completed the destruction of the Hill. As residents left, homes stood vacant and ultimately crumbled, part of a long-term decline that, between 1950 and 1990, created numerous but depressing "green spaces" where houses once stood, and caused the district's population to decline from forty-three thousand to just fifteen thousand.

The 1990s witnessed a modest reversal of fortunes. Two new housing developments inspired a local paper to pronounce "The Re-Birth of the Hill." Crawford Square, a government-private partnership, built attractive townhouses over a ten-block stretch eastward from the Civic Arena, and Oak Hill replaced the massive Terrace Village housing project with similar townhouses. Rebirth or not, by 2005 it is expected that some two thousand units of new housing will have been built, meaning that the Hill, with its attractive new townhouses, abundant green spaces, and still commanding views of downtown, may indeed have entered a new phase in its long historical evolution—and perhaps be on the verge of coming full circle.

LAURENCE GLASCO

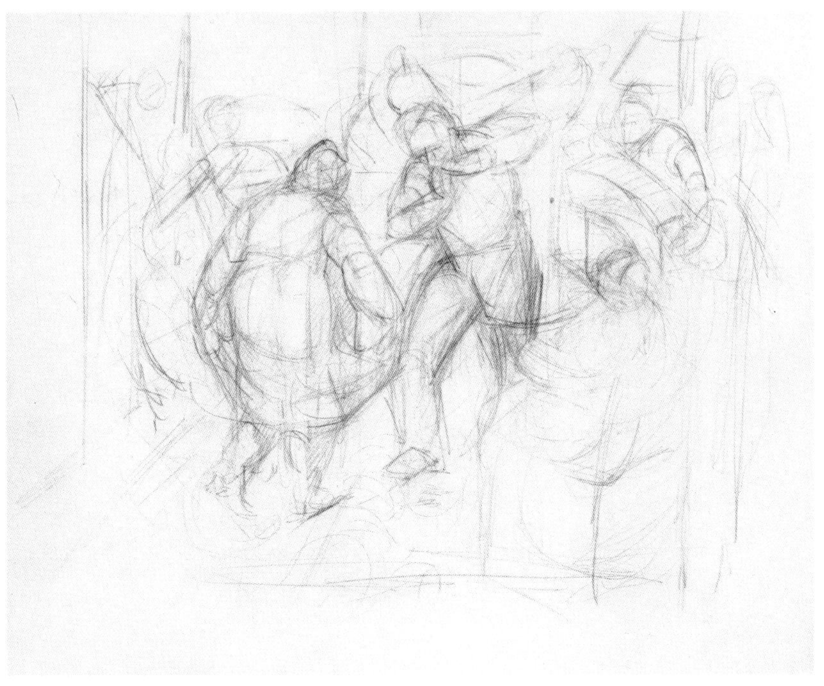

FIG. 29. *The Dance* (preparatory study), 1939. Pencil on paper, 10 x 12″.

The optimism that had accompanied the rise of a new American aesthetic would, unfortunately, disappear with the entry of the United States into World War II. By the 1940s, the American Scene movement had lost its momentum. Artists instead turned their attention to a more personal, introspective expression of their emotions. At the same time, the Hill District in which Rosenberg was so rooted was disappearing to urban renewal. A writer for the *Pittsburgh Sun-Telegraph* wondered where Rosenberg would go in search of subjects so dear to him. But as we will see, Rosenberg went in another direction entirely.[77]

Allegory to Abstraction: 1940s

On February 14, 1936, the first Artists' Congress met in New York and Lewis Mumford opened it with these words: "We are gathered together tonight for the first time partly because we are in the midst of what is plainly a world catastrophe."[78] Fascism, war, and economic depression were at odds with all the forces of human culture. The following year, Hitler staged the famous Degenerate Art exhibition, which showed work unacceptable to the Third Reich. The exhibit included 650 works, by artists including Marc Chagall, Max Ernst, Wassily Kandinsky, Paul Klee, and Edvard Munch.

As the 1930s continued, Rosenberg also became increasingly concerned about the growing threat of Hitler, and his paintings reflect that. Hitler had begun his war against the Jews immediately upon his coming to power in March 1933. By April there had been a boycott of Jewish businesses, wholesale dismissals from civil service work and book burnings. In 1935 the Nuremberg laws separating Jews from Christians took away German citizenship from all German Jews. In 1936, Sam's father, who had emigrated from Vienna over forty-five years before, died. Ironically, that same year Hitler marched in and annexed Austria to the Third Reich. Overnight, Vienna and all of Austria became a hell for Jews who were suddenly attacked in unrestrained violence by storm troopers on the streets. Just three years later, war broke out. By 1941, the fate of the Jews was sealed as Hitler and his henchman embarked on the "final solution," the murder of every Jewish man, woman, and child caught in their vise. In Minsk, where Rosenberg's mother had come from, the killing, looting, and raping began in 1941. The terrified Jews locked behind ghetto walls in Minsk included not only the thousands of Jewish city residents, but also those thousands who had been deported there from various places in Europe, including from Vienna. The killing did not end until all the Jews of Minsk had been killed outright or deported elsewhere and killed.

BARBARA BURSTIN

With the stress of the world at war, and man's hatred of man, artists could not help but be emotionally charged in their response to world events. Conflict and crisis took over the art world as artists attempted to come to grips with current conditions. They were searching for new values and new ways to express those values in their art. The entry of the United States into World War II presented American artists with several choices: they could use art to celebrate American values; they could use it as an escape mechanism from world events; or they could bear witness to the unsettling realities of the time. In the hands of social realists, art of the 1940s was satirical, loaded with biting sarcasm. Realists such as William Gropper, Jack Levine, and Ben Shahn used an 'in your face' style to protest what was going wrong with the world. Other artists responded to the question "What can I do?" through the organization Artists for Victory, a membership group which sponsored national exhibitions of contemporary paintings and the graphic arts in which war was a theme. A national war poster competition was held in 1942, and the entries were shown at the Museum of Modern Art in New York City. Among the themes presented to the artists for interpretation were War Bonds, The Nature of the Enemy, Deliver Us from Evil, and Sacrifice. Because of its popularity, the exhibition traveled to museums and galleries around the country, including the

Carnegie Institute in Pittsburgh in the spring of 1943. In that same year, an exhibition of prints that addressed "America in the War" appeared simultaneously in twenty-six cities around the country, from Scranton, Pennsylvania to Seattle, Washington. And at the end of 1943, Artists for Victory sponsored a large-scale exhibition of fifteen hundred contemporary American paintings, sculpture, and graphic arts, which opened at the Metropolitan Museum of Art in New York City.[79] The idea was not only to make art accessible to a broad public, but also to provide a way for artists to express their feelings about the war.

Rosenberg did not involve himself politically in the war effort nor did he participate in the Federal Art Project of the WPA, as did fellow Carnegie Tech faculty members Vincent Nesbert, Kindred McLeary, and Christian Walter. Instead, Rosenberg underwent a more emotional, inner response to world events, perhaps because of his ancestry, perhaps because of his kind, gentle nature. While socially conscious subject matter carried over into Rosenberg's work of the 1940s, as did images of Pittsburgh (until 1943), Rosenberg made a dramatic stylistic shift from direct observation of his subjects to predominantly allegorical depictions in this decade. Rosenberg's transition from the urban landscape of the previous decade was a result of his reaction to world events. Imbued with sadness, his paintings of this period are timeless metaphors for the ongoing suffering, poverty, and pain of this emotional decade. Rosenberg was searching, he said, for a more perfect language in his art that would best speak to his own growing concepts and impressions.

Rosenberg's paintings spoke for him. Some of his paintings are ambiguous in their reference to social issues and conditions of the day, but collectively, these paintings represent an expression of universal mourning. His subjects, while devoid of any overt political message, are commentaries on the human condition. While Rosenberg's work was not blatantly obvious in its symbolism, his characterizations of individuals drive home a message that was not lost on the audience of the day. Rosenberg was not as direct as Daumier and Goya, but his work contained a subtler symbolism that emphasized the sadness of the times, the despair, lack of hope, and bleakness of the day. He sympathized with the people of the world as well as those in stress at home. Even though the paintings are small in scale, Rosenberg's figures achieved a monumentality that conveyed the artist's message. In *Fear,* 1944 (plate 52), the viewer can almost feel the trembling of the group of figures who huddle together, afraid of the unknown that lies outside the picture plane.

While the colors in Rosenberg's paintings of this decade are often loud and even garish at times, the message is quite the opposite. His characters convey a very real sentiment, but do so without dramatic gesture or literal commentary. Rosenberg did not sensationalize. He did not paint about the activity of war, nor did he specifically address any world event; rather, he expressed his genuine concern for the time in which he was living through emotionally charged imagery. His paintings are comprised of opposites—contrasts of light and dark and clashing complementary colors that translate into an iconography of good versus evil or weak against strong. Caricature, while it did not predominate in his work, did not escape his brush either, and in such paintings as *Some Have Meat,* 1943 (plate 47), *Generalissimo (Man of Importance),* 1944, and *False Gods,* 1944, Rosenberg utilized this means to address injustices of the period. His raw, rich color scheme and subject matter call attention to his personification of gluttony, fascism, and the worship of riches. He also humorously, yet quite graphically, disparaged three generations of one family in his painting *Family Portrait* of 1946.

The themes of Rosenberg's paintings made during the war years were more universal and did not share the specificity of location or the narrative aspect of his work of the previous decade. His subjects were no longer indigenous to Pittsburgh. Indeed, the titles of his paintings during the decade, *Protest, Fear, Conflict, Bread, Flight, My Brother, Some Have Meat, Whither?, Israel,* and others, according to a reporter for the *Bulletin Index* in 1946, "recorded the trek of the world's homeless, intensity of hunger and pain and the stalking terror and horror of war."[80] While Rosenberg still seemed intent on leaving a record of things, his imagery of this decade reveals more of what he felt than what he saw. Harry Salpeter, who wrote a comprehensive article on the artist for *Esquire* magazine in 1945, noted that according to his wife, Libbie, Rosenberg "was intensely agitated over the things that were happening abroad and at the approaching shadow of war, and that this agitation was reflected in a struggle toward reorientation of his painting."[81] When referring to the work of that decade, Ralph Brem wrote in 1965, "They also carry the theme of sadness like *Eviction,* but colors are brighter, the concept simplified. Where *Eviction* strikes a poignant chord, these sear the eyes and ram the message home."[82]

In this decade, Rosenberg's compositions become much more simplified, and vibrant color, line, abstract shapes, and patterns dominate his work. His paintings become less about a person or a specific place and more about expressing emotion. Human beings become the primary force in these paintings and the landscape or background plays a less prominent, secondary role. Whereas in his paintings of the previous decade, his human characters were an integral part of the urban landscape, now the figure

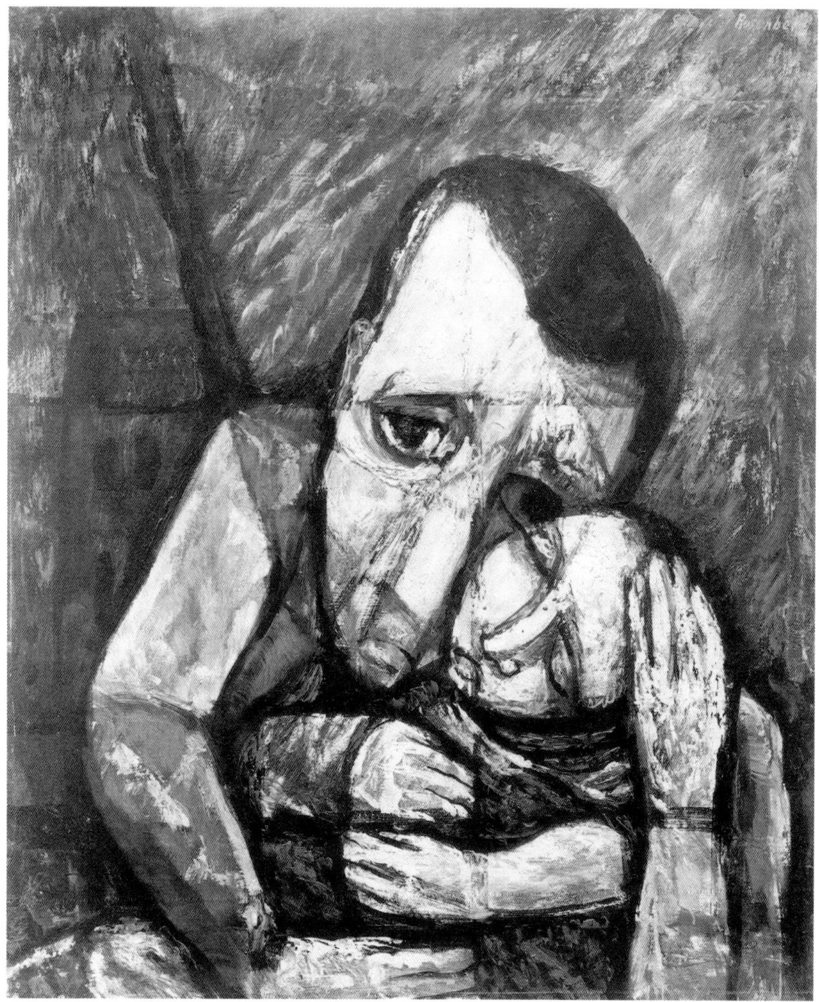

FIG. 30. *The Father,* 1945. Oil and tempera on masonite, 30 x 25″.

grows substantially in scale and dominates the pictorial space in his work. Pushed emphatically to the front of the picture plane, his large-scale men, women, and children are abstractions, situated in front of a structured yet undefined background. He injects his work with emotion through fundamental means: application of paint, color, strength of line, and combinations of pattern. He uses color chiefly for its emotional impact. His paint application is more vigorous and his brushwork more painterly than in previous years. Tragic overtones prevail in paintings such as *My Brother* of 1943 (plate 48), in which two men attempt to lift their fallen brother, or *The Father* of 1945 (figure 30), in which a parent holds his son tightly in his arms to protect him from the savage world around him.

A parent/child theme symbolizing trust, protection, and love reoccurs throughout the decade in paintings with titles such as *The Lesson* (1942), *Out in the Night* (1943) (figure 33), *Implicitness* (1943) (plate 45), *O, Mother* (1944),

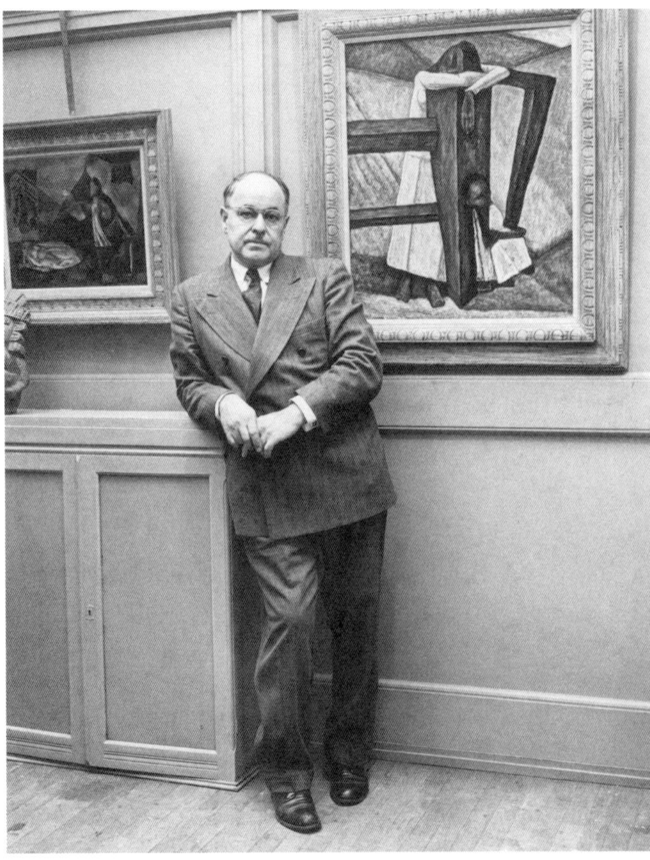

FIG. 31. Rosenberg with *Long on the Way*, 1947. Oil on masonite, 30 x 25″.

The Threshold (1944), *Long on the Way* (1947) (figure 31), and *The Present* (1949). While all of these paintings share an overwhelming sense of melancholy and human pathos, there is a faint undercurrent of hope in them, too. In *The Lesson,* a young mother oversees her child's reading lesson in a series of simplified forms. In the preparatory drawing for this painting (figure 32), the two figures are sitting upright; the background, while scumbled, is abstract in its arrangement of hard-edged geometric shapes. In the final painting (location unknown), Rosenberg lowered the woman's head more dramatically to emphasize the mood of the moment. A bright light illuminates the woman's face, her hand, and the pages of the book, calling attention to the subject. A subtle light filters softly through the less-defined color planes comprising the background, implying that learning goes on even in the darkest hour. In a somber scene entitled *Out in the Night* (figure 33) of 1943, Rosenberg sets a family against a fortress-like wall, unable to continue on to their destination. Rosenberg said he used the wall as a "barrier, physical or spiritual, which exists among us humans. In this case, the barrier shuts the family out, forcing the group to travel in space, searching for an opening that will let them in, to home, comfort, and warmth. As is

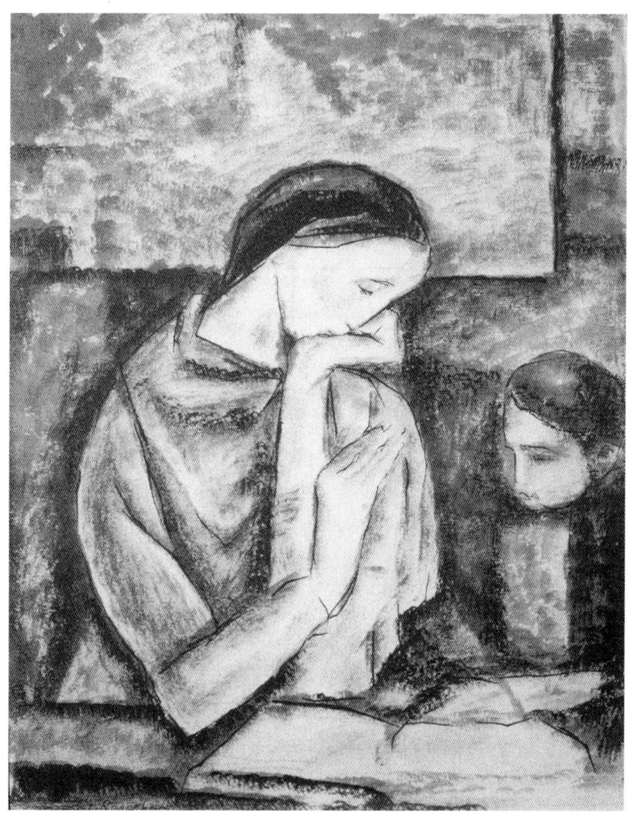

FIG. 32. *The Lesson* (preparatory study), 1942. Ink and conte crayon on paper, 20 x 16″.

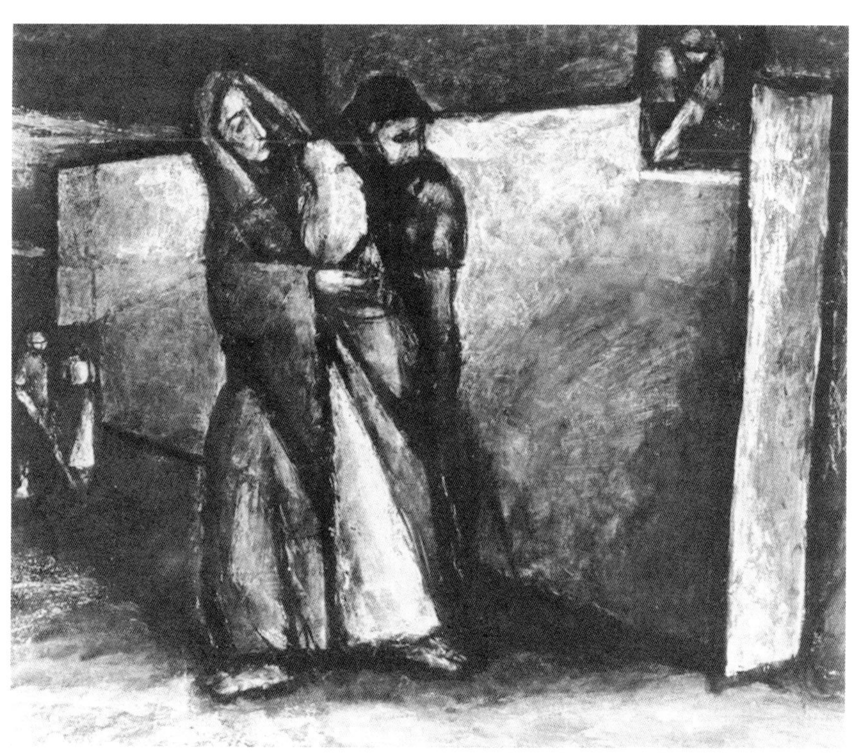

FIG. 33. *Out in the Night,* 1943. Oil on masonite, 20 x 24″.

my custom, I have allowed the mood to dictate to me the technique, the color and the composition."[83]

The majority of Rosenberg's paintings of this decade seem to have been intended to serve as a catharsis to release his own worries and inner tensions. *Bread No. 2* of 1942 (plate 43), is a poignant reminder of both the poverty that the masses suffered during the depression and the horrific events of World War II, specifically Rosenberg's reaction to the effect of war on humanity. While the figures in the composition are androgynous, their facial expressions dramatically illustrate the struggle of men, women, and children during these two critical events in world history. Crowded into a small space, and surrounded by a concrete wall, the figures, with outstretched arms, reach for loaves of bread that have been placed just beyond their grasp. They are trapped in a container-like structure, unable to reach the other side. Their gaunt, mask-like faces reveal the agony that they feel and their expressions are all powerful. On the one hand, it is logical to interpret this painting as a reflection of the continued effect of the depression on Pittsburgh, when Rosenberg witnessed firsthand the poverty that consumed the Hill District while he was painting in the streets there, and which was still widespread in the 1940s. The act of reaching for the bread that is unattainable is a viable way of expressing those times. Rosenberg painted a full-color preparatory study for this painting early in 1942 (figure 34), which supports the idea that he was referring to the ongoing need in Pittsburgh. On the other hand, while Rosenberg never specifically referred to the Holocaust or the annihilation of the Jews in concentration camps in any interviews of the period, it is conceivable that he may also have been addressing his feelings about the events in Germany in this and other paintings of the decade. Information on the massacres and the extermination camps was officially available in the United States as early as November 1942, but, according to the reference librarian at the United States Holocaust Museum, many in the United States were aware of camp activities in Germany much earlier.[84] The first Nazi camp in Poland was liberated by the Soviets on July 24, 1943, a fact that would not have escaped the Jewish population of Pittsburgh. These forced-labor camps were instituted as early as 1933, to handle the masses of people arrested as alleged political opponents of Hitler's regime. While no visual records were available, general information about starvation and the depravity of human life was. It is not unreasonable to think that Rosenberg may have symbolized his awareness of those events with androgynous figures whose outstretched arms reach for the bread as well as for help and freedom that is unattainable. The strong, rich color palette, combined with dynamic line and ab-

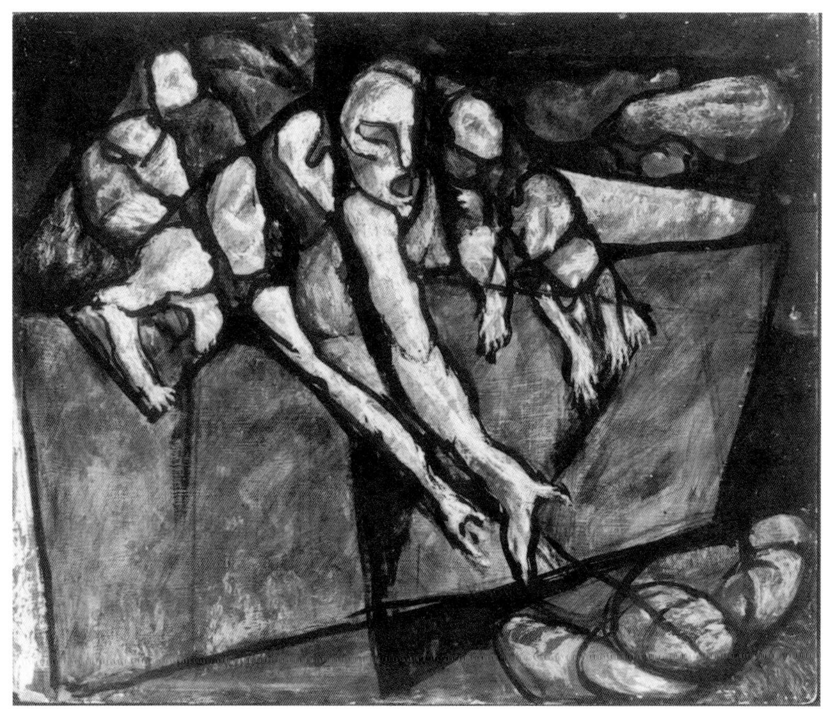

FIG. 34. *Bread No. 1*, 1942. Oil and tempera on masonite, 20 x 24″.

stract patterns convey Rosenberg's intensity of feeling. The Mannerist technique that Rosenberg used in elongating both the faces and limbs of the human figures in this painting heighten its expressive power. His images of this period do not allow his viewers to remain indifferent to the world situation.

Contemporary critics of the period saw both interpretations as plausible. Penelope Redd of the *Pittsburgh Sun-Telegraph* commented that in *Bread*, Rosenberg "adopts an archaic formality and the resonant color of stained glass to ejaculate his biblical wrath against the plight of the Hitler oppressed." And four years later, when the painting was included in Rosenberg's second solo show in New York City at the Associated American Artists Gallery, the *New York Herald Tribune* noted how powerfully Rosenberg conveyed the impression of starving humanity. In the *Pittsburgh Press*, Douglas Naylor called *Bread* "a garish, shuddery reflection on human life," and compared the composition to Reginald Marsh's painting *No. 6 Bowery* that was in also in Painting in the United States at the Carnegie Institute in 1944. This was the fourth in a series of exhibitions that the Carnegie Institute mounted to replace the annual Carnegie International that was suspended due to the war. Naylor continued his commentary by observing that Marsh's street scene was a "bit milder" than the "biting realism" of Rosenberg. It is interesting to note the headline of Naylor's article on the exhibition that read "Show Indicates That Most of Painters Are Unaffected by War's Turmoil." Naylor wrote that the viewer would "immediately forget there is such a catastrophe," the show "is so quiet and peaceful."[85] Rosenberg was one of the few artists in the show whose works revealed an awareness of the world crisis.

As early as 1939, with his painting *The Books Burn* (location unknown), Rosenberg was dealing with the subject of what Hitler was doing in Germany. Rosenberg's awareness of the plight of his fellow Jews in Europe is revealed in many of his paintings of the 1940s and in a few that carry into the next decade, as well. This is the only time in Rosenberg's artistic career that he utilized this subject matter and perhaps it was his way of retaining a connection to his Jewish heritage. Sam and Libbie identified with the Jewish experience and respected their cultural heritage. Rosenberg's paintings of this decade are populated with men with long white beards wearing prayer shawls and yarmulkes, and holding the Torah, reading books, or contemplating a skull. Rosenberg's selection of stereotypical Jewish figures gives these paintings an Old-World quality, as if he is looking back to an earlier time.

In *The Covenantor* of 1942 (figure 35), an Orthodox Jewish man wrapped in a large prayer shawl clutches the Torah close to his chest, cradling it like a baby. The prayer shawl, or *tallith,* is worn for morning worship services so that the wearer might separate himself from the world around him. The open book, which Rosenberg included in many of his paintings of this period, may represent the Book of Life, in which, during Rosh Hashanah, the deeds of the past year are recorded. Because the book is not sealed until Yom Kippur (the day of atonement), there is still time to make changes in the lives of those recorded inside. Once it is closed, the deeds inside are permanently written. Moreover, the title of the painting underscores man's connection to the covenant, or man's covenant to God, in the five Books of Moses given to Israel at Mt. Sinai. The Torah that the Covenantor holds is especially small compared to an actual one, which may indicate the difficulty of holding on to Jewish tradition during this period, even as the subject of the painting, and perhaps the artist, too, tries to do so.[86] While this painting has not been located, the *Pittsburgh Sun-Telegraph* indicated that it contained glazes of deep rich colors, and *Carnegie Magazine* noted that Rosenberg achieved the effect of light transmitted through rich and glowing color by glazing pure color over white.[87] Rosenberg won second prize for this painting when it was exhibited in the Associated Artists of Pittsburgh Thirty-sixth Annual Exhibition in 1946.

Rosenberg references a popular seventeenth-century subject in his *me-*

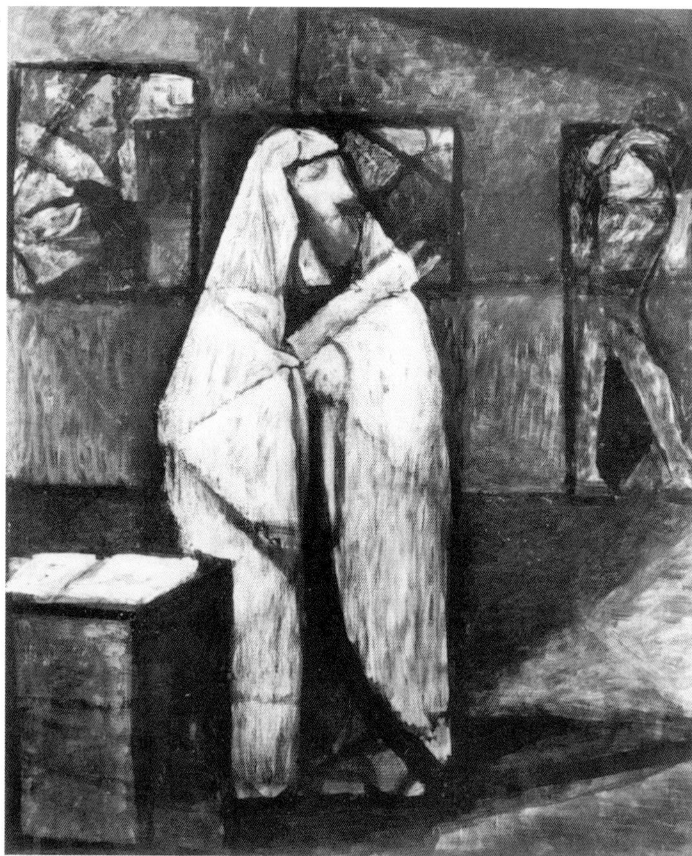

FIG. 35. *The Covenantor,* 1942. Oil and tempera on masonite, 30 x 25″.

mento mori still-life composition, *The Connoisseur (The Skull),* of 1944 (plate 51). Here, a man stares at a skull, with an "Alas, poor Yorick" expression on his face, perhaps in contemplation of his own death.[88] In *Patriarch,* 1944 (plate 50), the head of the household, in the midst of a Sabbath meal, reads the prayer book, illuminated only by a pair of candles. This man might be perceived as the almighty Father of the human race, praying for a world at peace. The powerful halo created by the candles suggests a spiritual light.

Rosenberg's characters in *The Counselors,* 1945 (figure 36), stand on either side of the seated king and appear to be whispering conflicting advice to their leader. The one on the left actively holds a sword, the symbol of war, while the figure on the right stands passively at the king's side with no weapon. This painting may well be Rosenberg's reference to the decision by the United States to use the atomic bomb to end the war with Japan, as well as the general concept of war and peace. Whatever this king's decision, it will impact the next generation of children who are starving and dying behind him.

The essentially monochromatic painting of a Jewish scholar reading the scriptures in *The Word,* of 1947, shimmers with light, color, and texture. As late as 1949, Rosenberg was still dealing with this subject, clearly dear to his heart, with *The Book* (plate 57), which depicts a Jewish man contemplating pages that seem to have been torn asunder.

Rosenberg's shift in subject matter during this decade parallels a shift in his painting technique. The majority of the work that Rosenberg created during this period was painted with a combination of oil and egg tempera, using masonite as a support instead of canvas. In addition, he switched from a direct painting method to an indirect one of building up layer upon layer of paint and glaze. While world events can explain the artist's change to more religious subjects relating to his Jewish ancestry, they do not explain his unexpected shift to abstraction nor his change in technique. Abstraction may well have been the only way he felt he could convey his subjective message without the distraction of an identifiable figure. His figures became more universal representations that mark a significant moment in history. One of Rosenberg's former students suggests that his shift in style was brought on by exposure to other artists' work in the annual Carnegie International exhibitions. With their broad scope, these exhibitions presented a climate of new possibilities and exposed its audience to most of the current artistic trends in the world.[89] In fact, it was during the 1939 International that Rosenberg came in contact with the French modernist Georges Rouault (1871–1958) and his painting *The Old King* for the first time. This particular work profoundly affected Rosenberg, and he acknowledged the painting's impact when he told a student, "It freed me to find myself."[90] The Carnegie Institute purchased Rouault's painting for its permanent collection in 1940, and Rosenberg referred to it often in his teaching when making points about layering, underpainting, and overglazing. He admired the work greatly and was pleased that he would have the opportunity to study it often in the museum, a method—learned at an early age from Coblens—that he continued to employ. Rosenberg and Rouault might even be considered kindred spirits, as they shared not only an inner vision and perception of the world around them, but a similar approach to achieving that vision. In Rosenberg's painting of 1947 entitled *Dedication* (figure 37), Rosenberg pays homage to the elder artist by incorporating a Rouaultesque painting on the back wall of the artist's studio he is depicting. The subject of the painting holds a large book, reading to continue his learning and development, as Rosenberg instructed his students to do. Not to be underestimated, Rosenberg's comprehensive awareness of what was going on in the art world, something he maintained for both his own intellectual growth and to assist him in his teaching, may have played a

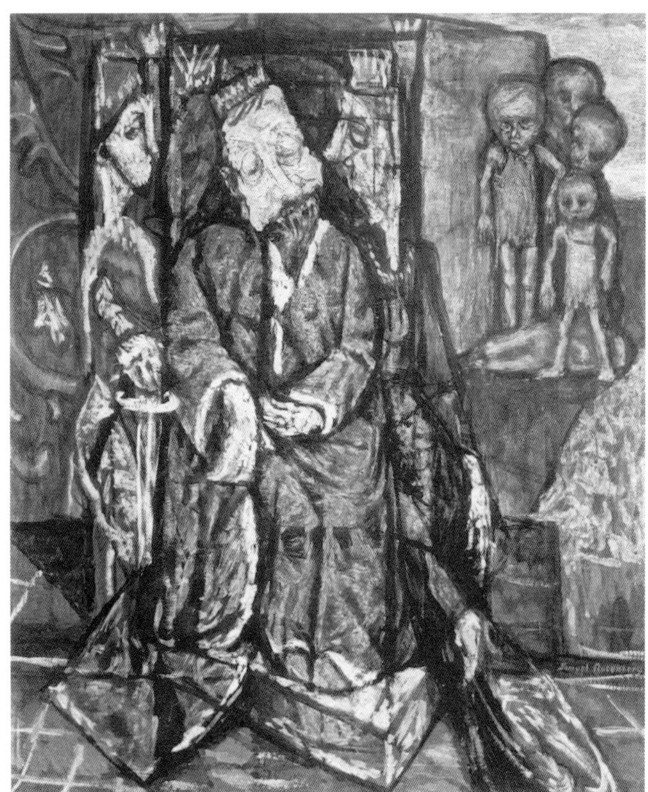

FIG. 36: *The Counselors,* 1945. Oil and tempera on masonite, 29 x 23″.

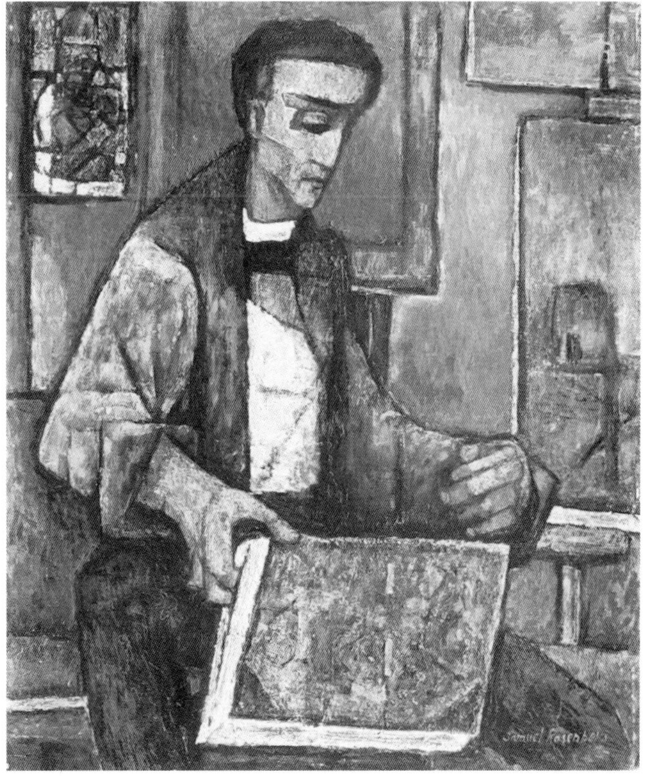

FIG. 37. *Dedication,* 1947. Oil on canvas.

significant role in his stylistic development. The idea of remaining static in this regard was the antithesis of Rosenberg's artistic personality. Contemporary critics in Pittsburgh, and those outside the city, commented on the stylistic affinity between Rosenberg and Rouault. Rosenberg never denied this association, but he never really acknowledged it, either.

Rosenberg said that he preferred painting using the Renaissance method of egg tempera underpainting and overglazing, as it allowed him to achieve the depth of emotion that his subject matter of this period required.[91] Rosenberg created a dialogue between underpainting and overglazing and perfected his technique of placing light colors over dark without creating muddy tones. It was through his thorough experimentation with myriad applications of paint that he arrived at this formula: opaque lights over transparent darks. By starting with a white-gessoed ground and letting some of the ground show through to the top layers, Rosenberg achieved a quality in composition that made the paintings appear to glow from within. In later years, Rosenberg's paintings would even more strongly reveal this quality.

Rosenberg was a skillful craftsman and highly organized in his approach to painting. His process in making a painting was a methodical one. Each painting progressed in layers, beginning with a white or lightly tinted ground. The first layer of underpainting was comprised of thin washes of monochromatic or neutral tones of muted color of egg tempera or casein. The second layer of color was thinly glazed on, so it would remain semi-transparent and receive the multiple layers of either pure or diluted color to follow. The final layer of paint was more thickly applied with a palette knife in small amounts of broken color to achieve opaque highlights. These areas of impasto pigment would then be scumbled, incised, or rubbed away in spots to allow the layers of color underneath to show through. He manipulated the glazes in a similar manner, rubbing some of the glaze off in areas so that a thicker layer of pigment could be applied. Rosenberg did not believe in making arbitrary decisions with regard to color. His was always a well-thought out and intentional course. Central to his premise was that opposing chromatic forces created powerful graphic tensions, so he emphasized complementary color relationships throughout his painting. If the undertone was cool in color temperature, then the overtone or overpainting should be warm, and vice versa. Warm lights equal cool shadows; opaque highlights offset the luminous darks. With this interplay of opposites, he achieved balance in his compositions. His transparent luminous darks were the result of multiple layers of glaze, one floating over the other. He always followed his cardinal rule of "fat over lean," a process that he ingrained in his students as well. This resonance of complementary colors was especially useful to him in achieving the emotional impact he was seeking in his paintings of the 1940s.[92] The luminosity that viewers comment on when seeing these paintings is the result of his use of the egg tempera medium and complex glazing combinations. Rosenberg's utilization of this time-consuming technique was one of the reasons he often worked on up to six paintings at one time. Rosenberg's painting process also included working with a mirror behind him so he could see his painting in reverse. He said it gave him a better sense of balance in the composition. His approach was to work all over the canvas at once, and, as he suggested to his students, he even turned the painting upside down at times to get a better sense of the whole without being distracted by the subject or form.[93]

This stage in Rosenberg's development has been repeatedly referred to as his "stained glass" period. The way in which Rosenberg "built" his paintings in layers has much in common with the way that a stained glass designer fabricates a window in multiple plating layers. Using sequential layers of translucent color and transparent glazes, some of them blending with one another, some remaining independent, Rosenberg was able to achieve a shimmering effect similar to that of light as it passes through layers of multicolored glass. This transmission of light was his primary goal. Like a window, his paintings seem to emit light rather than reflect it, and this aspect of his art would dominate his later work. The dark, heavy outlines that Rosenberg used to define his figures resemble the leading that is used to separate glass panels in a stained glass composition. Rosenberg incorporated this linear device to divide his compositions into abstract sections, so that when put together, they narrate the story he was trying to tell (very much the way in which a stained glass window is "read"). Rosenberg's students remember him referencing the glowing colors of Romanesque stained glass windows in his classes, and although they don't recall him specifically talking about their linear quality, he obviously studied their drawing stylization as well.[94]

Critics tried to draw parallels between Rosenberg and Abraham Rattner, a New York artist whose work also resembled stained glass, but Rosenberg responded with displeasure to the comparison.[95] Philip Pearlstein, who was a student of Rosenberg's, has suggested that it may have been this unwanted association that pushed Rosenberg to experiment with nonobjectivity in his paintings at the end of the decade and in the decades that followed.[96]

Two years after the United States entered World War II, Louise Bruner wrote that war as a theme was "strikingly absent" from paintings included in the Painting in the United States exhibition of 1943, but Rosenberg's painting *Whither? No. 1* of that year (plate 44) "cries out against the fate of the Jews in an abstract composition designed like a stained glass window with the stylized head of ancient Jews as the center of interest." And the following year, when the painting was included in Rosenberg's first solo show in New York City at Associated American Artists gallery, the *New York World Telegram* recognized the painting's luminosity: "the paint is so luminous, you feel almost as if a light must be shining behind.[97] In this painting, Rosenberg has compartmentalized the composition in a more deliberate manner, making an even stronger allusion to stained glass. Its quality of light, as well, suggests the effect of light filtering through colored pieces of glass. Once again, the open book figures prominently in the foreground of this composition, suggesting there is still hope for change in the midst of despair.

For *Israel* of 1945 (plate 53), Rosenberg portrays another Old-World image in his half-length portrait of an observant Jewish man in yarmulke and prayer shawl, who sits with his head in his hand, staring blankly out at the viewer. An open book in his hand, he has been interrupted from his reading by his thoughts; overcome by his emotional state. *Israel* is the immediate expression of a man with the weight of the world on his shoulders, whose spiritual and physical strength has been seriously tested. It is a burden that seems too heavy for one man to carry. Is Rosenberg perhaps expressing his awareness of the Jewish people and their struggle for independence? His fellow Jews were in the process of asserting their independence in their homeland for which statehood would be granted within three years. Rosenberg has translated his idea through his use of strong complementary colors, extreme contrasts of light and dark, and layer upon layer of thinly applied transparent glazes and thick opaque texture. His technique gives the painting a depth that allows the viewer to look deep inside the sitter, as if to reveal an inner truth. Rosenberg often said that he let the mood of his subject dictate to him which method to use in depicting it and in his paintings of this decade he allowed the interaction of color to convey the intensity of that mood. The background of *Israel* is an undefined series of abstract shapes that does not distract the viewer from the subject at hand. Consistently, Rosenberg pulls the subject to the very front of the picture plane so no one can escape its message. Background becomes simply background in many cases, as no reference to the subject or representation is made. The incorporation of figuration with abstraction is a route Rosenberg would take beginning with this work of the 1940s, sometimes veering from the path entirely into a nonobjective world of pure paint. He never abandons representation altogether, however. Just when you think he has made the leap to nonobjectivity in his art, the human form reemerges. This movement back and forth between figuration and nonobjectivity would occupy him for the remainder of his life. Just as giving up commissioned portraits lifted many of the restraints put on the artist, Rosenberg's move to abstraction allowed him a similar freedom and more flexibility in his work. It seems to have been a natural move for him and one he adapted to readily. As witnessed in his work of the previous decade, he made the transition to abstraction gradually. His new style evolved slowly over a period of years. From 1942 onward, the decade was filled with paintings that show his experimentation and continual progression in this direction.

Israel is the single most reproduced of all Rosenberg's work. It made a strong impression on the art critics of the day, who agreed that it conveyed a deep religious quality. In an article published in *Carnegie Magazine,* the author suggests "The scholar is almost a mood, certainly a type rather than an individual, and here personifies the whole heritage of sorrow and tribulation that is associated with Israel." And according to Dorothy Grafly for *Christian Science Monitor,* Rosenberg reveals a "basic appreciation of the trials, hopes, and fears of the Jewish people."[98] A reporter for the *Bulletin Index* thought that *Israel* depicted "the eternal struggle of the Jewish race in the world."[99] And Mary M. Davis for the *Toledo Sunday Times* described the painting more universally, as "symbolic of a race, it does not matter which he is, for he is thought itself, the link between man, the greater universe, and its Creator."[100] A second painting of the same year, *Chosen Land,* which was also known as "The Promised Land," may also have been a reference to Israel's approaching statehood.

Rosenberg was awarded First Honorable Mention for *Israel* in the Painting in the United States exhibition of 1945 at the Carnegie Institute. The Carnegie purchased the painting for its permanent collection but returned it to the artist in exchange for *Time Echoes* (plate 63).

Even when the war ended, and optimism prevailed in the country, very little of that hopefulness was expressed in his work. For *Astrea* of 1945, as its title would suggest, Rosenberg extracts a recognizable symbol from Greek mythology to comment on justice (or the lack of it) at the war's end. A woman, enveloped in a composition of abstract geometric forms, cradles her ill or mortally wounded child in her arms. In *A King* of 1946 (plate 54), the subject is so deep in his own thoughts that he is unaware of the writhing skeletal symbols of death swirling all around him. The death and destruction he presumably has caused has come back to haunt him.

Pittsburgh was not particularly receptive to abstract art in the 1940s. In an article for the *Pittsburgh Press,* Douglas Naylor used the headline "Saint-

Gaudens Asks 'Peace' with Foes of Abstract Art," adding that "Saint-Gaudens asked for an armistice in the widespread attack on ultra-modern art." The uproar was over the fact that first prize, one thousand dollars, had been awarded to Karl Knaths for his abstract painting *Gear,* which was shown in the Painting in the United States exhibition of 1946 at the Carnegie Institute. Artists of the city responded to the implication that abstract art was somehow less significant than representational art. In an interview with Naylor, Rosenberg defended Knaths's painting: "You can't talk art; you just do art. It has a language all its own and it is difficult to find another kind of language to explain it." Rosenberg felt that no picture was more deserving than Knaths's *Gear*. "*Gear,*" he said, "is painted according to the first truth of the painter; the organization of the painter's visual language comprising the relationship of line, form, and color."[101] During an interview for *The Arrow* in 1945, Rosenberg told his Pennsylvania College for Women students that he believed emotion was by far the most important element of painting. He also told them that his work was becoming "more abstract and impressionistic." "I cannot be sure what will occur, for studied change is not desirable. Change, however, is very important and I hope that my work will continue to change."[102]

Near the end of the decade change indeed occurred. Light as a subject became more important to Rosenberg and would become a dominant factor in his paintings of future years. His style shifted again and his color palette and mood lightened. As was his custom, Rosenberg did not make any advances in his art without retreating once or twice to an earlier investigation. Rosenberg implies rebirth and perhaps a regeneration of the world in *The Leaf* of 1948 (plate 56), his only painting of the decade from which he drew his subject literally from nature. In his painting of a bearded Jewish man entitled *Amos,* of 1949, we see the beginning of Rosenberg's fourth stylistic transition. While the figure still looms large at the front of the picture plane, it is now blending into or merging with the background. The high contrast of light and dark is gone, as are the vibrant colors, and a light, seeming to come from within the canvas, illuminates the figure. This is a more upbeat image than earlier portrayals of similar subjects and suggests an emergence from the darkness of previous years. Rosenberg's emotionally laden subject matter and heavily outlined forms disappeared gradually in the first few years of the new decade and his application of paint became even more spontaneous and painterly. He was on his way to creating his own brand of abstract expressionism.

Rosenberg's work of the postwar period took another sudden and no less dramatic turn in his artistic development. By the time the decade came to a close, Rosenberg had moved on to explore painting techniques used by the abstract expressionists. Artists everywhere felt alienation following the war. There was no longer a common cause to direct them in their efforts. Painters turned inward, attempting to find themselves and their individuality. The world had changed and would never be the same again. Their turning back to an earlier, simpler time was in the past. Artists such as Jackson Pollock, Willem de Kooning, Mark Rothko, Franz Kline, Robert Motherwell, and others pushed forward to create unique, individual expressions, not the mutual expression of a nation. Rosenberg was no exception. In a series of eight paintings, all referred to as *Untitled Composition 1949 No. 1* (plate 59) through *No. 8*, he initiated his inward search and outward journey to make light the subject of his work. These paintings reveal Rosenberg's obvious awareness of the automatic writing of the surrealists and perhaps the poured and drip techniques utilized by Hans Hofmann and Jackson Pollock. Rosenberg only ventured into this pouring, dripping, and staining arena for the better part of one year, and appears, from the work that remains, to have never returned to it as a means of expression. In all eight paintings, from *No. 5*, the smallest, which measures eight inches by six inches, to *No. 8*, the largest, at thirty inches by twenty-five inches, Rosenberg is clearly making a break with the past by experimenting with a new method of applying paint. He continues to use masonite as his support for these works, but now relies only on oil paint as his medium, laid on thickly in some areas, and so thinly in others that it resembles a stain. Once the paint was applied, Rosenberg incised, scrubbed, and scraped the layers to achieve a balance in color, texture, and line. Again we see the resonance of opposites with his use of complementary color combinations, but the line has now become the lighter, negative space as opposed to the dark positive. He utilized the uninterrupted movement of one continuous line to maintain a unified surface of color, shape, and texture in which organic and geometric shapes float in the same two-dimensional pictorial space. Rosenberg's spontaneous use of line is the common thread that ties seven of the eight compositions together. The figure, which appears in three out of the eight paintings, faintly emerges in *No. 2*, is abstractly suggested in *No. 3*, and has become a fully recognizable female form in *No. 5*, the most representational of the group, resembling a mosaic in its all-over patterning. The artist's only experiment with staining can be seen in composition *No. 7*.

> Art—in painting—is the highest level of development of visual communication of the emotional and intellectual reality which the artist perceives. Art today concerns itself with the relationships of space-time, physical and psychological forces as expressed through the plastic means of line, form and color. At times symbols and images may be used, but the work of art must always stem from reality through creative activity and never from imitation.[103]

Rosenberg wrote this personal definition of the meaning of art in response to a request from *Carnegie Magazine,* which was planning an article on the subject, "After All, What is Art?" for their December 1948 issue. This statement identifies his lifelong artistic search.

With the economic boom overtaking Pittsburgh in the postwar decade, Rosenberg turned further inward to an even more subjective expression of his ongoing investigation of the formal problems of art. Social or political events of the day were no longer omnipresent in his work and he turned his attentions to an overall exploration of abstraction. When Rosenberg's work changes stylistically, it is neither all encompassing nor does it imply permanence. To be sure, after one year of experimentation with looser methods of paint handling, Rosenberg moved forward, but not without taking a few steps back. His stylistic course is far from a straight one, but filled with curves and outright detours along the way.

By 1950, the figure predominated once again. In Rosenberg's first two paintings of the decade, he references a familiar subject on the streets of Pittsburgh, the balloon vendor. No longer allegorical, but at the same time not a literal representation either, his *Balloon Man No. 1* and *No. 2* (plate 60), both of 1950, are abstract, cubist-inspired arrangements of the human form, set against a background "city" of broken, flat color planes. Both the heavy figure moving through space and the background are comprised of simplified and stylized geometric shapes. In *No. 1,* foreground figure and background are weighted equally, and are balanced from front to back; while in *No. 2,* the balloon man is more dimensional; each is situated before a gridded patchwork of colored blocks. *Balloon Man No. 1* was purchased by Abbott Laboratories of Chicago in 1955 and reprinted as a poster in limited edition made available to their employees for a minimal fee. Emily Genauer, art critic for the *New York Herald Tribune,* wrote a short summary to accompany the painting when it was reproduced on the cover of the company's quarterly publication, "What's New," in 1957. Commenting on

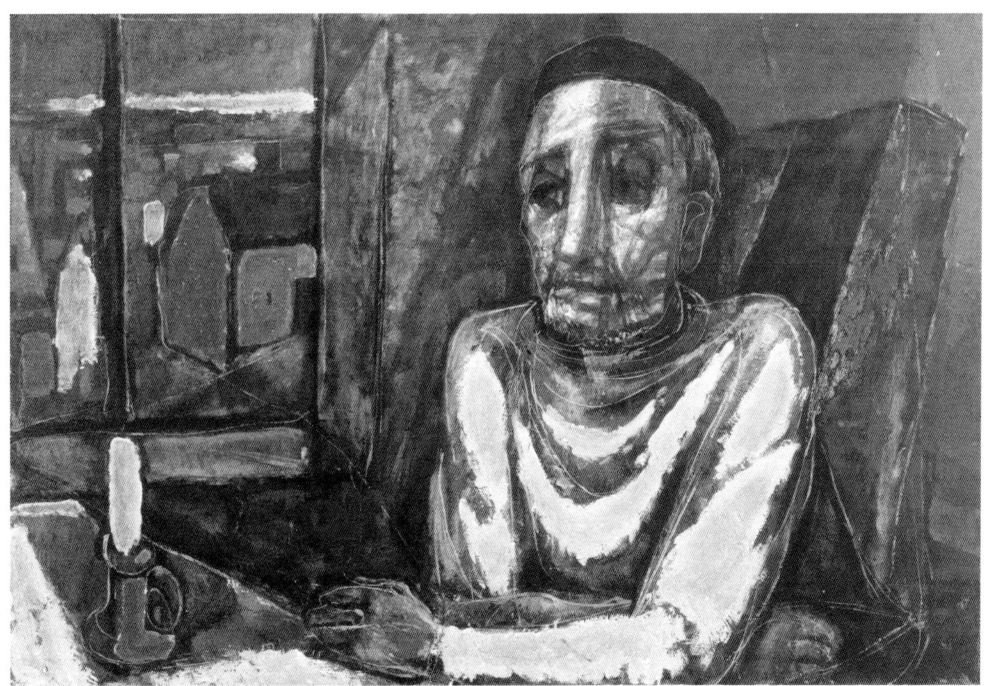

FIG. 38. *Brief Candle,* 1950. Oil and tempera on masonite, 32 x 48″.

the subject, she wrote, "But there are painters who refuse to stop at the obvious aspect of the subject, however pleasing. Samuel Rosenberg . . . is one of them. Although this nationally known Pittsburgh painter started his career about thirty years ago with just such simple, warm, spirited, realistic city scenes, today he sees his material symbolically. He is concerned, he says, with 'relationships of space and time, with physical and psychological forces expressed through line, form, and color.' Beyond that, he says, the pictures must speak for themselves."[104]

Religious subject matter continues to appear in Rosenberg's work of the 1950s, and while it is only during the first few years that literal religious references take precedence, the spiritual quality persists in his later works, as well. Two other paintings of 1950, *Brief Candle* (figure 38) and *Light Transcendent,* show Rosenberg reverting to familiar subjects from the previous decade. In the former, a man in yarmulke sits before a burned-out candle. Vibrant primary and tertiary colors of red and chartreuse dominate this painting but do not negate the overwhelming sense of melancholy expressed by the figure, who is in a state of total grief or resignation. A view out the window to the neighborhood alludes to a new day dawning, even while the candle has burned out. In the latter painting, two rabbinical figures in prayer shawls and yarmulkes conduct a worship service. The elder of the two men holds his hands up, in the gesture of blessing the people that takes place at the end of the worship service. The title, also, intimates God's blessings "shining" on all people. The younger male, standing with his arms crossed in a stance of defiance, may be a reference to the old versus the new ways, or tradition versus new ideas.

Religious imagery remained a part of Rosenberg's oeuvre for several more years, as evidenced in a mural he completed for the entry to St. Henry's Church in the Allentown section of Pittsburgh (plate 61). In 1951, the Pittsburgh firm Marlier and Johnstone Architects commissioned Rosenberg to paint the ten-by-twenty-two-foot, oil on canvas mural depicting Christ teaching the children. The subject of the mural, "Suffer the little children to come unto me and forbid them not: for of such is the Kingdom of God," is taken from Mark 10:14. In a statement that accompanied the work, Rosenberg wrote:

> The painting depicts Jesus as the source of the light that emanates from the right of the panel. This light, brilliant white and yellow, shines from His head and figure, enveloping the people and landscape about Him. It falls on the figures and on the landscape with its Pittsburgh hills and mills, its bridges, its rivers, and buildings. The light penetrates the shadows and the clouds, making them rich and luminous. The children and other people close to Jesus merge with the light and lose their earthly form as they turn to Him. The mills, the hills and the bridges almost dissolve in the light. On the left side of the canvas where the figures are farther removed from Him, the light from the right cascades and billows through the canvas, across, around, and through the little children caught in the moment of their play with their pets, their wagons, and their toys, or with their books.[105]

Rosenberg used some of the parishioners and local children from St. Henry's elementary school next door as his models for the abstract composition. It was the goal of both the architects and the artist to make the wall that opened into the church a living and vital part of the community. Wearing baseball caps and blue jeans, the children included in this historical biblical reference are expressions of their own time. The mural was mounted in the narthex of the church so that visitors must pass through it to enter the nave. One of the exciting features about the construction of the church, according to Dorothy Kantner, was that it was a "church of collaboration." The *YM&WHA Weekly* also noted that "the architects, Marlier and Johnstone, one a Catholic, one a Protestant," had "commissioned Samuel Rosenberg, whose most famous internationally distinguished paintings have been closest to his own Jewish heritage . . ."[106]

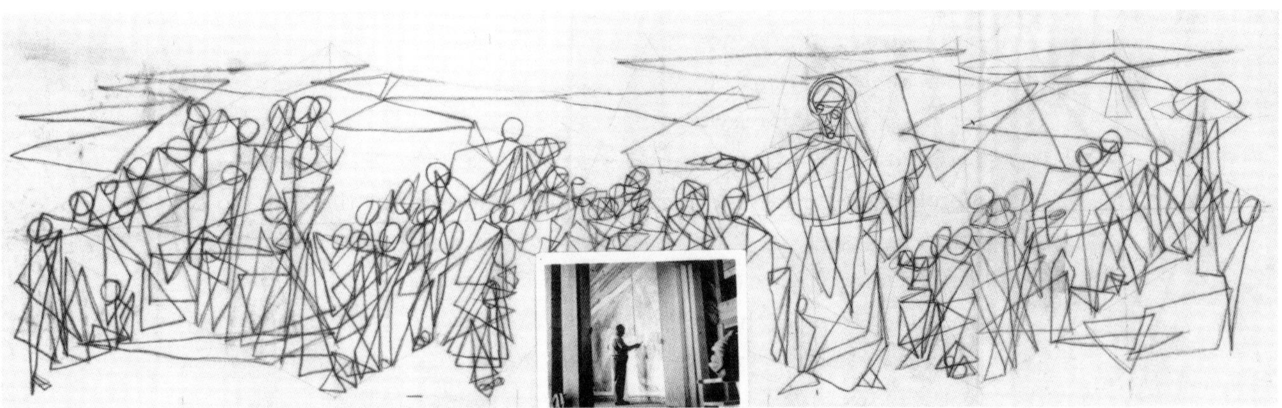

FIG. 39. *Christ Teaching* (preparatory sketch for mural with photograph of Rosenberg painting mural in Kindred McLeary's former home in Humbert Valley, Somerset County, Pa.), 1952. Pencil on paper, 10 x 30″.

Rosenberg made sketches and drawings for six months before beginning on the canvas that would take him a full year to complete. He carefully organized the pattern of light in his composition so that it would fit with the architectural pattern and structure of the church, to preserve the architect's conception. Rosenberg worked closely with the architects during the execution of this commission. He studied the church as it was being built and carried the yellow color of the exterior brick as well as the yellow marble of the altar into his mural for continuity. In this complex composition, Rosenberg successfully orchestrated the activity of the welcoming figure of Christ with the large number of children being shepherded to him from both sides by adults.[107]

Rosenberg made at least five large-scale cartoons or preparatory studies in oil (and watercolor) for the mural and one large pencil sketch. The oil studies show the artist's intentions in color palette and pattern, as well as the evolution of the composition and the spiritual light emanating from Christ (plate 62). The pencil cartoon is also revealing. This ten-by-thirty-inch sketch appears to have been executed quickly with one continuous line and constant movement of the hand. The line's vitality carries through the drawing from left to right across the surface of the paper, in the same direction in which the children are moving toward the figure of Christ. While only a preliminary study, the drawing suggests all the components that would comprise the final work of art (figure 39). The substructure for the completed composition is delineated in this drawing and remains visible in the final painting.

As evidenced in this mural, and as referenced earlier, Rosenberg's palette became increasingly lighter as he delved deeper into utilizing light as his subject. Although much less recognizable than before, there is still an emphasis on the human form in his work. The artist's continual search leads him back and forth between what appears to be the earthly realm of figuration and the spiritual realm of nonobjectivity. From 1952 on, with a few exceptions (as always), Rosenberg proceeded to merge abstraction and figuration to achieve a unique visual language. By this time, his figures begin to dissolve into his backgrounds, and once in a while, they disappear altogether, only to reemerge again in another canvas. When figures reemerge, they are not literal representations; while still rooted in realistic observations, they become more mystical in nature. In his reticent style of communication, Rosenberg maintained that his aim as an abstract painter was "a matter of artistic efficiency"; he was merely expressing what he saw and felt "in the simplest terms." Rosenberg's move to abstract expressionism would dominate his output for the last twenty years of his life.

Rosenberg eliminated any sense of dimensionality in favor of a planar structure for his life-size canvas *Time Echoes* of 1952 (plate 63). His use of a cubist analytical framework allowed him to build this composition architectonically. Utilizing cubism once again, Rosenberg began to break down his figural forms into a series of flat, angular shapes that exist in a shallow, light-filled space. His faceted female form, suggestive of the Madonna and Child, enters into a dialogue with the background, and with this composition, Rosenberg initiates his synthesis of the two. Life-size figures advance from and recede into the picture plane, creating an ambiguous pictorial space. In this kaleidoscopic arrangement of fragmented color, Rosenberg references his earlier investigations of transparency and translucency, the complexity of which rely on the artist's methodical painting process of applying layer upon layer of thinned pigment to build the composition. Reduced to a series of abstract forms, Rosenberg has abandoned modeling and anatomical accuracy in favor of a dynamic reordering of the female form, which practically dissolves into the undefined background. Rosenberg began his initial exploration of the possibilities of cubism nearly twenty-five years earlier in two previously discussed portraits of 1928 and 1931, *Around the Corner (Derelict)* (figure 11) and *My Friend Twiggs* (figure 12).

Rosenberg's loose interpretation of cubism in his paintings of the early 1950s was only one stop in his sequential progression. Subsequently, he would eliminate the underlying structure altogether, and through a modified abstract expressionist vocabulary, Rosenberg would find his own mature style. Rosenberg followed the same advice he gave to his students; he did not experiment with abstraction until he had a firm grasp on realism. It was Rosenberg's temperament that allowed him his slow and steady growth in his work, and perhaps even his teaching helped in that regard, as it gave him time during the academic year to think about the possibilities of what was to come next, and make sketches and drawings of his thought process. No stylistic change was abrupt because there was always some re-examining of earlier efforts.

Rosenberg abandoned his indirect method of overglazing and underpainting with his work of the 1950s, turning instead to the direct method of painting with oil on canvas. According to his son Murray, Rosenberg found that he could achieve the same luminosity of his earlier work with color juxtapositions and by applying paint in short brushstrokes with a variety of homemade spatulas and knives. In preparation for much of his work of this period, Rosenberg made small collages as his starting point. Cutting and tearing scraps of colored construction paper, newspapers, magazines, and tissue allowed him to investigate not only the interplay of color but spatial relationships, as well, prior to working on a larger scale. With these thin layers of paper, he could experiment with the shallow depth he was seeking in his painting. Once put together, he painted and drew on them to create a final study that approached the techniques he would use in his paintings. A preparatory collage for an earlier painting, *The Grandfather,* is tiny, measuring only four by three inches, but contains all the elements of the final painting. Patches of irregularly cut construction paper are laid over one another to organize the basic shapes of the composition, and then details such as hands, face, and shadows are filled in with pencil and charcoal. As many as four layers of paper are evident in some areas of this miniature composition. His collages are helpful in illuminating the artist's method of building his paintings. Several tissue paper collages are especially revealing in this regard.

Rosenberg's depiction of the human form as a series of angular flat planes also suggests the expressive possibilities of African sculpture. His reduction of human anatomy to a series of angular planes is similar to the way African sculpture is carved away to reveal the human or animal form. Rosenberg owned a number of African sculptures and masks that he had purchased from the estate of his late friend Kindred McLeary. While Rosenberg never discussed those sculptures with regard to his own work, they were important to him and he often talked about them when students, friends, and family came to the house.[108]

The Madonna and Child are once again referenced in his painting *Emergence No. 2* (plate 64) of 1953, now with a heightened sense of color. Whereas in *Time Echoes,* the tones were muted, this light-filled composition is comprised of patches of luminous complementary colors. In his paintings of these years, Rosenberg no longer attempts to recreate the visual world inside the boundaries of the canvas, but to have his figures become one with the picture plane and their surrounding pictorial space. Chiaroscuro and modeling are eliminated and the structure of his composition relies completely on the interplay of light and color as he continues to deal with the formal art-making problems of color, line, texture, and design.

Rosenberg's abstract expressionist period, which essentially began with his experiments of 1949, was often referred to as his "light period," although it had always been a major factor in his work. Rosenberg revealed his interest in light as early as 1922 in a painting entitled *Reflected Light* (location unknown). A reporter for the *Sentinel* said of Rosenberg, "Running through all his work . . . from early views of millworker homes lined along the valleys to late figure studies made alive with a flick of paint on eyeball, arm, or thigh—is a marvelous light that springs from the canvas."[109] With Rosenberg's stylistic transition in the 1950s, however, came a new title. Referred to as the "painter of light" repeatedly in these years by colleagues and critics alike, Rosenberg spoke to Sam Hood about the limitations of such an allusion. During an extensive interview with Hood in 1957, Rosenberg said "Light is one thing, paint another. Art cannot compete with nature. I never saw a painting that made me squint like when I look at the sun or even a lighted candle."[110]

From 1953 to 1956, figuration in Rosenberg's paintings comes and goes before backgrounds of geometric shapes. In paintings such as *Fleeting Substance* of 1954 (plate 66), and *The Seed* of 1955 (plate 67), Rosenberg's work no longer offers a view, however abstracted, into the natural world; instead it tenders a glimpse into a subjective world of his own design. Through plastic means, Rosenberg created colors that emanate light from within. The quality of light in each color, overall compositional balance, and harmonious color relationships are the substance of this mature work. Even when the titles of the works reference nature, in paintings such as *Sunlit Rhythms, The Pool,* and *Season's Turnings,* the paintings themselves are about relationships of light, color, and texture. The physicality of the dense and tactile surfaces of impasto pigment underscore Rosenberg's continual search to convey meaning with the act of painting as opposed to the suggested subject, as his paintings were often titled upon completion in collaboration with his wife.

In *Fruit in Evening Light,* completed in 1955, Rosenberg returns to a theme he referred to often in the 1930s. The fruit and vegetable markets he depicted twenty years prior were expressive studies of Hill District residents, their cultures, and identities. In this work, Rosenberg is no longer trying to literally represent the subject; rather, he concentrates on the formal attributes of pattern, color, and the play of light on the fruit, and not the fruit itself. In an interview with Douglas Naylor, he describes his intent in this painting: "I saw the display of fruit when a storm was coming up, and casting a peculiar light through the clouds. This was a mood of nature created by the play of light on form. I was interested in the cold light playing on the angular lines of Downtown buildings in the background and the warm colors of the curved fruit in the foreground." Naylor continued the interview with the question: "What's wrong with painting fruit that looks like fruit?" Rosenberg responded: "Most people in looking at a painting ask 'What is it?' These are curiosity values. The real truth of a painting is shape, color, line and texture. It is not the fruit that counts, it is the spot of color on the canvas in relation to all the areas of color which create balance and feeling."[111]

As Ralph Brem wrote in his review of an exhibition of Rosenberg's work at the Hewlett Gallery in 1965: "By 1954, Rosenberg was looking for some way to catch the light and shapes that play constantly across people's lives. *Green on Yellow* of 1957, which he worked on for three years, is the turnaround painting from the figure to the abstract in the show. Still a hint of the real in the leaf forms and a bough, but green atop yellow was the problem he felt he must solve." Rosenberg himself expressed the importance of the painting *Green on Yellow* when he said, "It was the beginning for what I am doing now. Keeping the colors close together in hue." In *Composition* (plate 69) of 1957, two blocks of red are the same color but look different because of the colors that surround them. Rosenberg explained: "Sometimes I would set up a problem to solve, or I would just improvise. I suppose a composer does that too; one thing leading to another . . . balance, moving forms. It all has a lot to do with balance. That's how it was with *Crescendo*" (plate 70). According to Brem, the artist "pointed out a tiny block of green and said the picture would fall apart without it."[112] Two years later, Rosenberg would write, "I feel that I am right now in the full flush of my painting career, that I am reaching the fruition of the many years of search and discovery."[113]

From his series of figures dissolving into abstract backgrounds, Rosenberg proceeded to figures set in motion, as in *Becoming* (figure 40; plate 68) of 1956. Then he began on a series of completely nonobjective paintings. In 1957, Rosenberg made a conservative adjustment in his investigation of color, in keeping with Joseph Albers's investigations of the properties of color, and especially Hans Hofmann's push-pull theory of the recession and advancement of cool and warm colors. According to Hofmann, color

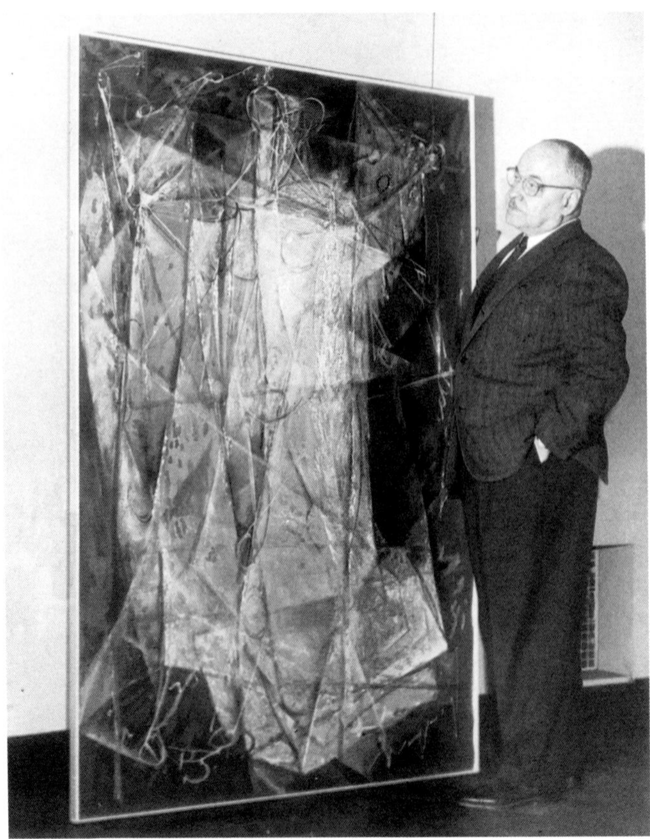

FIG. 40.
Rosenberg with *Becoming*, 1956.
Oil on canvas, 71 x 46″.

plays "an active part in that magic phenomena of push-pull which creates the pulsating quality of pictorial life." He also said that "Only from the varied counter play of push and pull, and from its variation in intensities, will plastic creation result." Hofmann elaborated: "Push is answered by pull, and pull with push."[114] Like Rosenberg, Hofmann was both a committed teacher and an artist who believed that painting could reveal both a physical and spiritual reality. Rosenberg understood this and worked toward that end in his paintings as well. The two artists both made their way to abstraction in the 1940s and were especially interested in unifying color, form, and space. They shared other achievements as well; each was given his first one-man show in New York City in 1944, Hofmann at Peggy Guggenheim's Art of this Century Gallery, and Rosenberg at Associated American Artists Gallery. Rosenberg obviously studied Hofmann's color theory; each successive Rosenberg painting appears to be a chromatic experiment with another set of colors, shapes, space, and light. Moreover, Rosenberg shared Hofmann's ideas with his students at both Carnegie Tech and the YM&WHA. Yet there were some differences between Rosenberg's approach and Hofmann's. Whereas Hofmann was trying to capture the pulsating quality and movement of color, Rosenberg was attempting to stabilize the picture plane through his color relationships, to create harmony as opposed to tension. In Rosenberg's work of this period, heavy outlines are gone; squares, rectangles, and triangles all float together on a common plane. No sense of three dimensions is present in this work, and all colors relate so that the neutral surface is preserved.

In 1957, Rosenberg eliminated referential titles, calling his paintings of the next three years *Composition, Blue in Black, Crescendo, Light Transcendent, Magic City,* and *Blue Beyond Blue,* among other nonobjective designations. In these paintings, Rosenberg temporarily eliminated heavy texture in order to more closely consider color and its relationship to the picture plane. And while the human form (and any reference to it) is completely purged from this series of paintings, there remains a verticality and a spatial configuration that suggests the underlying presence of the figure. *Tuscan Light* of 1959 has a faintly visible Madonna and Child completely enveloped in a radiant glow of yellow pigment. This may have been the artist's response to his trip to Italy the previous year.

According to Jeanette Jena, the "New York School" of painting dominated the jurors' selections for the Associated Artists of Pittsburgh Fifty-first Annual Exhibition in 1961, to which Rosenberg's nonobjective composition *Arrival* was accepted. The painter Theodoros Stamos, sculptor David Smith, and craftsman David Campbell, jurors of the exhibition, were responsible, she said, for the large number of so many well-known artists not included in the show. Jena continued: "I must say that this is a very handsome exhibition, for the most part. It has all the light and color and movement of this very active and important school of modern painting; that dramatic impact and ability to open up physical and spiritual vistas, which is an important aspect of the best abstract expressionism."[115]

Rosenberg continued his investigation of both nonobjectivity and figural abstraction in a dozen or so paintings for the remainder of his career. *Personages* of 1964 (plate 74) reveals the vaporous presence of two human figures that emerge from a veiled background of scumbled color. A white light emanates from their nonphysical forms.

In *Through Eastern Windows* and *Afterglow* (plate 71), both of 1964, we see the artist's harmoniously balanced composition of secondary color combinations. In the latter painting, two large orange squares float weightlessly in a field of blue-green pigment underneath which the orange "afterglow" is apparent, providing overall balance and symmetry to the composition. This painting took Rosenberg years to complete. He first painted it in 1958, however, due to his dissatisfaction with it, he repainted the entire canvas six years later. Rosenberg was known to rework and touch up his canvases from time to time, but it was not often that he reworked them altogether. *Fleeting Substance* is another canvas that was painted twice—in 1954 and again in 1971. When friends of the artist bought the painting, they invited Rosenberg to see where they would hang it. When Rosenberg saw it, he told his new collector that he wanted to reframe the picture. So he took it with him and when he brought it back, it was a completely different painting. He "reworked it," he said, "to improve it."[116] The strongly vertical *Bright October Morning* of 1968 (figure 41) ultimately became the horizontal *Interaction Blue and Red* of 1972 (plate 77), and the only reference to the earlier painting that remains is the one patch of red in the lower right-hand corner of the painting that began in the upper right of the original composition. Rosenberg worked on this painting from 1968 to 1972. Other works in Rosenberg's list of paintings took years to complete as well, presumably because he was continually reworking them.

As their titles suggest, in *Interaction Blue and Red* and *Importance of Red,* 1969 (plate 78), Rosenberg emphasizes his concentration on color interactions. In the former, primary colors interact, while in the latter, complementary colors come together. They overlay one another yet sit harmoniously on the same plane. The red band at the top offsets the two complementary rectangles in the center. And even though the red band is a brighter hue than both the orange and blue, because of its proximity to the white and multicolored background field, it is seen as equal in value. Rosenberg applied a second small patch of red to a darker area of blue to balance the entire composition. Echoing his earlier comments about *Crescendo,* Rosenberg said of *Importance of Red* that if he removed the spot of red in the painting's lower right, the composition would fall apart.

Rosenberg continued this thorough investigation of color throughout the remainder of his life. In paintings such as *April No. 1,* 1969 (plate 76), and *No. 2,* 1970, Rosenberg examined the subject of springtime light, but moved from an easel-sized composition to one that is larger than life. The natural world is also present in *Heart of the Rock* (plate 80) of 1970. Light emanates out of a multifaceted rock from a central interior source and illuminates the rock from behind as well. Whether Rosenberg is referencing the natural world or his own subjective world, a majority of his late paintings share this ethereal, soft, white light that radiates from within the canvas. In *Clearstream No. 2* of 1972, that ethereal light takes on the ghostly shape of a human figure and shares the metaphysical quality of his other paintings of this period. Rosenberg's late works operate on many levels and

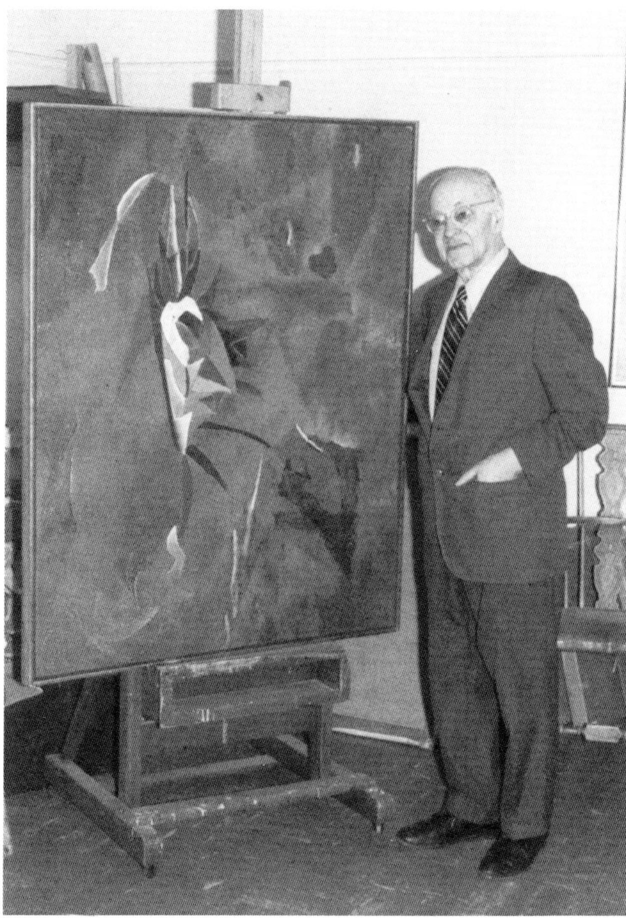

FIG. 41. Rosenberg with *Bright October Morning (Interaction Blue and Red)*, 1968–72. Oil on canvas, 48 x 38″.

can be interpreted literally, symbolically, and emotionally, sometimes all within the same composition.

Only three years into his retirement from teaching, in 1967, Rosenberg suffered his first major heart attack. He experienced a slow but steady recovery, and even as he recuperated, his output did not diminish, nor did his continual experimentation. He tried acrylic paint for the first time in 1967 and used it to make five paintings between that year and 1970. As was Rosenberg's lifelong custom, he worked on several paintings at one time, so at the time of his death, a number of them remained in progress in his studio. His last eight paintings of 1972, with titles and subjects such as *Clearstream No. 2, Elusive Image, Interaction Blue and Red, Light and Image* (plate 81), *Perpetual Light No. 2, Untitled Composition, Wedding in the Garden,* and *Man by the Sea No. 2,* all reveal that the artist's investigations—of color, the figure, and the relationship of each to space—were ongoing. *Elusive Image* conveys these investigations, as the mysterious presence of a figural form seems to appear and then disappear. At the time of Rosenberg's second heart attack in 1972, from which he did not recover, he was working on three paintings. *Wedding in the Garden* (plate 82) and *Man by the Sea No. 2* were late figural references to subject matter of an earlier period. The former, a composition of two shadowy figures both emerging from and merging into a multicolored background, is luminous. Stimulated by the upcoming wedding of his grandson Joel in 1972, Rosenberg created the painting that year and it was given to Joel and his wife Dorothy following the artist's death. *Man by the Sea No. 2* was a recreation and reinvestigation of the primitive man he had painted in *Man by the Sea No. 1* of 1965 (plate 75). *Untitled Composition* was on Rosenberg's easel at the time of his death. To Libbie, these last paintings were full of the joy of life.

Rosenberg created over 400 sketches during his lifetime; 346 were donated to Carnegie Museum of Art by Libbie and Murray Rosenberg after the artist's death. These preliminary ideas for paintings or subjects reveal the artist's thought process as well as his proclivity for experimentation. Nature studies, street scenes, figures in motion, buildings, portraits, the Hill District, fruit markets, vacations in Mexico, Gloucester, Somerset County, and abstractions exist from every period in his career, many with annotations of the colors he would use in the final painting. He made drawings and sketches in pastel, ink, pencil, crayon, and collage, sometimes appropriating the shapes of a color reproduction from a magazine as his starting point.

Teaching

Rosenberg embarked on his nearly five-decade teaching career in the heart of the Hill District at the Irene Kaufmann Settlement (IKS), where he founded the Neighborhood Art School in 1917. Hired by resident director Sidney Teller at age twenty-one, Rosenberg directed the IKS's art program for the next twelve years. The art program at the settlement continued well beyond Rosenberg's tenure there, until the IKS merged with the YM&WHA in 1961. Rosenberg himself had benefited from a similar class at the Columbian Council School, forerunner to IKS, when he was about eleven years old. Having experienced the school as a young man, it is easy to understand why he would have been interested in perpetuating that experience for others. According to Libbie, Rosenberg taught five nights a week at the settlement.

The Irene Kaufmann Settlement was originally founded as the Columbian Council School and Settlement, which formally opened through the

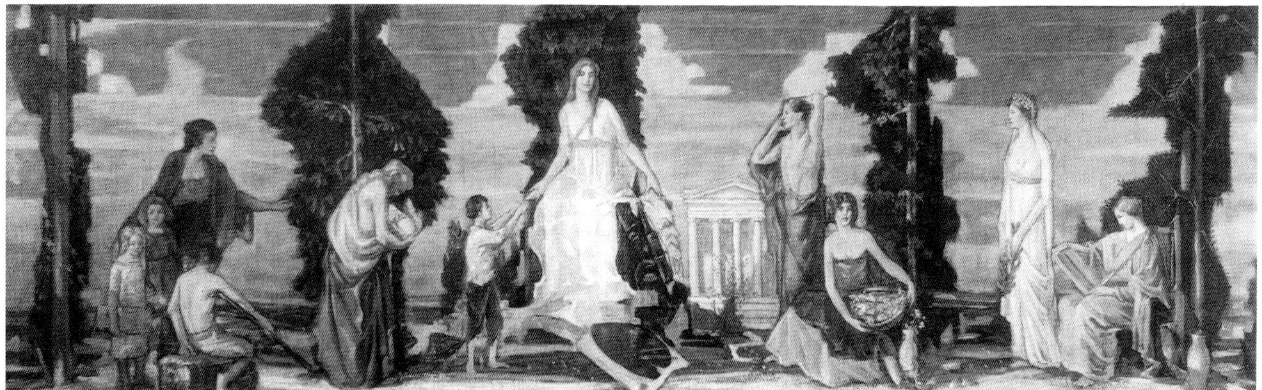

FIG. 42. *The Spirit of the Settlement* (mural for the former Irene Kaufmann Settlement, 1835 Centre Avenue, Pittsburgh, commissioned by Sidney A. Teller, Resident Director), 1922. Oil on canvas.

efforts of Rabbi Lippman Mayer, who developed the school for Jewish immigrant children, and Mrs. A. Leo Weil, president of the Columbian Council. Rosenberg painted a mural design entitled *The Spirit of the Settlement* in 1922 (figure 42), and would paint Rabbi Mayer's portrait some time later (plate 10).[117]

The influence of the IKS in the Hill District was pervasive and had an impact on generations of the multiethnic population. With offerings of job training, English language and citizenship classes, free public baths, nursing care, a better baby clinic, race relations classes, interreligious activities, athletics, art classes, a summer playschool, a library, concerts, lectures, and a theater, IKS became one of the largest settlements worldwide.[118] Although a Jewish-sponsored organization, it was a community center that served the diverse neighborhood regardless of the color, creed, race, or nationality of its inhabitants.[119] Sidney Teller took pride in his position as director of the settlement, and it was his goal to improve living conditions for inhabitants of the Hill. He organized the demolition of unsafe, substandard housing and instituted a campaign to "Clean Up! Paint Up! Plant Up!" the neighborhood.[120] In an attempt to eliminate the negative forces that contributed to the delinquency of children and adults in the Hill, he sponsored the Better Neighborhood Contest in the early 1920s. Initiated through the Pittsburgh Public Schools, this program encouraged kids in the city, and especially the Hill, to beautify their neighborhood by planting flower and vegetable gardens. (These gardens would also provide food for residents caught in the depression during the following decade.)

Teller had been appointed director of IKS in 1916, and it was his inspired idea to teach art at the settlement. Rosenberg and other Pittsburgh artists, including William Schulgold, who helped plan the classes, William Wolfson, Frank Vittor, and Nathaniel Spear, as well as an advisory board composed of community leaders and artists, initiated a creative outlet for

During the 1930s, Rosenberg painted a variety of scenes of the Hill, particularly of Jewish and black neighborhoods. The Jews were moving away from the Hill by the 1920s, although elderly, poor Jews still remained; the Hill was increasingly taking on the flavor of an all-black neighborhood. Rosenberg was very sympathetic to the hardships and difficulties of the district's residents, and painted a number of scenes of black life on the Hill. His sensitivity reflected the concern of many Jews at the time to issues of discrimination and hardship which affected both the black and Jewish communities. The IKS where Rosenberg worked for over a decade did not admit blacks as members, but it was the first such institution to offer its facilities for use to blacks. There were blacks in some of the classes and the black community was enormously helped by the health and nursing programs offered at the IKS. One longtime observer noted that if it weren't for the IKS, the black community would have been devastated by typhoid, a real threat in Pittsburgh at the time because of unfiltered water (Frank Bolden, former city editor for the *Pittsburgh Courier*, interview by Barbara Burstin, 20 December 2001). S. Leo Ruslander, a prominent Pittsburgh Jewish attorney who was president of the IKS board, wrote in his memoirs, *The Life and Times of S. Leo Ruslander*, that once the pastor of the black Baptist Church in the neighborhood complained that he had no available facilities for baptizing the members of his congregation. In response, it was decided to open up the swimming pool during stated hours at night to the pastor and his flock. By the 1950s, when the IKS had long since stopped serving a Jewish neighborhood, the IKS—under the presidency of Julian Ruslander, S. Leo's son—rented its buildings on Centre Avenue to the black community for one dollar a year for five years. In addition to the IKS, the nearby Montefiore Hospital, which had opened its doors on Centre Avenue in the Hill in 1908, admitted black patients, most of them free of charge. As noted in an article by Ida Cohen Selavan ("Jewish Wage Earners in Pittsburgh, 1890–1930," *AJHQ* [March 1976]: 283), the Labor Lyceum, which opened in 1916 and was frequented by the Jewish labor union members, was the first white organization in the city to rent a hall to black groups.

BARBARA BURSTIN

both children and adults. The Neighborhood Art School, which operated annually from October to May, offered instruction in illustration, poster design, pen-and-ink sketching, charcoal drawing, pastel, oil painting, and modeling.[121] The IKS newsletter, which was published monthly, did not list all courses taught by each instructor; instead it provided a general list of course offerings. Rosenberg and Schulgold taught drawing and painting to children from ages six to seventeen in the evenings from seven o'clock to ten o'clock, but the newsletter does not specify when or how many classes each instructor taught. Rosenberg tutored his students in painting and drawing from plaster casts and sculptures, from still life arrangements, and

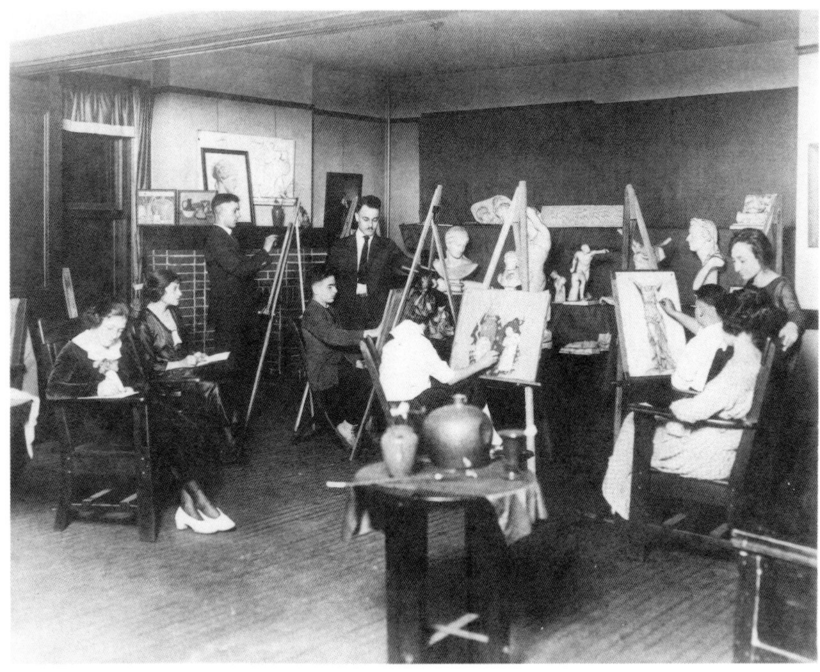

FIG. 43. Rosenberg teaching art class at the Irene Kaufmann Settlement, 1920.

live models. He even assisted for a time in the modeling classes taught by Vittor.

Rosenberg organized the IKS art students into a club and encouraged them to hold meetings to openly discuss their problems and exchange opinions on matters pertaining to art. In 1923, the club, whose name had changed to Junior Associated Artists, had sixty members with a goal of one hundred.[122] Rosenberg also promoted his students' work through regular art exhibitions at the settlement. As head of the art school, Rosenberg also gave lectures on the history of art and art appreciation that were not limited to art school students, and attended the thirteenth conference of the National Federation of Settlements in Washington, D.C., in 1923 as a delegate for IKS. He brought artwork by his students to be included in an exhibition of art created in settlements nationwide.[123]

Milton Weiss, Dr. Herman Gordon, Sam Filner, and Leonard Kessler were among Rosenberg's early students at the IKS art school. According to Kessler, Rosenberg saved some photographs of a mural Leonard had made when he was nine years old and presented them to him when he was a freshman at Carnegie Tech saying: "I kept these all these years . . . I knew you would someday study art."[124] Carnegie Tech recognized the work that the IKS Art School was doing and sent groups of their students to study drawing there. By 1924, the art school had sixty students enrolled and had reached its capacity limit.

Among all the learning activities for both children and adults were the IKS art classes. Sidney Teller, the dynamic director of the IKS who took over in 1916 (and retired twenty-six years later), recognized the talent and efforts of the young Samuel Rosenberg who by 1917, at the age of twenty-one, was already establishing a reputation for himself. He asked Rosenberg, a former IKS student, to teach art classes at the IKS which Rosenberg did until 1929.

The IKS not only provided the struggling young artist with some income, but it also doubled as his home for a year after his marriage to his wife Libbie. Sam had been eying his future wife at the Carnegie and Wylie Avenue Library where she had become a librarian after graduating from high school in Pittsburgh. But it was not until her cousin invited Sam to a party that they officially met. Libbie in her reminiscences commented that everybody thought Sam was very nice and handsome, but that he was very poor, too poor to be a good prospect for a husband. But that didn't bother Libbie. She decided to marry Sam against the wishes of her mother who feared that as an artist, he would never make a proper living. When Libbie took sick with what appeared to be typhoid soon after their marriage, their dire economic circumstances compelled them to live at the IKS. This was a very difficult time for the young couple until they were helped out by a loan from one of Libbie's sisters, Celia, and her husband, Abraham Seder. He was the younger brother of Isaac Seder who in 1907, the same year Sam had come to Pittsburgh, started a retail business with J. Frank. The business developed into the Frank and Seder department store, one of several Jewish-owned downtown department stores. Abe was a lawyer and manager of the store. Sam's name would be linked again with the Seders just a few years later. Meanwhile, in 1924, just two years after their marriage, Cantor Joseph Levin, Libbie's father, offered the young couple an apartment in a duplex he built at 340 Coltart Street in Oakland. The Rosenbergs lived upstairs and Libbie's other sister, Belle, and her husband, Max Levy, lived downstairs.

BARBARA BURSTIN

Beginning in 1919, Rosenberg also taught life drawing at a school for veterans on the G.I. Bill subsidy. In 1923, Rosenberg was dismissed abruptly from this position, but because he had a signed contract from the school, he took them to court and won. While he did not get his job back, he was paid his full contract salary. Rosenberg then made his one and only attempt at self-employment. He opened and directed the Art Student's Guild downtown, where he taught fine and commercial art to veterans. Located at 1015 Fifth Avenue, this was to be a short-lived venture, lasting only two years and ending when his only child, Murray, was born.

Rosenberg was still teaching at the IKS and the Art Student's Guild when he accepted the added responsibility of a third teaching position. In

1924, he became an instructor of drawing in the Department of Architecture in the night school at Carnegie Tech (now Carnegie Mellon University). His drawing class in the Department of Architecture did not emphasize preparation for easel painting; rather it stressed the amplification of drawing skills. Rosenberg alternated teaching the course with Ray Simboli and shepherded the architects through life drawing every morning from ten until noon. According to a former student, his common-sense approach required students to parse the body into solids; to carve it up in much the same manner as a sculptor would. Rosenberg wanted his students to see beyond the shadows on the body and look at reflections on the solid being portrayed by varying light conditions. It was in one of these classes that Rosenberg took the liberty of emphatically drawing contour lines directly on the nude model to make his point on volume and weight of the form to a student who could not see beyond the two dimensions of her paper. According to one of his students, "There was a moment you could have heard a pin drop. I think we all learned a bit about loosening up while drawing."[125] Rosenberg also gave a bonus lecture to these students on the Renaissance painting method of egg tempera, which he demonstrated, showing them the multiple stages in the process. In addition, he gave a private lecture in two sessions on the technique of Leonardo as he saw it. Rosenberg said he knew how the Mona Lisa was painted.[126]

When the lack of a college degree threatened to disqualify Sam from his appointment as instructor in the night school at Carnegie Tech in 1924, he returned to classes to earn his B.A. degree. Because of his years of experience and reputation as an artist, his exhibitions and awards, the school allowed Sam two years of course credit as a replacement for classes in art. Subsequently, he had only to take academic courses, such as English composition, esthetics, French, and the history of art, to satisfy the degree requirements. It seems that they completely ignored his lack of a high school education.[127] Despite teaching at IKS during the day and at Carnegie Tech in the evening, Rosenberg made time to attend school and earned his degree in 1926. When Rosenberg was a student at Carnegie Tech, faculty members included Russell "Papa" Hyde, Charles Taylor, Wilfred Readio, Everett Warner, Ray Simboli, Norwood MacGilvary, and Edmund Ashe. For the next forty years, Rosenberg would share faculty status with Hyde, Readio, and others including Robert Lepper, Kindred McLeary, Roy Hilton, Russell Twiggs, Roger Anliker, Howard Worner, Esther Topp Edmonds, William Libby, Clarence Carter, Balcomb Greene, and Robert Gwathmey.

The fact that all of the faculty members in the Department of Fine Arts were practicing artists was an inspiration to their many students. In her review entitled "They Practice What They Teach," Jeanette Jena noted that the work of Carnegie Tech Department of Fine Arts faculty at the Carnegie Institute demonstrated that in their "variety of personalities of different ages and philosophies," they indeed practiced what they taught their students. She continued, "An instructor who keeps on experimenting in his chosen field, whether for industry or personal pleasure, is certain to have a healthy influence on the next generation, be they painters, designers, art teachers, or business men."[128]

Rosenberg taught evening courses at Carnegie Tech's night school for twenty-three years, from 1924 to 1947, alternating between classes in painting and illustration (drawing), painting and decoration, and architecture. As evidenced by the teaching notes that the artist made and kept in his possession, he put a great deal of effort and creative energy into the preparation for those courses. Specific problems reproduced on mimeographed sheets include "What is a Line?" "The Picture Plane," "What is a Volume?" "Translation and Rotation," "Picture Mechanics," and "Simple Cubic Spacial [*sic*] Conception." These indicate the basic principles of art that Rosenberg was trying to impart to his night school students. A glossary of terms was also included in the assignment packet.[129] By 1925, Rosenberg was listed in the bulletin of evening and part-time courses as assistant professor of architecture and also as assistant professor of painting and decoration. The courses offered at that time included architectural design, shades and shadows, perspective, watercolor, freehand drawing, and the history of architecture. According to his son, Murray, Rosenberg taught the course in freehand drawing to budding architects. According to the bulletin, the night course was "intended primarily for men engaged during the daytime in the offices of architects, and therefore unable to attend the regular day course of the department." The course was a fundamental one, "to improve . . . their ability in freehand drawing" and was "arranged with a view to develop skill in draftsmanship, rendering, and design.[130] The class was scheduled on Tuesday and Thursday evenings from seven-thirty to nine-thirty.

Night classes in the Department of Painting and Decoration offered a series of subjects "which lay a broad foundation for professional practice in painting, illustration, decoration, and related fields." Courses offered included drawing, anatomy, figure construction, still life painting, life painting, pictorial and decorative design, advanced design, figure construction, and decoration problems, among others. While the course offerings do not list the professor who taught them, Rosenberg most likely taught

Drawing I, "a basic course in representation, including drawing in outline and full value from still life objects, casts, and the human figure; freehand perspective. Charcoal, pencil, and other media are used. For students without previous training, this course will be considered prerequisite to all other courses in the department."[131] Students were required to complete a satisfactory year of this work before scheduling any of the advanced courses. But his detailed teaching notes could also have been used for the course called Pictorial and Decorative Design which was described as "a basic creative course stressing the principles of organization and their application to the problems of decorative and pictorial design. Problems in line, value, mass, and color."[132] Additional problem headings in Rosenberg's notes included projection, personal and pictorial perspective, balance, spatial planes, harmonic structure, parallel rhythms, expansion, rotation, optical illusion, and color. He referenced such artists as Giotto, Holbein, Botticelli, Dürer, El Greco, Cézanne, and Leger to make his points about issues such as opposition, pictorial perspective, and lines of continuation.

In 1926, the same year that Rosenberg was awarded his B.A. degree in art, he was listed for the first time in Carnegie Tech's personnel directory as a "new appointee."[133] It was in that year that he began his four-decade teaching career as an official part-time instructor in the College of Fine Arts. Now, Rosenberg taught both day and night classes. He was promoted to instructor of architecture in 1927; to assistant professor of architecture in 1930; assistant professor of painting and design in 1944; associate professor in 1947; and full professor in 1952. While I have been unable to determine either the exact number of classes that Rosenberg taught in the College of Fine Arts over the years, or his exact course schedule, it is evident that Rosenberg spent a major amount of his time teaching at Carnegie Tech. According to Libbie, Rosenberg taught at Carnegie Tech five days a week, and his daily routine was always the same; he left the house around ten in the morning and returned home around five in the afternoon.

Rosenberg taught upper-level courses in painting, primarily to juniors and seniors. The College of Fine Arts at the time offered three career options to their enrolled students: art education, industrial design, and painting and design. The idea of becoming a full-time fine artist was not an option. The career objective for art students majoring in these subject areas was to learn a commercial skill from which they could earn a living upon graduation. It was necessary for students to choose a major by their junior year, so Rosenberg did not often see students before their major was selected. However, by the 1950s, there appears to have been a shift in philosophy about the career goals in the Department of Fine Arts. At that

One of the aspects of the Carnegie Tech faculty that impressed me the most was its variety of stimulating art instructors, who ran the gamut from realism to the abstract. Among them, Roy Hilton and Russell Hyde, who taught perspective and anatomy, respectively, required that at least a portion of their classes stress visual accuracy. And Howard Worner, who had just resigned as art director for the Armstrong Cork Company to join the Tech faculty, shared his professional experience in teaching pictorial design. At the other end of the spectrum was Balcomb Greene, who was named one of the ten best artists in the United States by *ARTnews*. Although he taught the history of painting and sculpture, all of us were aware of his large canvases of figures whose forms were partially intersected and dissolved by intense white light.

In between were an abundance of creative problems to solve. Esther Topp Edmonds had a cot rolled into the drawing class, directed a student to jump onto it and throw back the covers, at which point we were told to sketch the complex network of folds on the sheets and pillow in charcoal. On the other hand, William Libby emphasized spontaneous on-the-spot sketches in pen-and-ink, while Wilfred Readio's Mediums & Reproduction course exposed us to creating everything from blockprints and lithographs to monoprints. In C. Kermit Ewing's course, Pictorial and Decorative Design, there were constant mental challenges, such as his early project in organization that involved mounting three rectangles on a piece of paper so that not only were all three shapes of different sizes, but the spaces between them varied as well.

A year-long challenge conceived by Robert Lepper was the so-called Oakland Project, a thorough study of that portion of Pittsburgh lying just beyond the campus. No simple collection of sketches this, for the challenge involved our becoming sociologists and anthropologists, organizing the life and views of the area into categories: people, goods and services, shelters, topography, public service, ceremonial observances, and government activities. Between regular critiques by Lepper, we would fan out along the main streets of Fifth and Forbes Avenues, and all those connecting them, to find and record the life and times of the area in a variety of media. Further along into the project, Lepper advised us to select a specific house and show how it is constructed, how the windows and roof fit, its solidity. And finally the class was directed to depict a single room inside, based upon what we thought the people who lived there would be like, from their furniture and wallpaper down to the knickknacks. What an ingenious and stimulating project.

And then, of course, there was Sam Rosenberg.

Rosenberg's continual encouragement of our choices of varied media and subject matter caused me to produce large compositions that were different as night and day. One was a nighttime view of slag pouring, in which a glazing technique similar to his was employed in order to attain the glow from molten waste cascading down a hillside like a waterfall of fire. Another was an impasto painting of a busted pipe in a fraternity house wall, revealing lath, plaster, and a porthole view of a toilet.

For me, one of the major attractions of Carnegie Tech's Department of Painting and Design was the combination of art with academic subjects: Thought and Expression, Arts and Civilization, Social Orientation, and Psychology.

The majority of the country's art institutes, such as the one in my native Baltimore, taught just art.

Carnegie Tech was the recipient of my only college application. In high school I was enrolled in a college preparatory art curriculum, coincidentally funded by the Carnegie Foundation, which offered a different area of concentration each semester: Painting, Sculpture, Architecture, Commercial Art, Theater Art, and Textiles.

Just prior to graduation, a four-year scholarship to the local art institute was offered to me, but in conversation with the Director of Art Education for the public schools, Dr. Leon L. Winslow, I determined not to accept it. "If your parents can afford to send you to an out-of-town art school," he said, "I'd suggest Carnegie Tech." He then added: "I believe it to be the best art school in the country."

I happily took his advice and have never regretted that decision.

BENNARD PERLMAN

time, students who chose to major in painting and design had every intention of becoming artists when they completed their degree and they understood that the school expected that same result.[134] One student commented that in choosing painting and design as a major, they understood that there were probably few other schools of art that offered Samuel Rosenberg's expertise.[135]

Rosenberg taught oil painting to students in their junior year and it was during this year that students also participated in Robert Lepper's sociological Oakland Project. During their senior year, Rosenberg concentrated his efforts on teaching them mixed media, egg tempera, glazing and underpainting techniques, and other technical exercises.

Many students, especially World War II veterans who returned to school following the war, described the 1940s at Carnegie Tech as a revolutionary period. A more mature student body lent an air of sophistication to the experience. Veterans and non-veterans alike felt that it was a volatile time and that they were moving in a charged environment at an accelerated pace. Some students said they felt threatened by it; others grew from their encounters.

In his classes, Rosenberg drew on his encyclopedic knowledge of contemporary art and art history when trying to illustrate important points. His reference library, which contained hundreds of books on art and artists, exhibition catalogs, and periodicals, is telling in this regard. He discussed other artists and their work, from the Old Masters (Giotto, Titian, Botticelli, Michelangelo, Leonardo, Vermeer, Rembrandt) to the Modern

Masters (Goya, Cézanne, Matisse, Picasso, Roualt, Bonnard, Klee, Kandinsky), and showed examples of their work in reproduction form. He never showed slides nor lectured to his students per se; he would just fit in the topics he wanted to discuss when "talking" with them individually about their work. Rosenberg admired myriad artists for as many different reasons and he would stress specific artists when trying to make critical points. For example, he often described the color of Rubens, Delacroix, and Matisse; the spontaneity of Frans Hals; chiaroscuro of Rembrandt (who Rosenberg said was the consummate master of luminous darks); the light source of Vermeer; the structure of Courbet; and the underpainting of Rubens and Roualt. Rosenberg brought Paul Klee's *Pedagogical Sketch Book,* published in 1923, to class for one of his students who was especially interested in the power of line.[136] He often referenced American artists such as Whistler and Eakins, as well as the abstract expressionists, Pollock, Kline, de Kooning, and Hofmann. Rosenberg seemed to very much believe in the approach of Henri, the inspirational teacher of the early twentieth century, who stated, "I have little interest in teaching you what I know. I wish to stimulate you to tell me what you know," and also, "The Old Masters made their language. You make yours. They can help you. All the past can help you."[137] Rosenberg spent as much time explaining the drive and muscularity of Kline and de Kooning as he would the complexities of underpainting and overglazing expressed in the work of the great Venetian painters, Tintoretto and Titian.[138]

From California to New York, from Vermont to Florida, former students from thirteen states remember Rosenberg as an inspirational teacher. Known as a man of few words, Rosenberg was more of a guide, and, as one of his students suggested, you learned from him by "enigmatic osmosis." That is not to say that he didn't teach about specifics, but it was a relaxed transfer.[139] This idea of osmosis is interesting, as it seems to be the natural way that Rosenberg imparted knowledge to his students. It appears to be a common thread in his teaching style, wherever he happened to be at the time. While he did not consider himself a strong verbal communicator, Rosenberg nevertheless successfully transferred his ideas about art to his students. Even after nearly sixty years in some cases, his students still draw on and remember many of the things he told them. Much like Henri, Rosenberg encouraged his students to follow their own emotions, reflect upon their own personal experiences, and paint from their hearts. He would direct them to look at their own work, to create their own personal style, rather than imitate his or another artist's style.

The majority of Rosenberg's students from the 1940s to the 1960s remember their teacher fondly, as a quiet force who inspired them to create. Always dressed in a suit, white shirt, and tie (with plastic covers from his wrists to his elbows to protect the cuffs of his shirt), he demonstrated painting techniques, showed them examples of other artists' work, discussed both current and historical ideas, and critiqued students' work on a regular basis. One of his students wrote, "It was reassuring yet quite intimidating to see his neatness before a canvas while creating those rich, luminous paintings while I was getting the pigment all over me as I produced timid, tentative first efforts.[140] Although his appearance was formal, his manner was kind, gentle, sympathetic, and encouraging.[141] Rosenberg never imposed his belief system on students; rather he encouraged them to experiment with different media and different styles. This self-exploration would allow them to find themselves in their art. It is clear that Rosenberg felt it was the responsibility of each student, by his or her senior year, to be self-motivated, to have grasped the fundamentals of art-making from the previous three years of instruction, and to have formed his or her own style. It was not necessary for Rosenberg to take students by the hand and lead them in a specific direction. It was up to them to find their own paths, and then follow them. Of course, there were probably periods of time in which Rosenberg was not the most attentive teacher, as he was stretched too thin, teaching elsewhere, preparing for exhibitions, and making his own art. A few students made this observation, but for the most part, his students throughout the years enjoyed the fact that they were learning from a professional artist, who was actively making art every day, exhibiting it, and selling it.[142]

It was not an easy task getting accepted to Carnegie Tech in the first place. Each applicant was required to take one full week of technical tests in drawing and design prescribed by the faculty. For five solid days, prospective students worked out assignments, and by the end of the week, they had amassed portfolios from which they were accepted or rejected. Students in the first year were monitored very closely. At the end of the first semester, it was necessary for them to be invited back in order for them to continue with the second semester. At the end of the year, students were either formally invited back for their sophomore year or not.[143] Students at Carnegie Tech learned through doing. In an article he wrote for *Carnegie Magazine,* Wilfred Readio, head of the Department of Painting and Design, stressed that "the acquisition of the power to analyze and criticize his own work can give the student the ability to continue to learn from his own experience as a well-rounded artist and human being."[144]

As a teacher, Rosenberg was an enabler, a gentle motivator who possessed the natural ability to inspire his students. Described as shy and easygoing, with a nurturing temperament, he never critiqued his students' work in a negative way; rather, he always responded positively to it. His critiques were constructive and he did not exploit his instructor's position to denigrate or disparage. If he had difficulty with a painting, he would ask the student a question about it, so that he or she would have to identify and solve the problem. His students said they felt free, yet focused on their work. Rosenberg was highly organized, but this was deceptive because of his low-key approach to teaching. Exercises he gave dealt with multiple layers of interacting color, how light falls upon a form, the complex relationships between positive and negative space, the interplay of light and shadow, and movement and countermovement, among other topics. He demonstrated specific techniques in his classes such as how to make gesso from rabbit skin glue and chalk; how to prepare a canvas or masonite panel; how to grind and mix color pigments; the sequential build-up of paint layers; *a la prima* and *bravura* paint application; the use of casein underpainting; and how to make frames from raw moldings. He provided the recipes for the Renaissance painting method of egg tempera emulsions and glazes and instructed in their use; and he showed students how the positioning of special underpainting with neutral pigments would produce evanescent tones without disaster.[145] He explained the unknown dangers facing artists who were not knowledgeable about the chemistry of pigments, oils and other binders, and while he encouraged students to try new techniques in their painting, he did not require it.[146] He also provided warnings about the toxicity of certain pigments, mediums, and solvents, and other strictly technical matters.[147] He did not tell a student how to work or what to paint; nor did he ever mark on a student's paper or canvas. (Another faculty member, Esther Topp Edmonds, who taught watercolor classes, was known for drawing on a student's work.) His technical demonstrations were not dry and removed from the creative act, but integrated into the creative pursuit of making art.[148]

During class, Rosenberg would circulate unobtrusively around the classroom, stand behind each student's easel for a time to observe, and then softly discuss the work in progress. The fact that other students in the room benefited from his observations was an added bonus.[149] If he had a specific point to make with one student's work that was relevant to the others, he would occasionally call the rest of the students over to take part in the discussion. Classrooms were located on the fourth floor of the Fine Arts Building and students negotiated their places in the large painting studio. Students constructed open cubicles that gave them private studio spaces where they could hang preparatory studies, keep supplies, and store the wet paintings on which they were working. Students said that this arrangement allowed them their privacy, and gave Rosenberg a more complete idea of the directions they were taking with their work. While Rosenberg treated all his students individually, each with their own set of problems, the classroom environment was a learning one, where camaraderie existed and students learned from each other even though they were not working in the same manner. A group critique occurred at the end of every painting session, in which Rosenberg encouraged open discussion of the work. It was all very low-key.[150] Rosenberg wanted all his students to become thinking artists and encouraged them to stretch to reach their next level of performance. As one student recalls: "I can still see him standing in front of the class explaining this concept: 'Your goals are here,' raising one hand to his shoulder level. 'Your performance level is here,' then he would position his other hand at a lower level. 'This is the dynamic of your discontent and the format for your growth. As you continue to practice, your performance level goes up, but this same practice also allows you to understand more and your goals also rise.' He demonstrated this by raising both hands higher, but with the performance level still below the goals. 'This is the way it should be, the one always above the other. This is the architecture of growth, the goals much exceed your grasp. This dynamic discontent is essential for improvements to take place.'"[151]

Rosenberg never attempted to mold his students or force them to conform to any artistic ideal or format, nor to his ideas or formulas. He did not feel it was the teacher's responsibility to transfer his or her attitude or style to the students. It was the teacher's responsibility to guide students and expose them to the use of materials and techniques that would allow them to explore their own concepts in art. Rosenberg was a perceptive teacher and drew out each student's individual potential. He exposed them to concepts, and to other artists, materials, and technical processes, but the students had to decide what issues to deal with and what materials they would use to convey those ideas. Every exercise was geared as an introduction to the next. A teacher can show what a teacher does, but that is only technique and materials. The teacher simply guides students beyond their limited framework and provides them with the means to solve problems. Rosenberg gave his students the freedom to search for meaningful ways to express their own unique painting styles and techniques. He never imposed his own views, but helped students clarify what they were trying to achieve.[152] He assisted with the student's process of self-discovery. Rosenberg rarely used his own work as an example in class; instead, he taught by analogy, showing pertinent examples of work by an artist who had inspired him. Students have said that by the time they were in their senior year at Carnegie Tech, they were expected to know the artists that Rosenberg was showing to them.

Rosenberg treated all of his art students as peers, not underlings. He and his students shared mutual respect for one another. The students felt that Rosenberg respected their opinions, and he often repeated that he learned as much from his students as they learned from him. He treated his students with old-fashioned courtesy. He referred to them formally as Miss or Mr. and they addressed him as Mr. Rosenberg (behind his back though, they referred to him affectionately as 'Sam'). One of his students recalled that it was "joyous torture trying to paint masterpieces under the guidance of Samuel Rosenberg. He gave when you needed him and withheld when he knew you didn't since he respected the privacy and individuality of each student."[153] Even those Carnegie Tech students who did not study with Rosenberg felt his influence.[154] Rosenberg often invited students home to dinner where they could continue to discuss painting trends and participate in problem-solving sessions.

It was the brutal "judgment" that students dreaded in the Department of Fine Arts. At the end of each term, students were required to put work from all their classes up on panels in the hallway of the fourth floor. Senior faculty members would then be pushed along the panels on a bench with castors to review the work presented. All the professors would discuss the work and then come to a consensus for the student's final grade. As a result of the end-of-year judgment in 1946, Andy Warhol was not going to be invited back for his sophomore year. Rosenberg's was the kindest, gentlest voice of the entire faculty, and, together with "Papa" Hyde, he supported Warhol.[155] Because of their intervention, suggesting to Warhol that he retake his Drawing I course in summer school, Andy was subsequently invited to continue his education at Carnegie Tech. Rosenberg saved some of Warhol's early drawings and kept them in his possession until his death (they are now in the collection of the Andy Warhol Museum). When critics said Warhol worked as he did because he couldn't draw, Rosenberg would bring out his drawings and show them how fine a draughtsman he was. Libbie later wrote to Warhol that Rosenberg thought him to be "one of the finest of the day . . . better in fact than some of the faculty who insisted that the student make a product, one that would be saleable and would look well in a portfolio for presentation to a prospective buyer."[156]

Rosenberg's students were supportive of him, both as an artist and a teacher. They sent congratulatory telegrams on the occasion of his exhibition at the Associated American Artists Gallery in New York City. In 1948, the first year that long-playing records were introduced, the students raised money to present Rosenberg with a sound system and several LPs because they knew he loved music.[157] If ever his students were critical of Rosenberg at all, it was because they thought he didn't try to make it big as an artist in New York City as Balcomb Greene had. They believed he could have accomplished this if he wanted to. Rosenberg mentioned to several of his students that he liked to visit New York, but the sensory overload there was too great and he couldn't absorb what he wanted to absorb.[158]

One anecdote repeated by a number of Rosenberg's students speaks to his good-humored personality, although it does not support the description of him as shy. At the end of the semester one year in the late 1940s, the art students produced a stage production that parodied their faculty's teaching methods. According to one student's recollection, "the impersonator of Samuel Rosenberg delivered a truly masterful performance. Responding to a 'student work' that was, literally, garbage, Rosenberg's grave observations of the piece's potential in its subsurface rhythmic patterns brought the performers and audience to helpless howls of laughter that I can still hear." Aware of the student's theatrical plans, the faculty produced skits of their own and the climax, it seemed, was Samuel Rosenberg, outfitted in a grass skirt, lei, and flowers in his hair, dancing the hula.[159]

While still teaching at the IKS and at Carnegie Tech, Rosenberg took on yet another teaching position at the Young Men's and Women's Hebrew Association (YM&WHA, hereafter referred to as the Y). In 1926, he became Director of the Fine Arts Department of the Isaac Seder Educational Center for the Y at 315 South Bellefield Avenue in Oakland. Over the years, he taught a variety of courses including Elementary Drawing and Painting; Advanced Drawing and Painting; Modeling (with Frank Vittor, 1926 and 1930); a sketch class (1926); Poster Design (1926 and 1927); a special course in anatomical drawing for professional men, including doctors and dentists (1931); and Criticism and Discussion of Art (1943). He also participated in the "Enjoyment of the Arts" series with a lecture on "The Language of the Artist" as an aid to the understanding of the arts and their meaning for everyday life (1945). When he started, he taught three evenings a week, and with the few exceptions noted above, he concentrated his efforts on two courses: Elementary Drawing and Painting and Advanced Drawing and Painting. In 1946, Rosenberg dropped the Elementary Drawing and Painting course and continued to teach only Advanced Drawing and Painting until his retirement in 1964. This course, which came to be known as the

It was no spur-of-the-moment decision, for like college sophomores everywhere, Andy Warhol and I were faced with the career-affecting choice of selecting an area of concentrated study for our junior and senior years. As the two youngest male classmates in Carnegie Tech's Department of Painting and Design who had entered in September, 1945 directly from high school—the others were returning veterans from World War II—we had to make up our minds: Would we pick Art Education, Pictorial Design, or Industrial Design?

In the school's friendly atmosphere, where meetings with faculty members could be had without appointments, the two of us sought to elicit the advice of the senior professor with whom we were then studying painting. That individual was Samuel Rosenberg.

Sam Rosenberg was constantly challenging us in a variety of ways. On one occasion, soon after the opening of the fall term in October 1947, he directed the class to visit the *Painting in the United States* exhibition at the Carnegie Museum, choose a small portion of one of the works, then draw it, complete with shading and color notes, while still in the gallery. Once back in the studio we sought to duplicate the chosen fragment in oils, but if certain aspects were missing from both sketch and memory, a return trip to the museum was necessary.

The experience encouraged us to not only notice but remember such aspects as detail, brush strokes and texture resulting from paint application.

So it was that on a spring day in 1947, Andy Warhol and I walked down a hallway in the school's Fine Arts Building which contained studios for each of the instructors, and stopped at the one marked with his name. With a distinguished yet warm presence, he opened the door, his countenance carrying with it a pleasant smile, his attire consisting of a three-piece, pinstripe suit, as was his custom.

Upon entering I was dazzled by an array of Rosenberg's luminous canvases, works that seemed to have been created with a palette of crushed jewels. Sam Rosenberg had taught at Carnegie Institute of Technology since 1924—four years before the two of us were born. Now we were prepared to place our futures in his hands.

Andy, being a shy and hesitant introvert at the time, left the conversation to me. "Mr. Rosenberg," I began, "we would like to become artists, but how do you earn a living from painting?" He replied succinctly: "Well, look what I'm doing."

Although my goal from the outset had been to become a practicing artist, Andy's was to train as a teacher. Rosenberg's words must have been reassuring to him, yet my classmate had little awareness as to the demands of the profession. When a fellow art student once asked Warhol about his life's ambition, he answered that he wanted to teach children to play.

The routes to this defining moment in our lives had been dissimilar, to say the least. Andy had, indeed, set his goals on teaching, having already applied during his senior year in high school to do so—at the University of Pittsburgh!

That decision had been made in combination with his best friend, Nick Kish, who lived near the Warhol home, which was located at 3252 Dawson Street in Oakland, a short distance from Pitt. The two had much in common, for as Kish told me: "Andy and I were both outcasts, which is why we sort of got together."

As graduation from Schenley High School approached for the two of them, Kish chose the University of Pittsburgh and Andy, intent on becoming an education major, followed suit. Both were accepted to enter in the fall of 1945.

Then Uncle Sam intervened. Kish, who was older than Andy and eligible for the draft, received his induction notice in July, leaving Andy with the prospect of going it alone to the University, whose School of Education enrollment was as large as the total student body in some small colleges.

Andy opted instead to seek admittance to less-threatening Carnegie Tech (just a few blocks further than Pitt) where he intended to enroll in the Art Education option in his junior year. Now Sam Rosenberg's common-sense advice convinced him otherwise, and he chose Pictorial Design, as did I.

BENNARD PERLMAN

"artists' workshop," would be Rosenberg's greatest contribution to the Y's curriculum and the class for which he is most recognized today. Students from this class still recall how important the experience was for them and how much they developed as artists because of their participation in Rosenberg's workshop.[160]

The Art Department of the Y was unique in that it was the only school in Pittsburgh for adults that gave "authoritative instruction to amateurs with no professional or commercial aim." A diverse group of art lovers utilized the Y for their artistic gain, including "physicians, lawyers, teachers, businessmen and business girls, and professional artists who had to give it up."[161] The purpose of the YM&WHA art classes was to bring a "keener sense of the value of beauty through actual participation in drawing, painting, sculpture, scene painting, stage craft, each of which has a class of laymen who pursue art for the sheer esthetic joy it gives them."[162] The Isaac Seder Educational Center offered courses throughout the year in two fifteen-week semesters, from October to December, and from March to May. The weekly newsletter of the Y explained, "Although instruction on the highest level, the primary aim of the educational center is to provide the opportunity for all adults to get personal pleasure from creative activity, not the preparation of professional artists."[163]

In his second year at the Y, Rosenberg taught a course in painting and drawing that met one evening a week for two hours. His description of the course, published in the *YM&WHA Weekly*, reveals his comprehensive purpose in teaching the fundamentals of art. Rosenberg designed this course "to develop the student's ability to observe and select from what is before him, the characteristics with which the artist is concerned, and step by step train his mechanical skills in the expression of his personal interest. As a

Anyone who knew Andy Warhol in those days would have immediately noticed that his soft-spoken, timid, and naive demeanor ill-prepared him for teaching in a classroom, even in an era when student deportment was unlike today's.

Sam Rosenberg did his part in bringing reality home to his pupil. The professor had been instructing adult classes for years at the Young Men's and Young Women's Hebrew Association, located across the street from the Carnegie Museum and Pitt, so he arranged for Andy to teach a class of teenagers there after school. The experiment was short-lived.

Of even greater import was Rosenberg's action after Andy nearly flunked out of Carnegie Tech at the end of his freshman year. Left unchallenged, the low grades may well have resulted in the termination of his art education and any hope for the creative development of a future Pop Art superstar.

When classes had begun in October 1945, Andy and I, plus fifty-eight other students, the vast majority of whom were coeds, were enrolled in Drawing I, Pictorial and Decorative Design, Color, Thought and Expression (English), Physical Education, and Hygiene. While it is unlikely that all of us would have returned the following fall to become sophomores, that eventuality was made certain by the Head of the Department, Wilfred Readio, who addressed the assemblage the following February.

Three hundred returning veterans had applied for admission to Carnegie Tech's Art Department and it was decided that fifteen of that number would be admitted at midyear into a separate class, continue their studies during the summer, and they would then replace the lowest fifteen in our class at the beginning of the sophomore year.

On May 29, 1946 Andy received his report card. It was bad news, for all of the grades were C's and D's, plus an R, which meant repeat, in Thought and Expression.

A notation read: "Suspended until advancement in Drawing I."

Several days later Sam Rosenberg appeared in the Drawing studio just as Andy, there by himself and sobbing, was cleaning out his art locker. The professor asked what was wrong, and Andy explained that he had flunked out. Rosenberg

result of this comes a perception of the finer quality of form and color, of the significance of masses in composition, and of the value of tones. The principal training is from life in the study of the head or figure—from life or the cast. Students of drawing are permitted to paint as soon as they are able to draw well enough not to be too much confused by the additional difficulties of color."[164] Rosenberg taught a second course that year in poster design, which was also scheduled one evening a week for two hours. This was a purely technical course that stressed the arrangement of letters in conjunction with pictorial design—methods of laying out and completing posters. Eighty-five students, many with no previous training, ranging in age from nineteen to forty, were enrolled in Rosenberg's two art classes counseled him to attend summer school with the veterans, receive a passing grade in Drawing, and he would be readmitted.

Andy did just that, and when a grade of B was attained in the make-up class, he rejoined the rest of us in the fall.

The reprieve allowed Andy to be himself. Now the nonconformist, he was nevertheless often ahead of his classmates, and sometimes the instructors as well.

Examples abound. One of Sam Rosenberg's painting assignments was to produce an oil self-portrait using only the tubes of black, white, and burnt sienna. Because Andy had produced many likenesses of himself when he and Nick Kish worked together on their own, he now chose experimentation over realism. When the class efforts were lined up along a classroom wall, someone blurted out: "Who the hell is that? Is that your sister?"

Andy replied very matter-of-factly: "No, I always wanted to know what I would look like if I had long hair and was a girl."

In our final two semesters, Rosenberg once again taught the course in Painting. By now we seniors were allowed to create subjects of our own choosing, and Andy was in his element. For one composition he brought in a statue, no larger than his finger, of Shiva, the Hindu god, plus a huge piece of floral fabric, then chose to paint them with the sizes reversed. On another occasion Andy splashed red, yellow, and blue on a canvas, allowed the colors to run down and form a pattern of droplets. He titled it *Rain*.

There was yet another painting without an assigned title for which our class was to produce a flat pattern of colors similar in light and dark value. Andy chose warm variations of light red, orange, and yellow, then combined them with pale Indian red and alizarin crimson. His canvas glowed, in part because it was overpainted with a pointillist technique. As if this abstraction were not sufficiently creative, Andy dubbed it with the title "A Sow with Six Suckling Piglets."

Under Rosenberg's tutelage, a student's ingenuity and originality were constantly encouraged. Little wonder that Andy labeled Sam his favorite among the art faculty.

BENNARD PERLMAN

in 1927. The demand for his classes in drawing and painting was so great that year that he agreed to give up another evening the following year (1928) in anticipation of a still larger enrollment. This course, which laid the foundation for his Advanced Drawing and Painting workshop, met on Monday and Thursday evenings from eight o'clock to ten o'clock. On Monday evenings, Rosenberg offered individual instruction to his students and on Thursday evenings they often worked on their own. Some students went to the Y every day to continue their work without supervision. From that point on, with the exception of one or two years, Rosenberg would teach two courses per term, Elementary Drawing and Painting and Advanced Drawing and Painting. The elementary class, listed as a class for beginners, offered instruction in drawing from brief poses, and from the figure in motion in pencil, pen, chalk, and brush. The advanced class offered instruction in drawing and painting from life.

At the beginning of the term in 1929, Rosenberg had fifty students enrolled in his two classes. By the end of the second semester, he had seventy students enrolled in Advanced Drawing and Painting and twenty-eight in Elementary Drawing and Painting. Whenever Rosenberg was referenced in the *YM&WHA Weekly*, he was referred to with accolades. He was called "one of the most successful teachers on the Y educational faculty," and the newsletter explained, "Mr. Rosenberg believes in following out a well-balanced program in the teaching of his courses. Besides the actual brush, crayon, and charcoal work, there are illustrated lectures on technique, style, design, and color, supplemented by the occasional excursions to the galleries where the different schools of painting are represented." Further comments revealed what it was like to witness Rosenberg's teaching: "Perhaps the secret to his success with his students is the deep personal interest he takes in their work. The visitor to the class is amazed at the zeal with which he goes among his class, suggesting, explaining, assisting, and sometimes correcting. He never tires. His job is no easy task. And that is why this same visitor leaves the classroom convinced that here is a man who can manufacture artists, if anyone can."[165] During the 1929–1930 academic year, Rosenberg taught three classes.

The 1933–1934 term was considered the most successful in the eight years of the center's existence. Two hundred and fifty students were enrolled, and twenty-five courses were offered over the two semesters. As a result, the art department was enlarged again, and the fees were raised to twelve dollars per semester, or twenty-two dollars per year.[166] In addition to his duties as an instructor, as Director of the Fine Arts Department, Rosenberg organized exhibitions of other artists' work and invited fellow artists to give lectures. One exhibit that Rosenberg helped to sponsor showed the work of two German artists in exile, Kathe Kollwitz and Otto Lange.

The Isaac Seder Educational Center was designed to offer college-level courses that would contribute to a well-rounded liberal education, either as a substitute for regular college training or as a supplement to or continuation of such training. The center was divided into five schools: Jewish Studies, Fine Arts (art, music, dance), Languages and Literature, Social Sciences, and History. It was a broad and liberal program where "people learn, experience, and create side by side as people in a completely democratic fashion under Jewish auspices."[167] They held roundtables on anti-Semitism, and conferences on interfaith and interracial understanding. J. Fred Lissfelt, music critic for the *Pittsburgh Sun-Telegraph,* taught music appreciation; Gladys Schmitt, a professor at Carnegie Tech, taught creative writing. The Y was also important to the community for the diverse array of speakers who were invited to give lectures on topics including "The Race Problem in America," "The State of the Jews in Europe and Atrocities in Germany and Austria and Jewish Refugees," "The Fascists Engulfing Europe," and "Problems of Jewish Living," among many others. The center celebrated the fifth birthday of the state of Israel in 1953.

By 1944, the faculty of the Fine Arts Department included three of Rosenberg's fellow faculty members from Carnegie Tech. Balcomb Greene joined the Y in 1943, and taught Appreciation of Art and Modern Painting; Robert Lepper taught Dimensional Construction from 1938 on; and Patricia Gormley taught courses in modeling and sculpture. Greene taught a new course in 1944 called New Directions in Modern Art, and the following year, the Y held an exhibition of abstract paintings by Greene's students. An unidentified writer for the *YM&WHA Weekly* noted that the exhibition was "indicative of the progressive principles in the Y program. Although abstract art has become an accepted form and makes up a large percentage of the paintings shown in the National art exhibitions, Pittsburgh has lagged behind in its appreciation. The Y can be justly proud that it is among the first to acquaint the public in Pittsburgh with such an important movement."[168] Greene would become the advocate for modernism at the Y and would give lectures on such topics as criticism, analysis of the modern painting, and what it was like to be a creative artist at that time.[169]

By 1948, Rosenberg was teaching fifty-four students in Advanced Drawing and Painting. The Y ended its biggest season that year with 3,300 students registered in all the Center's programs.[170] In 1950, the *YM&WHA Weekly* reported that Rosenberg had been named Man of the Year by the Arts and Crafts Center. According to the author of the article: "Professor Rosenberg's long association with the Y's Art Department has become a symbol of the kind of work that can be done in the arts in an informal educational setting. . . . Professor Rosenberg's excellence as a teacher of painting is matched only by his reticence about himself. Ask him for any specific details about his teaching or his work and the usual soft and considered reply is 'I only paint pictures.'"[171] In Rosenberg's twenty-sixth year of service, the *YM&WHA Weekly* reported: "Professor Rosenberg belies the oft quoted acorn of George Bernard Shaw 'Those who can, do; those who cannot, teach.' Of Professor Rosenberg it may be said that he can do and does, that he can teach, and does so beautifully." In the same issue,

Rosenberg's class was described: "Advanced Painting and Drawing meeting Monday and Thursday offers 75 hours of painting a semester, with constant use of live models. Low tuition fee for the quality and amount of art instruction Professor Rosenberg provides. The Educational Center considers this offering one of its major contributions to the cultural life in the community."[172] Another article called Rosenberg the "Dean of the Isaac Seder Educational Center faculty."[173]

Rosenberg's classes at the Y were similar in method to those he taught at Carnegie Tech—informal and simply structured. Most of the participants were practicing artists with prior academic training and professional experience. While Rosenberg encouraged experimentation with different media, he selected inexpensive, disposable materials for the purpose of this class: large sheets of white paper clipped to masonite backboards, housepainter's brushes, water-based poster paints, pencil, and charcoal. The class was held in one big room on the second floor of the Y, and the students worked in a maze of easels.

The format of the class was simple. Rosenberg would pose a problem for the evening session and the students would set about to solve it. There was no carryover to another session. He set a time limit of about an hour to complete the exercise, which added a degree of intensity and spontaneity to the experience. When the time was up, all of the unsigned work was pinned to the board at the front of the room, and Rosenberg critiqued each piece with regard to the imposed problem, commenting on the degree of success in dealing with it. If he did not comment on certain works, those students knew then that they had not been successful. An open discussion followed the critique, which often ran past the official end of class. Rosenberg's articulated his philosophy this way: "Every artist should have someone to stand behind him as he paints to say 'that's enough.' Reach the point of solving the problem then stop."[174] As at Carnegie Tech, the students learned from each other. An often-repeated comment was that there was no sense of inferiority in the class; if you didn't know what Rosenberg happened to be talking about, you just learned it. Rosenberg was rarely in a hurry to leave, and seemed to love the give and take of it all.

Rosenberg urged his students to see and think for themselves, not to do as he did. He taught by showing them reproductions of other artists' work, not so that they would imitate them, but so that they would learn from them. Specific problems he gave them for investigation included: expanding the possibilities of space; light and shadow; color harmony; color values; organic vs. man-made; curved lines vs. straight; soft vs. hard edges; and the plastic qualities of line, shape, and color. One night he made them draw with their eyes closed to teach them to loosen up. Students were also offered an additional weekly session in life drawing. Rosenberg did not supervise this class, but a model was available for students to enhance their eye/hand coordination and improve their observation skills.[175] Rosenberg felt that it was extremely important to draw, as evidenced in his own work, and catch a moving image on paper. He said, "You know, life doesn't stand still. The ocean didn't pose for Winslow Homer."[176]

Rosenberg encouraged his students to use a method he had used, by attending art exhibitions in galleries and museums in and out of the city and critiquing the work they saw there. He wanted them not just to simply look at objects, but to really see objects by studying and analyzing them. He did not want them to merely imitate what they saw, but gain insight into how each artist solved problems such as those he was discussing in class. Rosenberg's goal in this was to expand his students' perceptions and provide them with the analytical skills to solve problems that confronted them in their own work. He encouraged them to read, to discuss, and, most importantly, to think. Rosenberg's students often expressed that they felt intellectually challenged and stimulated by the range of experiences they were exposed to at the Y. "He created an environment of freedom which seemed to release one's conscious and intuitive instincts," according to one student.[177] Rosenberg instilled a sense of high achievement in all of his students. He had the uncanny ability to zero in on a person's specific need. His advice to his students (many of whom were women raising their children) was to continue with their work however they could. He stressed that they needed to fit it in somehow, even if it meant switching mediums. He told them to find a way to work even if circumstances inhibited them.[178]

The class explored contemporary art movements, especially the New York School in the 1950s. Abstract expressionists Jackson Pollock and Willem de Kooning were frequently discussed in reference to spontaneity in paint application; and Hans Hofmann's push-pull theory was discussed with regard to color harmonies and the sensation of color. When Rosenberg talked about experimenting with light, he referred to the Impressionists; when he needed to make a point about color relationships, he talked about Joseph Albers. And always there was Matisse, to whom Rosenberg returned whenever the class discussed the power of color. As he had at Carnegie Tech, Rosenberg provided recipes for egg tempera emulsions and glazes and demonstrated their application. He provided step-by-step instruction in the development of a painting, from the first drawn line to the final layer of pigment, and he always encouraged experimentation.

By 1959, adult classes at the center ranged from art to Zen Buddhism, with over eighty offerings and more than fifteen thousand students from every ethnic, religious, educational, social, cultural, and economic background within a seventy-mile radius of Pittsburgh. By 1960, Rosenberg's Advanced Drawing and Painting class was known at the Y as the artist's workshop and was described as "a focal point for experimentation with and exploration of modern concepts by many local artists of high standing who represent a cross-section of the Pittsburgh community. For many local artists, the Y Art Department, over the years, has played an important part in their development, with Mr. Rosenberg as the pivot of this phase of the Y's broad educational and cultural programs."[179] In 1961, the Y merged with the IKS to become known as the Y-IKC.

On October 2, 1964, the *YM&WHA Weekly* reported, "Professor George Abend, new professor of Painting and Design at Carnegie Tech, will take over Professor Samuel Rosenberg's Advanced Painting and Drawing Workshop."[180] Without fanfare, Rosenberg retired quietly from the Y after thirty-nine years of teaching. There was virtually no recognition of his contribution over the years with the exception of one article published in the *Jewish Chronicle,* in which Harris W. Sacks outlined Rosenberg's accomplishments and views on various subjects including Jewish or Israeli art, the meaning of universality in art, abstract art, young people, and Sunday painters. Sacks wrote: "Retiring this year from full-time teaching after 39 years, the man called 'dean of Pittsburgh artists,' has the background of canvas and classroom from which to survey the future in the serious artist's world."[181]

On September 15, 1964, Morton Rosenbaum, Director of the Isaac Seder Educational Center, sent a letter to the Advanced Drawing and Painting Workshop students in which he announced Rosenberg's sabbatical and the possibility of his permanent retirement. The two-page letter was to alert the students to the successful efforts that the Y was making to carry on "the most important advanced art workshop in the country." Rosenbaum expressed Rosenberg's concern about the continuation of the workshop and announced that the abstract expressionist painter, George Abend, would succeed Rosenberg as its instructor. The letter continued with the accomplishments of Abend. Only in the last paragraph did the director pay tribute to Rosenberg when he wrote: "Certainly we will miss Sam this year, but I could not have wished or dreamed of a better choice than George Abend. He and Sam seem to be cut of the same cloth in terms of their interest, points of view, their mutually stunning artistic and creative backgrounds, and conception of the teaching of and couraging [*sic*] of art, the relation to students, their warmth and reasonableness."[182] While Rosenbaum's letter made Rosenberg's sabbatical seem temporary, it was not; Rosenberg remained in retirement from teaching completely. In a letter to Arnold Auerbach, Director of the Y-IKC, of May 28, 1964, Rosenberg indicated his retirement would commence at the end of the June term. He also indicated he would be retiring from Carnegie Tech as he would be sixty-eight years old and he wanted to devote most of his time to painting. He had been Director of the Fine Arts Department and instructor of Y classes since he was thirty years old, and so Rosenberg's letter continued: "These classes and the workshop have become part of the warp and woof of our lives."[183]

Rosenberg's students, of course, recognized his achievement and remember well the role he played in their artistic development. Many are practicing artists who say they would not be pursuing art as a career had it not been for Rosenberg. His guidance let them be themselves as artists. His nurturing ensured that they stayed with it.

Rosenberg reached even more students through still other teaching venues. In 1937, he became Chairman of the Art Department at the Pennsylvania College for Women (now Chatham College, hereafter PCW) and was a part-time instructor in applied art there for eight years. Over the years he taught one course in drawing per semester, and team-taught a class in commercial design and lettering. By the 1942–1943 academic year, Rosenberg took over the course in the history and appreciation of art, which outlined the development of architecture, sculpture, and painting in France, England, and America. He was the only registered faculty member of the art department between 1943 and 1945. As the artist kept no specific records related to this period of his teaching career, it is not yet possible to completely reconstruct those years. He was, however, mentioned repeatedly in *The Arrow,* PCW's newsletter, which followed his exhibitions and accomplishments. *The Arrow* also printed a 1945 interview that Rosenberg's PCW students conducted with him on the occasion of his winning First Honorable Mention in the exhibition Painting in the United States at the Carnegie Institute.[184]

Together with two other teachers, Rosenberg also taught Saturday morning art classes for students from fifth grade through high school at the Carnegie Institute. This was Rosenberg's first encounter with Philip Pearlstein, who was about fourteen years old at the time, and would later become a student of Rosenberg's at Carnegie Tech. The classes were held

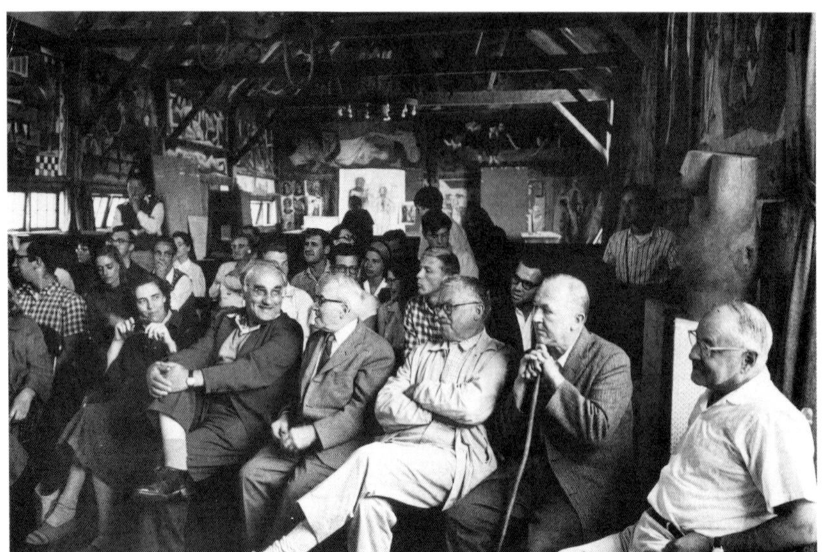

FIG. 44. Rosenberg (lower right) and others at Somerset Art School.

on the balcony of the sculpture court of the museum where students worked on a theme or assignment of the day. Rosenberg's son, Murray, also attended these classes.[185]

The Somerset Summer Art School, located in the valley of Laurel Hill Creek in Pennsylvania's Somerset County, opened in July and offered two six-week instruction periods in art, as well as private lessons, if desired. The school, which was operating by the summer of 1937, was the brainchild of John Scull, an art-loving local banker, who thought it would be a great spot for an art school, since many artists had summer homes in the mountains there. The school was housed in a former WPA Civilian Conservation Corps camp, and was complete with dormitories, a mess hall, and large studios.[186]

Over the years, the teaching staff included Rosenberg, Esther Topp Edmonds, and Robert Schmertz, all faculty members at Carnegie Tech; A. J. Kostellow from Pratt Institute, New York; Armando del Cimmuto of the Irene Kaufmann Settlement; and Carnegie Tech graduates Richard Wilt, C. S. McWilliams, and Richard Crist, who lived year-round in Somerset County. Rosenberg taught a class in tempera painting at the school off and on over the years, coinciding most likely with summers that he and Libbie spent in Somerset County, first with Kindred McLeary, and then later after they purchased McLeary's property near Confluence.[187]

The school not only offered art classes, but good swimming, boating, and other recreational facilities. It operated partially as a retreat for artists to escape the hot city during the summer months. The curriculum of the school included art instruction in all methods including drawing, painting,

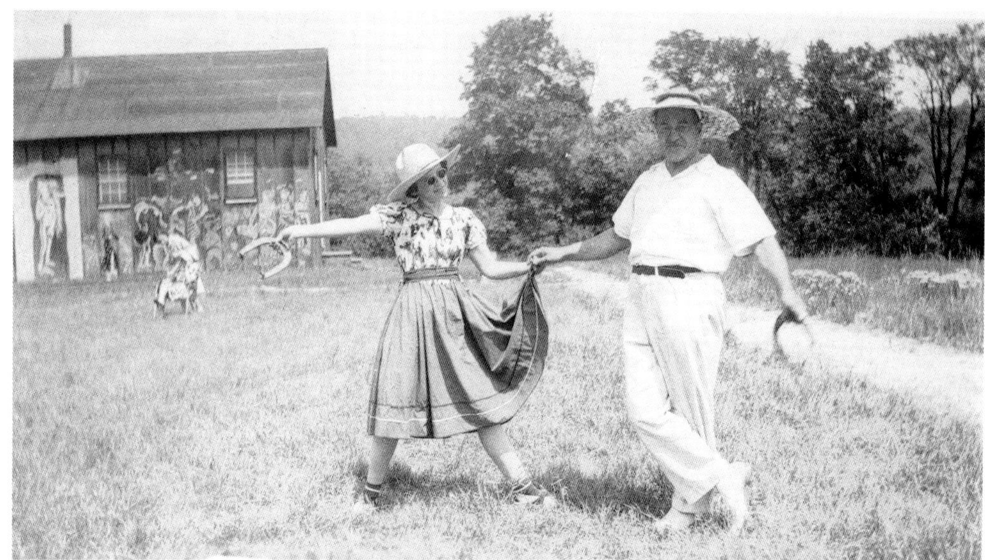

FIG. 45. Sam and Libbie at Somerset Art School.

sculpture, and watercolor. Artists instructed fellow artists in an open and informal environment. In a *Pittsburgh Press* article entitled "Somerset: A Painting Spot Rivalling Famous Cape Cod," Douglas Naylor discusses an exhibition at the Gillespie Gallery of work produced at the Somerset Summer Art School. He noted that this "proves that Western Pennsylvania is just as paintable as traditional haven—Cape Cod."[188]

For two consecutive summers in 1962 and 1963, Rosenberg was invited to teach in the Department of Fine Arts at the University of Southern California. He conducted a six-week session each summer in Life Drawing and Painting, four days a week, from one to five in the afternoon. At the time, Rosenberg had friends in Los Angeles, including William Wolfson, his childhood friend and fellow student at the NAD. Moreover, this gave Sam and Libbie the opportunity to travel in California, which they did after he completed his teaching assignment. The salary was very good for the time, as compared to his pay in Pittsburgh, and he received 1,525 dollars for his six-week effort. In a birthday letter he wrote to his son, Murray, in August 1963, Rosenberg discussed the six-week session at USC. "Finished my grades yesterday and can now breathe a bit easier. I always remained a little less scared than my students—though they never found out—I think. The first couple of weeks were the most difficult. I had to find out what they knew and how much they could take as the class was made up of people of such varied experiences as a Kansas farmer now teaching art in high school in Las Vegas. The other extreme in a young chap who studied with most of the teachers out this way, would work on canvases eight feet by six feet. He was a real athlete in paint. I admired his vigor. His approach is characteristic of the whole California school brush strokes about 4 or 5 inches wide. Brushes purchased at a hardware store. There is much to be said for this method. I remember Soudukine [*sic*] introduced me to it in Woodstock." This letter, like others that Rosenberg wrote to his son, included some aspect of teaching, for he seemed at all times to be the teacher. He knew Murray was always eager to learn, so he continually shared these experiences with him, and suggested ways for him to utilize the technique about which he was writing. In this particular letter, Rosenberg also discussed the different brush strokes of Delacroix, Van Gogh, and Rembrandt, stating that Rembrandt "can make a stroke have the texture of hair, cloth, skin, metal, any substance translates vision into paint." Rosenberg went on to say that he had sent Murray some large brushes to experiment with, and then continued with his instructional advice: "I think it's important to paint with your whole body, not just the fingers. Even drawing is fun that way. Students here bought a roll of white butcher paper 36 inches wide, pinned it on a 4 foot beaver board and drew with a 3" brush of black show card color getting grays by applying the brush dry. They made hundreds of drawings very fast. It freed them of tightness."[189]

Rosenberg inspired his students to teach as he did. Teaching enabled him to paint—the limited income that Rosenberg derived from his various teaching positions in Pittsburgh, as well as outside the city during the summer months sustained him and Libbie in their modest lifestyle. Portrait commissions that he accepted until 1942, the sale of paintings, and monetary prizes he won through the years also contributed to the financial stability of the family. Rosenberg suggested this path to some of his students, including Andy Warhol. Many followed in his footsteps and became teachers themselves while remaining painters all their lives.

Rosenberg dedicated his life to his art and to his teaching and his spirit indeed lives on in his students, but not his style! Rosenberg did not create replicas of himself, although, at one time in his career, newspaper critics commented about a "school of Rosenberg."[190] Leon Arkus, former director of Carnegie Museum of Art, remembered Rosenberg in a lecture of 1997: "He had a natural talent for helping students discover answers for themselves. And he didn't turn out little 'Sams.' All those students!" Arkus wondered if Rosenberg left enough time for his own art, and whether he gave too much of himself away.[191] Obviously, he did not.

Rosenberg kept an assortment of miscellaneous notes over the years, some from his students (but not necessarily from his classes), and some from his own lectures, as reference material. He kept them with him all of his life and they reveal the critical attention and tremendous effort he paid to his teaching. He saved a typewritten lecture on drawing, which included a definition, illustrations, and an outline for the first through fourth years of study. This may well have been a handout to freshmen in the Department of Fine Arts at Carnegie Tech, as drawing was a prerequisite for all other art courses, and may not have been initiated by Rosenberg. He kept a fifty-five-page treatise called "Painting—Transposition of the World as It Is in Terms of Flat Surface," which included such topics as potential dynamics, a plastic order within edges, position of the observer, organization of abstract shapes, and elements of color. Picasso, Ingres, Whistler, Raphael, and Van Gogh were referenced in the document. A very detailed typewritten set of notes prepared by an engineering student covered aspects of a freshman's education at Carnegie Tech with regard to color, including documents titled "Associative and Focal Attributes of Hue," "Effect of Illumination on Appearance of Colors," "Natural Order of Value of Colors," and "How We See Color," to name just a few. As color theory was not a course that Rosenberg taught, these notes most likely came from Wilfred Readio's comprehensive course on the subject.[192]

Several of Rosenberg's original lectures remain, including some of those prepared for the night school classes at Carnegie Tech. In another lecture to his class on December 4, 1933, Rosenberg began with "Space is the biggest problem a painter has to deal with. Two-dimensional space is only decorative, and while we see only two dimensions, we feel three." In this typewritten lecture, he addressed such problems as positive and negative space, cool and warm colors, diagonal composition, light, and the painter's use of line, form, and color to create plastic unity. He quoted Cézanne, "Work parallel to nature, do not copy it," and continued his instruction to his students with, "Character notes in portrait must carry far and not be lost a few feet away from the picture," as well as, "Tie your lights in a picture together, don't have them scattered meaninglessly, haphazardly," and "Do not be afraid to load some paint on to the painting. A few accentuated spots will help finish the picture. If you are painting with oil paints, let your work look like an oil painting, not thin and weak like a watercolor." With pencil drawings in the margins, he illustrated the various problems that he presented in this lecture.[193] The structure of these lecture notes seems incongruous with Rosenberg's informal teaching style, but since they were made early in his teaching career, the information they contained most likely became second nature to him. Without as much art school background, his night school students seemed to need more structure and this systematic approach was presumably taken for them.

Summer Travel

One might ask then, with all his responsibilities, when did Rosenberg find the time to make his own art? As a dedicated teacher, dividing his time between his various teaching positions, Rosenberg had little time to pursue his own art, except during the summer months when his output reveals a concentrated effort. During his short three months off, he would sometimes create up to twenty-five paintings.

Rosenberg's vacations from teaching were spent making sketches and paintings in a variety of locations over the years. Off and on, from 1926 to 1939, he, Libbie, and Murray spent the summer months in Woodstock, New York, a rural area about three hours north of New York City. An artist's colony had been established there earlier in the century and it was a conducive place for Rosenberg to paint. A sketching vacation in Mexico, where he examined the artwork of the leading Mexican artists and visited with muralist Diego Rivera, occurred in 1941 (figure 46). Rosenberg had met Juan O'Gorman in Pittsburgh and traveled to Mexico at his invitation. Rosenberg described Mexico as "a paradise for artists," and concluded that "some of the best painting in the whole world is being done in Mexico today." He was impressed with Jose Orozco's murals in Guadalajara and Rivera's early work in Chapinga.[194]

Travels to the western United States included a six-week, six thousand-mile tour of Taos, Santa Fe, Yellowstone, Salt Lake City, Colorado Springs, and other locations in 1938.[195] Numerous sketches and a few paintings reveal that Sam and Libbie also spent time in Gloucester and Rockport, Massachusetts, during the 1930s and early 1940s (figure 47).

During many summers in the 1940s, Sam and Libbie joined Kindred McLeary at his house in Lower Turkeyfoot Township, Somerset County. McLeary was an architect and a colleague of Rosenberg's at Carnegie Tech. They shared a studio on the fifth floor of the Fine Arts Building for a number of years. McLeary spent twelve years building the house, located in Humbert Valley, in the mountains near Confluence, but it was never completed. He died from an accidental fall while cutting branches from the trees that protruded through its roof. Influenced by Frank Lloyd Wright in his design, McLeary wanted both the inside and outside of the house to be continuous. He extended the flagstone floors to the outside with sliding glass doors that disappeared into pockets in the walls. There was no indoor bathroom facility, and no running water, only cold water with gravity feed to the house from a spring outside. This primitive lifestyle appealed to Rosenberg the artist, and satisfied his down-to-earth sensibilities. He

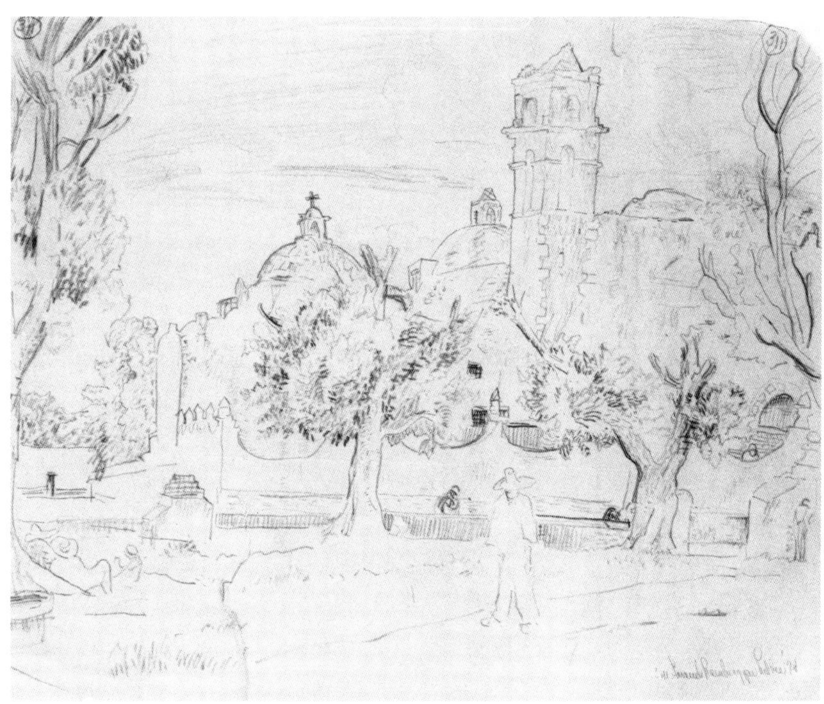

FIG. 46.
Mexican Village, 1941.
Pencil on paper,
9 9/16 x 11 13/16″.

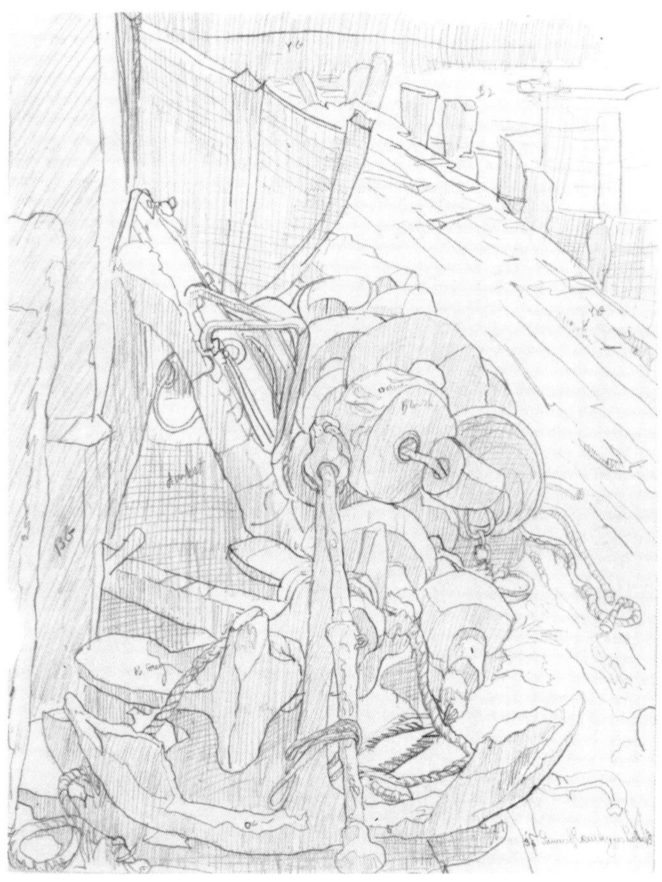

FIG. 47. *Gloucester Docks*, 1936.
Pencil on paper, 16 x 14″.

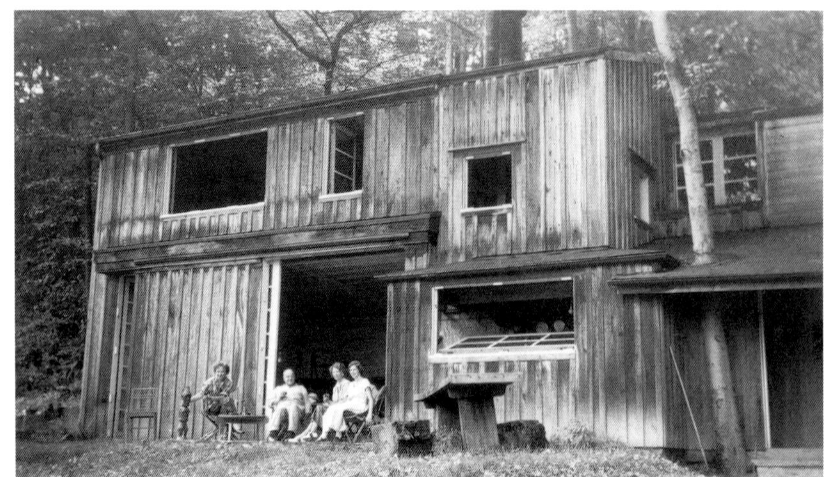

FIG. 48. Sam and Libbie with friends at Kindred McLeary's house in Humbert Valley, Somerset County, Pa., 1949.

painted well there, since he had much more space to create larger work. It was in the Humbert Valley studio that he completed the panels for the twenty-two-foot mural for St. Henry's Church and where he would complete *Israel,* one of his most important paintings of the 1940s. After McLeary's death in 1949, Sam and Libbie purchased the property and continued to spend the summer months there until 1952.[196]

From 1954 to 1957, Sam and Libbie spent their summers in Montauk, on Long Island, and along the coast of Maine. They made two trips to Europe, in 1958 and 1965, where they saw the American Academy in Rome, the Matisse Chapel, the mosaics at Ravenna, and the Dutch countryside where Rembrandt had lived and painted. In Madrid, Rosenberg spent time at the Prado looking at the work of his "old friend" Velázquez.[197]

Critical Reception and Patronage

Over the years, Rosenberg's art was reviewed in nearly all the periodicals of the day: *Art Digest* (*Arts Magazine* since 1955), *Art News, Art in America,* and *The Magazine of Art.* He held solo exhibitions in New York, Boston, Philadelphia, and Pittsburgh, and participated in a variety of notable exhibitions throughout the country. He was invited to participate in every Carnegie International from 1933 to 1964, passing the jury in both 1920 and 1925. From 1934 to 1948, Rosenberg's work was shown in New York six times, including aforementioned appearances at the MoMA, in two Whitney biennials, and at the 1939 New York World's Fair.

Over a three-year period, Rosenberg held two solo exhibitions in New York at the Associated American Artists Gallery (AAA), both of which were reviewed and received well by the New York press. His first show took place from May 22 through June 8, 1944. Howard DeVree, of the *New York Times,* called Rosenberg's initial exhibition "a Delayed 'First'," and referred to it as "another noteworthy one-man show . . . rich, deep color makes itself felt at once . . . Rosenberg's work has power and depth of spiritual conviction . . . very auspicious introduction." Under the headline "The Radiant Color of Samuel Rosenberg," Margaret Breuning of *Art Digest* wrote that her "first impression of Rosenberg's work is of sumptuous color, color that seems to radiate splendor from the canvases . . . in all the work the brushing is vigorous, conveying a sense of substance and tactile values to the canvases . . . organization of these paintings is excellent, even the emotional undercurrent felt in their subject matter and vehemence of presentment does not often impair the soundness and solidity of the able designs." Emily Genauer, for the *New York World-Telegram,* wrote that Rosenberg "weds heart and form," and noted the analogy of Rosenberg's work to stained glass, adding, "the paint is so luminous you feel almost as if a light must be shining behind. Now Roualt [*sic*] suggests stained glass too, and so does Rattner. Rosenberg is unlike any of them. From every point of view, this is a worthwhile and interesting exhibition, and Rosenberg ought to be better known in New York." The most flattering of all the reviews came in *Art News* when the magazine's writer called Rosenberg's paintings "among the most vital modern pictures seen this season," and referred to him as "an unusual thinker. He thinks with his emotions. He manages to do this in the language of paint by turning his subjects into themes—*Bread, Fear, My Brother, Conflict.*"[198] While all of the New York critics shared the same positive opinion about Rosenberg's use of color and brushwork, they too agreed that his ideas needed more clarity.

His second solo show at AAA, held from December 22 through January 17, 1948, was a tremendous success. Rosenberg exhibited fourteen paintings, eleven of which sold during the show's short run. The remaining three paintings were on loan to the exhibition. Gladys Schmitt, noted writer and fellow faculty member at Carnegie Tech, wrote the text for the brochure that accompanied the exhibition. This show, too, was well received by the New York art critics, such as Margaret Bruening, who called Rosenberg's colors "jewel-like . . . not only glowing on the surface but appearing to have lucent depths."[199] Sam Hunter of the *New York Times* wrote that Rosenberg made "an effort to poeticize the witch's mirror of expressionism into melancholy and sorrow." However, Rosenberg was also criticized this time for placing too much emphasis on form. One critic who wrote of Rosenberg's "rich fabric of loosely-brushed glowing colors" also disparaged his stylistic approach with the comment, "instead of letting his ideas dictate form, he has squeezed his into a rigid framework. His figures are tortured into attitudes and gestures of the saints in old stained-glass church windows."[200] B. F. Dolbin, for the German newspaper *Aufbau,* called attention to an aspect of the paintings that other critics had not recognized when he wrote, "The spiritual content of his paintings is furthered by a unique technique of painting, giving the painting an illuminating power, which appears to come out of his inner self."[201] Associated American Artists remained Rosenberg's dealer into the mid-1950s.

Rosenberg participated in group exhibitions throughout the country including the Albright Gallery, Buffalo, N.Y.; Corcoran Gallery, Washington, D.C.; Chicago Art Institute; Detroit Art Institute; Los Angeles County Museum; National Academy of Design; and the Walker Art Center, among many others. Rosenberg's work was selected by Pepsi Cola for inclusion in the corporation's Paintings of the Year exhibition in 1946; in 1947, when he won a five-hundred-dollar prize for his painting *Asleep* (plate 49); and again in 1948.

Rosenberg, as has been noted, had no shortage of patrons in the city of Pittsburgh. He sold paintings to the Chamber of Commerce, Carnegie Institute of Technology, University of Pittsburgh, the Hebrew Institute, Rodef Shalom Congregation, the YM&WHA, United Steelworkers, Latrobe High School, Allegheny County Bar Association, and noted collectors, including Harold and Katherine "Kitty" Ruttenberg, Gladys Schmitt, and Anita Morganstern, among so many others. Rosenberg's work was noticed outside the city as well, and was purchased by Allen Funt, director of *Candid Camera,* among others.

In the realm of corporate support, Abbott Laboratories and Encyclopedia Britannica, both of Chicago, commissioned Rosenberg to create specific works for their collections. Abbott Laboratories commissioned Rosenberg to paint two different subjects for publication in their corporate newsletter, *What's New,* in 1953 and again in 1957. The earlier painting was created to illustrate a poem written by Louis Untermeyer. Entitled *Nativity,* the painting was Rosenberg's expressionistic response to the words of the poet. Rosenberg's *Balloon Man,* as previously mentioned, was reproduced in the newsletter four years later.[202] The Encyclopedia Britannica collection, on the other hand, contained a broad cross section of contemporary American paintings. The company commissioned various artists to create paintings to illustrate specific sections in the new printing of *Britannica Junior.* According to Grace Pagano, "They decided that rather than the usual line drawings and photographs, *Junior* would be a more interesting edition if contemporary American paintings were used as visual explanation for certain subjects." Thomas Hart Benton painted *Boom Town* to illustrate an article on petroleum, and Alexander Hogue's painting described the subject of wind erosion. Questionnaires were sent to museum directors, artists, art critics, and others throughout the country to solicit the names of those artists they considered most important. Once the work had been reproduced, Britannica realized that the public should see more than reproductions, so they traveled the collection to cities and towns across the country on a five-year tour. The work was shown in museums, schools, and colleges so that the largest number of people and broadest possible audience could have the opportunity to see it. Encyclopedia Britannica's goal was to continue to collect contemporary American art in this manner in order to keep the collection vital. Unfortunately, the collection was broken up and sold at auction in the early 1980s and no information is currently available on its whereabouts. Rosenberg was the only painter represented from Pittsburgh, and his painting *Out in the Night* of 1943 (figure 33), was selected for the collection but its current location is unknown. Pagano, who wrote about each of the artists for the catalog of the Encyclopedia Britannica collection, thought that Rosenberg's work would continue to grow: "He never stays within boundary lines. He is never afraid to experiment, but always there is continuity in the change. He is a mature artist who handles social comments without indulging in soap-box posturing." When the collection was shown at the Carnegie Institute in 1945, the collection had grown to 135 paintings. Walter Read Hovey, a Professor in the Department of Fine Arts at the University of Pittsburgh, reviewed the exhibition for a Pittsburgh newspaper, and was enthusiastic about the collaboration between art and business: "When art and business get together anything might happen. The success of the present exhibition is perhaps an indication that each needs the other." In conclusion he wrote: "It is a formidable list [of artists] and more and more one comes to realize the power of American painting."[203]

Rosenberg was recognized twice for solo exhibitions at the Carnegie Institute, first in 1937, as only the third Pittsburgh artist to be so honored, and again in 1956. In 1950, three solo exhibitions of Rosenberg's work were held in the east: at the Boston Museum School; at the Cheltenham Art Center in Philadelphia; and at the Arts and Crafts Center in Pittsburgh, which had just named him Man of the Year. The latter exhibition was a retrospective that featured sixty-nine paintings ranging from his early Pittsburgh scenes to the more recent abstractions, and traveled to the Butler Institute in Youngstown, Ohio, later in 1950. In her review of that exhibition for the *Pittsburgh Post-Gazette,* Jeanette Jena spoke of the power of color

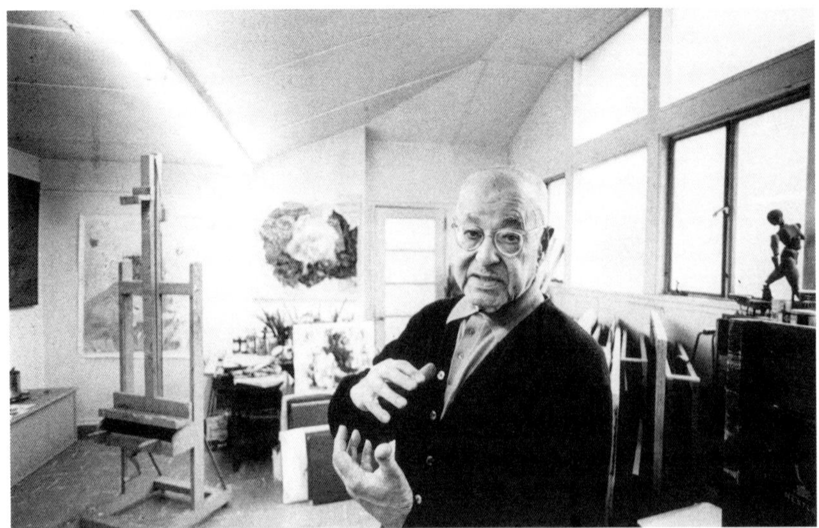

FIG. 49.
Rosenberg in his studio, 2721 Mount Royal Road, 1971.

in the artist's work: "Color is his creed, his inspiration, his means of communicating a sense of life as both immediate and evanescent. The relative power of color as an artist places dark against light; the absolute power of color as a shock to the senses."[204] Rosenberg was only the second Pittsburgh artist to receive the distinguished Man of the Year award from Pittsburgh's Arts and Crafts Center (now Pittsburgh Center for the Arts), and the tradition of this award continues after fifty-four years.

Samuel Rosenberg made art for sixty-five years, and never stopped experimenting, learning, changing, studying, and teaching. An ongoing discovery for him, it was, indeed, his life. "Every painting is an adventure," he said in 1957, and that adventure endured for him for a lifetime.[205] It lives on for us now in his work.

"For so many years I have painted, that I can scarcely remember the time when I did not paint. Painting leads me, and painting drives me; in painting, and in paintings, I find intensity and the struggle which expresses the joy of Life, the wonder of growth, the condition of man, the reality of Death. . . ."[206]

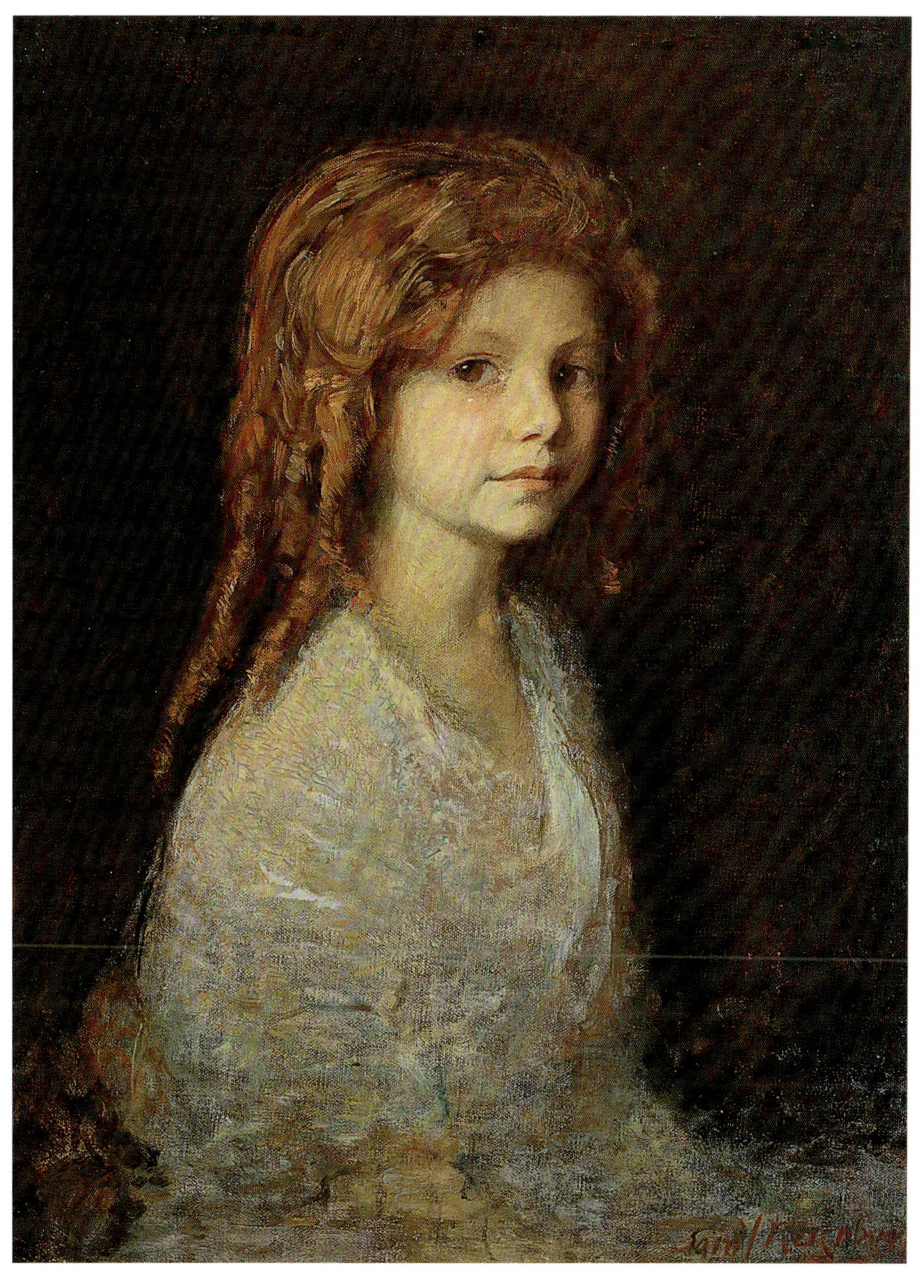

PLATE 1. *Portrait of Maxine,* 1919. Oil on canvas, 24 x 18″.

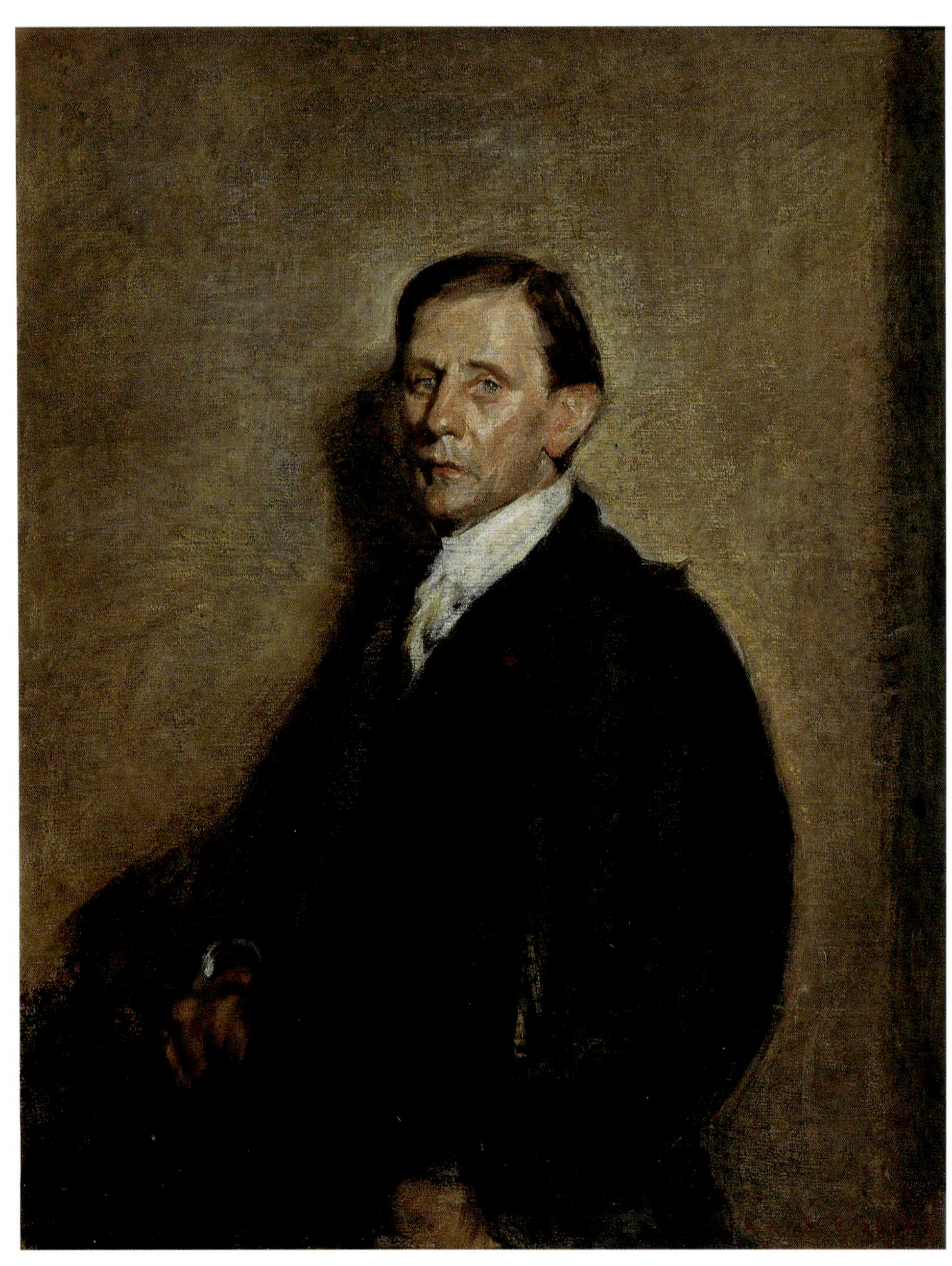

PLATE 2. *Portrait of Christian J. Walter,* 1921. Oil on canvas, 36 x 28″.

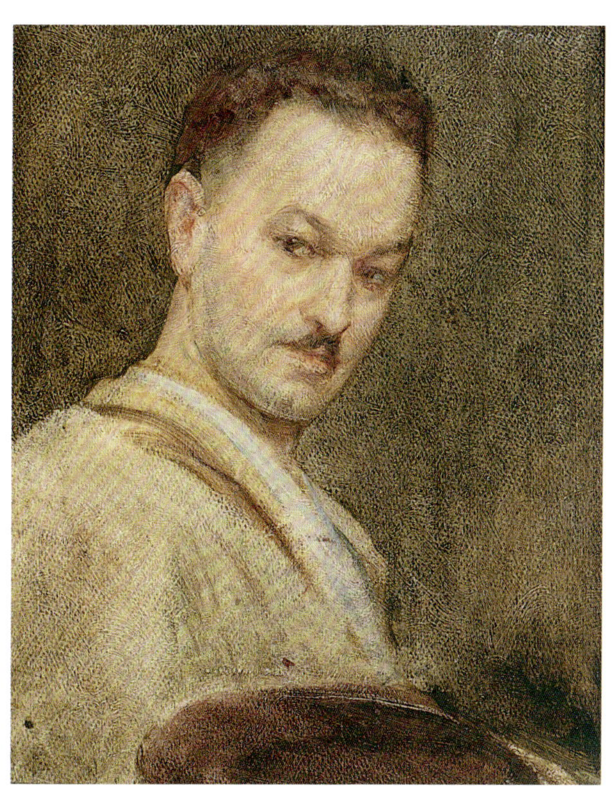

PLATE 3. *Self-Portrait with Palette,* 1923. Oil on board, 19 x 15″.

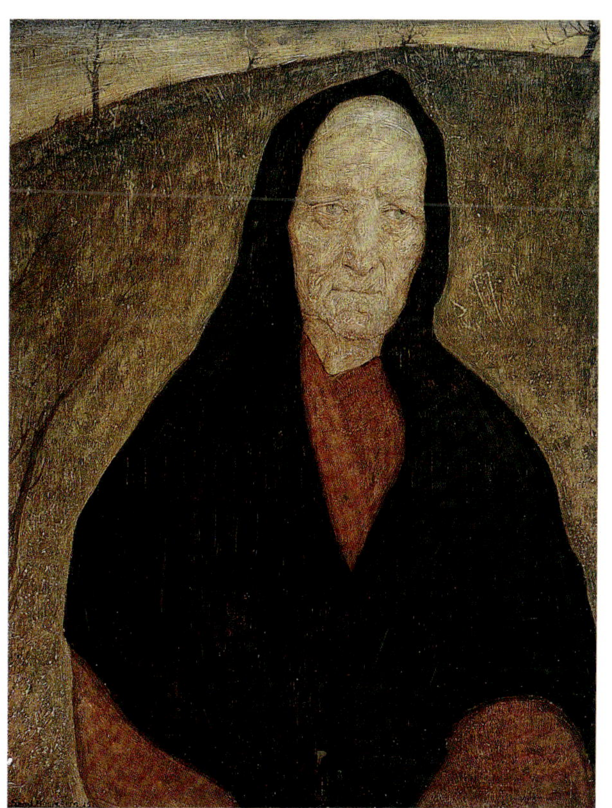

PLATE 4. *Marta,* 1925. Oil on wood, 24 x 18″.

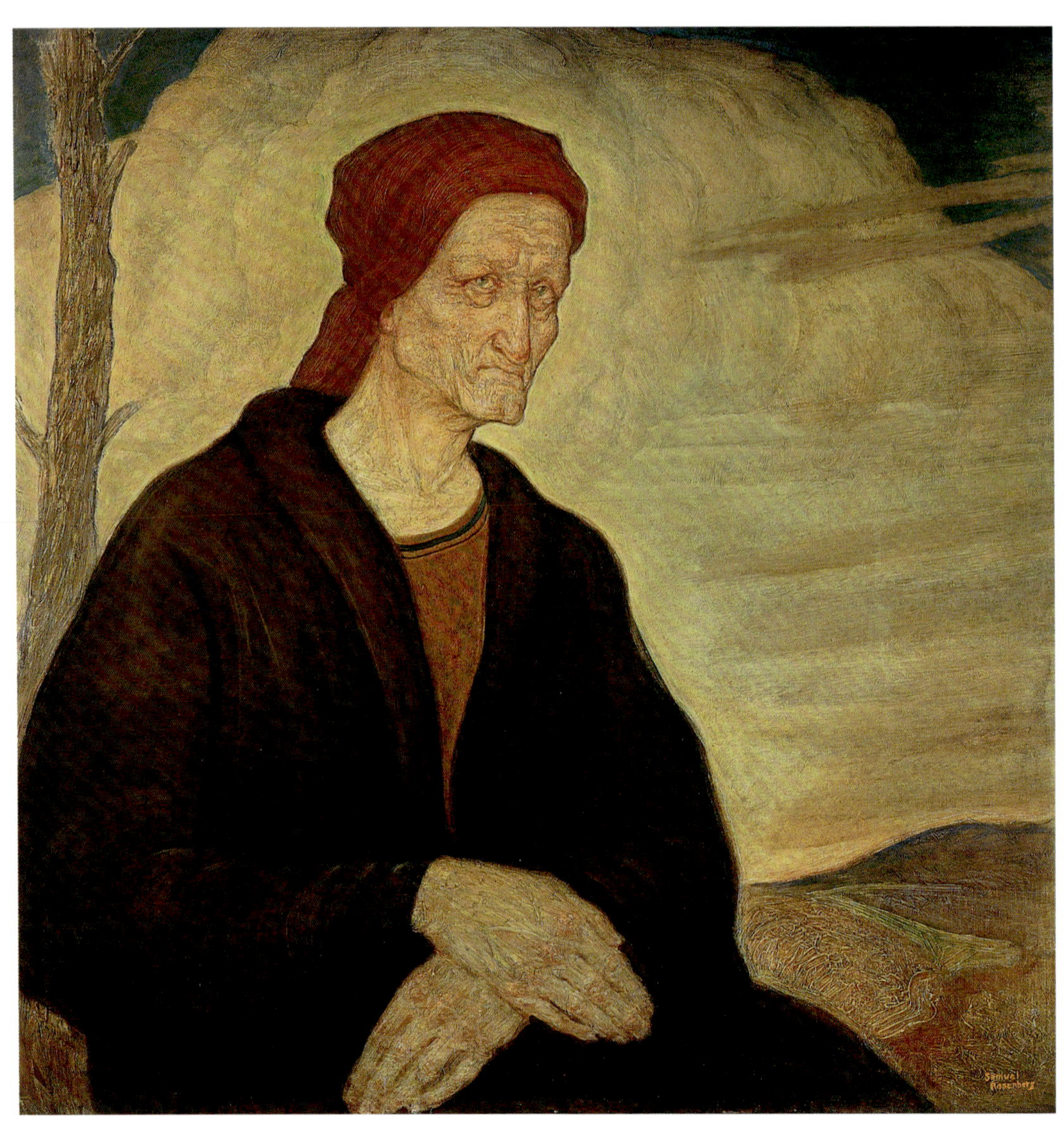

PLATE 5. *Helga,* 1925. Oil on canvas, 40 x 40″.

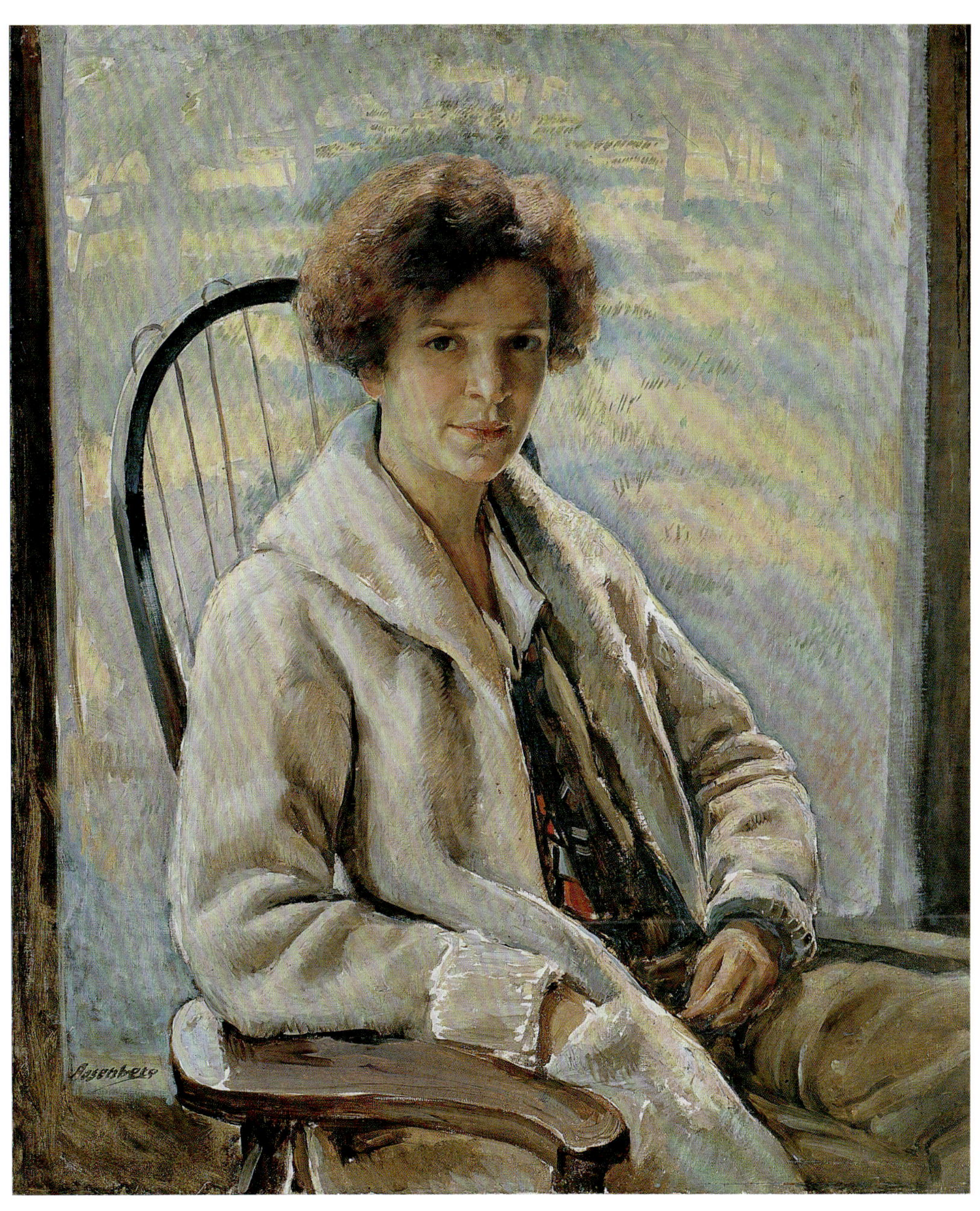

PLATE 6. *Portrait of Libbie in White Sweater,* 1926. Oil on canvas, 36 x 30″.

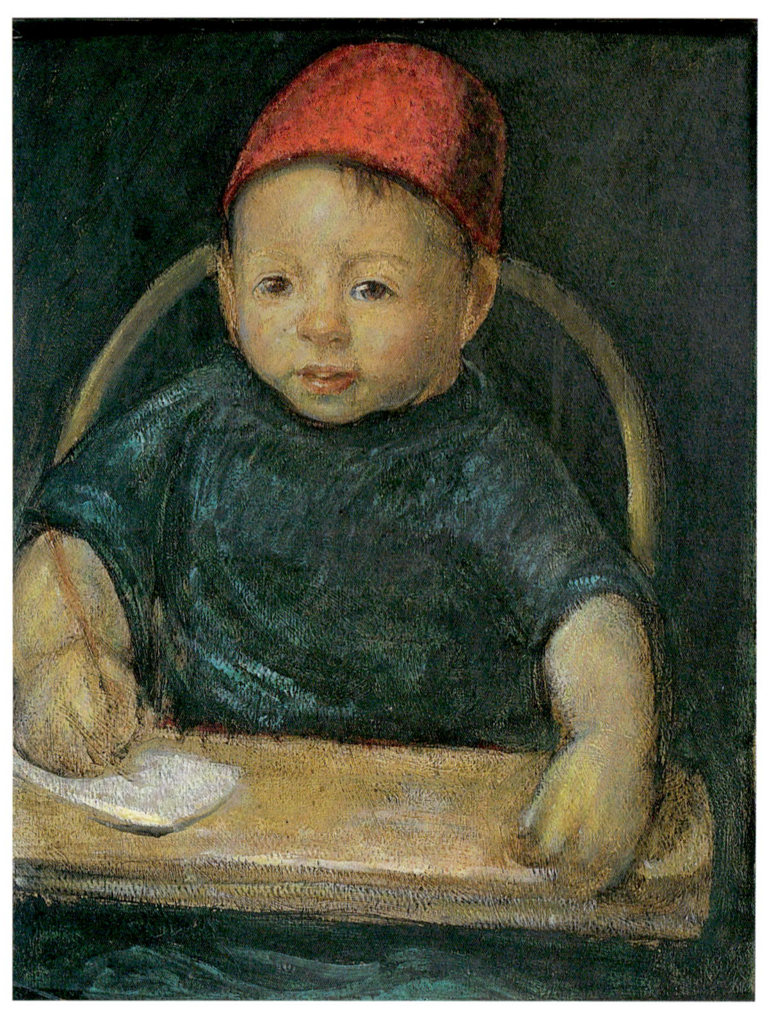

PLATE 7. *Portrait of Murray in Red Hat*, 1926. Oil on fiber board, 19 x 15″.

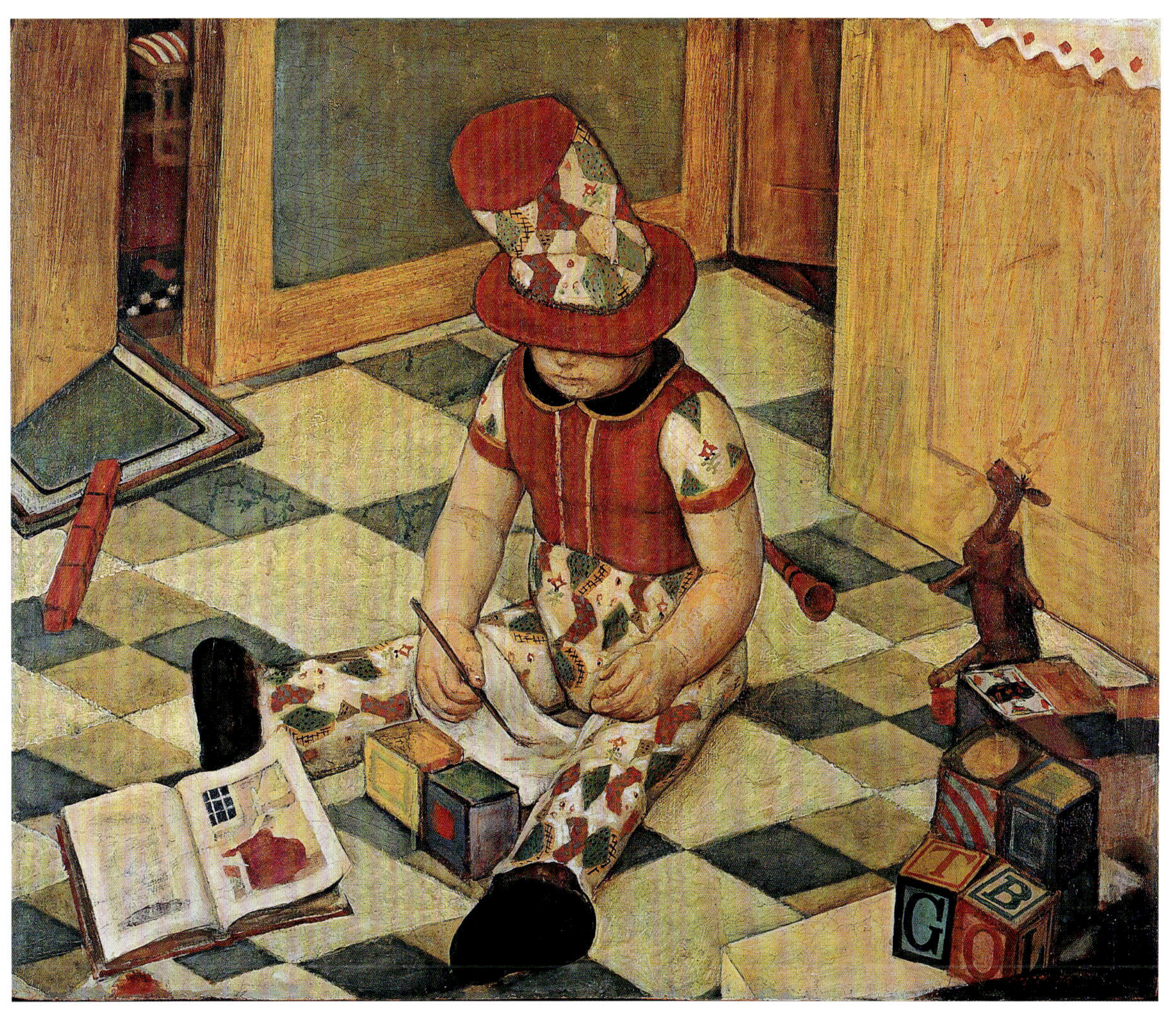

PLATE 8. *First Halloween,* 1926. Oil and tempera on masonite, 30 x 36″.

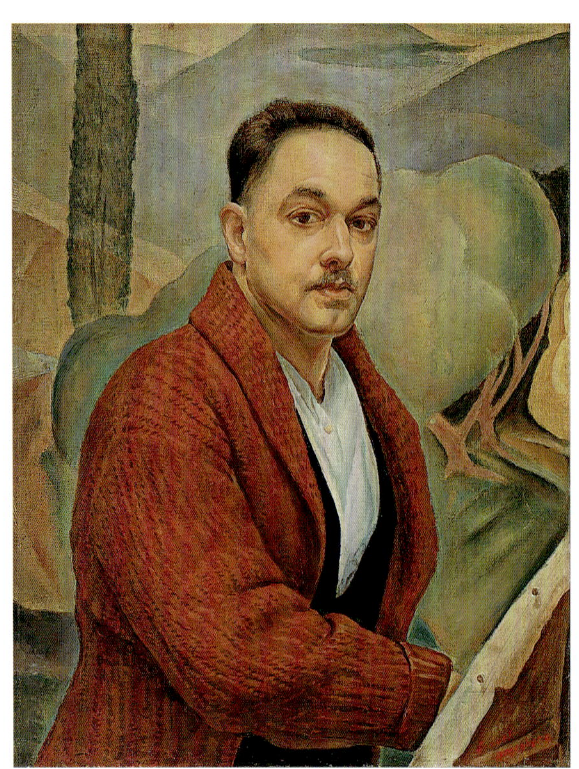

PLATE 9. *Self-Portrait in Sweater,* 1928. Oil on canvas, 24 x 19″.

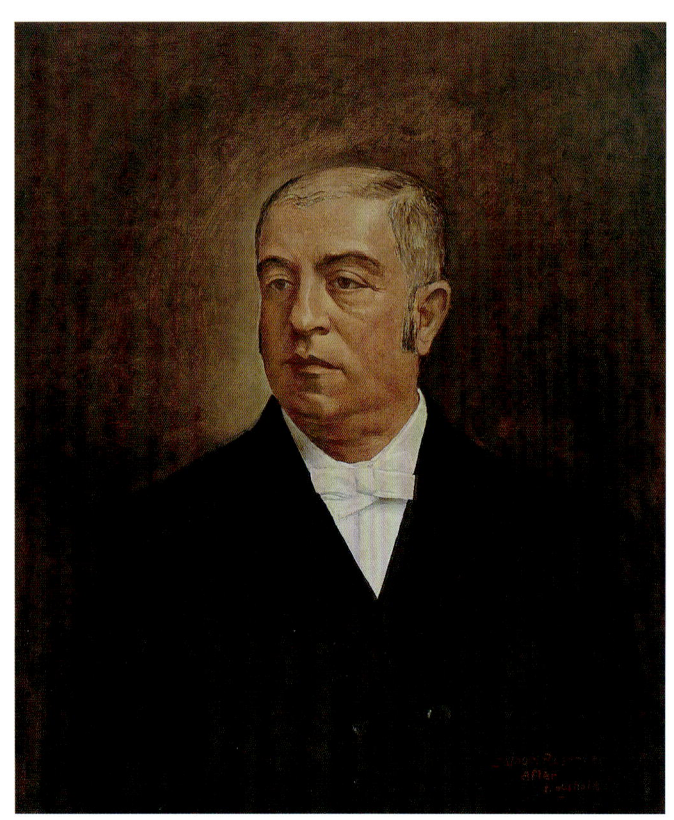

PLATE 10. *Portrait of Rabbi Lippman Mayer,* c. 1936. Oil on canvas, 36 x 31″.

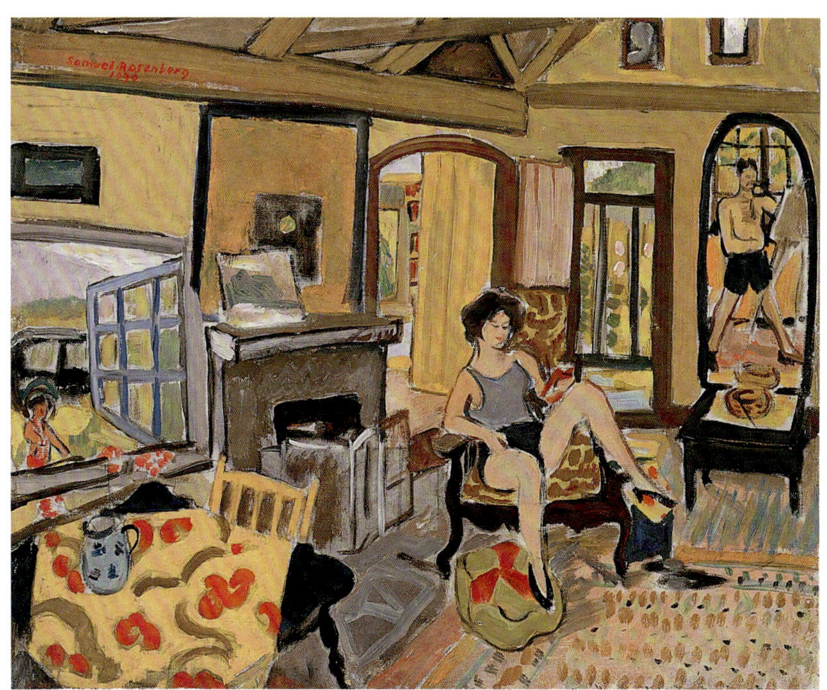

PLATE 11. *Vacation Days No. 1,* 1930. Oil on masonite, 19 x $23\frac{1}{2}$″.

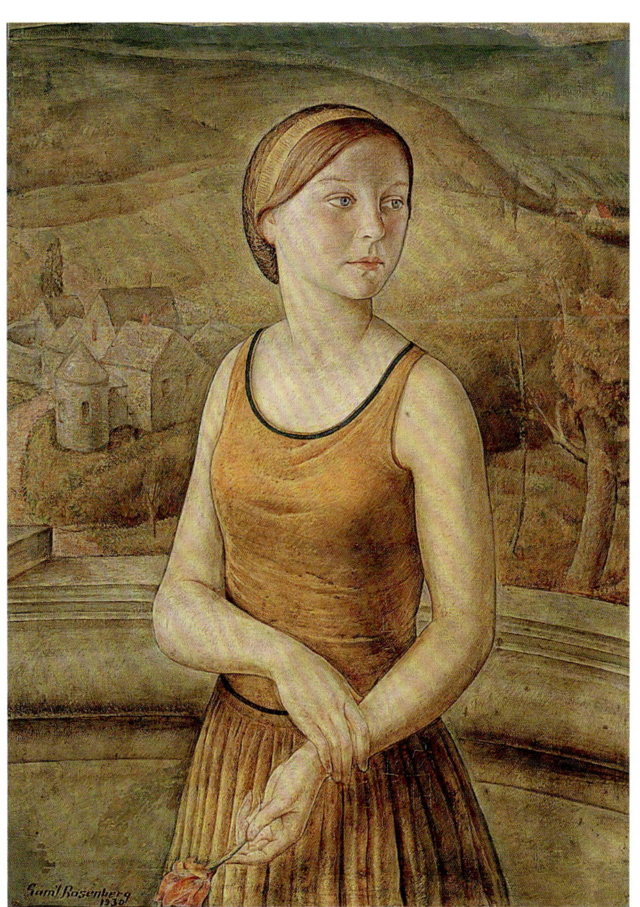

PLATE 12. *The Gold Gown,* 1930. Oil on canvas, 38 x 28″.

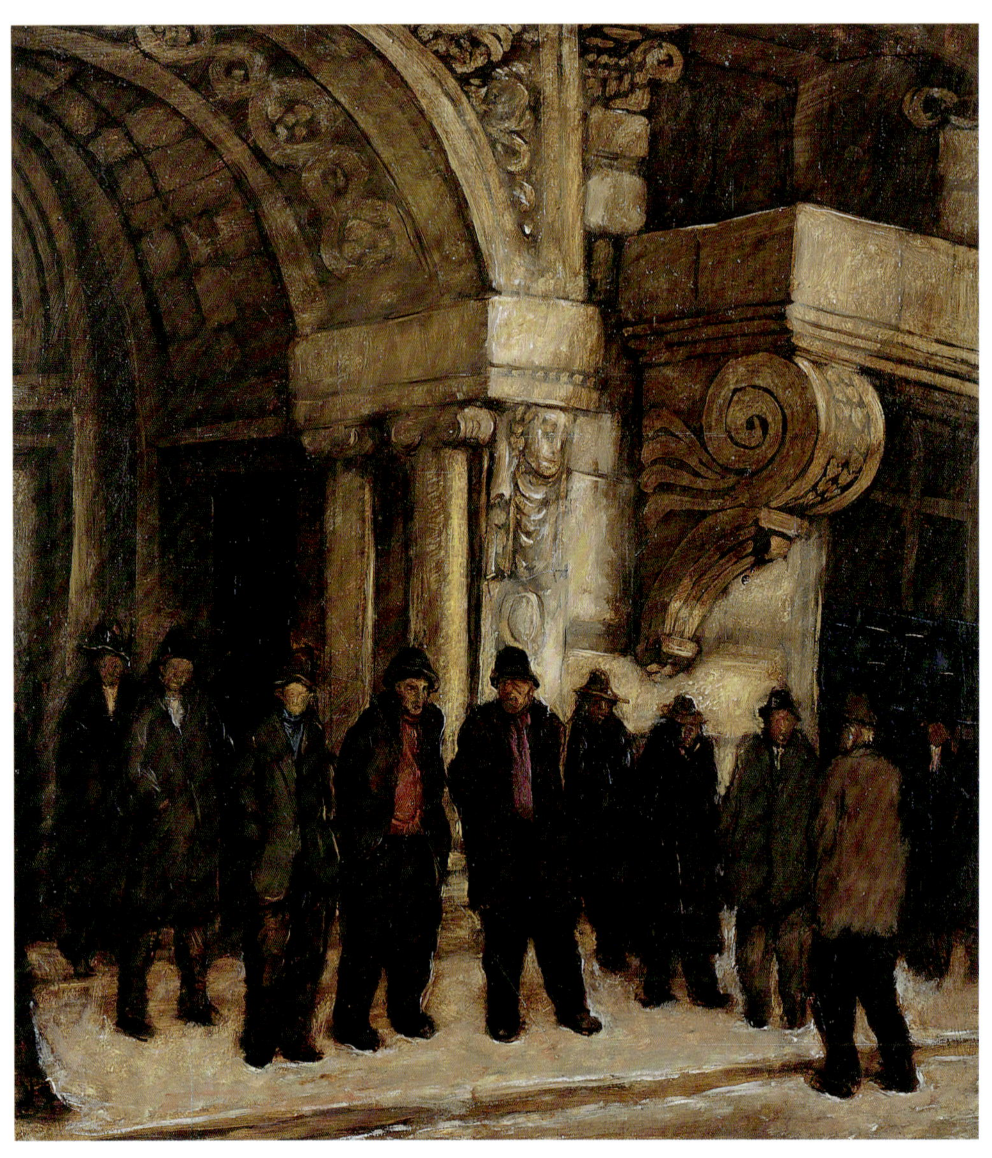

PLATE 13. *Yoder Hotel, Forbes Street,* 1930. Oil and tempera on masonite, 20 x 18″.

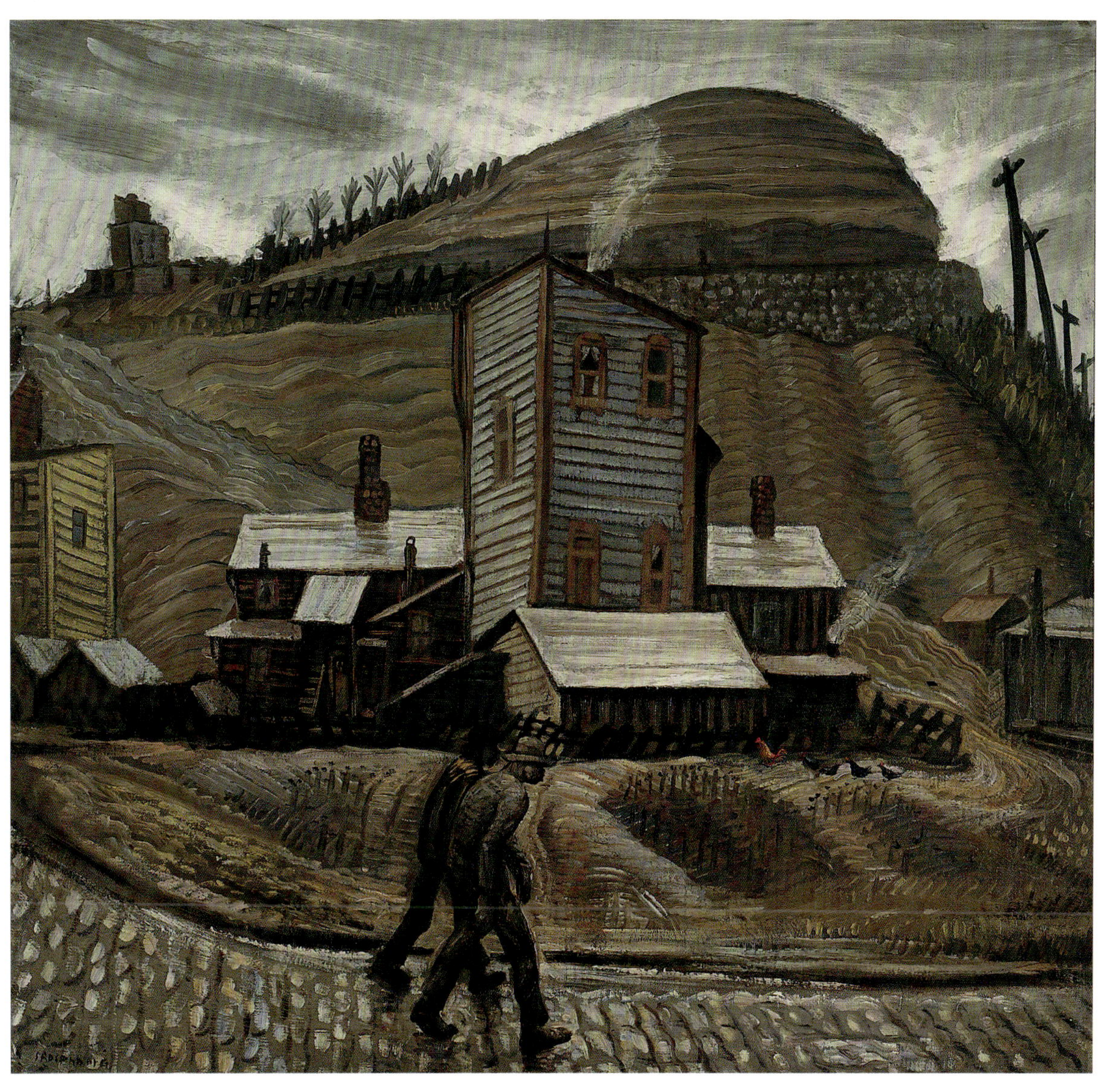

PLATE 14. *Greenfield Hill (Gazzam's Hill)*, 1932. Oil on canvas, 39 x 40½".

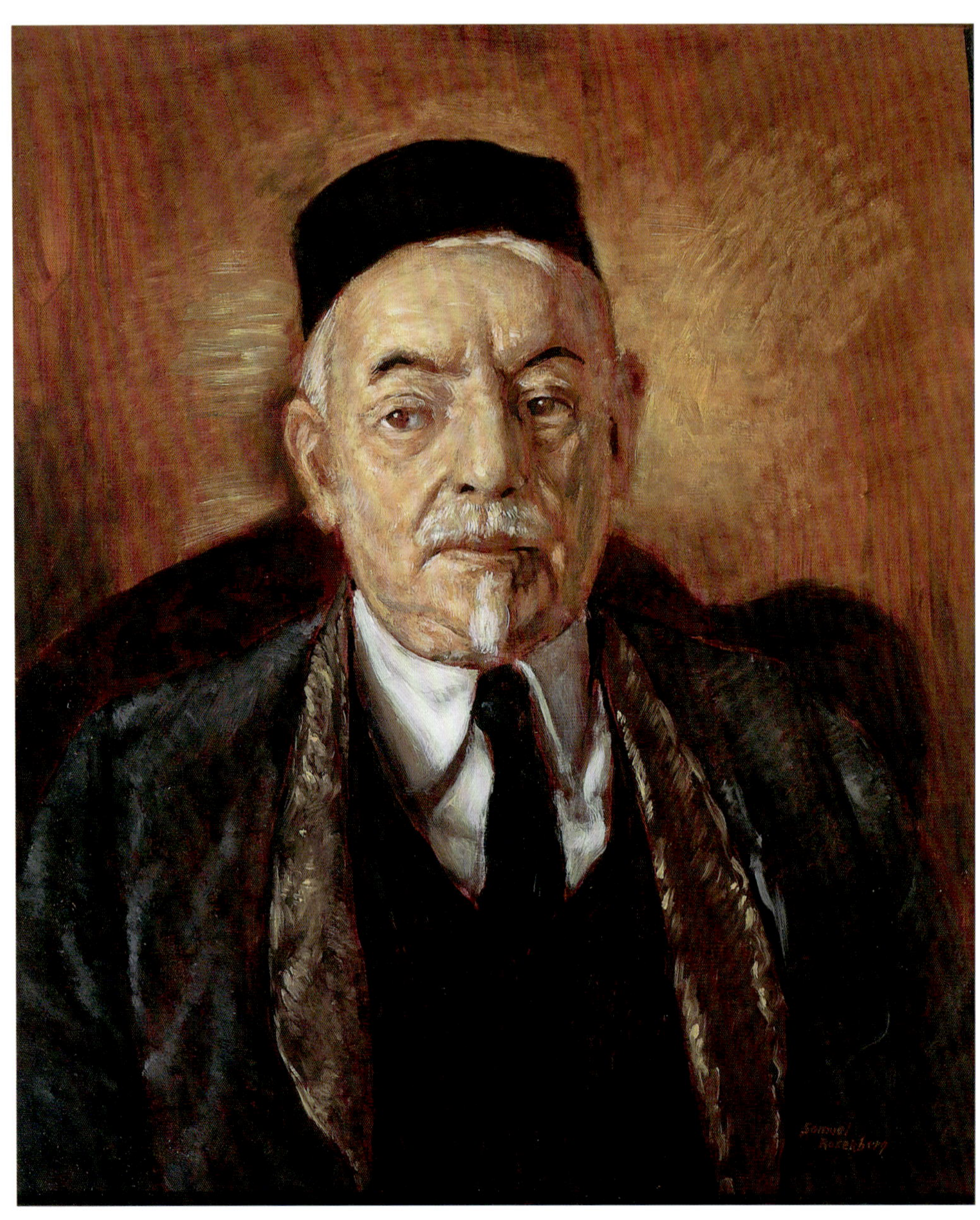

PLATE 15. *Portrait of Solomon Rosenberg No. 1*, 1932. Oil on masonite, 24 x 20″.

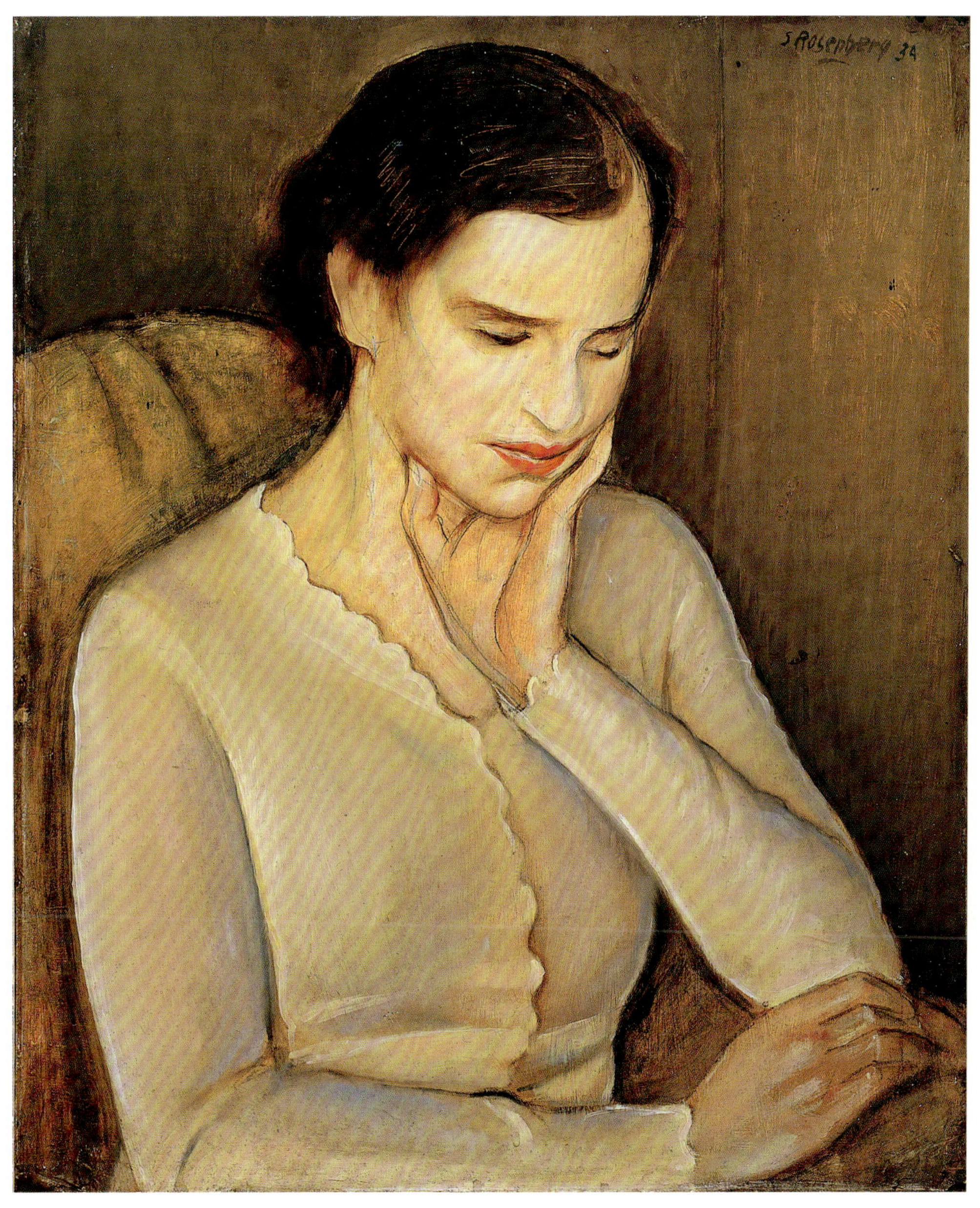

PLATE 16. *Meditation (Libbie)*, 1932. Oil on masonite, 24 x 20″.

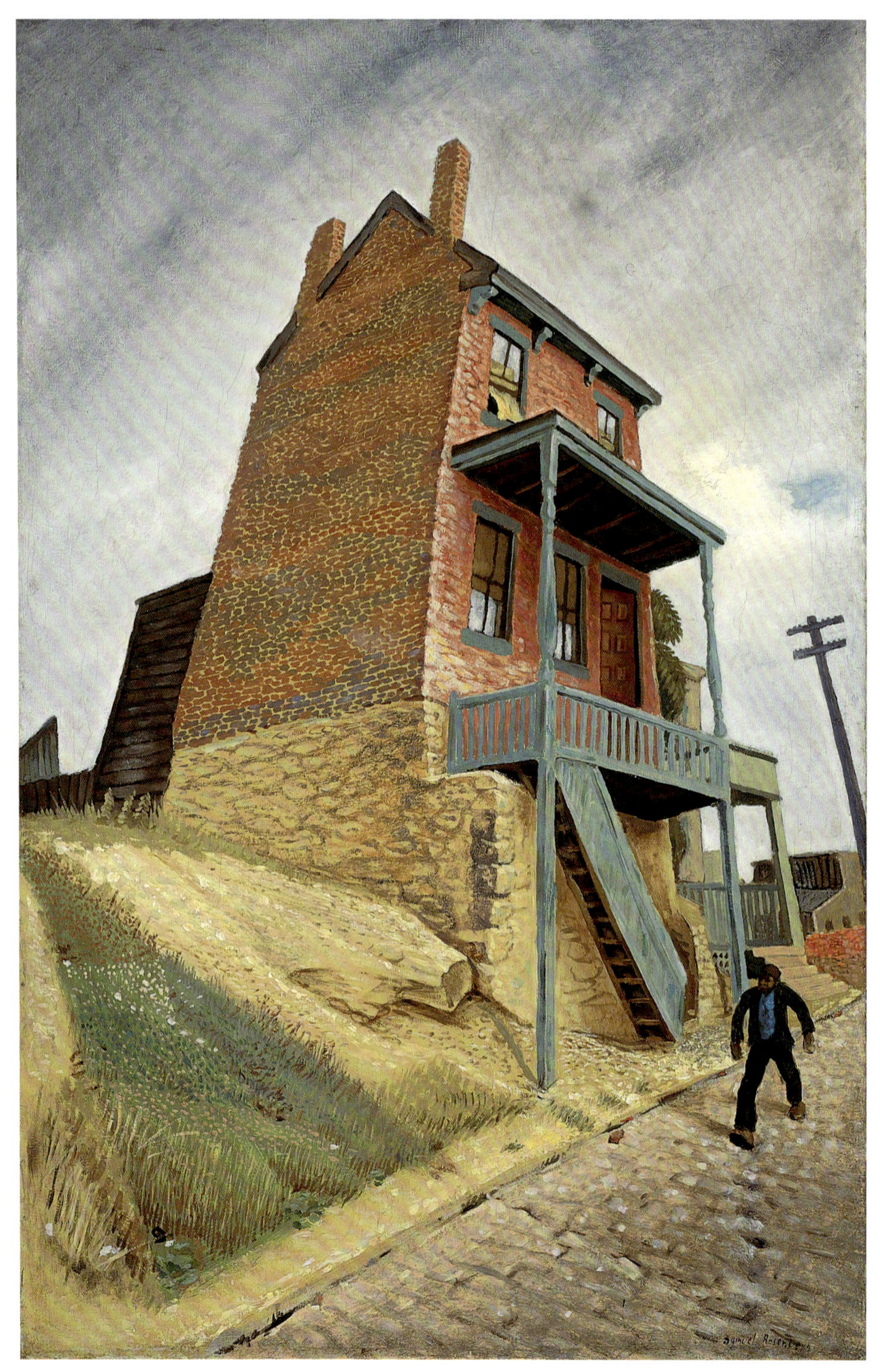

PLATE 17. *Webster Avenue House,* 1932. Oil on canvas, 40 x 26″.

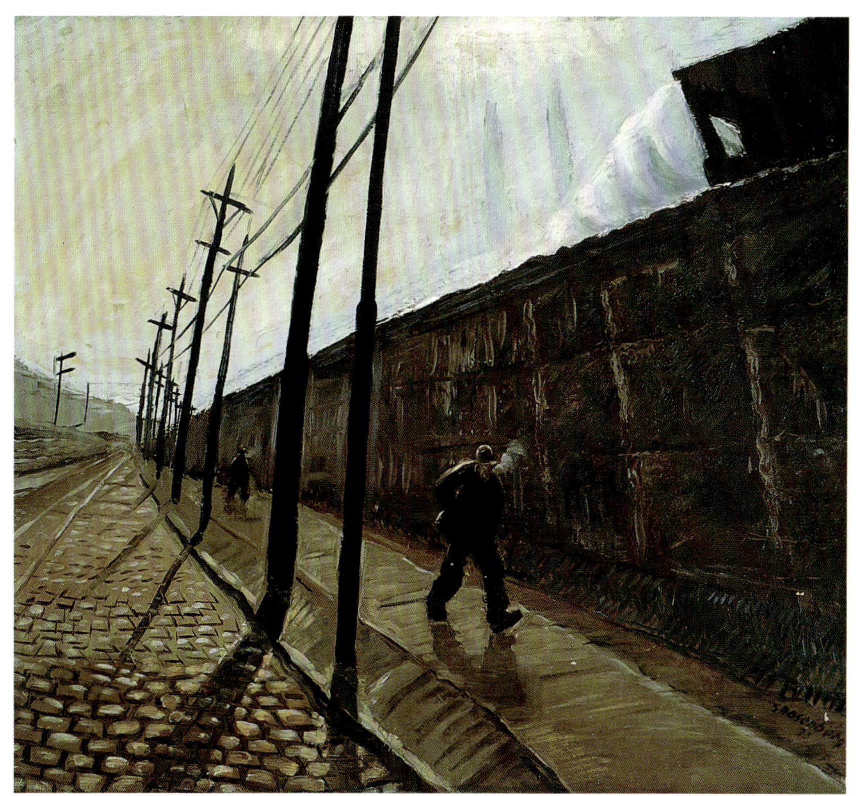

PLATE 18. *Second Avenue (Man-Made Desert, Street by the Mill)*, 1932. Oil on canvas, 36 x 41″.

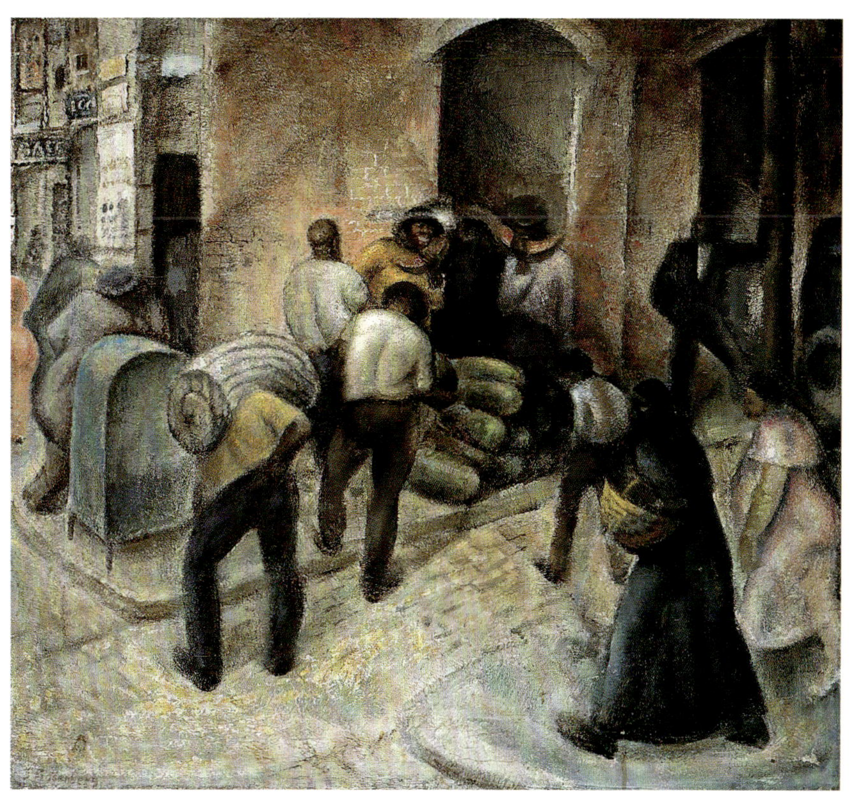

PLATE 19. *Watermelon Market*, 1933. Oil on canvas, 36 x 40″.

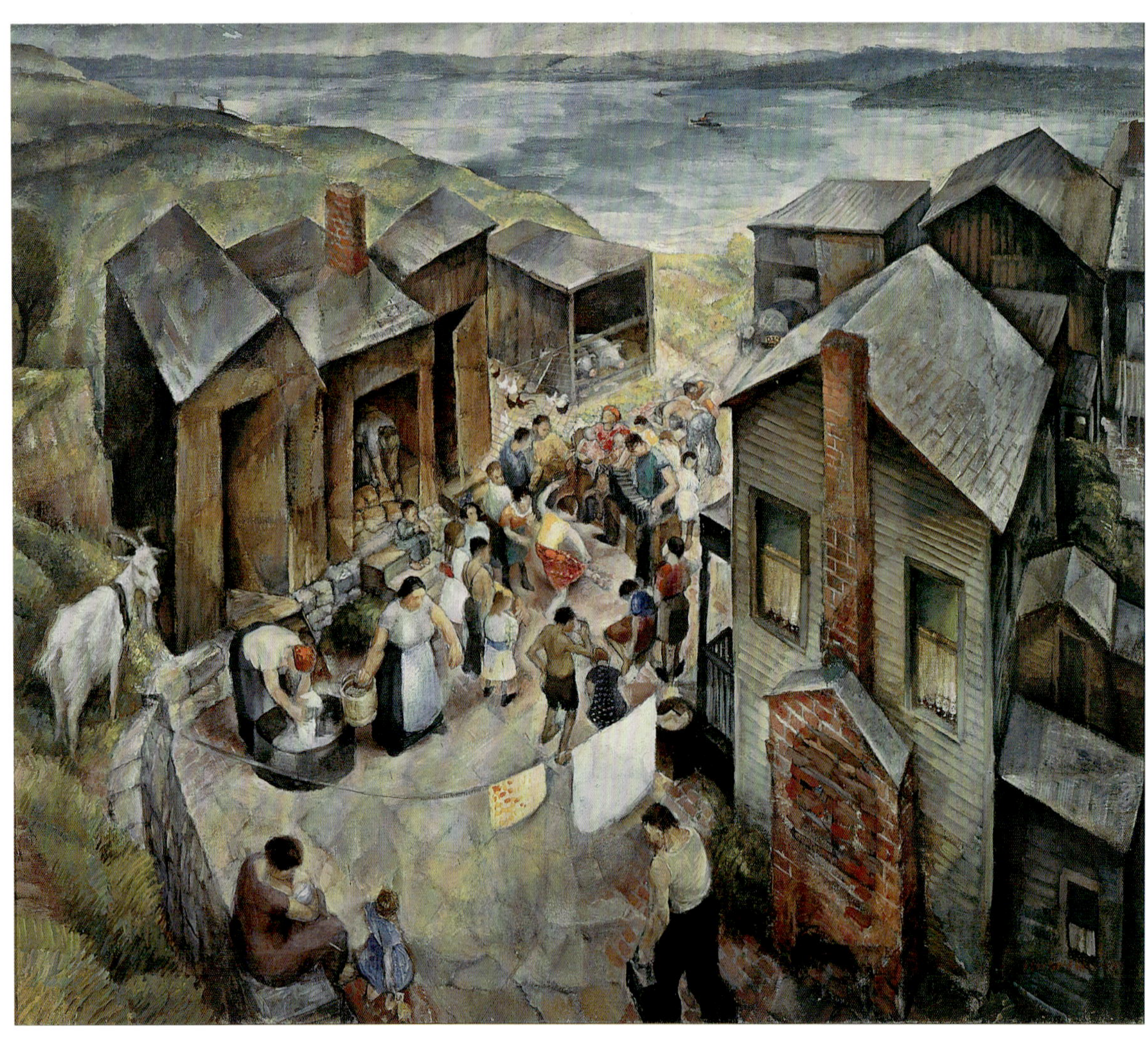

PLATE 20. *Settlement on the Hudson*, 1934. Oil on canvas, 38 x 44″.

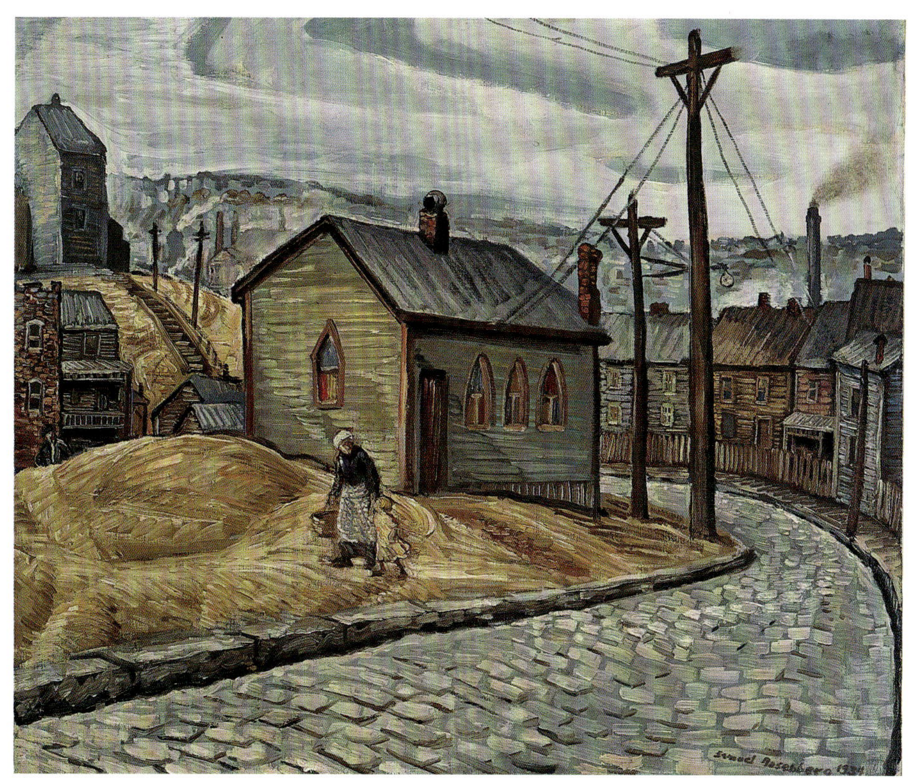

PLATE 21. *Near Herron Hill*, 1934. Oil on canvas, 32 x 38″.

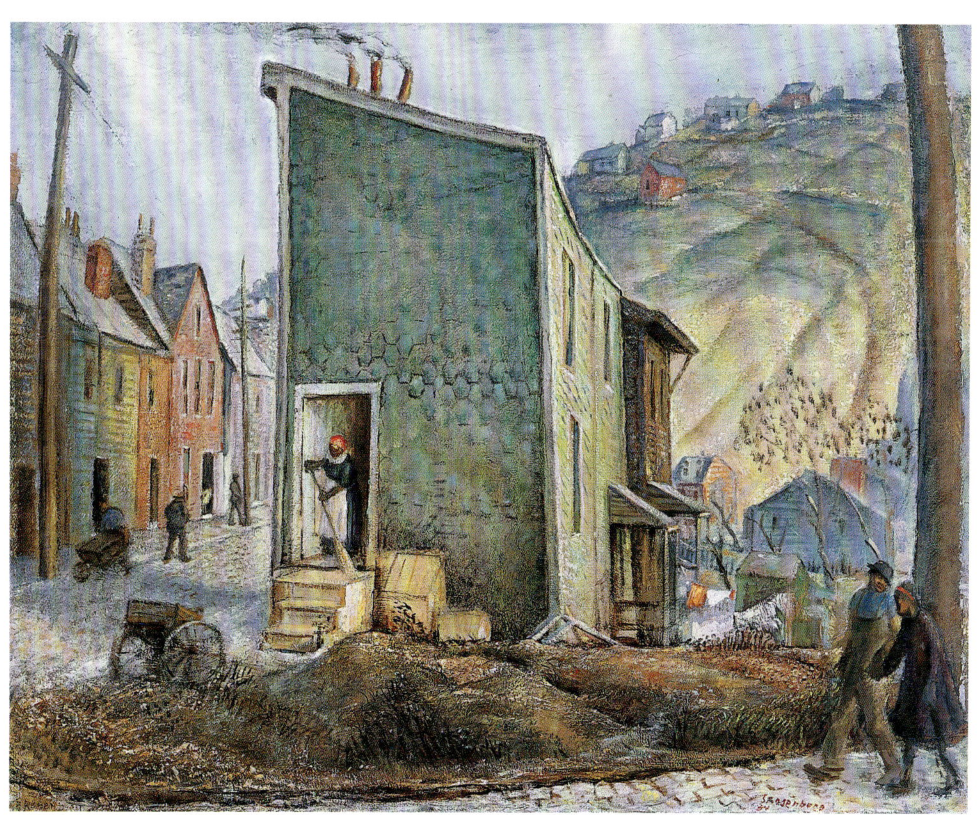

PLATE 22. *Soho*, 1934. Oil on canvas, 40 x 50″.

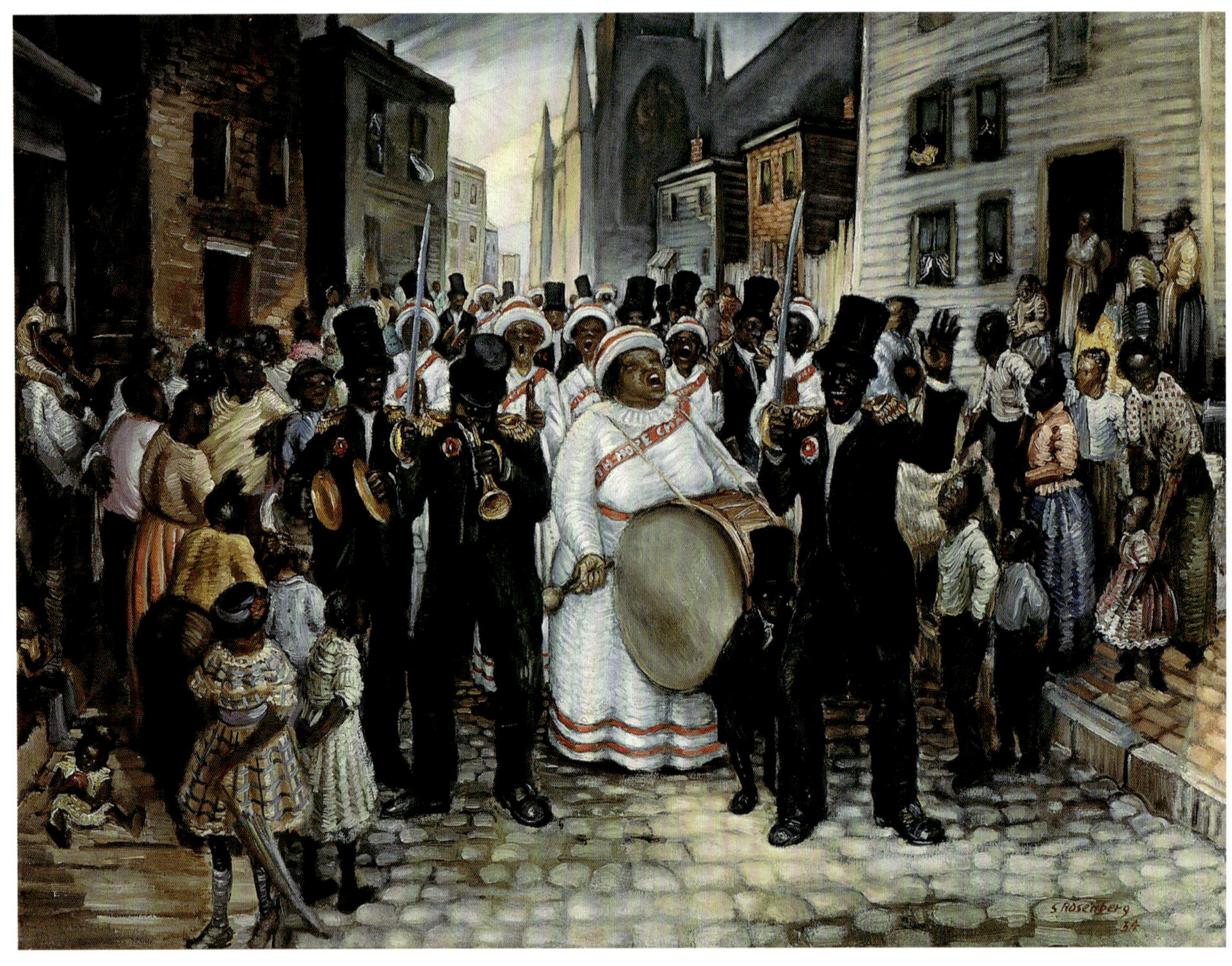

PLATE 23. *God's Chillun*, 1934. Oil on canvas, 36 x 48″.

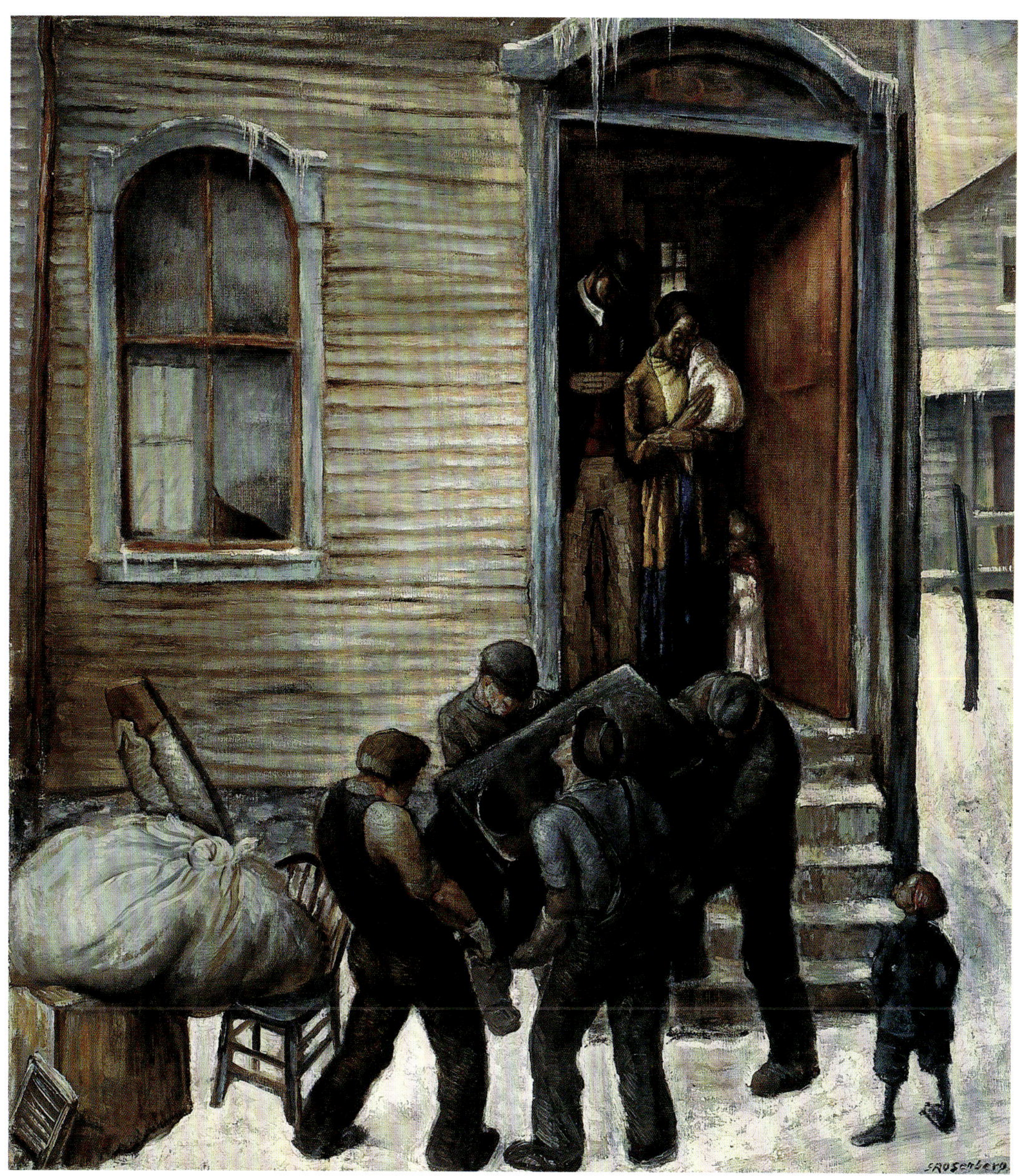

PLATE 24. *Eviction,* 1935. Oil on canvas, 40 x 36″.

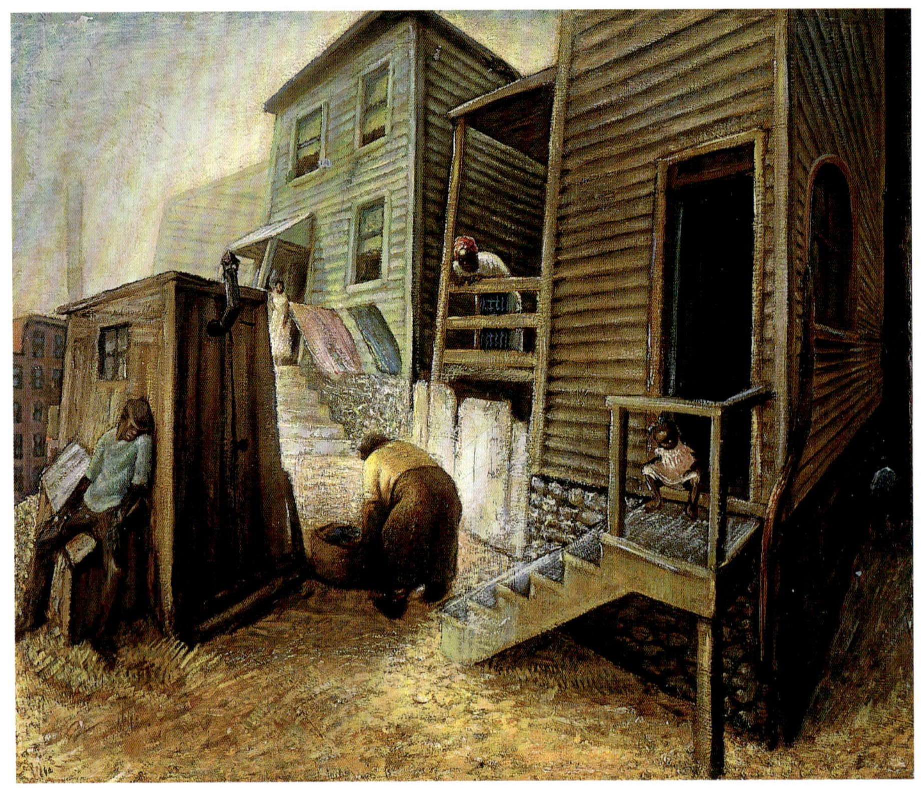

PLATE 25. *Monday Morning (After the Night Shift)*, 1935. Oil on canvas, 30 x 36″.

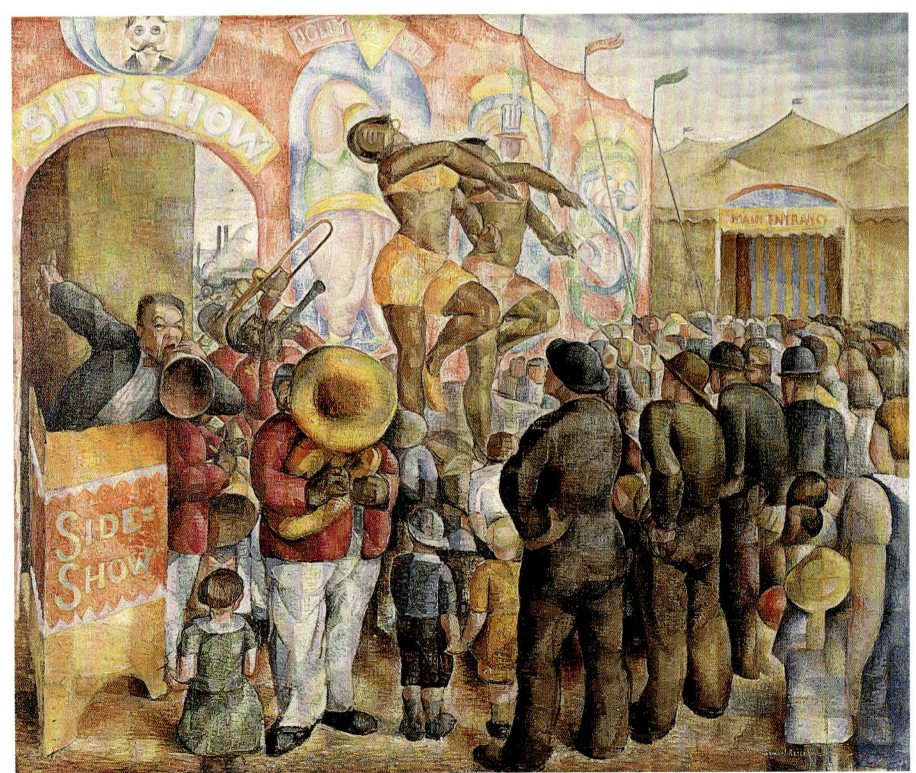

PLATE 26. *Sideshow*, 1935. Oil on canvas, 46 x 50″.

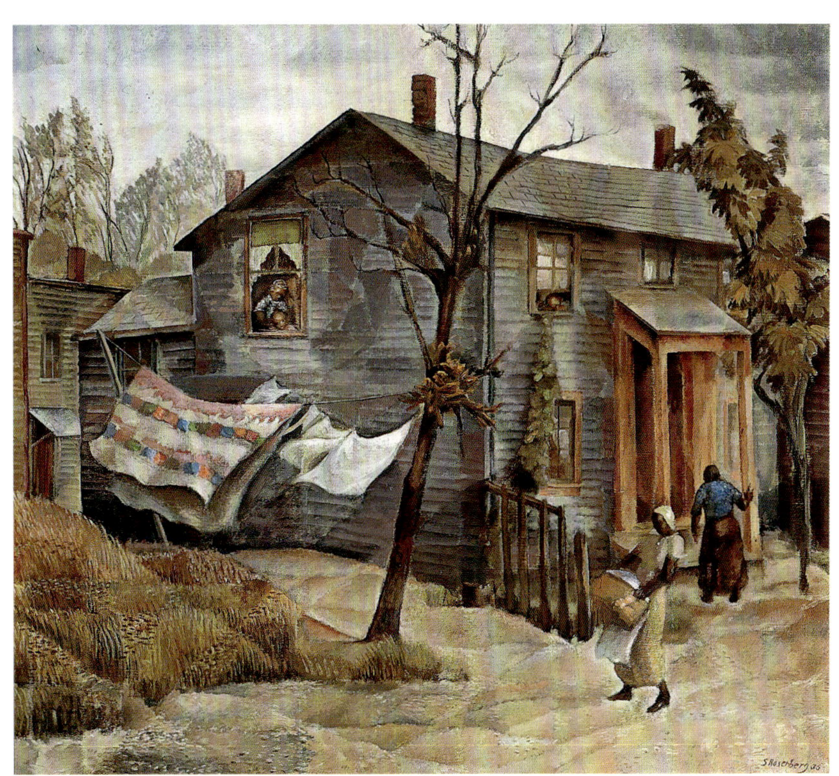

PLATE 27. *Autumn in Pittsburgh,* 1936. Oil on canvas, 25 x 28″.

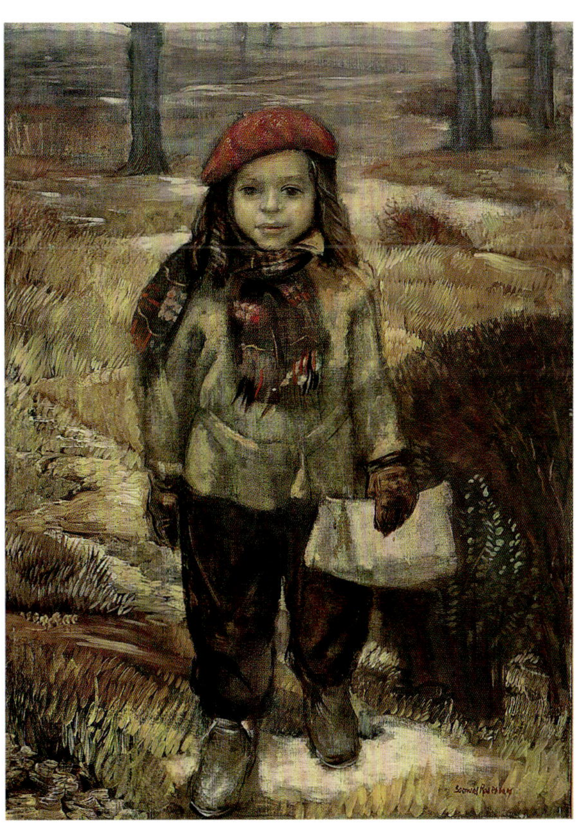

PLATE 28. *Coming Home from School,* 1936. Oil on canvas, 33 x 24″.

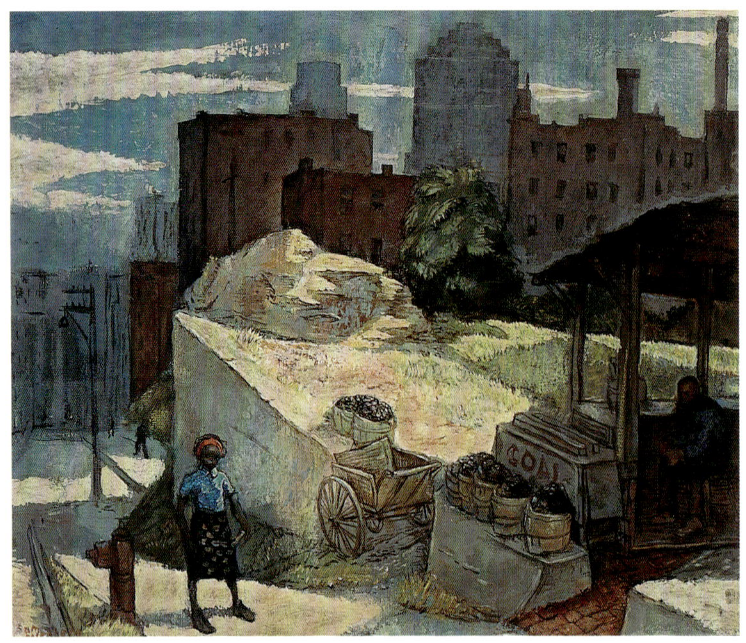

PLATE 29. *The Sun Shines in Pittsburgh*, 1936. Oil on masonite, 20 x 24″.

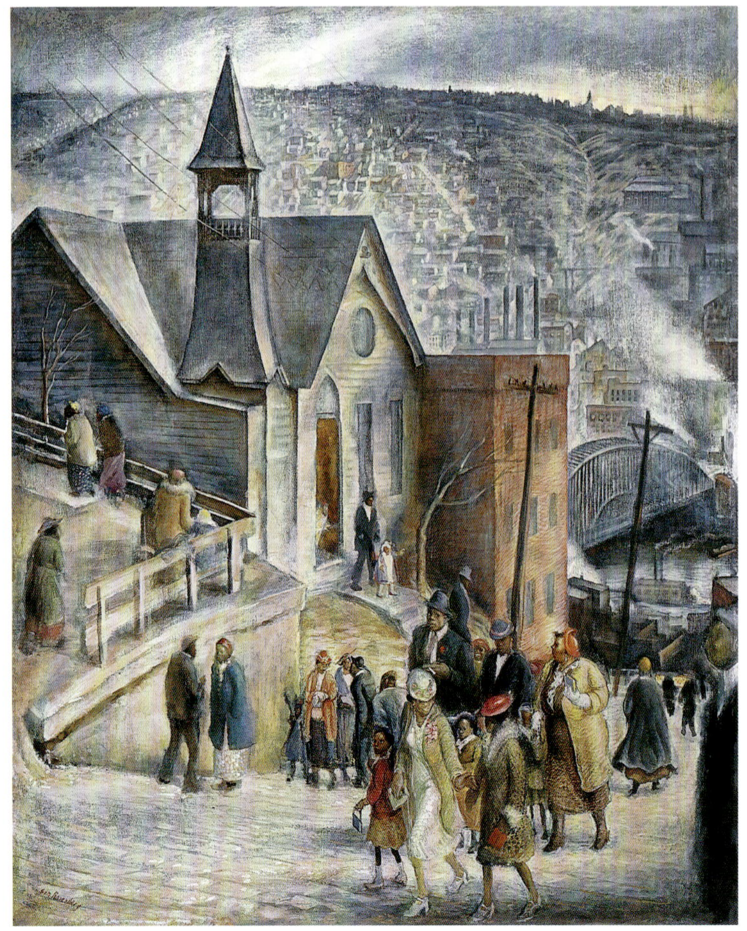

PLATE 30. *Sunday Morning*, 1937. Oil on masonite, 56 x 46″.

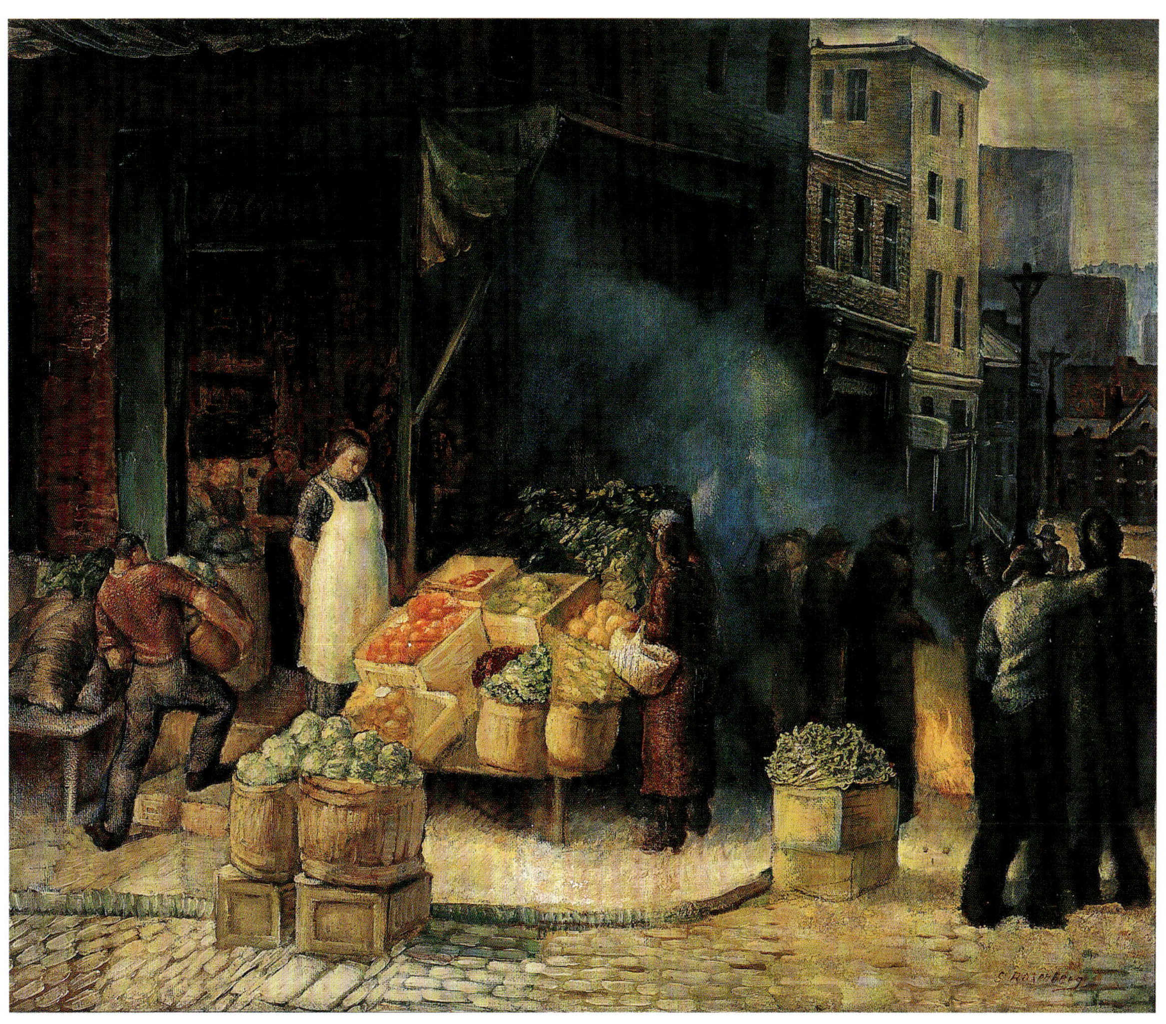

PLATE 31. *Fruit Market,* 1937. Oil and tempera on canvas, 30 x 36″.

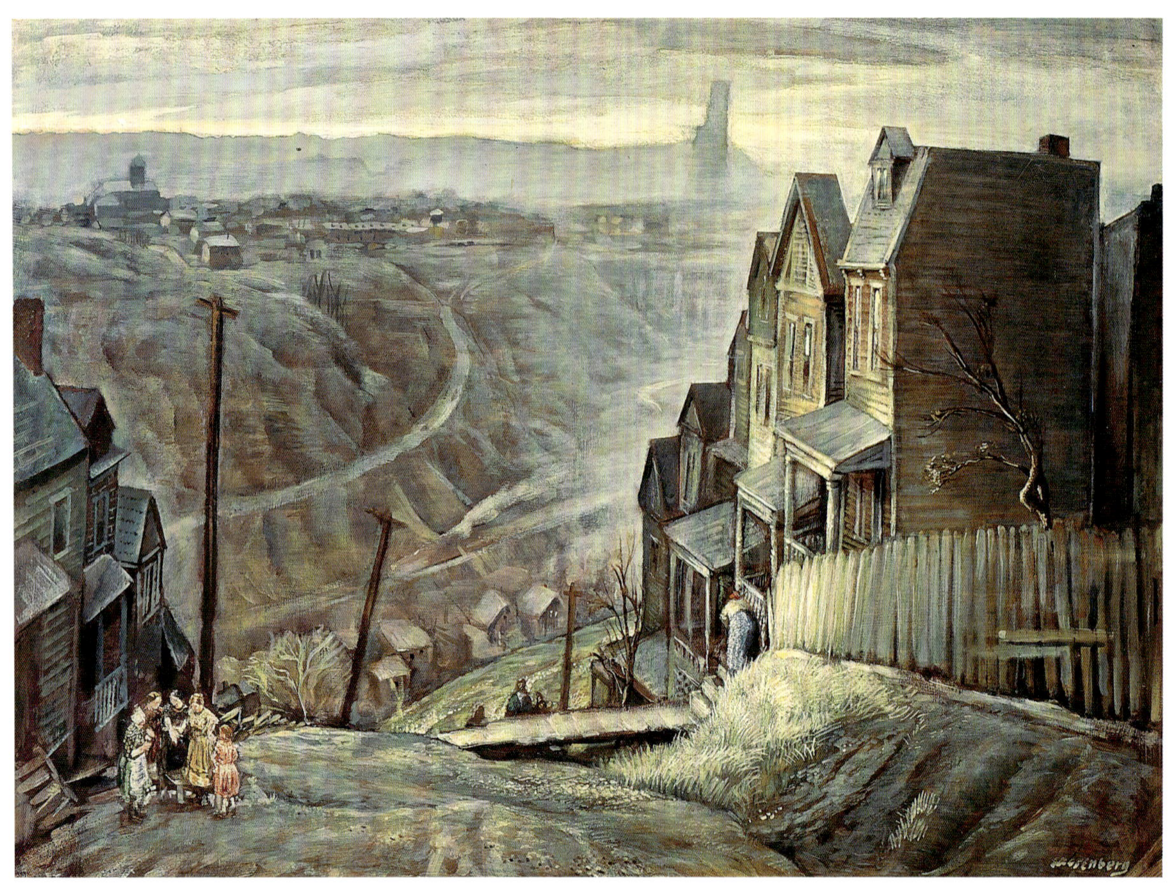

PLATE 32. *The Gossips*, 1937. Oil on canvas, 24 x 33″.

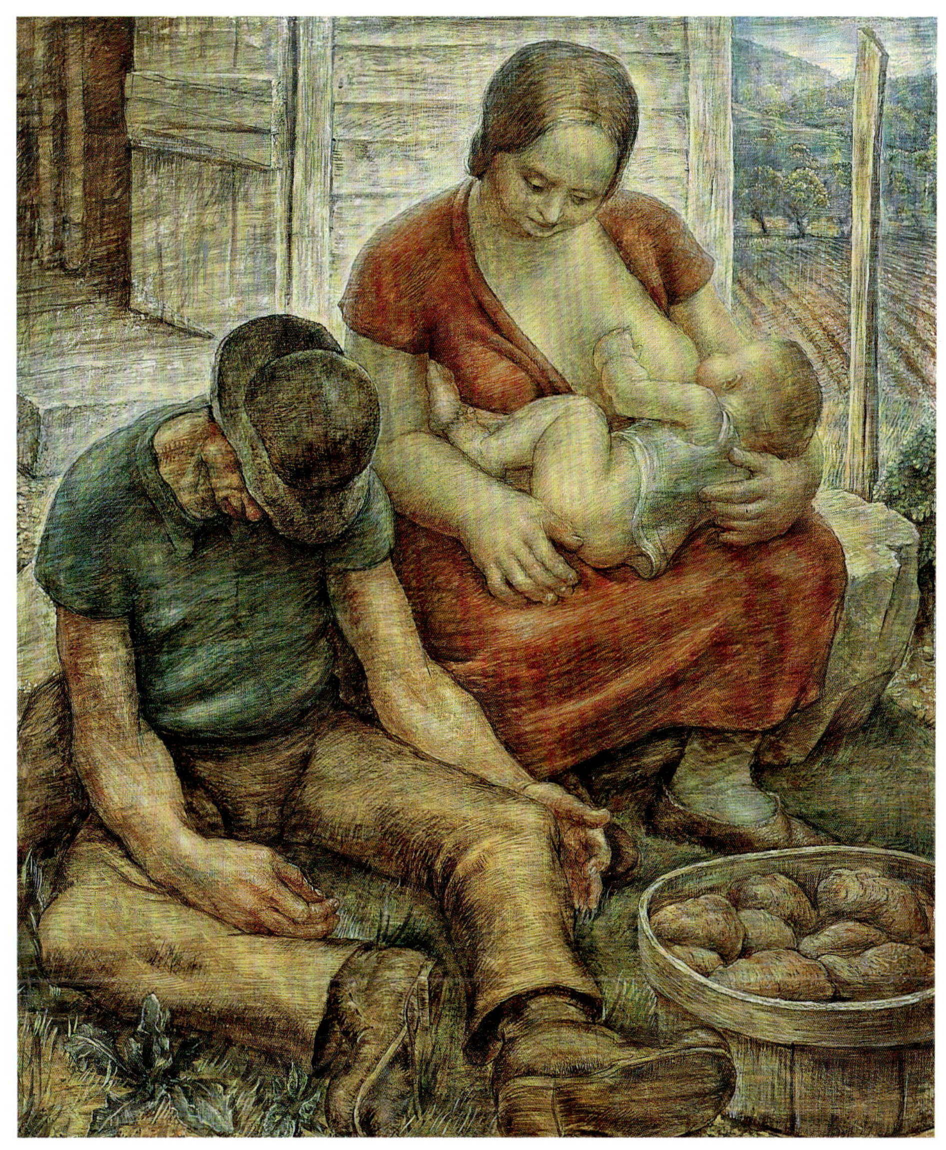

PLATE 33. *Rest,* 1938. Oil and tempera on masonite, 44 x 38″.

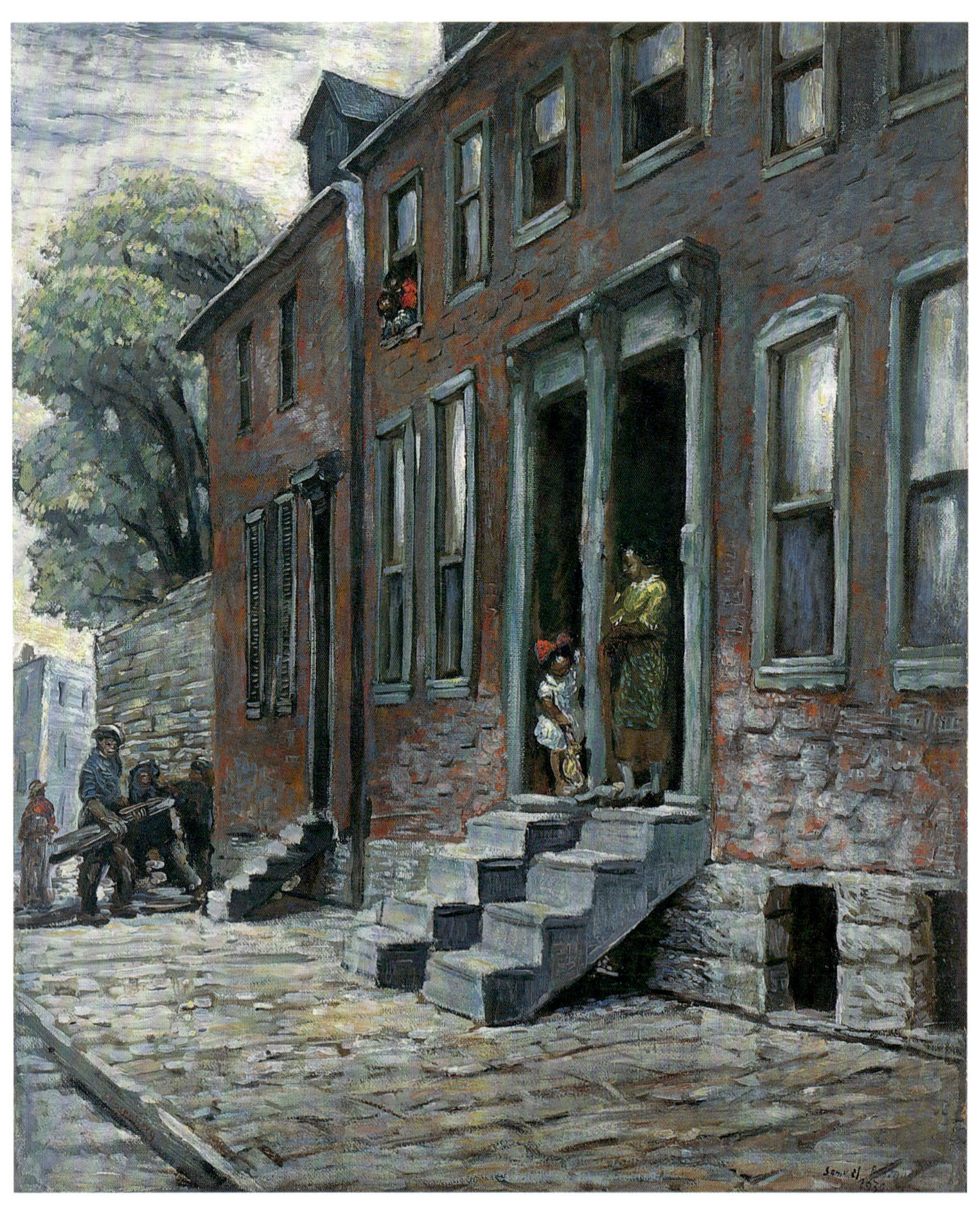

PLATE 34. *Doorways, Soho Street,* 1938. Oil on canvas, 36 x 30″.

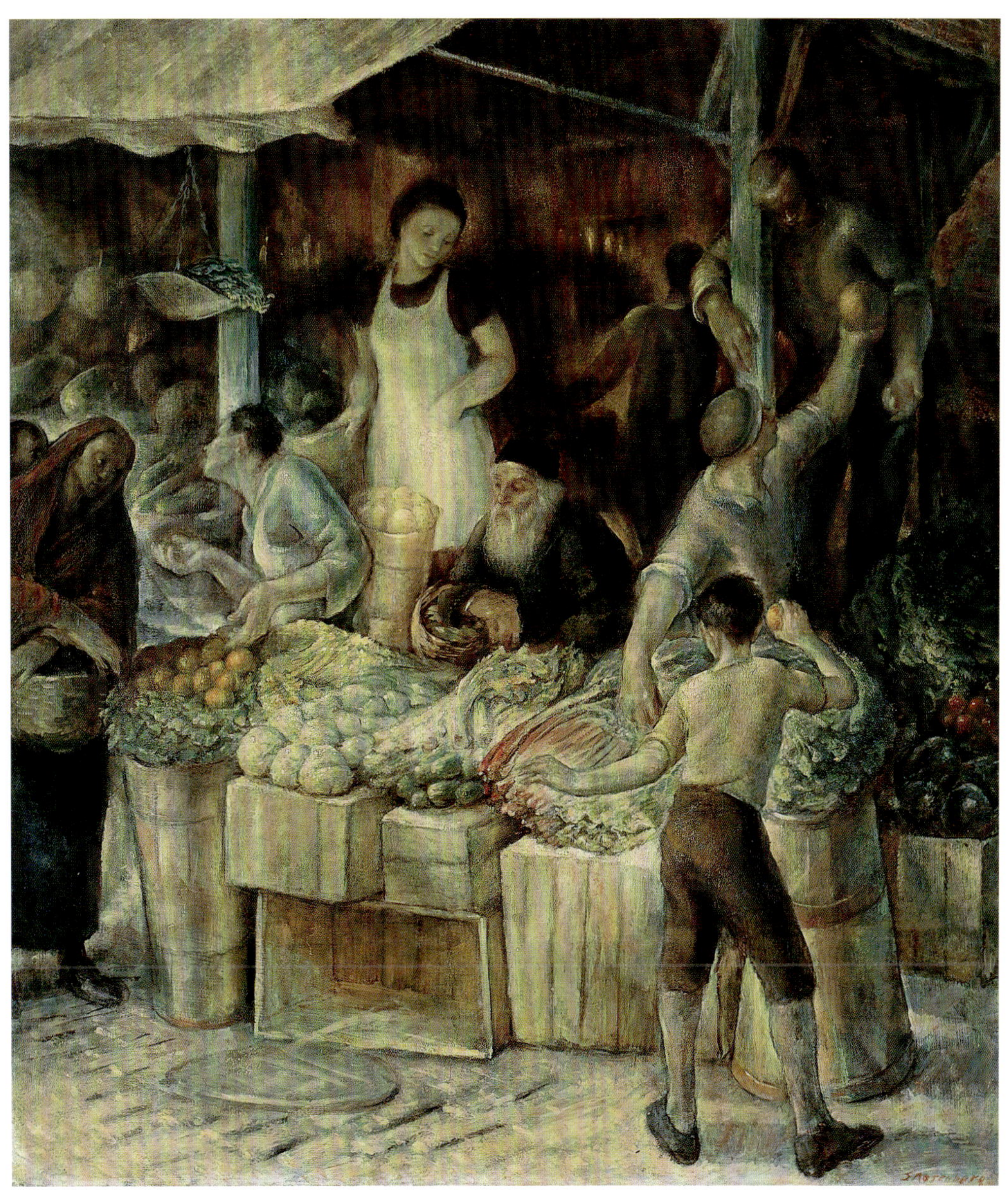

PLATE 35. *Fruit and Logan Street,* 1938. Oil and tempera on canvas, 54 x 48″.

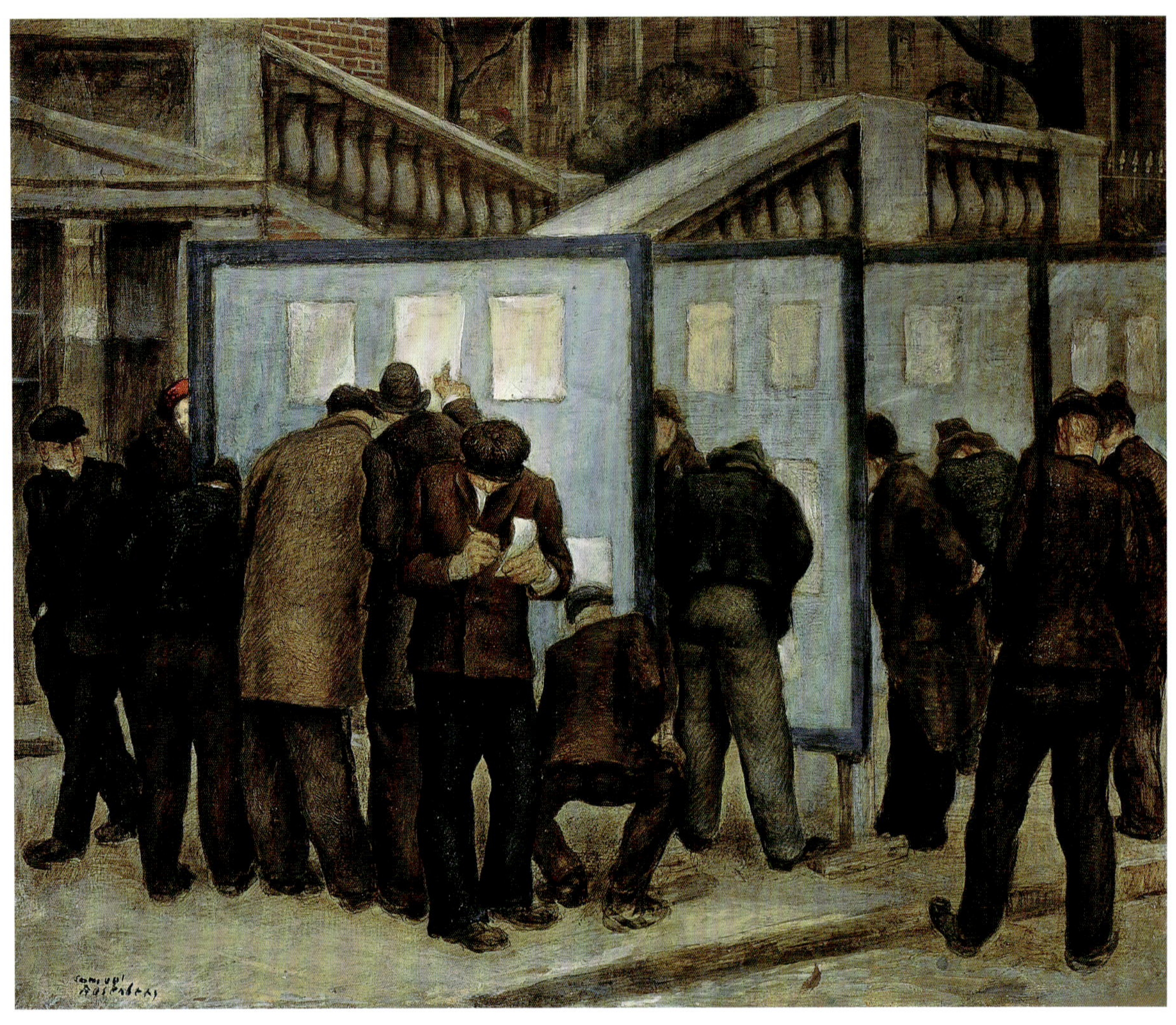

PLATE 36. *Job Lists*, 1938. Oil and tempera on masonite, 20 x 24″.

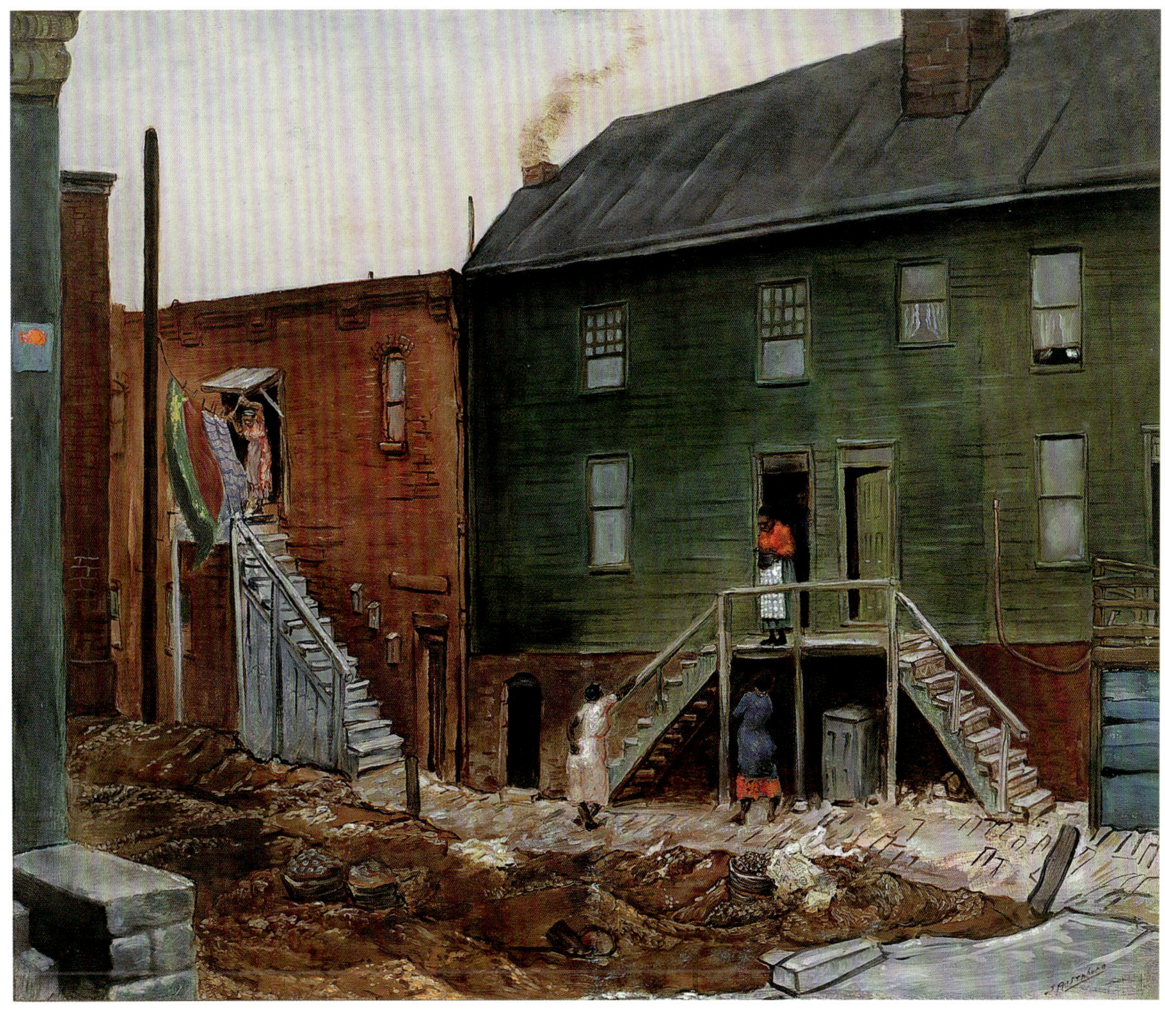

PLATE 37. *Mid-Morning Conversation,* 1939. Oil on masonite, 25 x 30″.

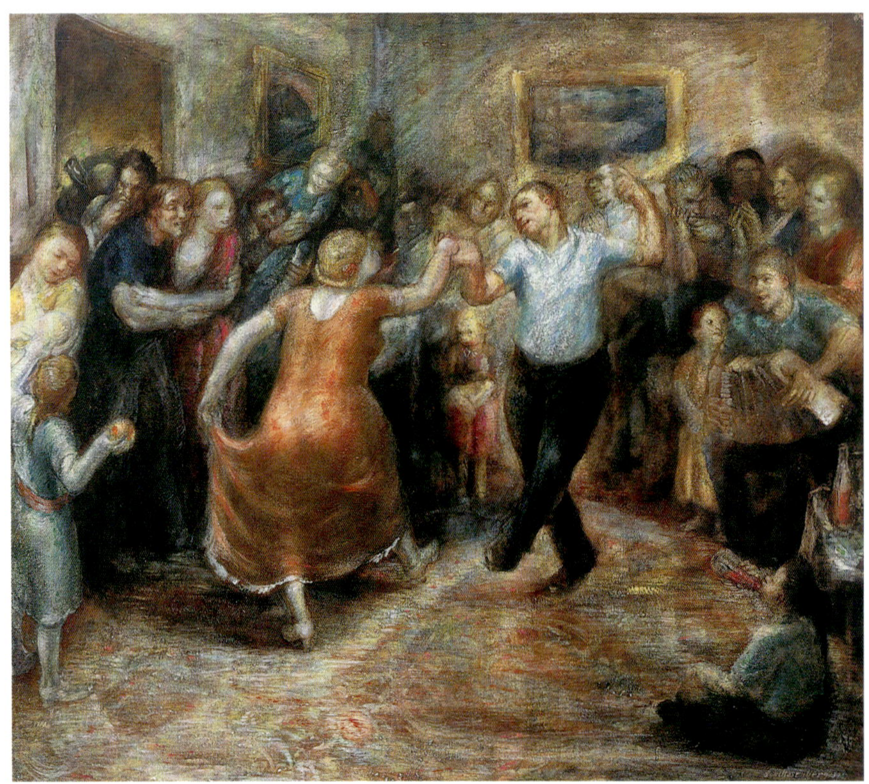

PLATE 38. *The Dance,* 1939. Oil on masonite, 42 x 48″.

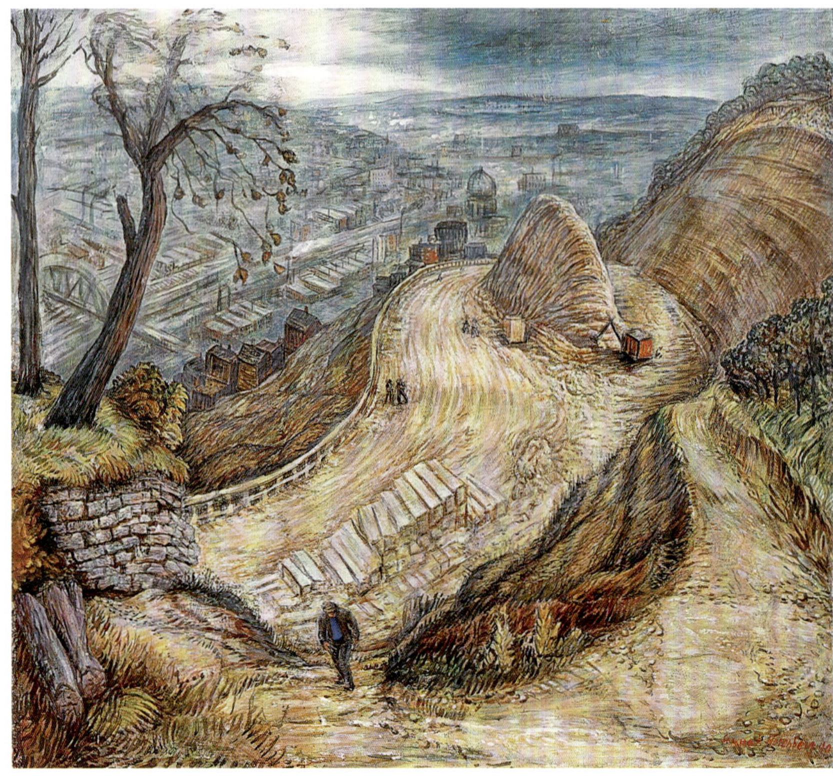

PLATE 39. *Bigelow Boulevard Under Construction,* 1940. Oil and tempera on masonite, 36 x 40″.

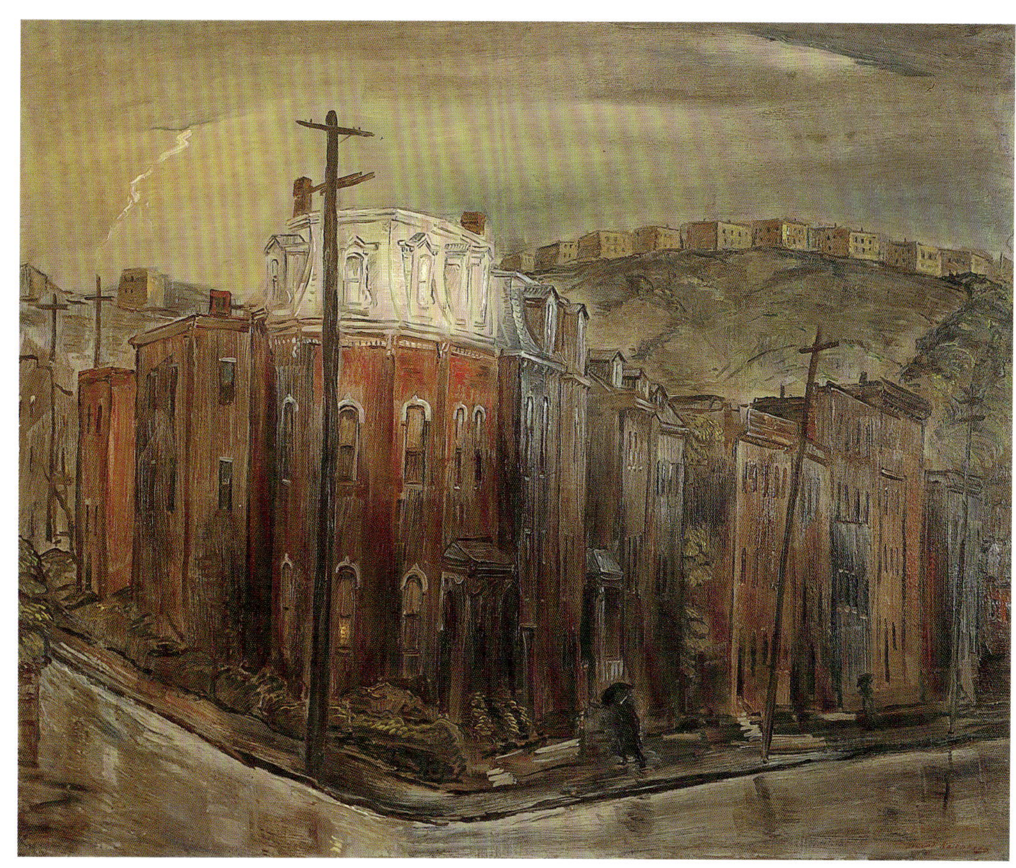

PLATE 40.
Roof Over Their Heads, 1940.
Oil on masonite,
46 x 52″.

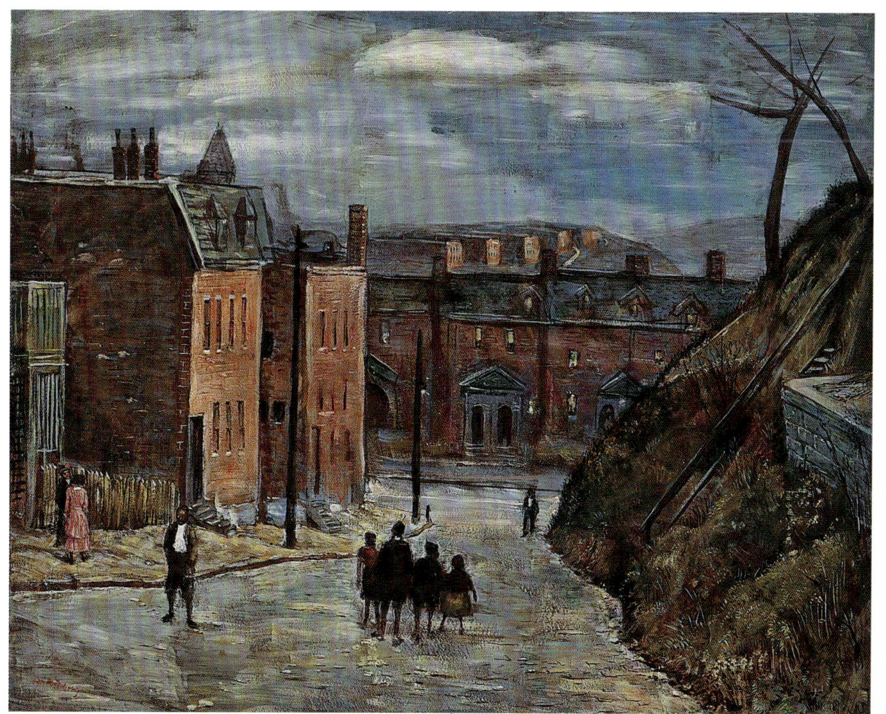

PLATE 41.
Evening Promenade, 1941. Oil on masonite,
24 x 30″.

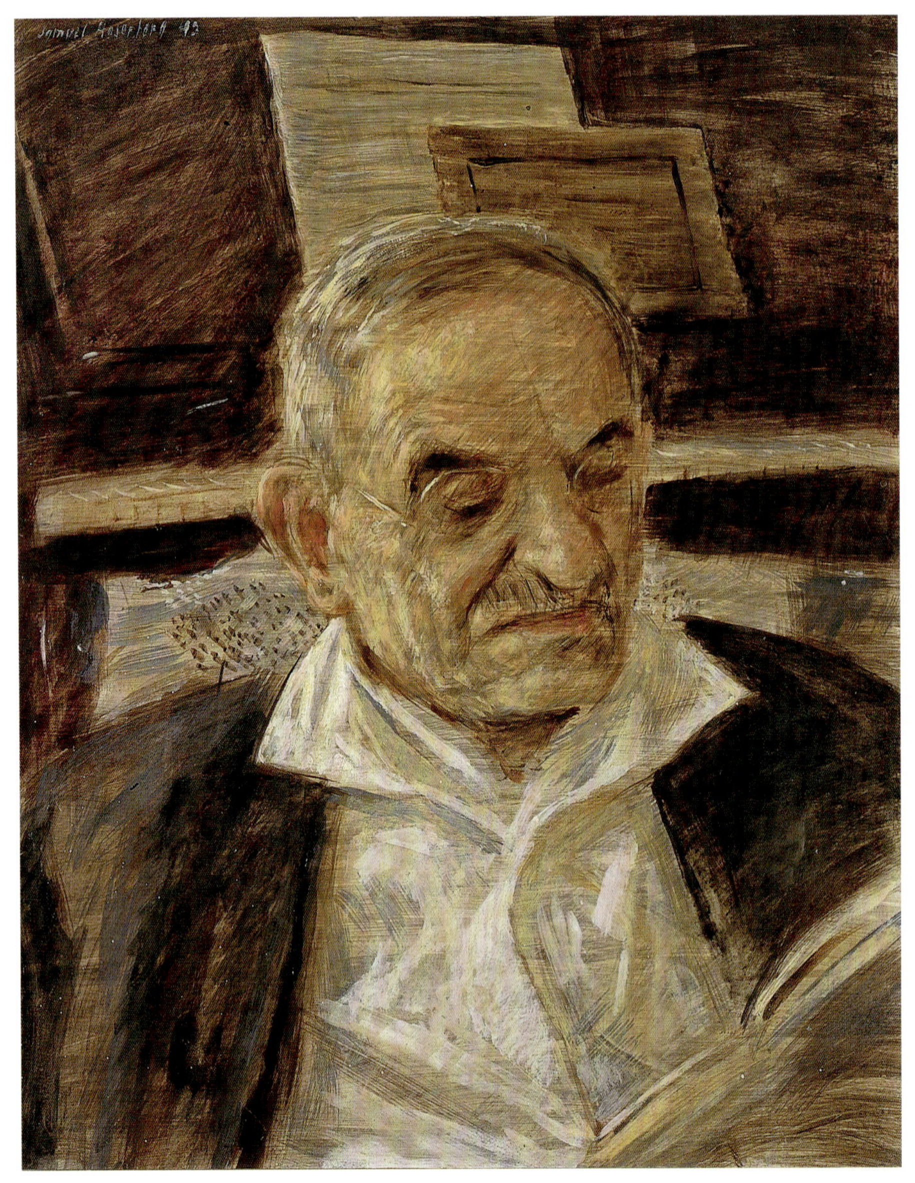

PLATE 42. *Libbie's Father (Joseph Levin)*, 1942. Oil on masonite, 20 x 16″.

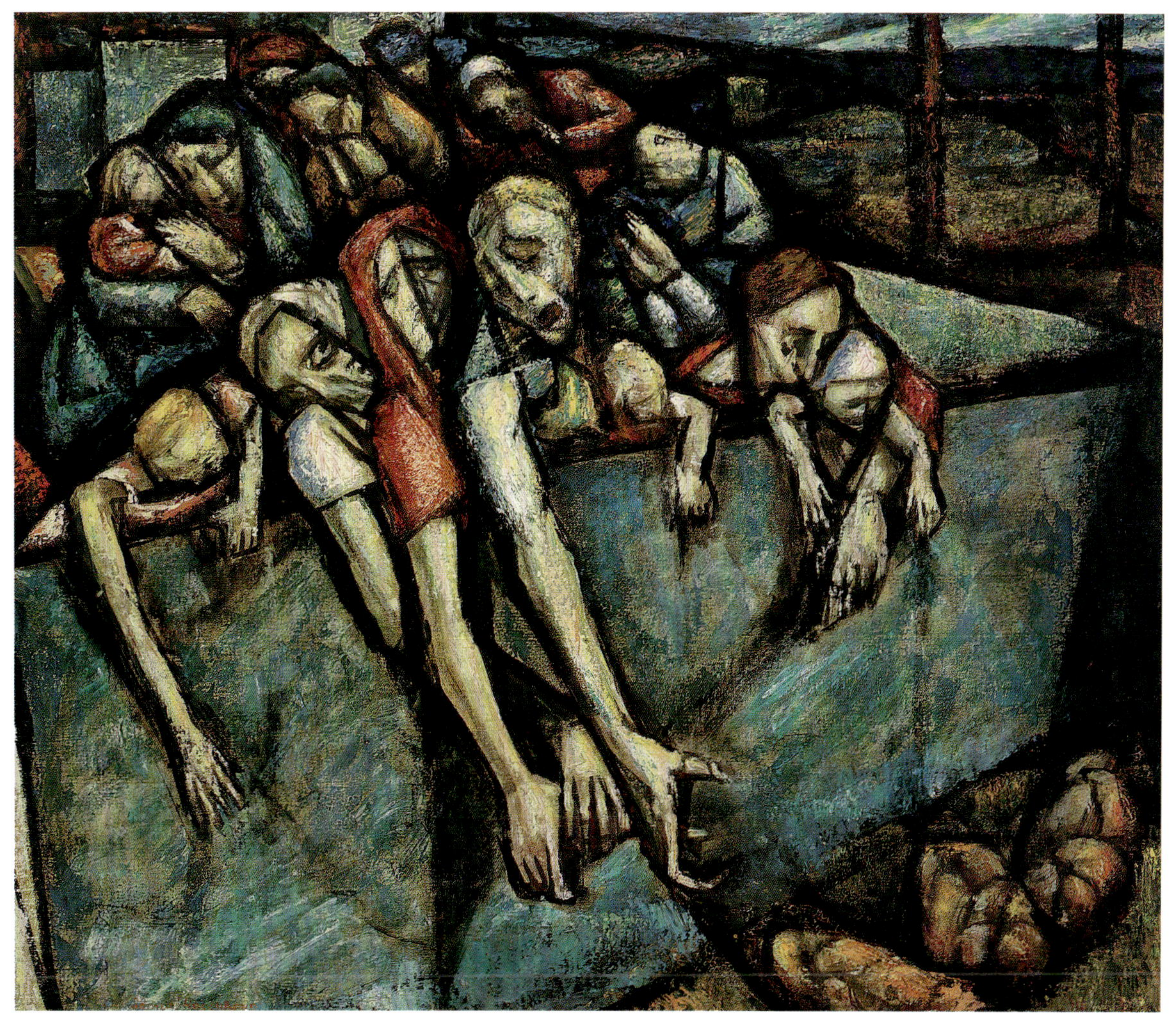

PLATE 43. *Bread No. 2,* 1942. Oil and tempera on canvas, 31 x 37″.

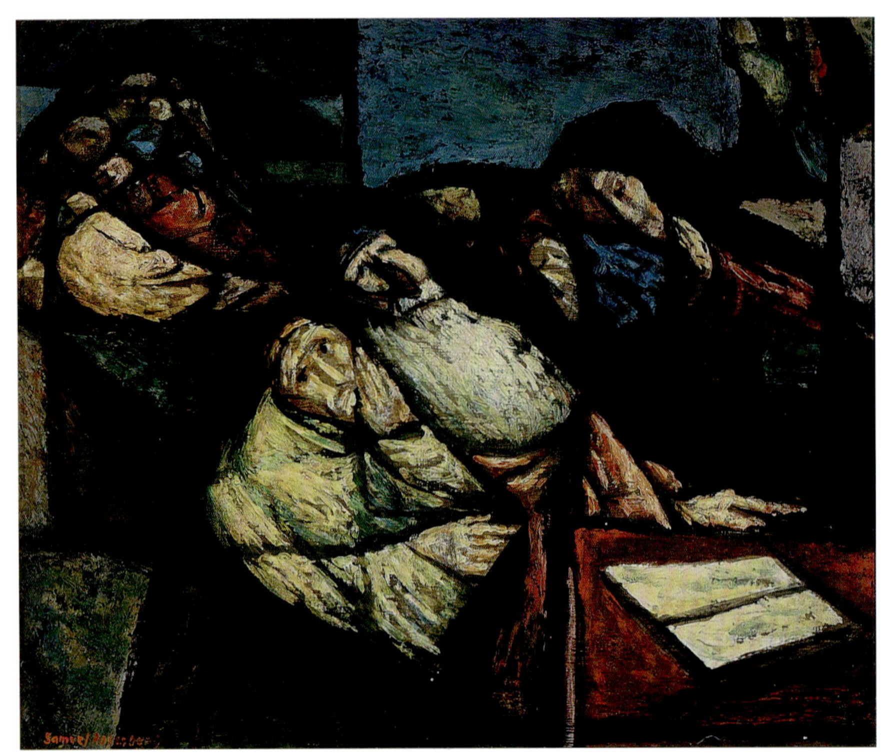

PLATE 44.
Whither? No. 1, 1943.
Oil on masonite,
20 x 24″.

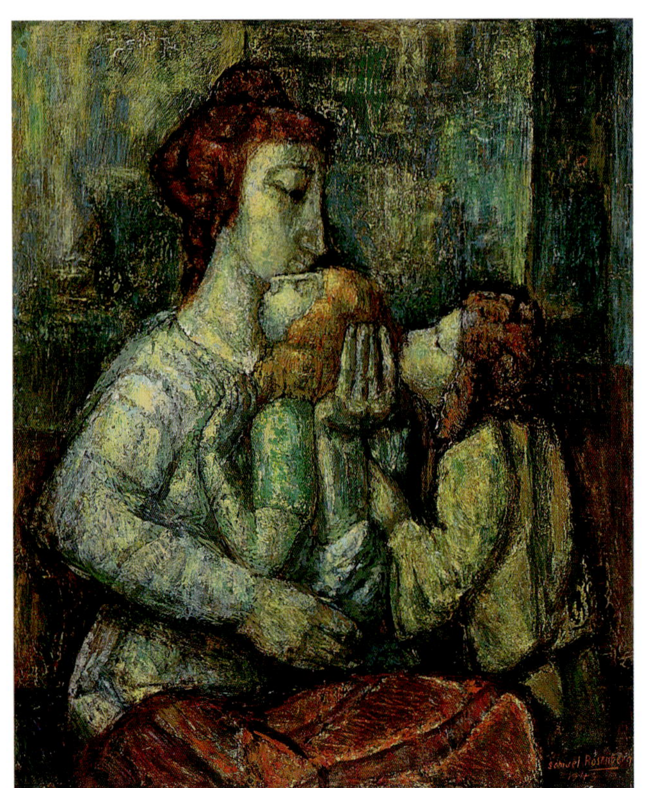

PLATE 45.
Implicitness, 1943.
Oil on masonite,
30 x 25″.

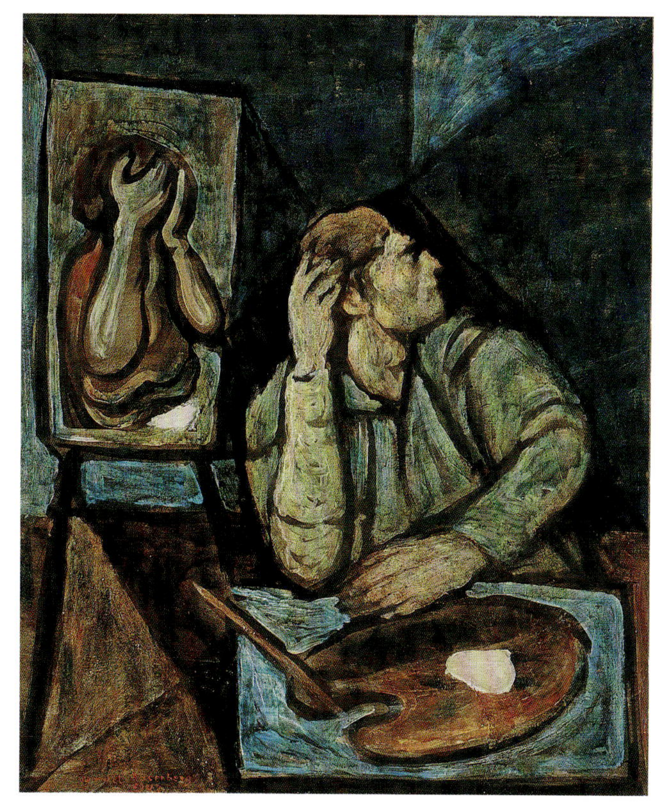

PLATE 46. *Conflict,* 1943.
Oil on masonite, 24 x 20″.

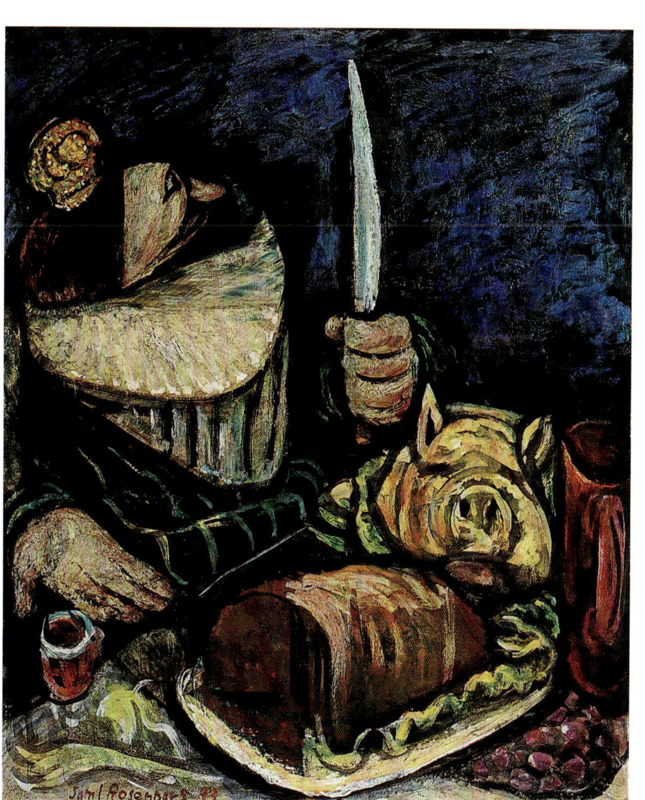

PLATE 47. *Some Have Meat,*
1943. Oil and tempera on
masonite, 24 x 20″.

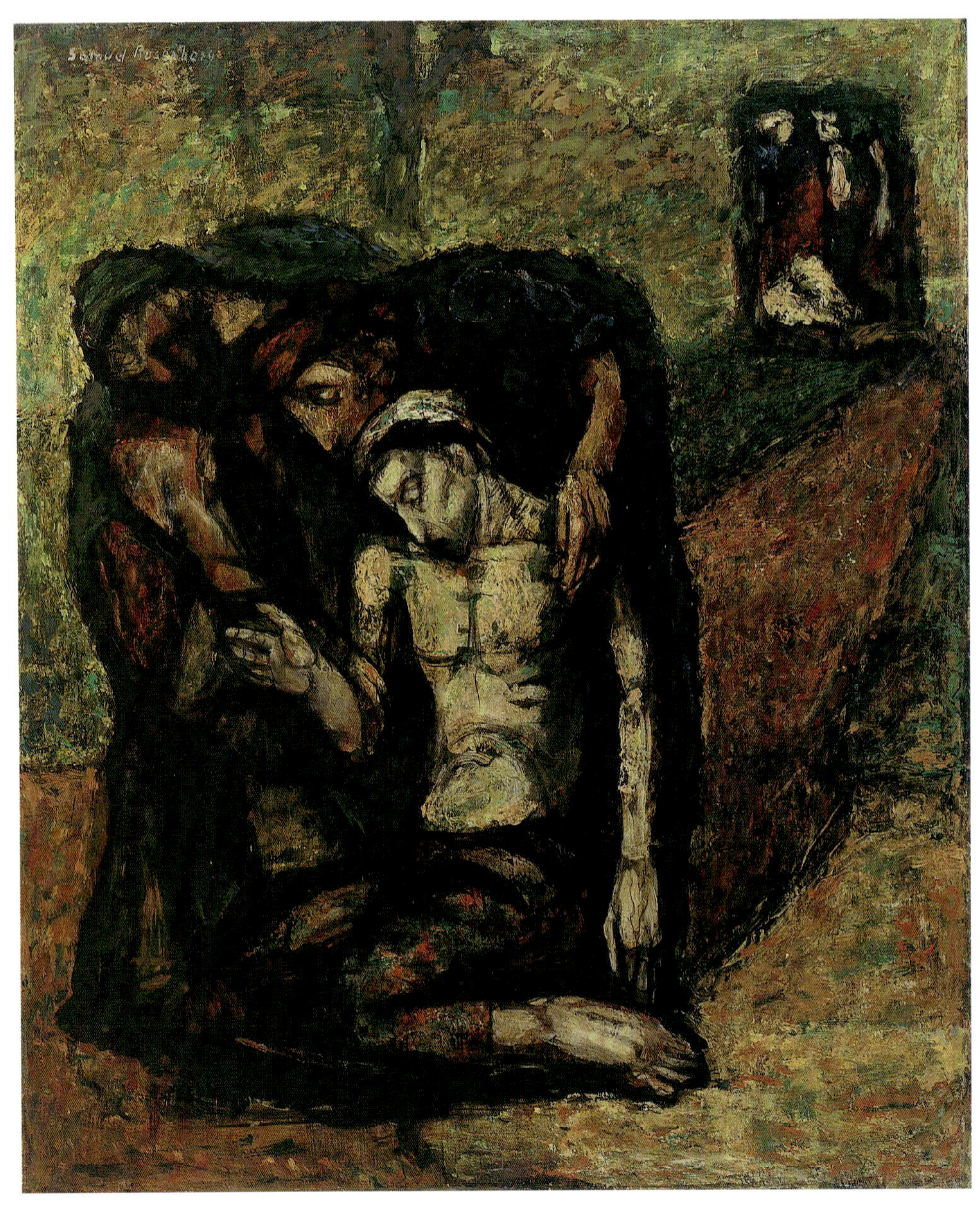

PLATE 48. *My Brother,* 1943. Oil and tempera on masonite, 24 x 20″.

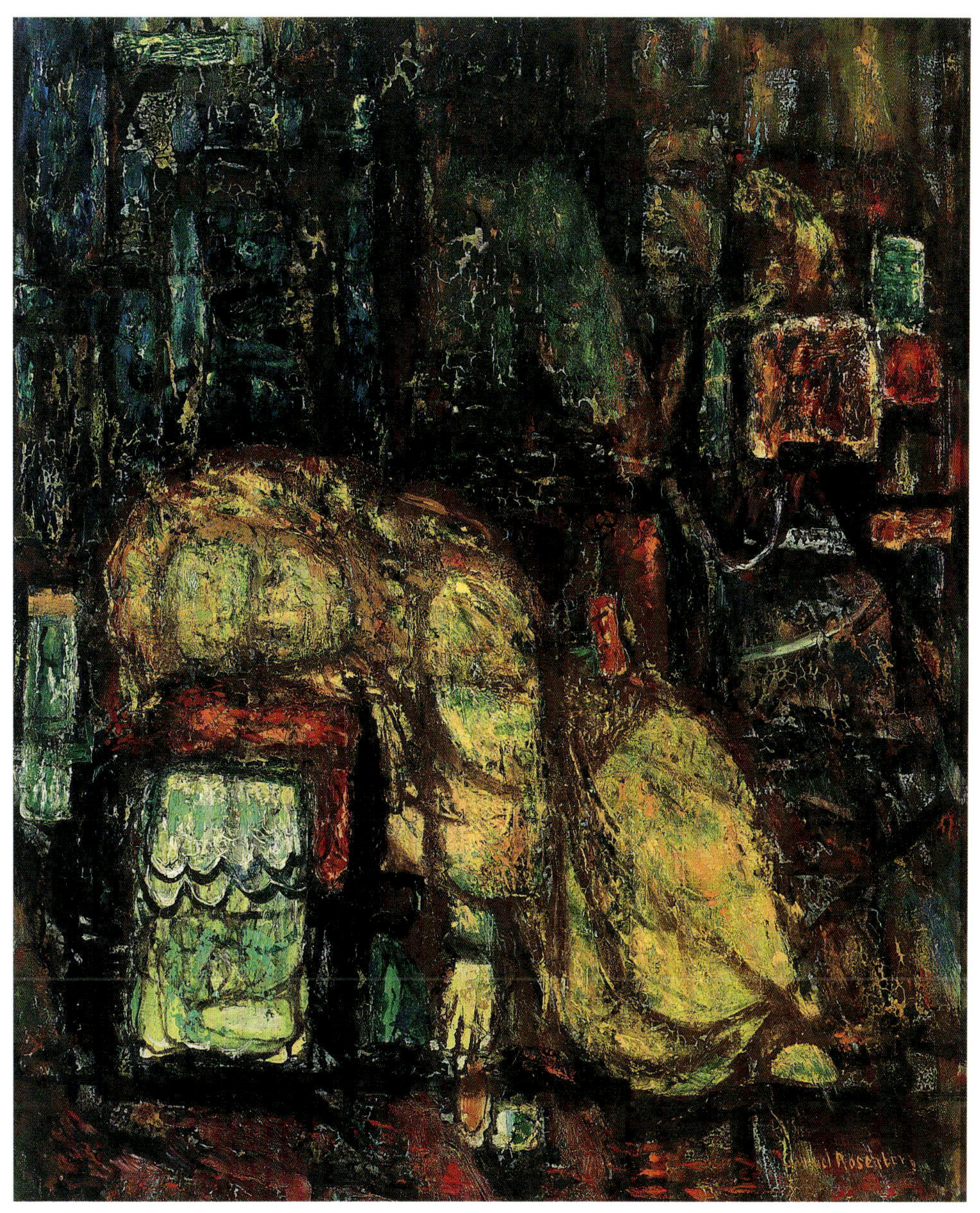

PLATE 49. *Asleep*, 1944. Oil on masonite, 24 x 20″.

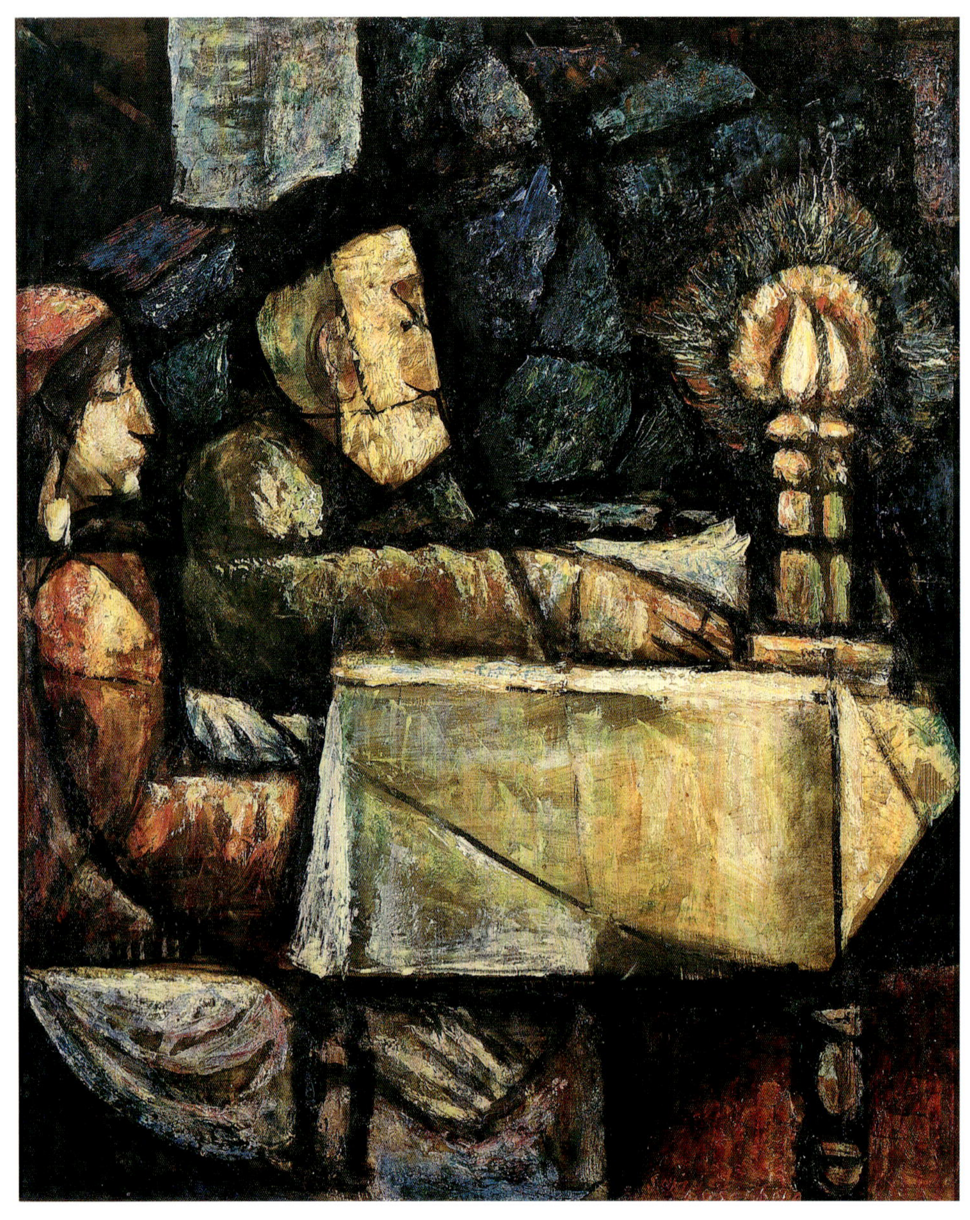

PLATE 50. *Patriarch,* 1944. Oil and tempera on masonite, 24 x 20″.

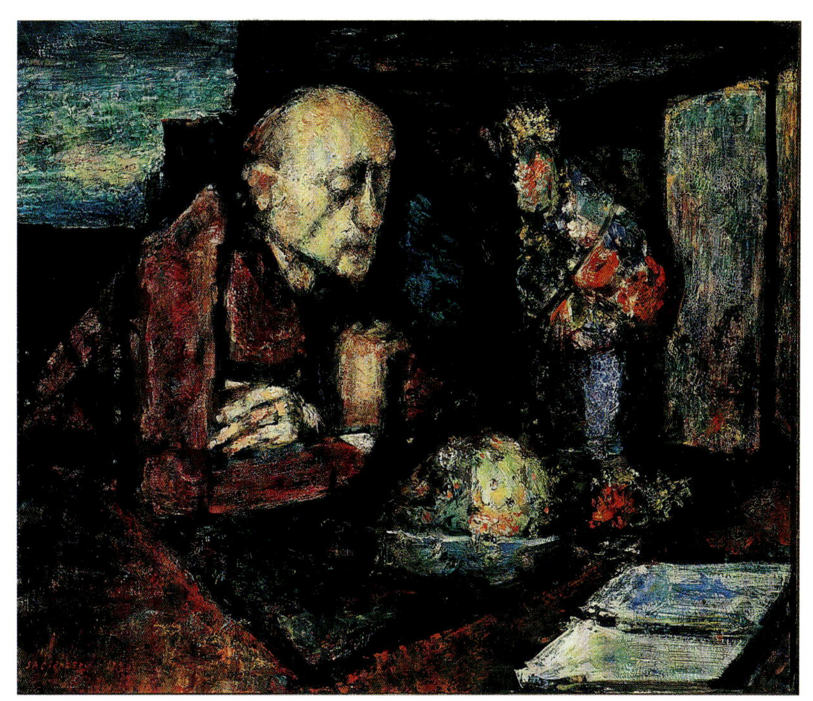

PLATE 51. *The Connoisseur (The Skull)*, 1944. Oil and tempera on masonite, 25 x 30″.

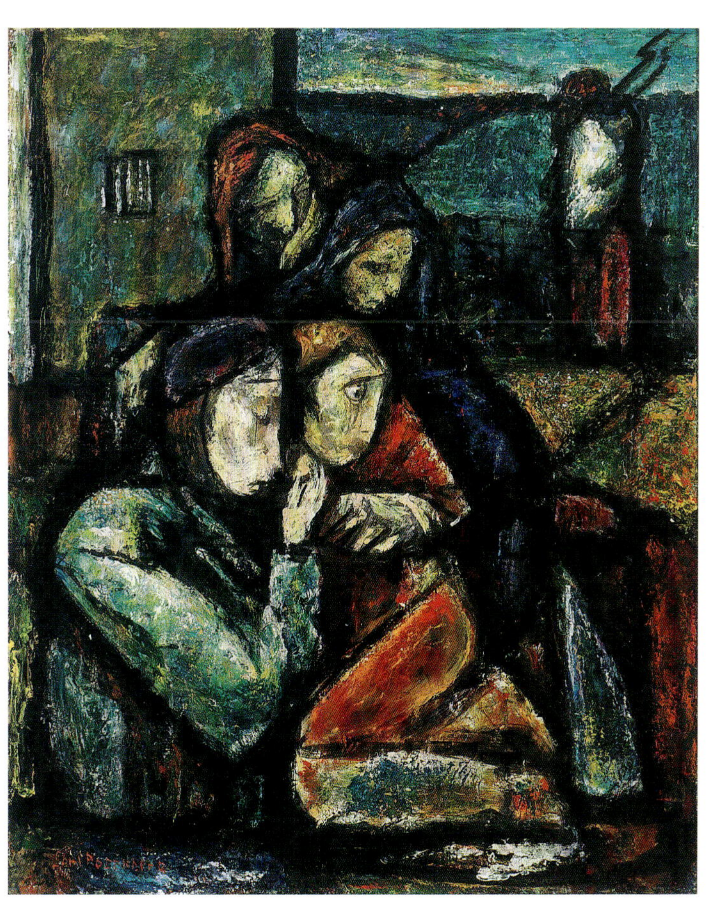

PLATE 52. *Fear,* 1944. Oil and tempera on masonite, 24 x 20″.

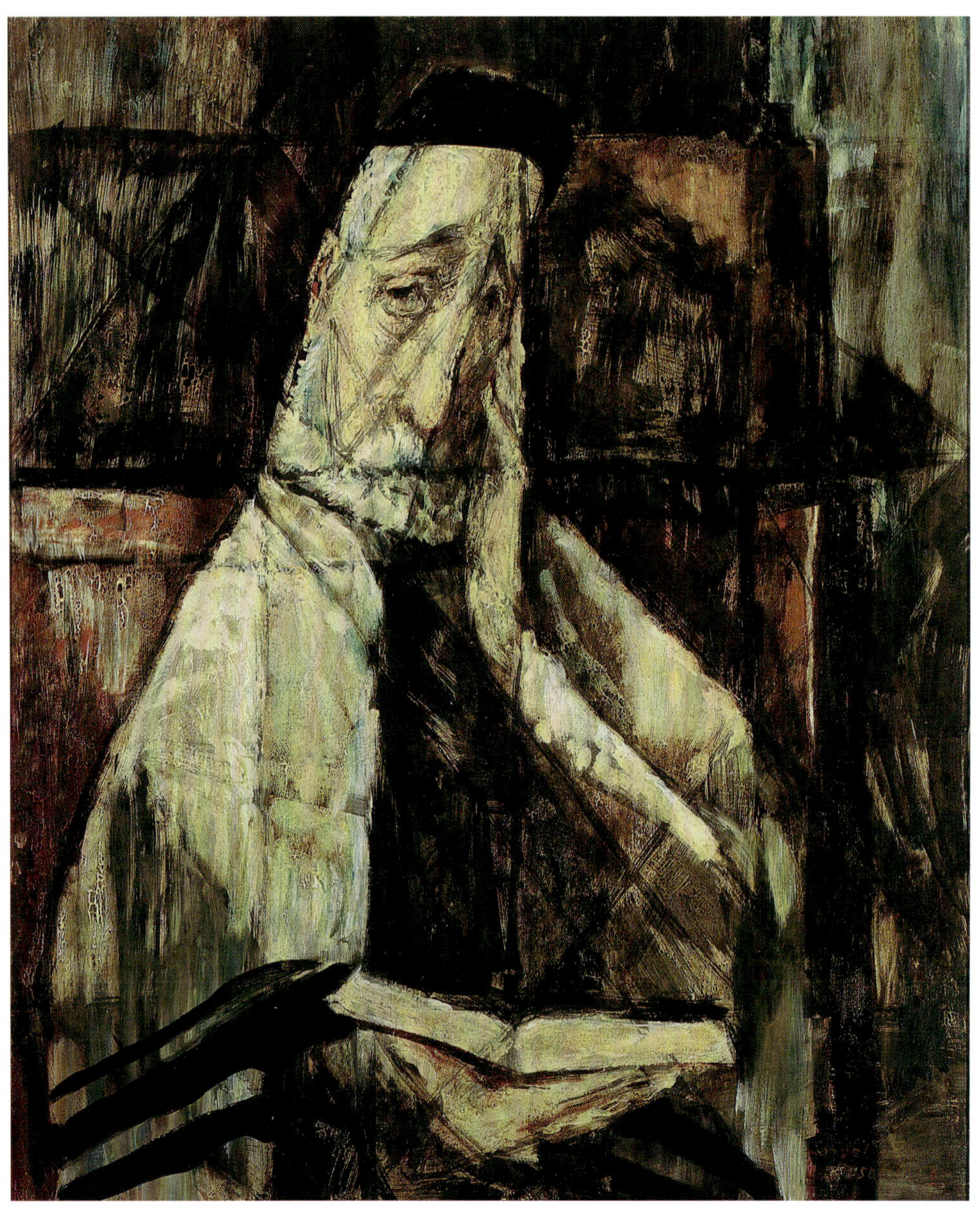

PLATE 53. *Israel,* 1945. Oil on masonite, 30 x 25″.

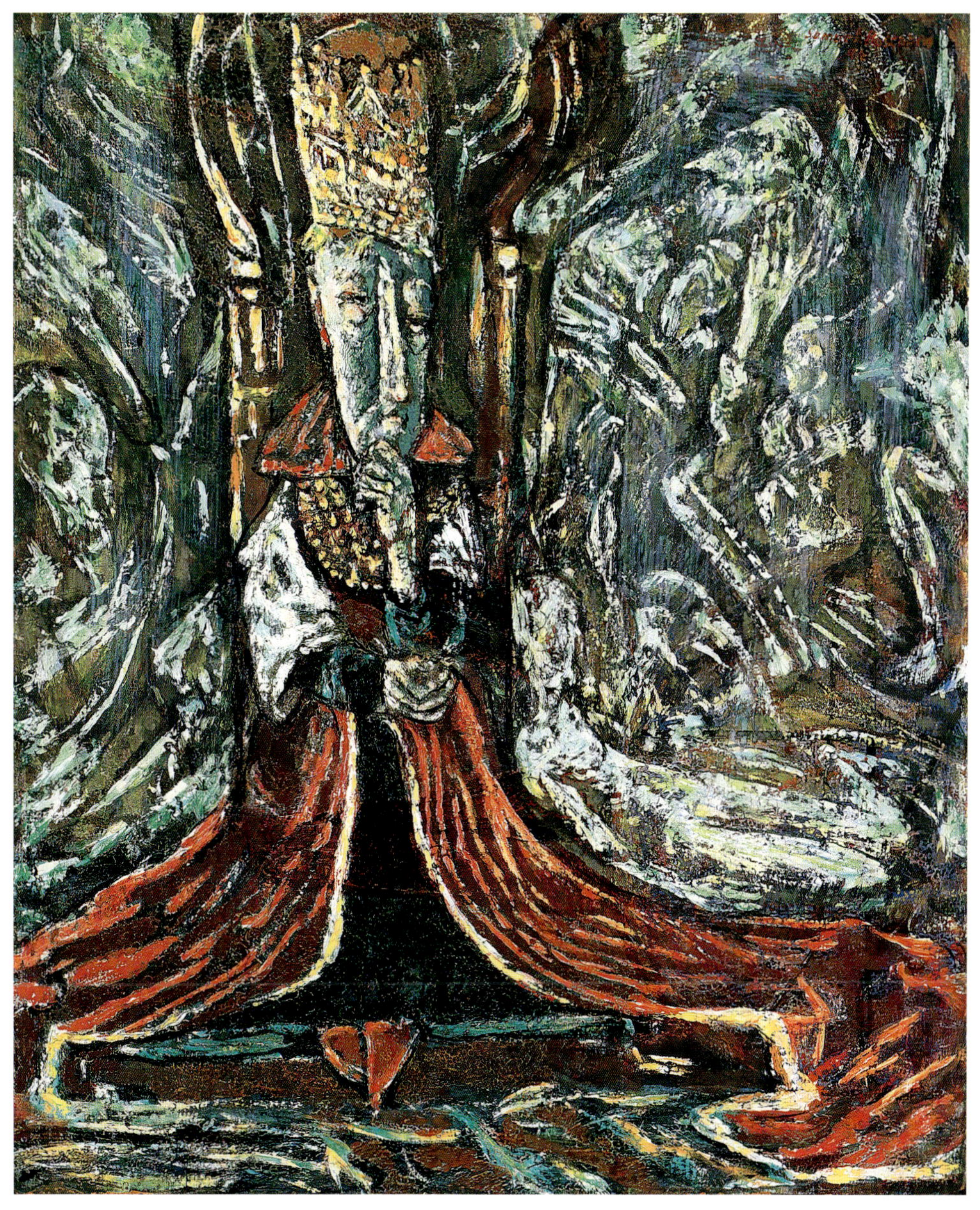

PLATE 54. *A King,* 1946. Oil and tempera on masonite, 30 x 25″.

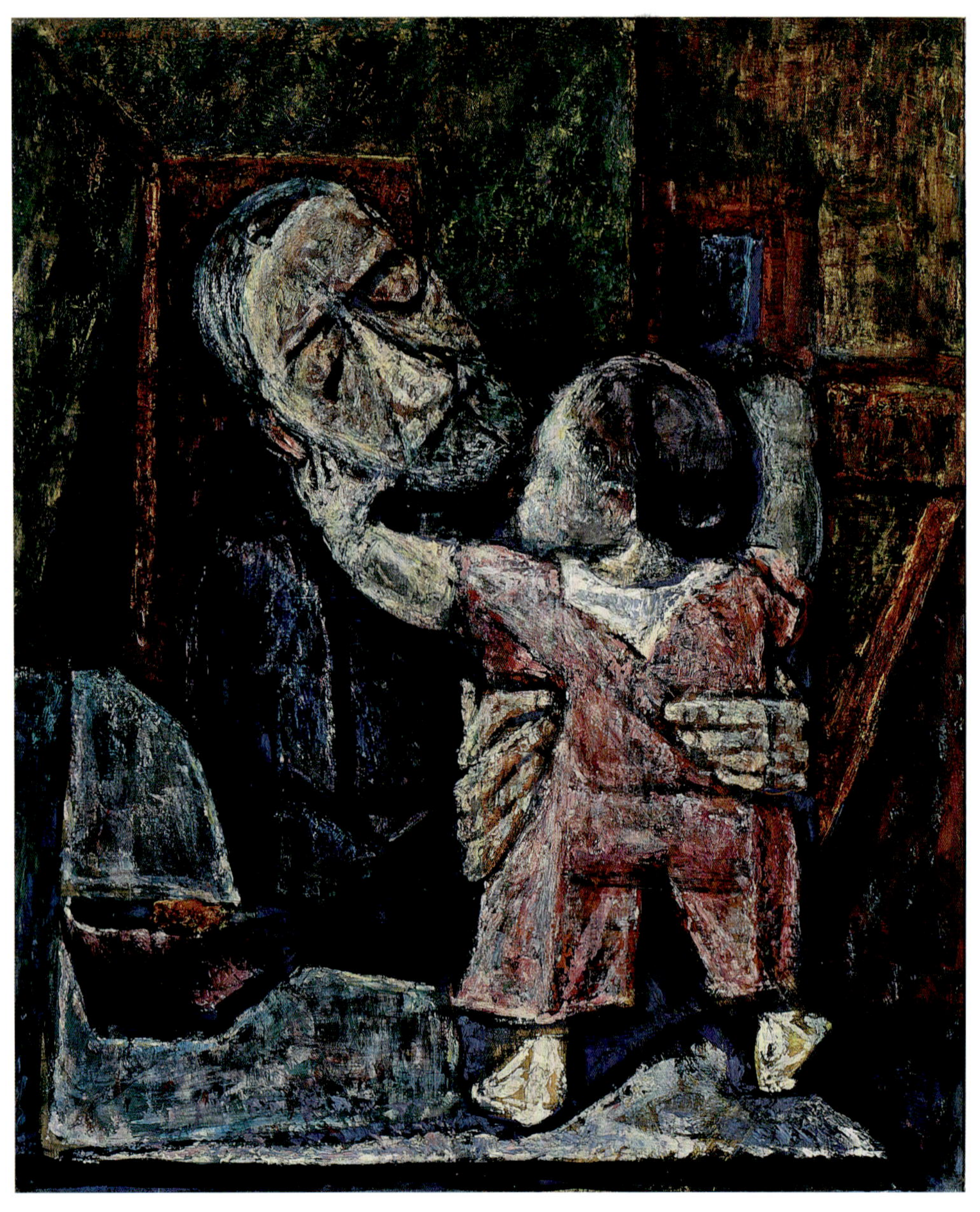

PLATE 55. *The Grandfather No. 2*, 1948. Oil on masonite, 30 x 25″.

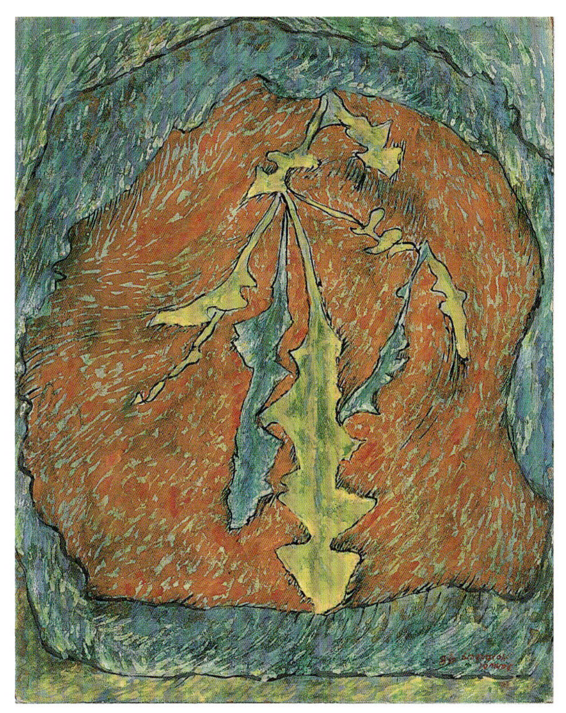

PLATE 56. *The Leaf,* 1948. Oil on masonite, 20 x 16″.

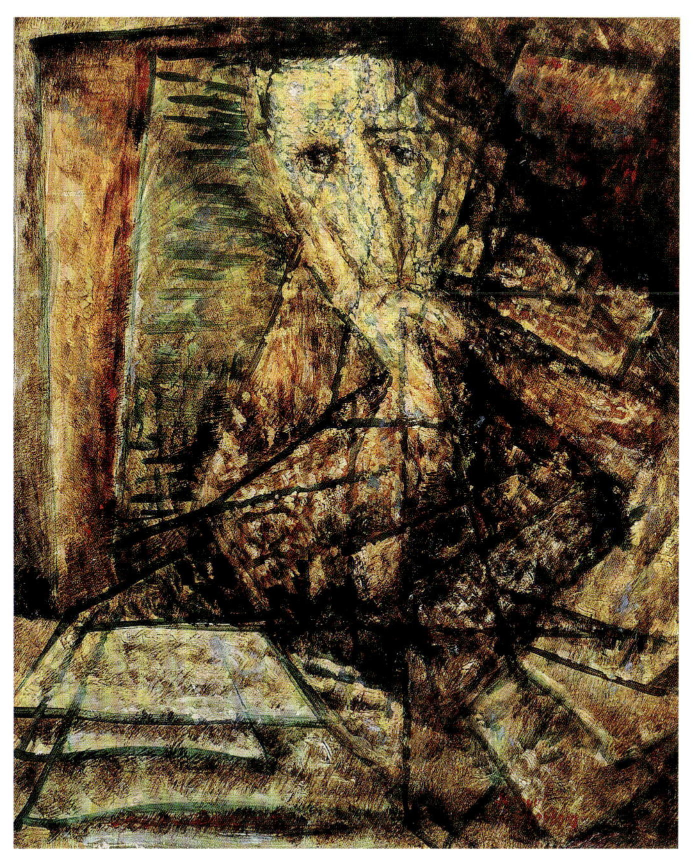

PLATE 57. *The Book,* 1949. Oil on canvas, 30 x 25″.

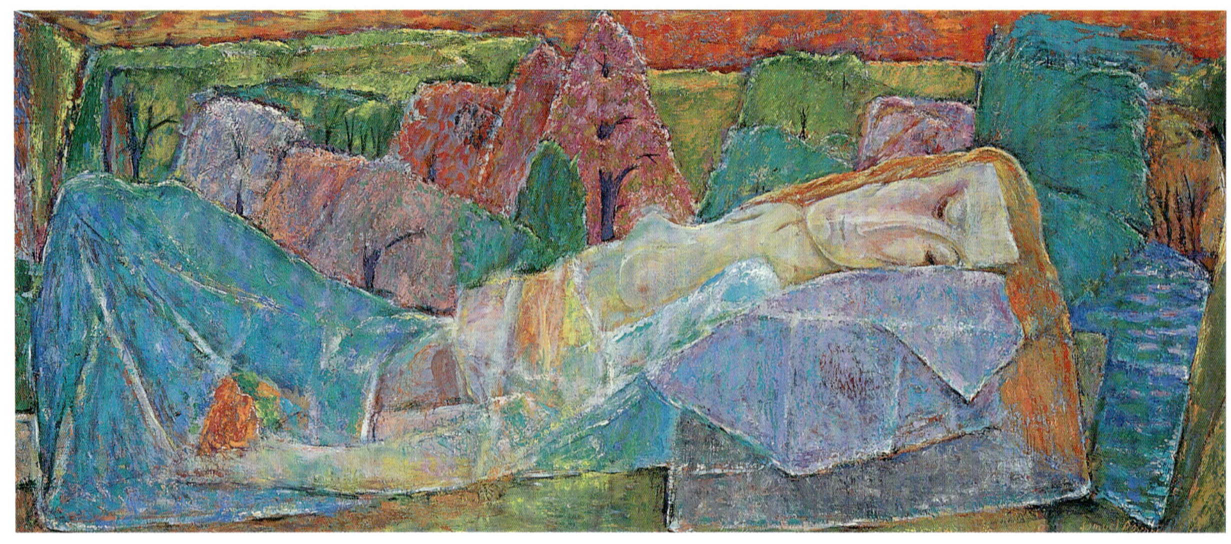

PLATE 58. *Awakening*, 1949. Oil on canvas, 20 x 46″.

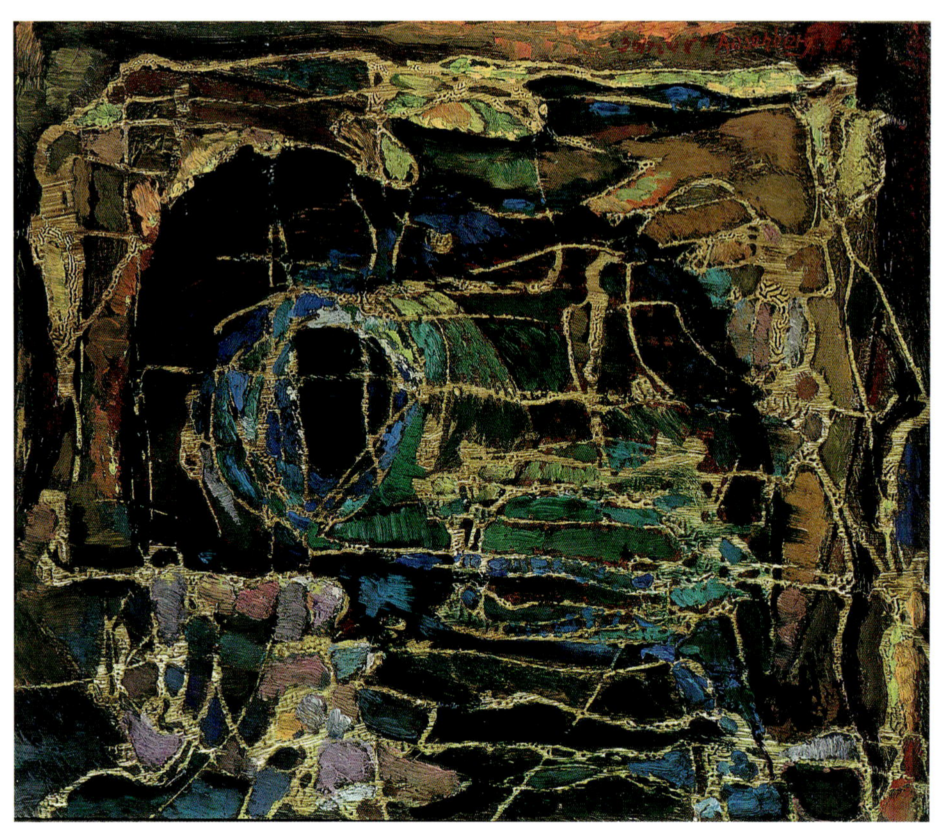

PLATE 59. *Untitled Composition 1949 No. 1*, 1949. Oil on masonite, 10 x 12″.

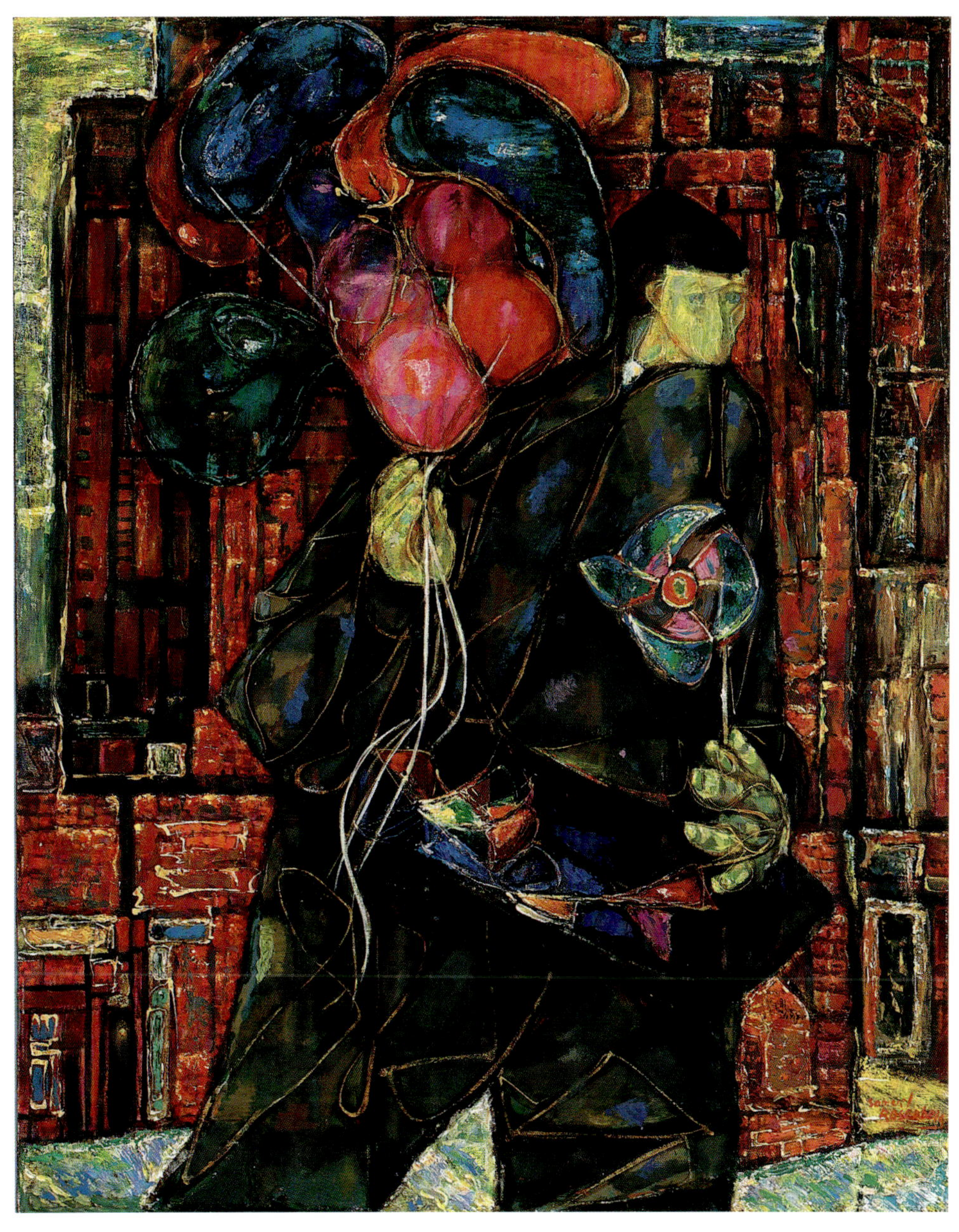

PLATE 60. *Balloon Man No. 2,* 1950. Oil on canvas, 46 x 36″.

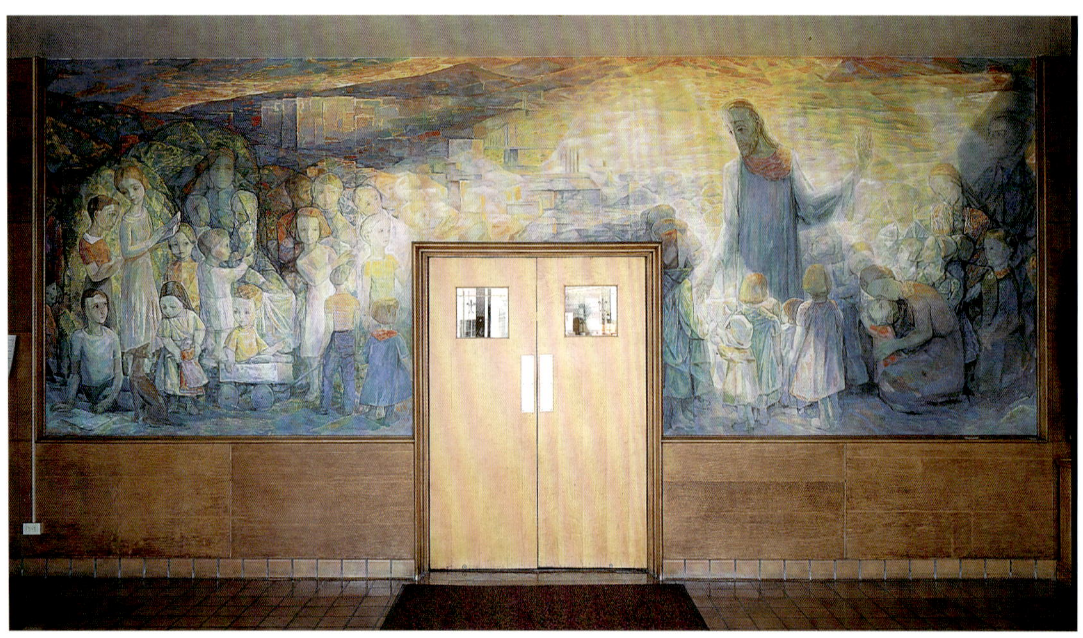

PLATE 61. *Christ Teaching* (mural), 1951–52. Oil on canvas, 120 x 228″.

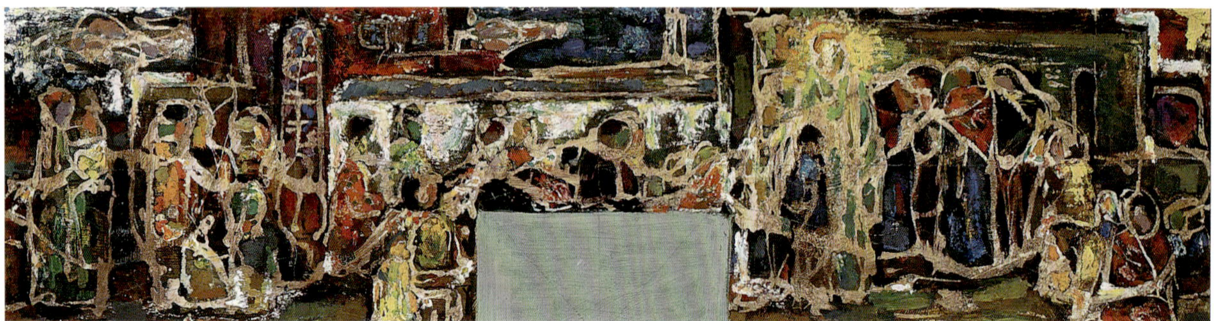

PLATE 62. *Christ Teaching* (sketch #2 in preparation for cartoon for mural), 1952. Oil on canvas, 8 x 30″.

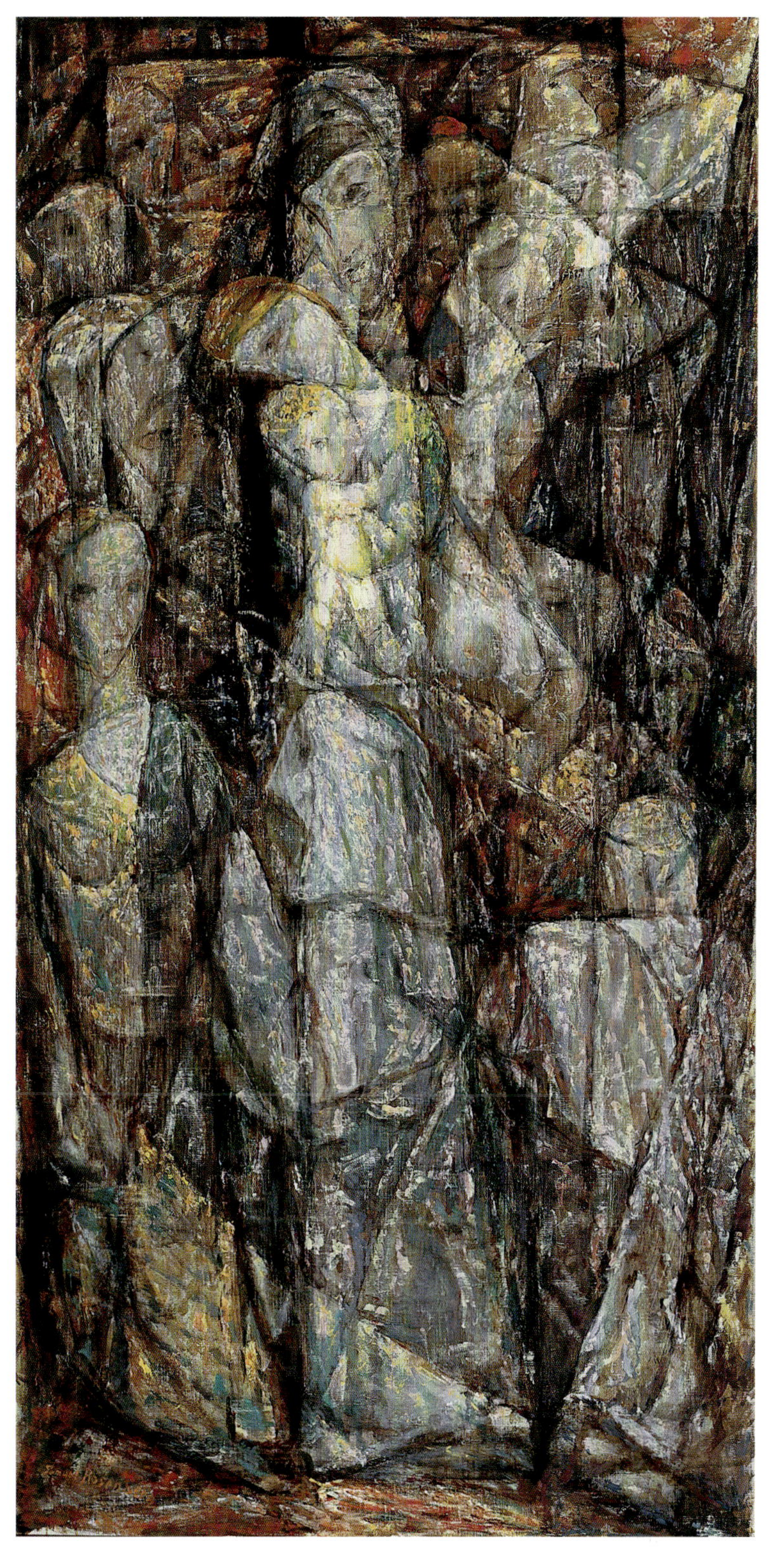

PLATE 63. *Time Echoes,* 1952. Oil on canvas, 72 x 36″.

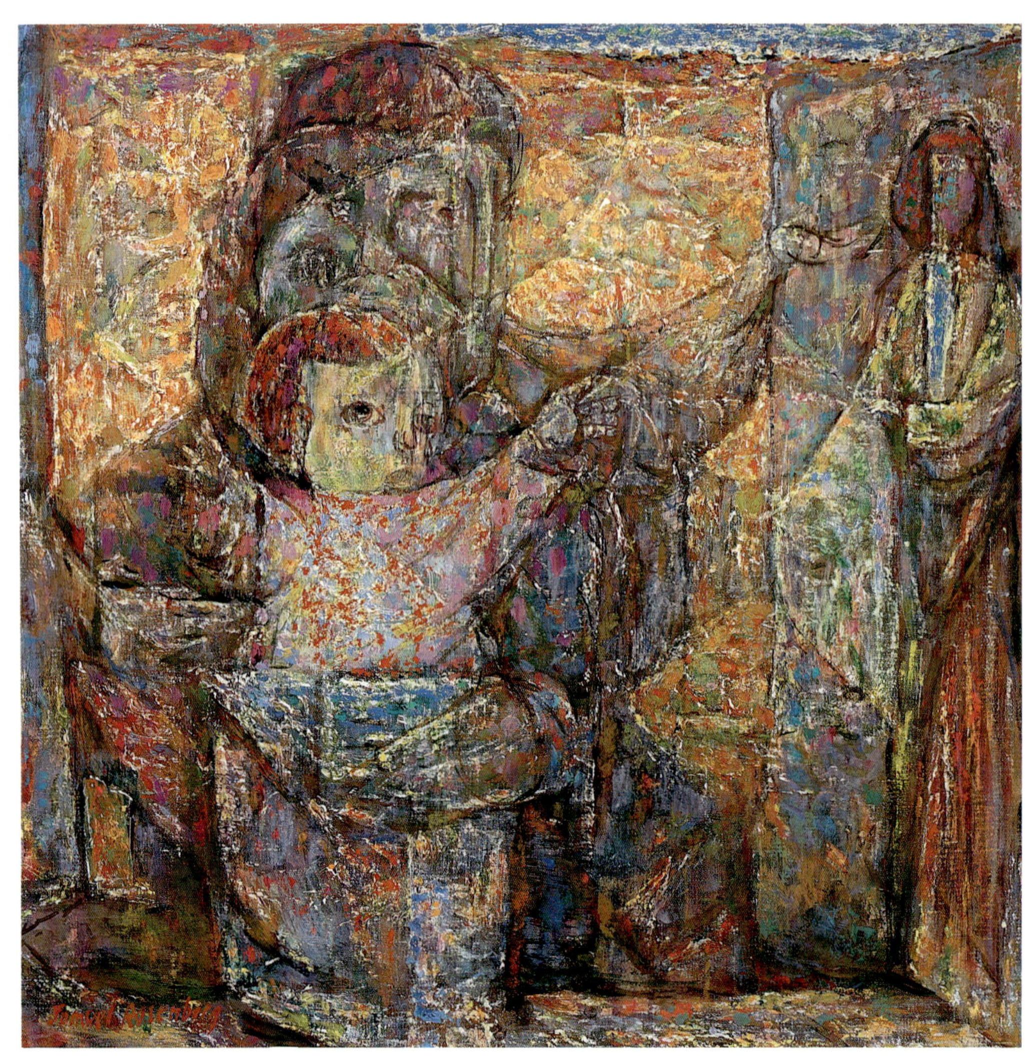

PLATE 64. *Emergence No. 2*, 1953. Oil on canvas, 30 x 30″.

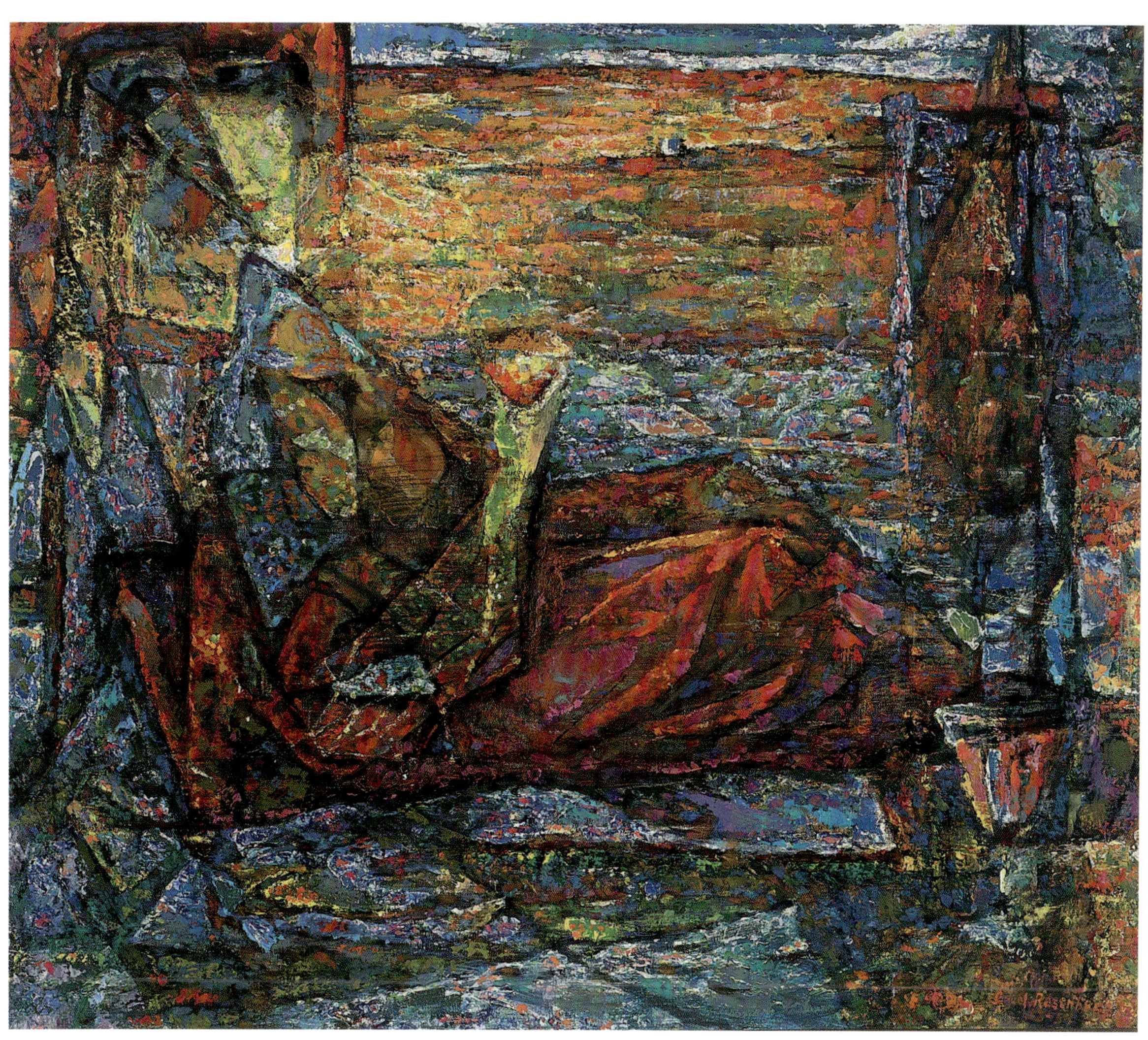

PLATE 65. *Horizons,* 1954. Oil on canvas, 36 x 40″.

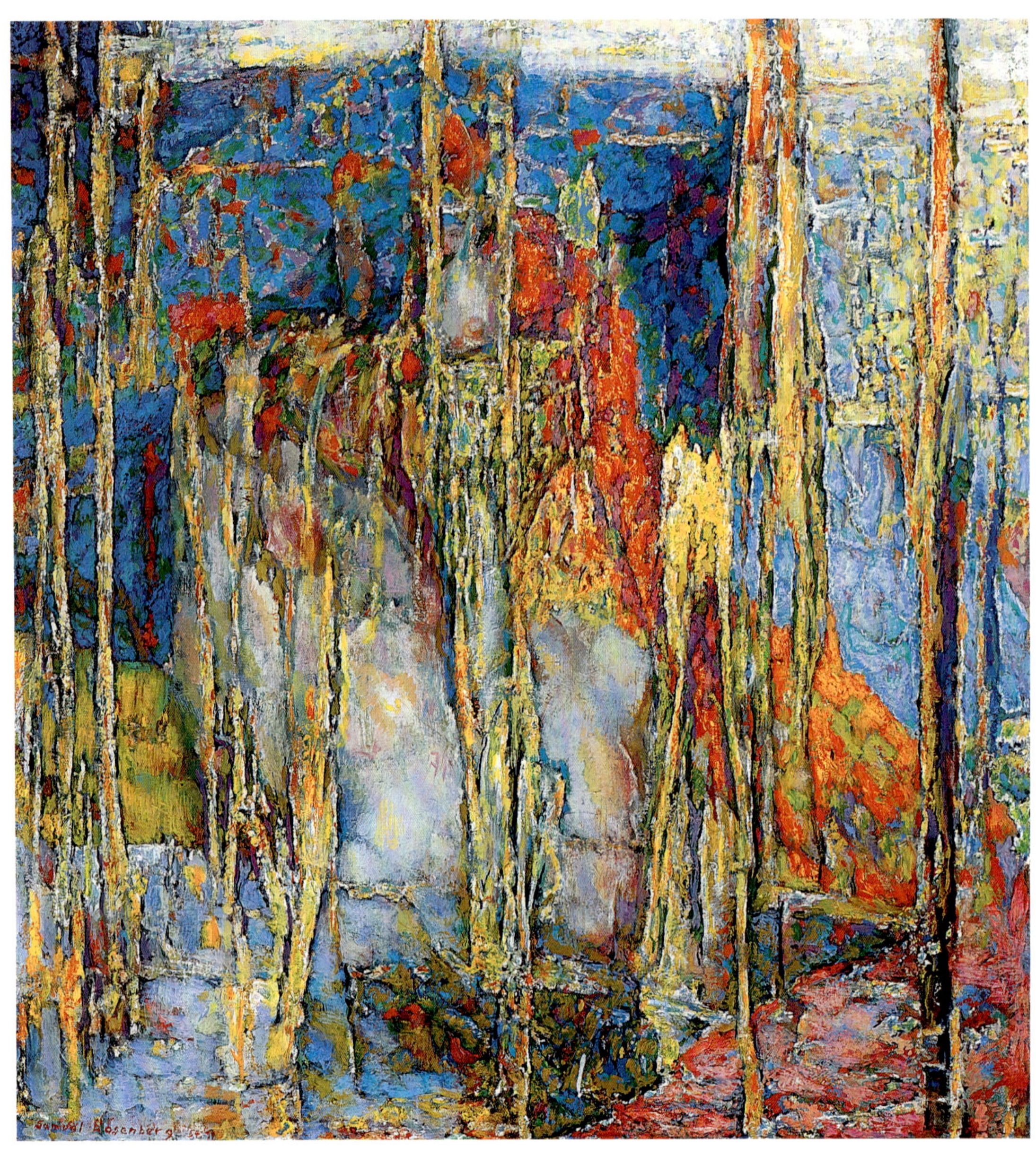

PLATE 66. *Fleeting Substance,* 1954–1971. Oil on canvas, 50 x 42″.

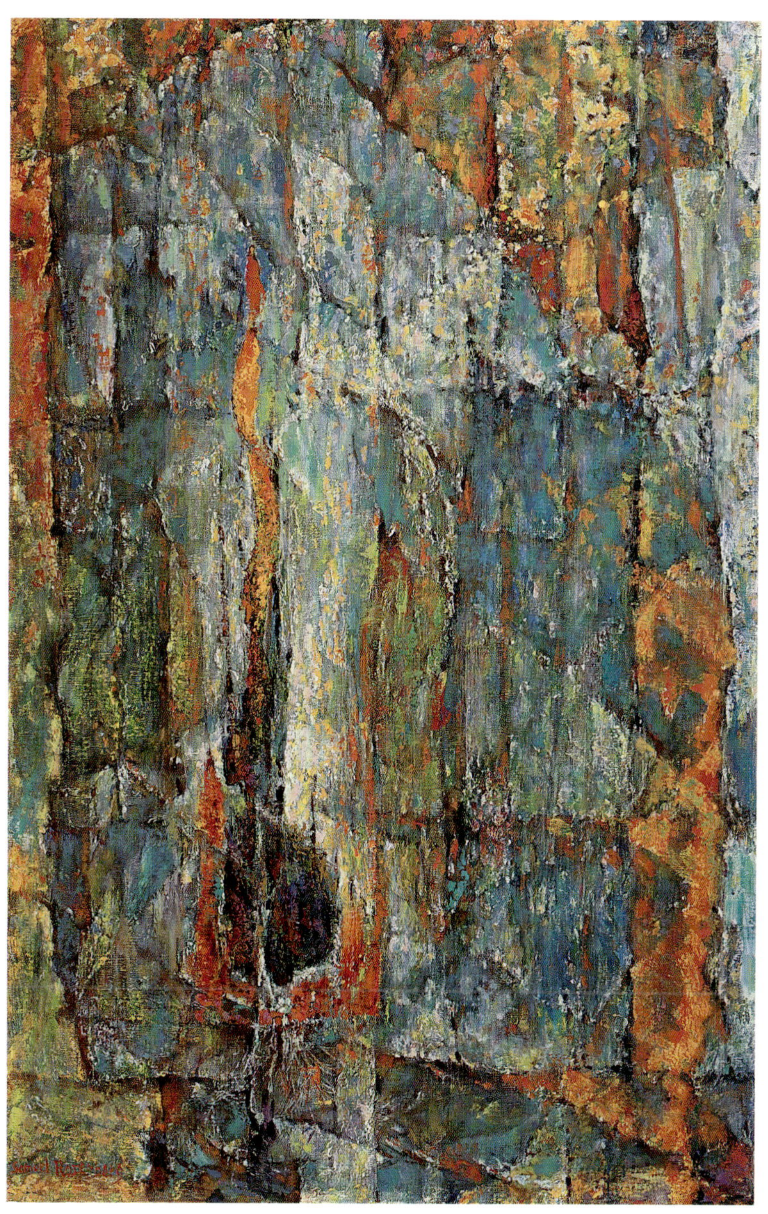

PLATE 67. *The Seed,* 1955. Oil on canvas, 46 x 30″.

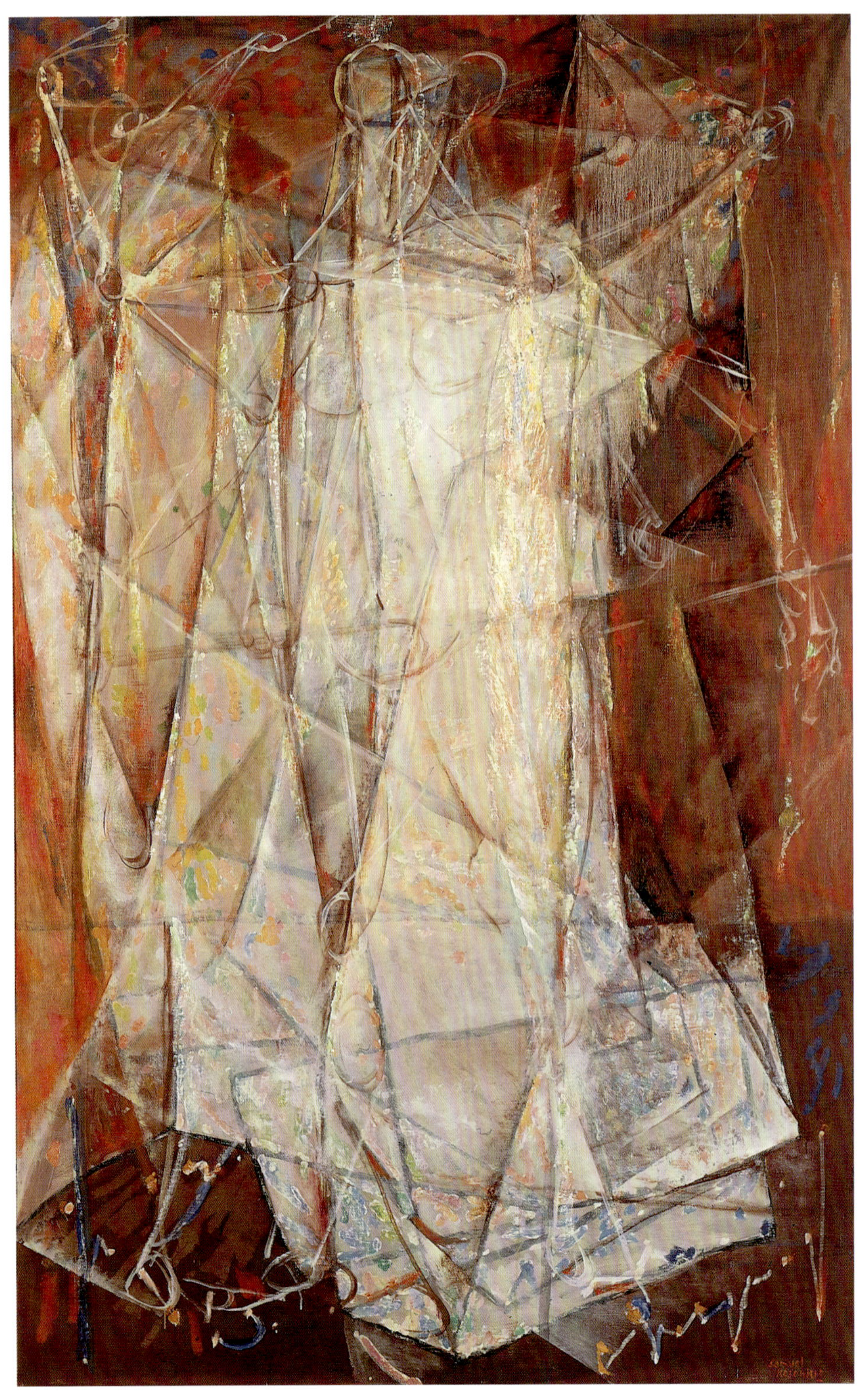

PLATE 68. *Becoming,* 1956. Oil on canvas, 71 x 46″.

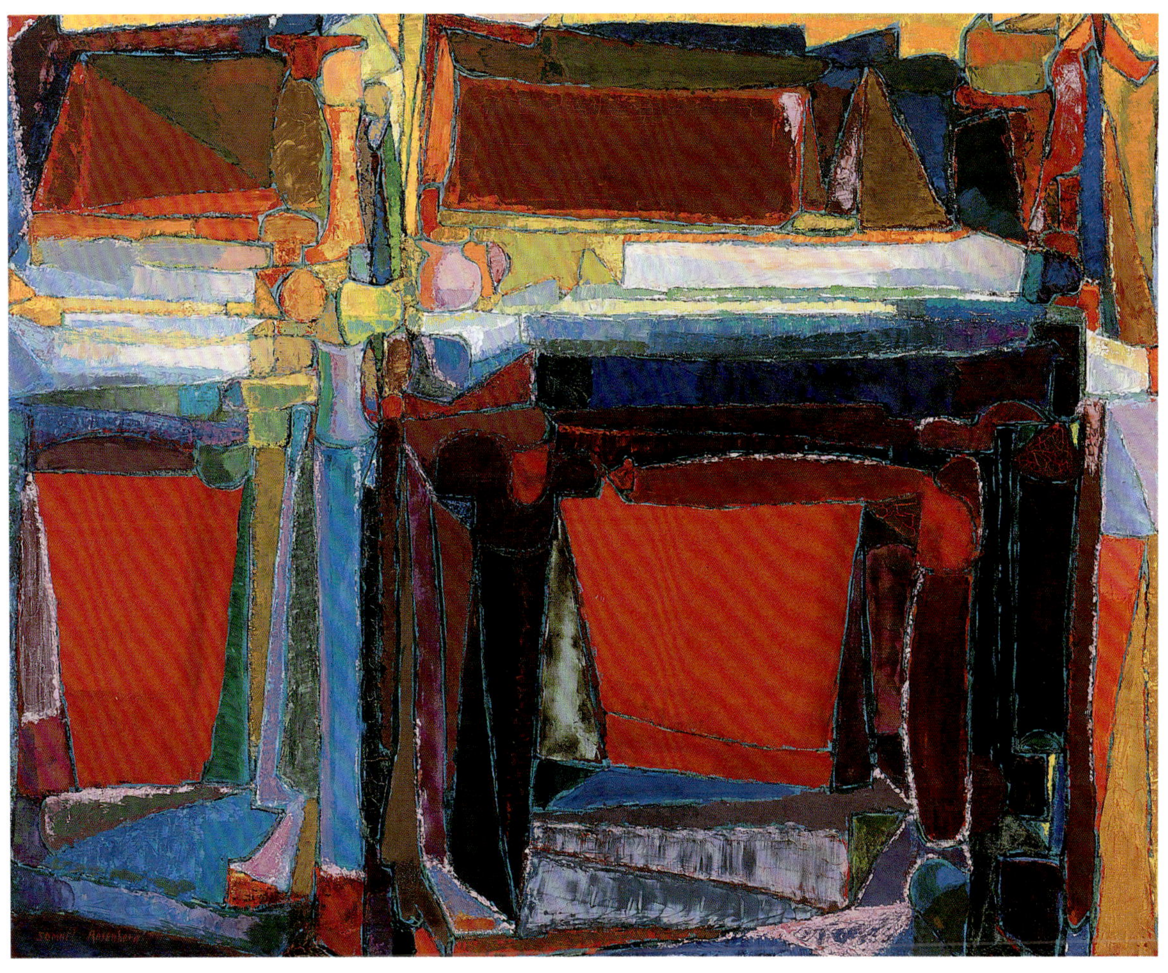

PLATE 69. *Composition*, 1957. Oil on canvas, 40 x 50″.

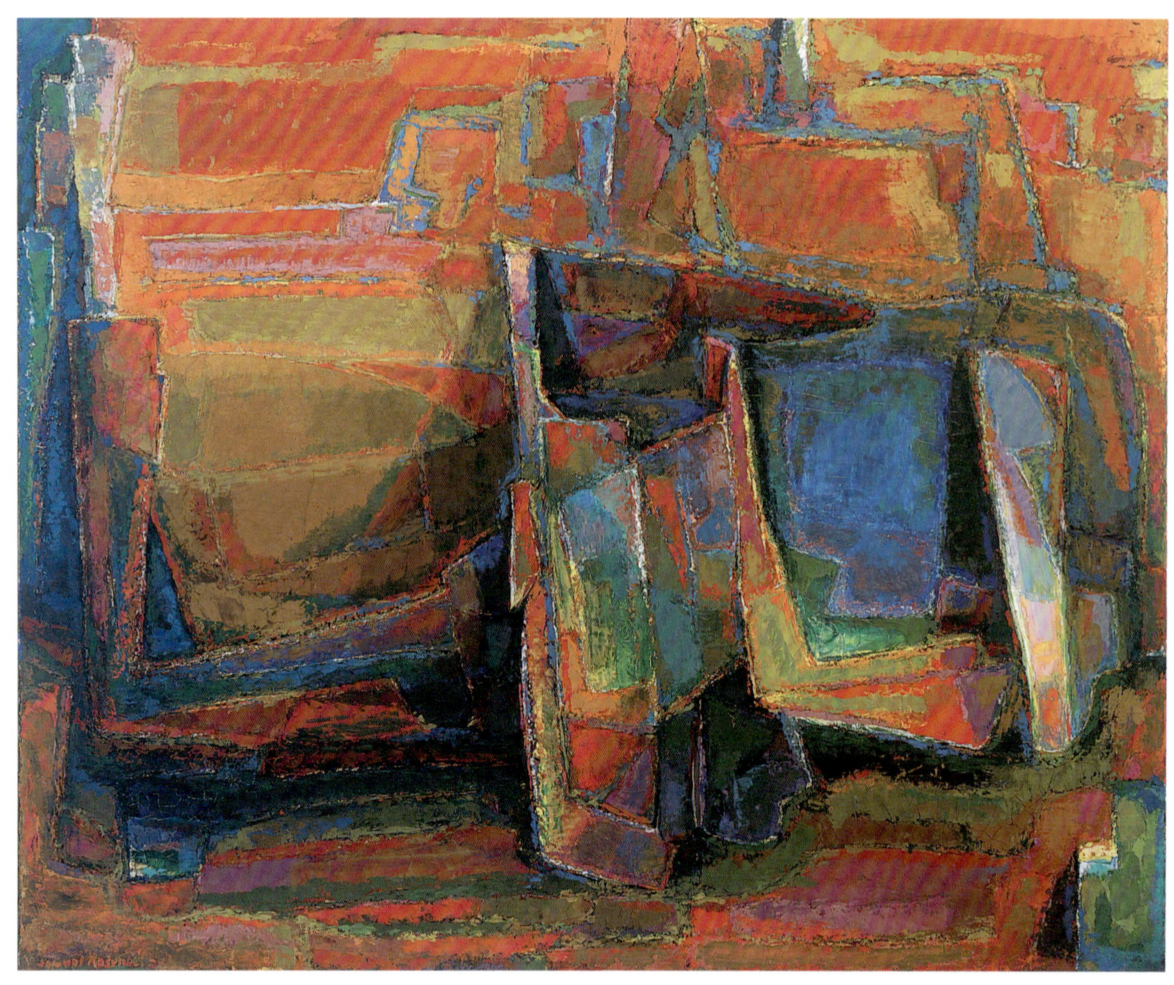

PLATE 70. *Crescendo,* 1958. Oil on canvas, 40 x 50″.

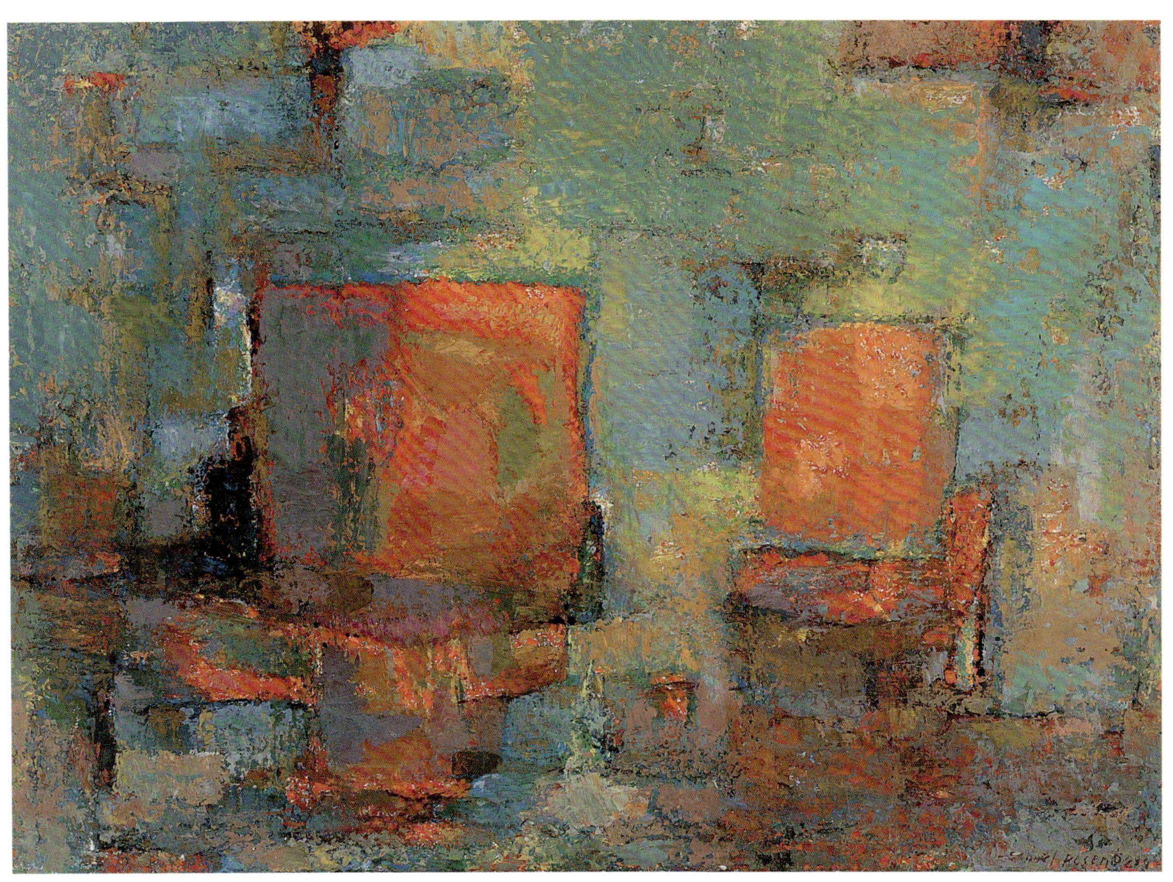

PLATE 71. *Afterglow,* 1958–64. Oil on canvas, 26 x 36″.

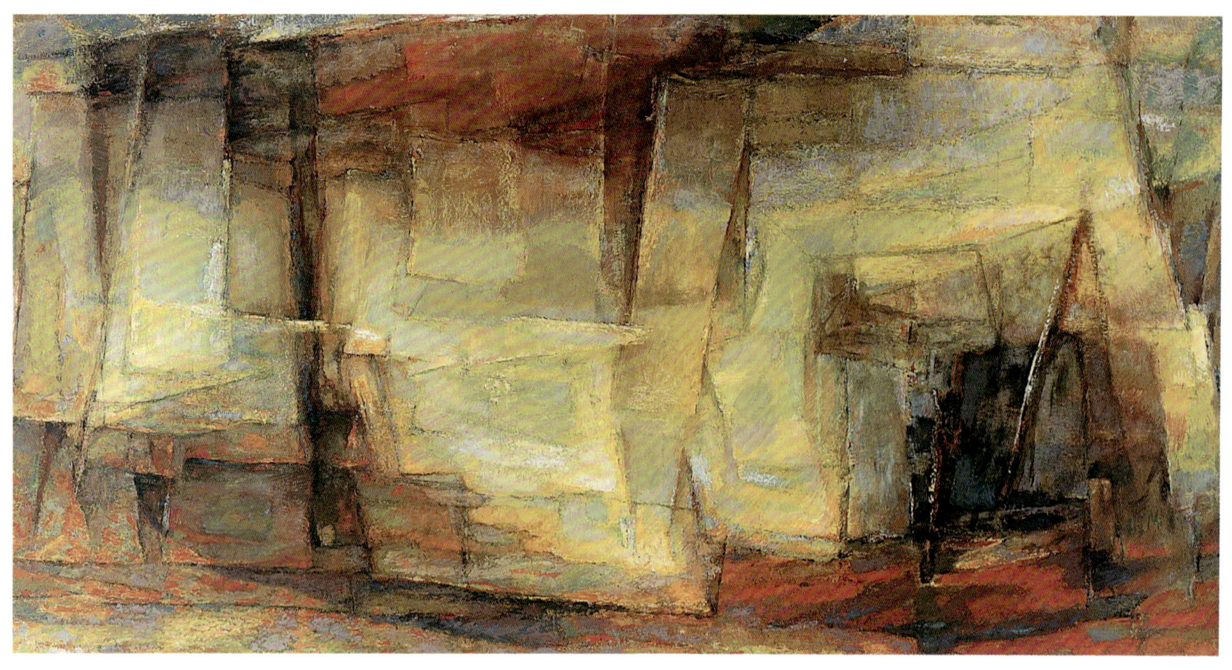

PLATE 72. *In the Beginning (Composition),* 1961. Oil on canvas, 56 x 93″.

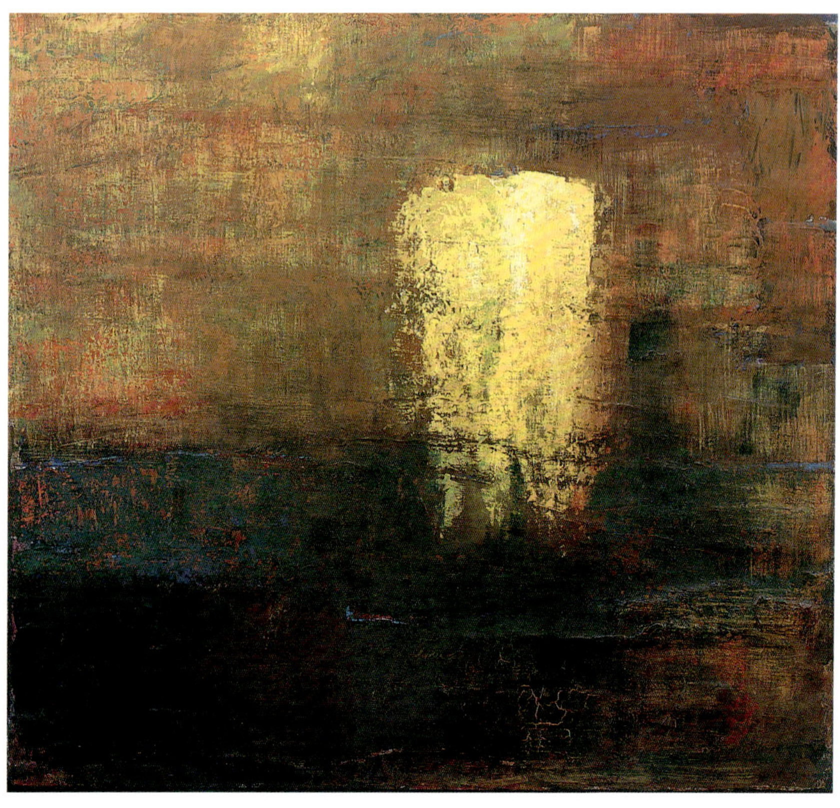

PLATE 73. *Horizon No. 2,* 1962. Oil on canvas, 36 x 40″.

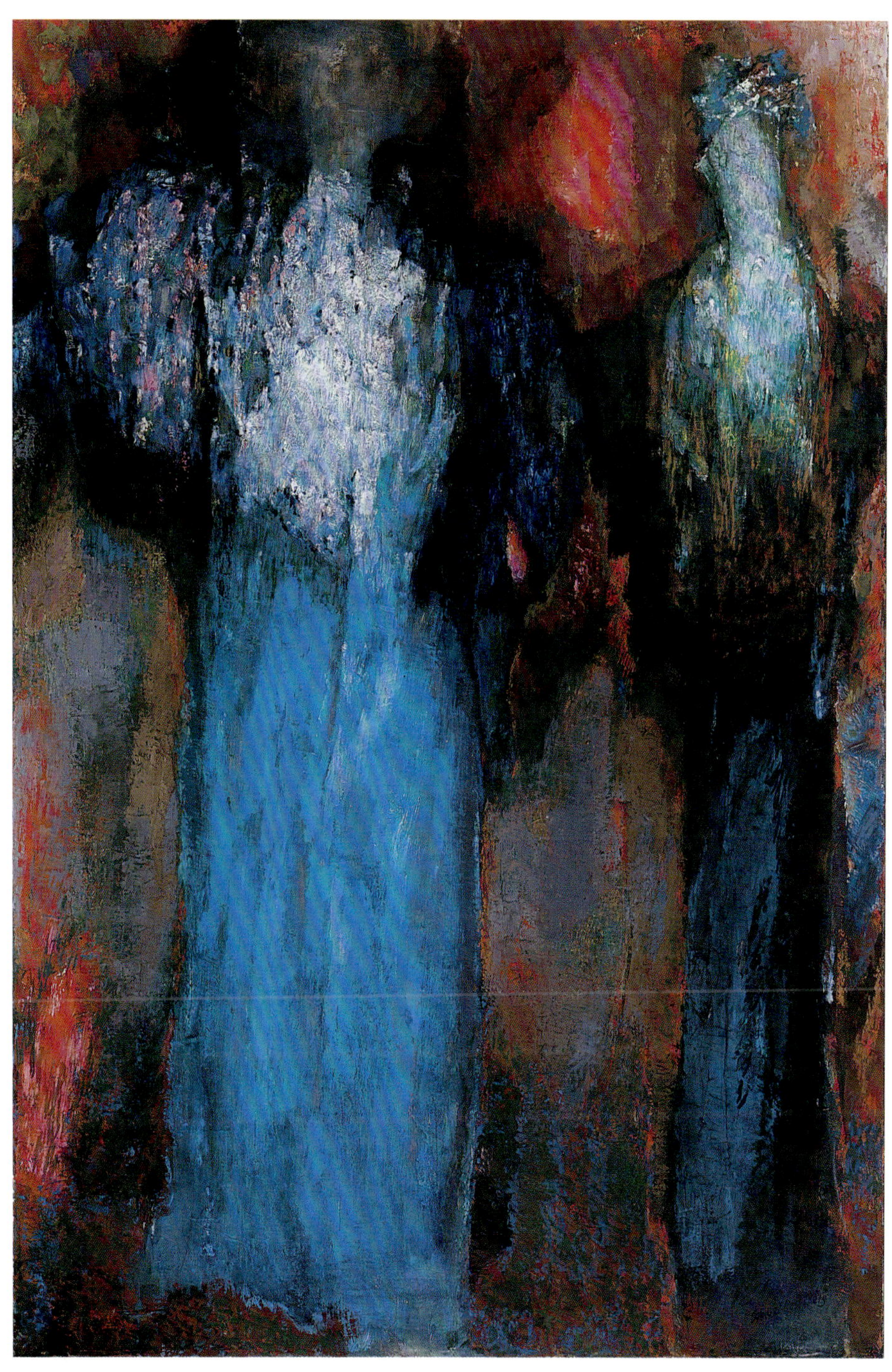

PLATE 74. *Personages*, 1964. Oil on canvas, 60 x 40″.

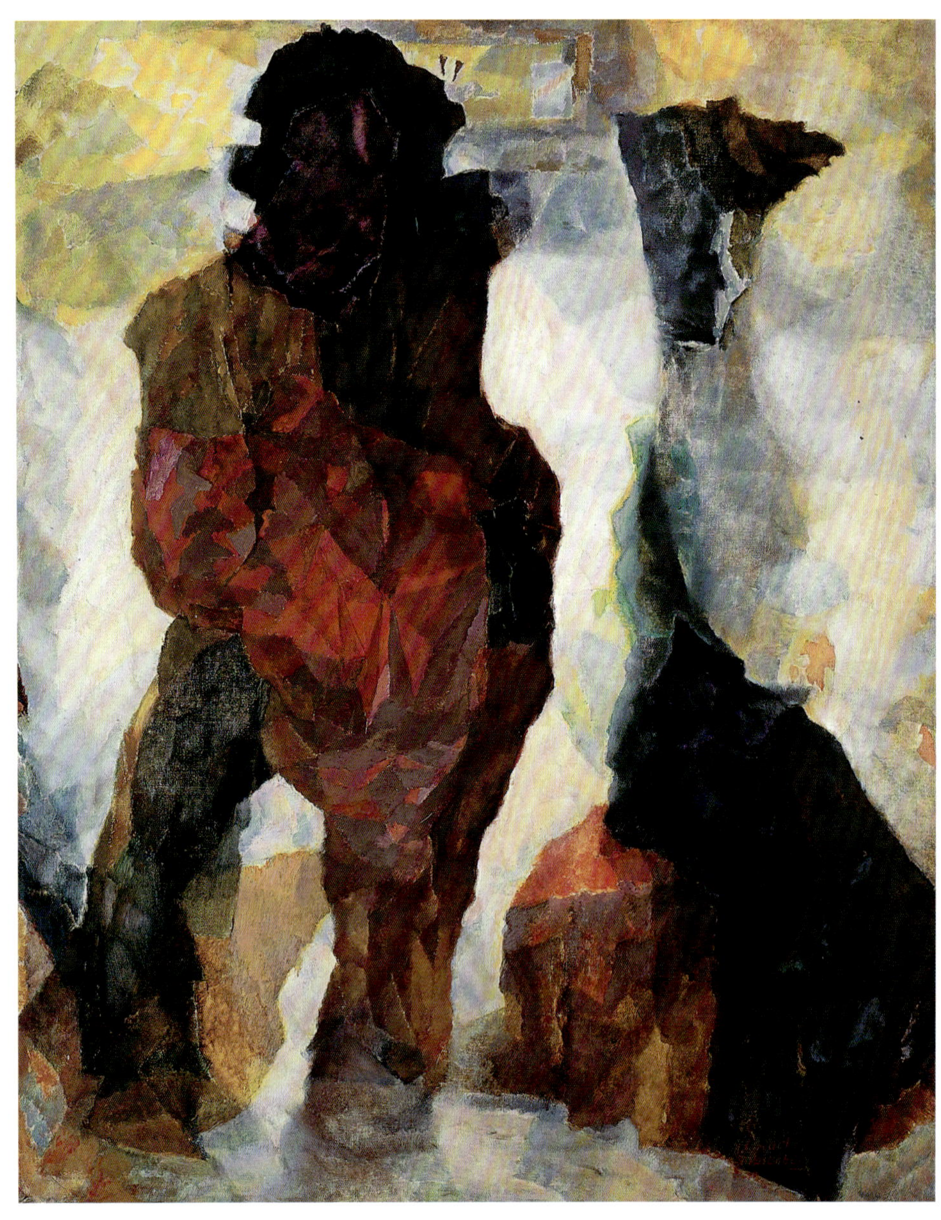

PLATE 75. *Man by the Sea No. 1*, 1965. Oil on canvas, 48 x 40″.

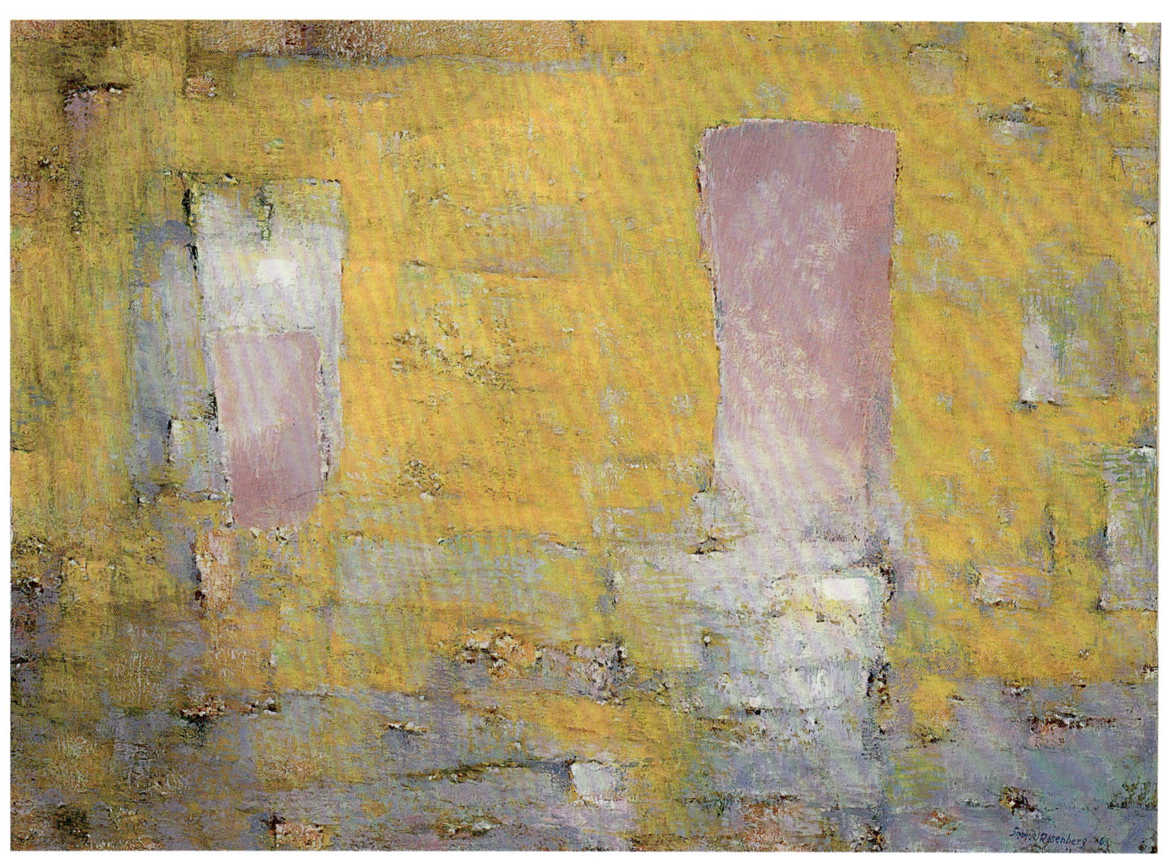

PLATE 76. *April No. 1,* 1969. Oil on canvas, 32 x 45″.

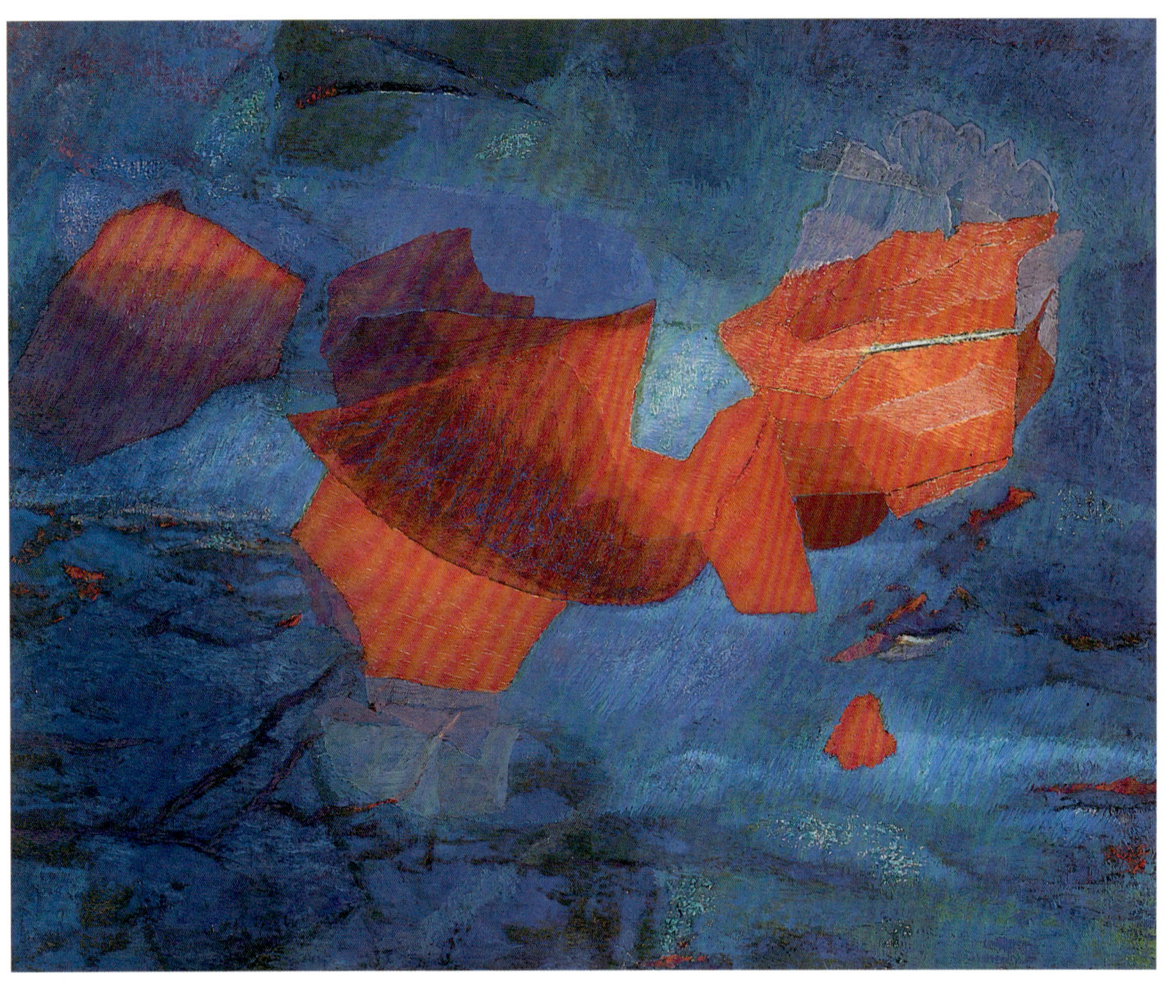

PLATE 77. *Interaction Blue and Red* (formerly *Bright October Morning*), 1968–72. Oil on canvas, 38 x 48″.

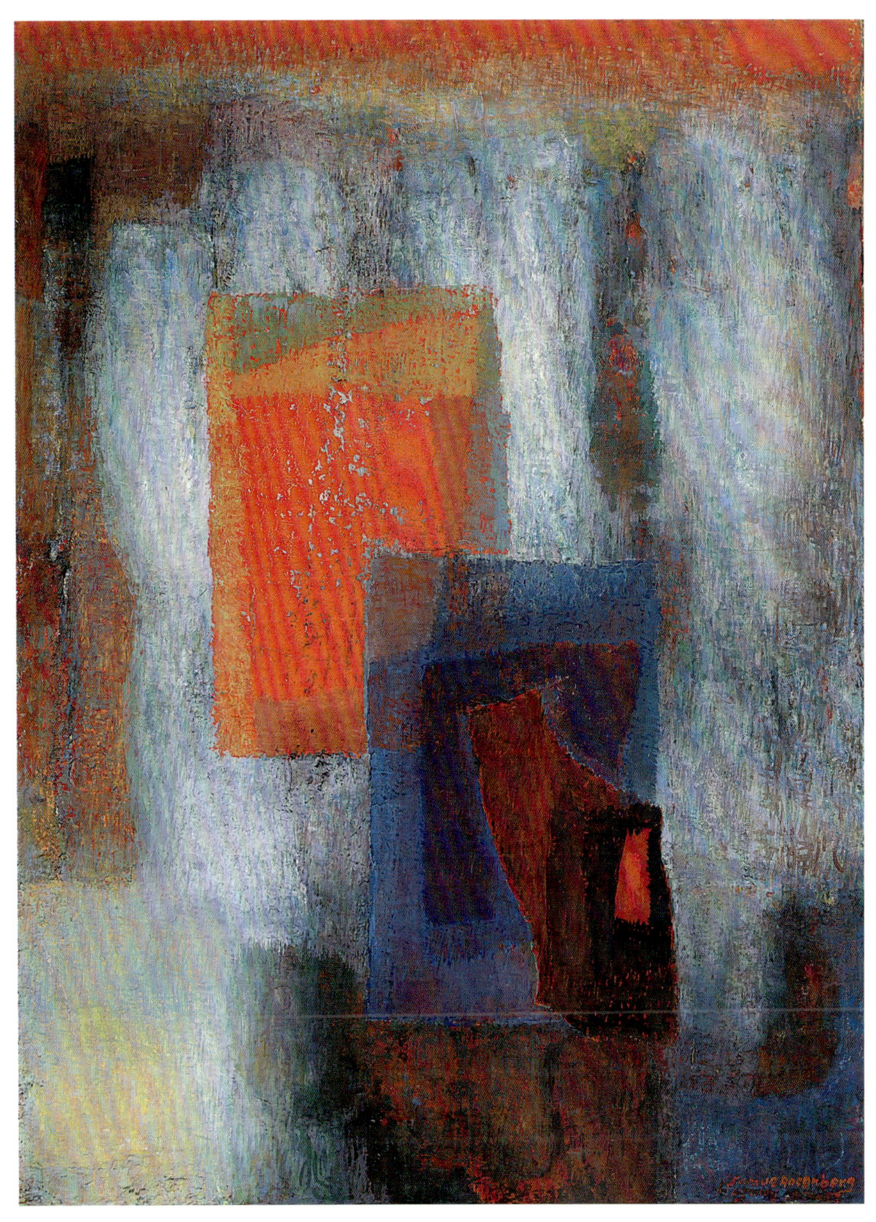

PLATE 78. *Importance of Red,* 1969. Oil on canvas, 48 x 35″.

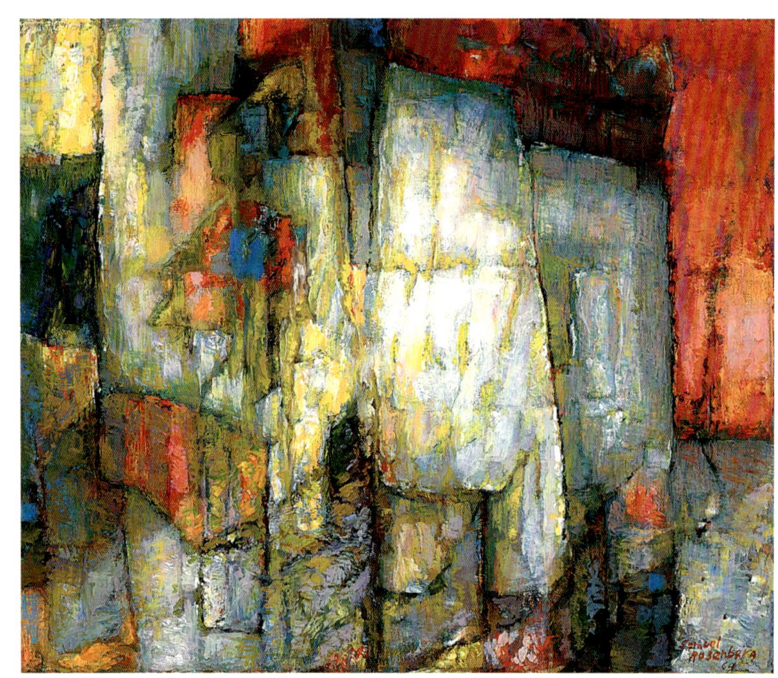

PLATE 79. *Painting 1969 No. 2*, 1969. Oil on canvas, 25 x 30″.

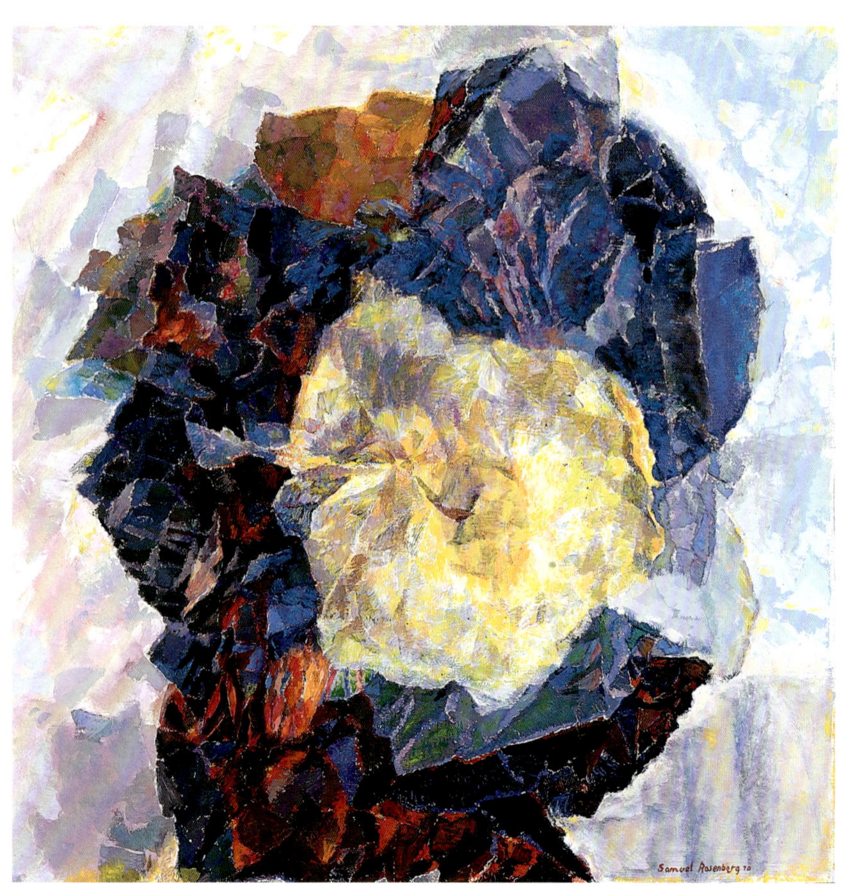

PLATE 80. *Heart of the Rock*, 1970. Oil on canvas, 40 x 40″.

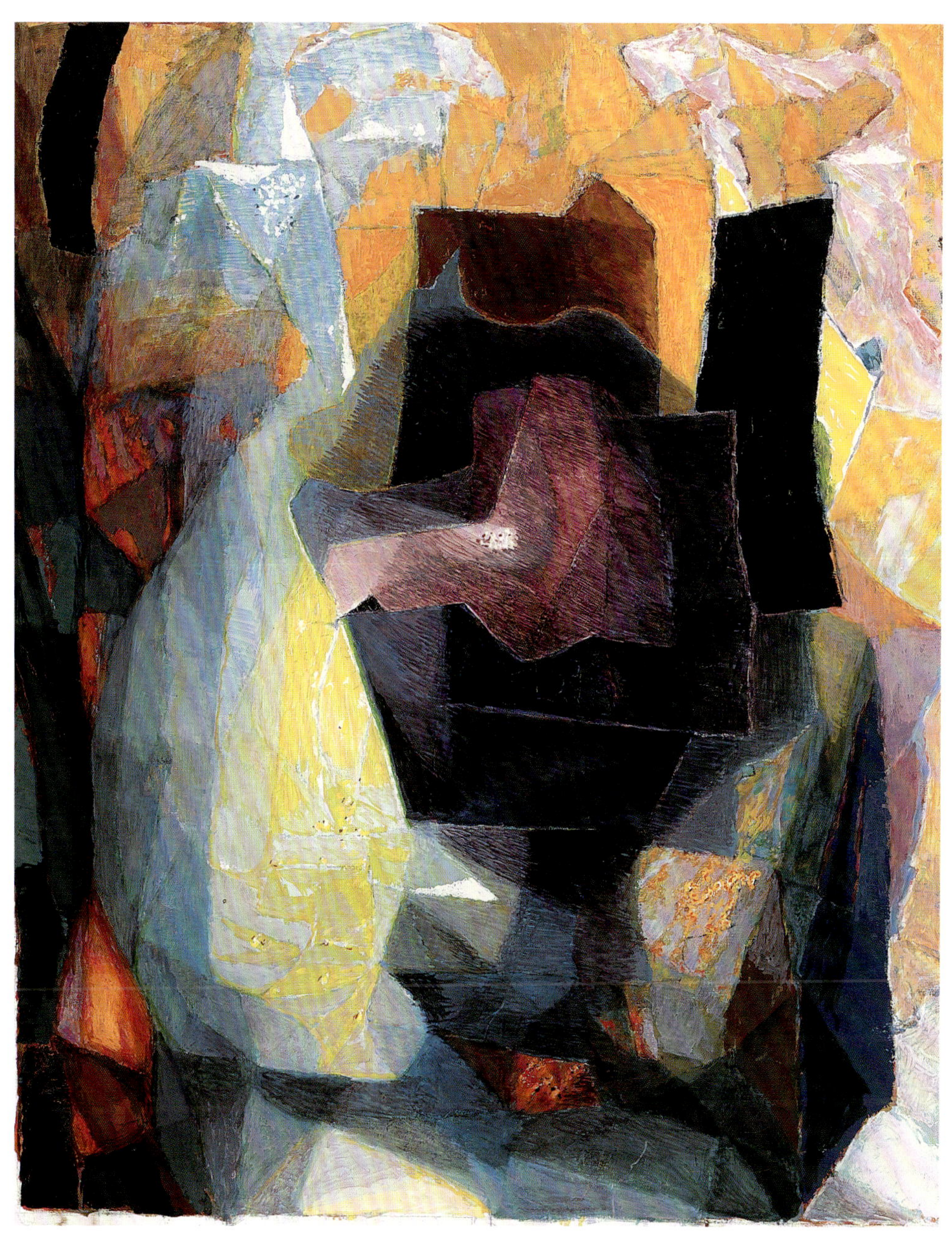

PLATE 81. *Light and Image*, 1972. Oil on canvas, 50 x 40″.

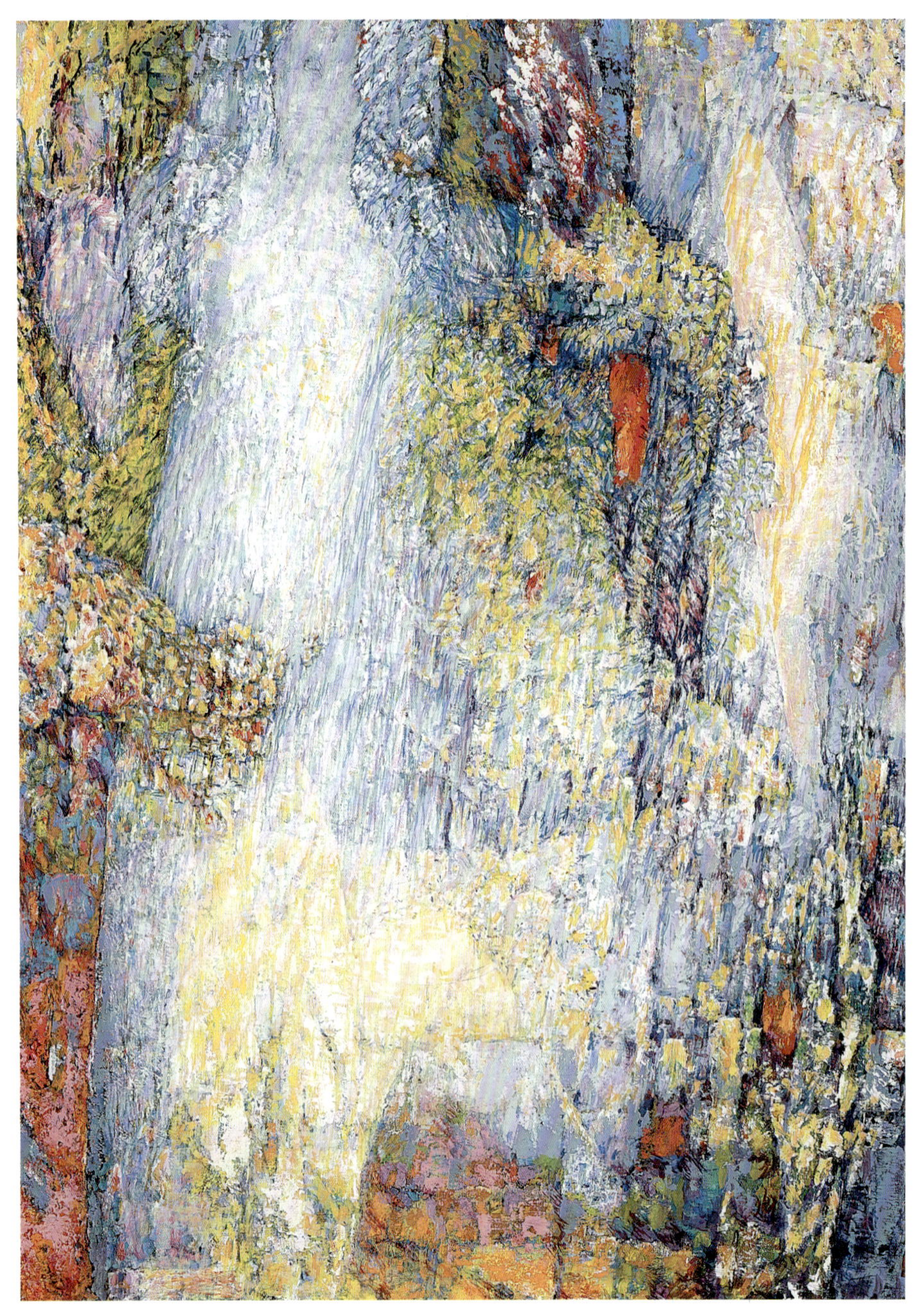

PLATE 82. *Wedding in the Garden,* 1972. Oil on canvas, 50 x 36″.

BIOGRAPHY

Biographical Information

1896	Born on June 28 in Philadelphia to parents Solomon and Anna Turetsky Dickstein Rosenberg, fifth of six children.
1898	Moved with family to Erie, Pennsylvania.
1907	Moved with family to Pittsburgh (North Craig Street at Centre Ave.); attended Osceola School; studied art at Columbian Council School, predecessor of the Irene Kaufmann Center.
1908	Tutored privately by Pittsburgh painter Jacques R. Coblens.
1911	Coblens moved to New York City, continued instruction by correspondence.
1913	Visited Coblens in New York and introduced to paintings at the Metropolitan Museum of Art. Acquired Japanese woodblock prints. Painted billboards in Pittsburgh.
1916	Enrolled as student at National Academy of Design in New York. Exhibited for the first time with Associated Artists of Pittsburgh.
1917	Exhibited with Associated Artists of Pittsburgh, awarded Second Honor. Founded Art School of Irene Kaufmann Settlement, served as director until 1929.
1918	Served four months in U.S. Army, stationed in Georgia, assigned to Camouflage Engineers.
1920	Passed jury and exhibited for first time in Carnegie International. First Prize in oil at Associated Artists of Pittsburgh annual exhibition.
1922	Married Libbie Levin of Pittsburgh (1898–1987).
1924	Moved to 340 Coltart Street in Oakland (Pittsburgh). Teaching appointment, Department of Painting and Design, Carnegie Institute of Technology (now Carnegie Mellon University), professor of painting and drawing until 1964.
1925	Birth of only child, Murray Z. Rosenberg.
1926	Received Bachelor of Arts Degree, Carnegie Institute of Technology.
1926–1939	Spent summers in Woodstock, New York, and Rockport, Massachusetts.
1926	Founded and became director of the Fine Arts Department in the Isaac Seder Educational Center of the Young Men's and Women's Hebrew

	Association (YM&WHA); taught there (including Advanced Drawing Workshop) until 1964.
1931	Right nephrectomy for pyonephrosis (Mercy Hospital).
1936	Death of father, Solomon Rosenberg.
1937	Director, Art Department, Pennsylvania College for Women (now Chatham College) until 1945.
1941	Spent summer in Mexico (three months).
1943–1951	Spent summers in Humbert Valley (Somerset County, Pa.). Tech students included Philip Pearlstein and Andrew Warhola (Andy Warhol).
1947	Death of father-in-law, Joseph Levin.
1949	Attended son's medical school graduation, Yale University.
1950	Son Murray married Arline Levinson of Pittsburgh.
1951	Birth of grandson, Joel Benjamin, in New Haven.
1952	Moved to 2721 Mt. Royal Road in Squirrel Hill (Pittsburgh). Painted mural for St. Henry's Church in Pittsburgh (begun 1950).
1953	Death of mother, Anna; birth of granddaughter, Sue Ann, in New York.
1954–1957	Spent summers in Montauk, Long Island, New York, and coastal Maine.
1958	First trip to Europe (Italy, France).
1962	Spent summer on West Coast: visiting professor, University of Southern California, Los Angeles; attended Seattle World's Fair; visited Mark Tobey in San Francisco and Los Angeles.
1963	Spent summer as visiting professor, University of Southern California, Los Angeles.
1964	Retired from teaching: Carnegie Institute of Technology (after forty years) and YM&WHA (after thirty-nine years).
1965	Second trip to Europe (Portugal, Spain).
1965–1972	Professor Emeritus, Carnegie Mellon University.
1967	First heart attack (Mercy Hospital).
1972	Died on July 23, following second heart attack (Montefiore Hospital).

Solo Exhibitions

1922	Honored Artist, Associated Artists of Pittsburgh at Carnegie Institute of Fine Arts (now Carnegie Museum of Art) (37 paintings)
1937	Carnegie Institute, Gallery H (30 paintings)
1939	Latrobe High School, Latrobe, Pa.
1940	Greensburg Art Club, Greensburg, Pa. (40 paintings)
1944	Associated American Artists, New York, N.Y.

1947	Associated American Artists, New York, N.Y.
1948	Bucknell University, Lewisburg, Pa.
1948	University of Tennessee, Knoxville, Tenn.
1950	Boston Museum School (26 paintings)
1950	Cheltenham Art Center, Philadelphia (26 paintings)
1950	Man of the Year, Arts and Crafts Center, Pittsburgh (now Pittsburgh Center for the Arts) (62 paintings); Butler Art Institute, Youngstown, Ohio (now Butler Institute of American Art) (62 paintings)
1950	Pittsburgh Playhouse
1951	Jewish Community Center, Cleveland, Ohio
1955	State Teachers College (now Indiana University of Pennsylvania), Indiana, Pa.
1956	Carnegie Institute, Pittsburgh
1957	Weirton Community Center, Weirton, W. Va.
1958	Hewlett Gallery, Carnegie Institute of Technology, Pittsburgh
1959	Baltimore Museum of Art
1960	Retrospective, Westmoreland County Museum of Art, Greensburg, Pa. (now Westmoreland Museum of American Art) (116 paintings)
1962	Honored Artist, Associated Artists of Pittsburgh, Carnegie Museum of Art (15 paintings); Pittsburgh in the Thirties, Pittsburgh Plan for Art
1963	Congressman Moorhead's Office, House Office Building, Washington, D.C.; Miami University, Oxford, Ohio
1965	Hewlett Gallery, Carnegie Mellon University, Pittsburgh
1972	Memorial Exhibition, Hewlett Gallery, Carnegie Mellon University, Pittsburgh
1974	Selected Paintings from Seven Decades, Sewickley Academy, Sewickley, Pa. (22 paintings)
1981	University of Connecticut Library, Storrs, Conn. (15 paintings)
1983	Carnegie Museum of Art, Pittsburgh (44 drawings)
1994	Jewish Community Center, Pittsburgh (29 paintings)
1996	Jewish Community Center, Pittsburgh (24 paintings, 1 drawing)

Group Exhibitions

Carnegie (Pittsburgh) International or Painting in the United States exhibitions: passed jury in 1920 and 1925; by invitation in 1933, 1935–1940, 1943, 1945–1950, 1952, 1955, 1958, 1961, 1964, 1967

Associated Artists of Pittsburgh Annual and Special Exhibitions: 1916–1967

Other Group Exhibitions (in alphabetical order):

Albright Gallery, Buffalo, N.Y. (1958)

Arts and Crafts Center, Pittsburgh, Pa. (1970)

Associated American Artists Gallery, New York, N.Y. (1945–1949, 1952)

Butler Art Institute (now Butler Institute of American Art), Youngstown, Ohio (1938, 1939)

Carlow College, Pittsburgh, Pa. (1969)

Carnegie Institute (now Carnegie Museum of Art), Pittsburgh, Pa. (1933, 1937, 1941, 1942, 1949, 1953, 1983)

Cincinnati Art Museum, Ohio (1944)

Cleveland Museum of Art, Ohio

Corcoran Gallery, Washington, D.C. (1934)

Chicago Art Institute, Ill. (1935, 1936, 1940)

Columbus Art Institute, Ohio (1947)

Dayton Art Institute, Ohio

Des Moines Art Center, Iowa

Detroit Art Institute, Mich.

Golden Gate International Exposition, San Francisco, Calif. (1939–1941)

Hebrew Institute, Pittsburgh, Pa.

Hewlett Gallery, Carnegie Mellon University, Pittsburgh, Pa. (1983)

Jewish Museum, New York, N.Y.

John Herron Art Institute, Indianapolis, Ind.

Los Angeles County Museum, Calif.

Memorial Art Gallery, Rochester, N.Y. (1940)

Lyman Allyn Museum, New London, Conn.

Miami University, Oxford, Ohio (1963)

Milwaukee Art Institute, Wisc.

Minneapolis Institute of Arts, Minn.

Museum of Columbia, S.C.

Museum of Modern Art, New York, N.Y. (1933)

National Academy of Design, New York, N.Y. (1946, 1947, 1948)

New York World's Fair (1939)

Pennsylvania Academy of the Fine Arts, Philadelphia, Pa. (1933, 1934, 1935, 1946)

Pepsi-Cola Company, Paintings of the Year (1946, 1947, 1948)

Philadelphia Art Alliance, Pa. (1966)

Pittsburgh Playhouse, Pa. (1956)

Riverside Museum, New York, N.Y. (1940)

St. Louis City Art Museum, St. Louis. Mo.

Smith Museum, Springfield, Mass. (1956)

Syracuse Museum of Fine Arts (now Everson Museum of Art), Syracuse, N.Y. (1948)

Three Rivers Arts Festival, Pittsburgh, Pa. (1960, 1964, 1965, 1972)

Toledo Museum of Art, Ohio (1946, 1949)

University Art Gallery, University of Pittsburgh, Pa. (1983, 1989)

University of Illinois, Urbana, Ill. (1952, 1953, 1955)

University of Nebraska, Lincoln, Nebr.

Virginia Museum of Fine Arts, Richmond, Va.

Walker Art Center, Minneapolis, Minn.

Westmoreland Museum of Art (now Westmoreland Museum of American Art), Greensburg, Pa. (1981)

Whitney Museum of American Art, New York, N.Y. (1934, 1936, 1948)

William Benton Museum, Storrs, Conn. (1977, 1980)

William Rockhill Nelson Gallery of Art (now Nelson-Atkins Museum of Art), Kansas City, Mo.

Public Collections (in alphabetical order)

Akron Art Institute, Akron, Ohio

Abbott Laboratories, Chicago, Ill.

Butler Institute of American Art, Youngstown, Ohio

Carnegie Mellon University, Pittsburgh, Pa.

Carnegie Museum of Art, Pittsburgh, Pa.

Dormont Manufacturing Company, Export, Pa.

Greater Latrobe School District, Latrobe, Pa.

Indiana University, Indiana, Pa.

Joseph M. Katz Graduate School of Business, University of Pittsburgh, Pittsburgh, Pa.

Jewish Community Center of Greater Pittsburgh, Pittsburgh, Pa.

Pennsylvania State University, State College, Pa.

Allegheny County Courthouse, Pittsburgh, Pa.

Pittsburgh Board of Education Administration Building, Pittsburgh, Pa.

Rodef Shalom Congregation, Pittsburgh, Pa.

Slippery Rock University, Slippery Rock, Pa.

Somerset Trust Company, Somerset, Pa.

Somerset County Schools, Somerset, Pa.
St. John Vianney Parish, St. Henry's Church, Pittsburgh, Pa.
Temple Sinai, Pittsburgh, Pa.
United Steelworkers of America Headquarters, Pittsburgh, Pa.
University of Pittsburgh, Pittsburgh, Pa.
Washington County Museum of Fine Arts, Hagerstown, Md.
Westmoreland Museum of American Art, Greensburg, Pa.

Awards: Associated Artists of Pittsburgh

1917	Second Honor (*Man with a Red Nose*)
1920	First Prize in Oil (*Self-Portrait*)
1921	Best Portrait (*Portrait of Christian Walter*)
1922	Honored Artist (37 paintings)
1928	Art Society of Pittsburgh Prize (*Portrait*)
1929	Second Honor (*Around the Corner [Derelict]*)
1930	Euphemia Bakewell Prize (*The Gold Gown*)
1935	Carnegie Institute Prize for Best Group of Paintings (*God's Chillun; Monday Morning; Portrait*)
1936	First Prize in Oil (*Autumn in Pittsburgh*)
1941	Martin Leisser Prize (*Walt's Place*)
1946	Second Honor (*The Covenantor*)
1947	Jacques Blum Prize (*The Counselors*)
1948	First Prize in Oil (*Abundance*)
1953	H. J. Grinsfelder Prize for Best Oil (*Light: Still and Moving*)
1954	Carnegie Institute Prize for Best Two Paintings (*Emergence; Unstilled Earth*)
1955	H. J. Grinsfelder Prize for Distinguished Painting (*Horizons*)
1962	Honored Artist (15 paintings)
1965	Honorary Life Active Membership
1966	Honored Artist for 50 Years of Membership (4 paintings)

Other Awards

1939	Butler Art Institute (now Butler Institute of American Art), Youngstown, Ohio
1943	Butler Art Institute (now Butler Institute of American Art), Youngstown, Ohio
1945	First Honorable Mention, Carnegie Institute, Painting in the United States

1947	Butler Art Institute, Youngstown, Ohio; Pepsi-Cola Company, Paintings of the Year, $500 prize for painting *Asleep*.
1948	Pittsburgh Junior Chamber of Commerce: Man of the Year
1950	Arts and Crafts Center, Pittsburgh: Man of the Year
1954	Pittsburgh Chapter of Hadassah: Citation of Achievement
1960	Westmoreland County Jewry: Citation of Achievement
1961	Carnegie Institute of Technology Alumni Federation: Award of Merit
1963	Carnegie Institute of Technology: Ryan Award for Meritorious Teaching; North Community Association: Man of the Year in Art
1965	Pittsburgh Chapter of Hadassah: Myrtle Award; Governor Scranton Award for Achievement in the Fine Arts

Memberships

1916–1967	Member of Associated Artists of Pittsburgh (AAP), founded in 1910.
1921	Founding member of the Artist Brotherhood, a group of Pittsburgh artists that included Malcolm Parcell, Joseph Bailey Ellis, Christian Walter, William Wolfson, Edmund Ashe, Raymond Simboli, Clifford Bayard, James Boudreau, D. Frank Sullivan, Donal Don, Eben Parcell, William Hyatt, and Berthol Nebel. Familiarly known as the "Tab Men," the goal of this group of young painters, sculptors, etchers, and gravers was to exhibit together in other cities. It does not appear that they succeeded in their goal, however, as the only recognized exhibitions of their work occurred in Pittsburgh. The first banquet of this Artist Brotherhood took place in May 1921 and their first exhibition was held at the Irene Kaufmann Settlement in the Hill District. Most of these artists were also members of the Associated Artists of Pittsburgh, or AAP (*Pittsburgh Sun-Telegraph*, 21 May 1921).
1922	Second Vice President of AAP, and chairman of the Associated Artists of Pittsburgh Thirteenth Annual Exhibition committee.
1944	Founding member, with fellow artists Russell Twiggs and Balcomb Greene, of the Abstract Artists Group (now called Group A) who broke away from the conservative AAP.
1951	Member of the Honor Society of Phi Kappa Phi, by election of the Chapter at Carnegie Tech.
1951	Honorary Fraternities: Phi Kappa Phi and Delta Phi Delta.

Other Involvements

1936	Juror: Greensburg Art Club.
1938	Juror: National Art Week.

1939 Rosenberg wrote a lengthy article entitled "Painting with Egg Tempera" for the September issue of the magazine *Art Instruction*, in which he illustrated the materials and the multiple steps involved in making a painting with this method. His article included a definition of tempera, recipes for gesso, the tempera emulsion, and instruction on overpainting with glazes, colors used in oil varnish glazes, as well as a second egg tempera method that more closely resembled direct oil painting. This was a method Rosenberg used in his own painting and taught to his students as well. He believed, as the Old Masters did, that this method aided in the longevity of color in the painting. Because egg tempera is a combination of egg, oil, and varnish, and is applied in thin layers, each layer of paint is protected from the elements. While later oil paintings have darkened with age due to yellowing of the final application of varnish, the color in tempera paintings remains brilliant, even after four hundred years (*Art Instruction* 3, no. 7 [September 1939]: 19–22, 36). Whether he was aware of it or not, Rosenberg was exactly in tune with his colleagues at other institutions in New York. In the June 1935 issue of *The Art Digest*, a brief article entitled "Teaching Tempera" was included under the heading "A Review of the Field in Art Education." It read, "A return to the painting technique and craftsmanship of Titian, Rembrandt, and Rubens is being fostered in the Cooper Union Art School, New York, where both the faculty and students are being instructed in the 'lost art' of painting with egg tempera" ("Teaching Tempera," *Art Digest* [1 June 1935], 23).

1941 Demonstrated to the Buckeye Art Club in Youngstown, Ohio, how to paint a portrait in two hours.

1945 Delivered an illustrated lecture with sketching and slides on "What Motivates the Artist?" at the Butler Art Institute (now the Butler Institute of American Art), Youngstown, Ohio.

1946 Participated in a ten-part series that KDKA "School of the Air" Radio produced under the title of "Art: A Design for Living," a program for the Upper Elementary and High School students in Pittsburgh which aired on Monday mornings from 9:45–10:00. Rosenberg's segment, "You and Art No. 6" was entitled "Artists are People" and aired on 20 May 1946. Two students visited Rosenberg's studio and discussed his art philosophy, his method of painting, and his family. While no transcripts or audiotapes remain of Rosenberg's interview, the program schedule reveals the features that were covered and outlined the activities that the students participated in for this component of the program. The *Pittsburgh Press* supported the radio program by publishing the illustrations that were to accompany each program in their Sunday Roto section prior to the Monday morning taping. Eleven of Rosenberg's paintings were reproduced together with a short article under the title "Why an Artist Paints Abstracts" (*Pittsburgh Press* [19 May 1946], 24, 25).

1946 Demonstrated how to make a painting at Clarion College, Clarion, Pa. In front of an audience, he quickly created a portrait of the model dressed in Turkish costume and left it with the school to be used for instructional purposes.

1946 Juror: Regional Art Show, Marietta, Ohio.

1947 Under his leadership, the Pittsburgh chapter of the Artists Equity Association (AEA) was founded in May of 1947. While not an artists' union, he and his fellow artists felt the need for such an organization in Pittsburgh to assist in gaining equality for artists with regard to employment (Beatrice Lewis, "Artists in Equity," *The Musical Forecast* [July 1947]). Other artists in the group included C. Kermit Ewing, Virginia Ward, Marty Cornelius, Aleta Cornelius, Harry Scheuch, Caroline McCreary, Louise Pershing, Robert Lepper, and Margaret Jensen.

1948 Juror: Poster Contest, B'nai B'rith Women's Council.

1949 Lecture on the "Organization of a Picture" at the Butler Art Institute.

1949 Featured speaker for the Indiana Art Education Conference held at Indiana State Teacher's College where he demonstrated "Painting a Portrait in Oil."

1949 Juror: College Art Students exhibition, Youngstown, Ohio.

1949 Juror: Thirty-first Toledo Artists Annual Exhibition, Toledo, Ohio.

1949 Juror: Fifth Annual Scholastic Art Awards.

1950 Lecture: Butler Art Institute when his "Man of the Year" exhibition traveled there.

1951 Lecture at the Jewish Community Center in Cleveland on the occasion of his exhibition there.

1951 Appointed by Mayor David Lawrence to serve as a member of the Pittsburgh Art Commission. He filled one of four vacancies that year together with Gordon Washburn, Fine Arts Director of the Carnegie Institute, John McKee, public relations professional, and B. Kenneth Johnstone, architect and President of the Local Chapter of the American Institute of Architects. (Johnstone commissioned Rosenberg to paint the mural for St. Henry's Church and other churches in the city that are yet to be identified.) Approval of the commission was required on the location and design of architecture and the artistic character of public bridges, buildings and memorials.

1953 Juror: The Human Equation exhibition, Akron Art Institute, Akron, Ohio.

CATALOG

This catalog includes all of Rosenberg's known paintings as well as many preparatory drawings, but does not include the complete collection of Rosenberg sketches and drawings held by Carnegie Museum of Art. Works are organized by year. When a date is uncertain, the work is listed under the year with a circa date. Works that span several years are listed under the last year of the span. Within each year, works are arranged alphabetically. When two works appear together, the work is listed under the date of recto work. All dimensions are image size, in inches, with height preceding width. Where information is missing, it is not known.

1915

Portrait of Patrick J. Byrne's Children
Oil on canvas

Portrait of Patrick J. and Eleanor Byrne
Oil on canvas, 35½ x 25½″
Collection: Linda Vogel McTall

Woman in Green No. 1 (Green and Gold)
Oil on canvas, 36 x 18″
Collection: Arline Rosenberg (Mrs. Murray)

1916

The Bridge No. 1 (The Viaduct)
Oil on panel, 27½ x 23½″
Collection: Frank Rosenberg

Man with a Red Nose
Oil on canvas, 30 x 25″
Collection: Carnegie Museum of Art, Pittsburgh, Pa.; Gift of Murray Z. Rosenberg, 1977.17

Portrait of Eleanor Byrne
Oil on canvas, 34 x 27″
Collection: Terri Vogel Gordon

Portrait of Eleanor Byrne with Doll
Oil on canvas, 27 x 22″
Collection: Aline Vogel Cunningham

Portrait of Master Paul Byrne
Oil on canvas

1917

Interior No. 1
Oil on canvas

Portrait of Father Graven
Oil on canvas

Portrait of Rhea
Oil on canvas, 15 x 16″
Collection: Mr. and Mrs. Jack Breskow

Portrait of Robert Phillips
Oil on canvas

1918

For a Boy in France
Oil on canvas

The Japanese Doll
Oil on canvas

Portrait of Miss Bierman
Oil on canvas

Portrait of Miss Mollenauer
Oil on canvas

Portrait of Patrick J. Byrne
Oil on canvas, 36 x 28″
Collection: Terri Vogel Gordon

Self-Portrait in Green Shirt
Oil on masonite, 17 x 16″
Collection: Arline Rosenberg (Mrs. Murray)

1919

Portrait of Arthur Watson Sparks
Oil on canvas, 25 x 20″
Collection: Margaret Vogel Coulehan

Portrait of Jerry
Oil on canvas

Portrait of Maxine
Oil on canvas, 24 x 18″
Collection: Maxine Cuden Goldman

Rose and Grey
Oil on canvas

Self-Portrait by a Window
Oil on canvas, 18 x 16″
Collection: Arline Rosenberg (Mrs. Murray)

Still Life with Flowers, c. 1919
Oil on panel, 19 x 15½″
Collection: Frank Rosenberg

1920

Man with a Vermillion Turban
Oil on canvas

Portrait of P. J. Byrne and Myself
Oil on canvas

Repose No. 1
Oil on canvas

1921

Blue and Gold
Oil on wood, 16 x 13″
Collection: Arline Rosenberg (Mrs. Murray)

Portrait of Christian J. Walter
Oil on canvas, 36 x 28″
Collection: Westmoreland Museum of American Art, Greensburg, Pa.; Gift of Murray Z. Rosenberg, 1977.49

Portrait of Yetta Malamud
Oil on canvas, 15 x 15″

Self-Portrait
Oil on canvas, 25½ x 18½″
Collection: Richard Avner

1922

After the Bath
Oil on canvas

The Blue Vase
Oil on masonite, 18 x 14″
Collection: Mrs. Laibe Kessler

The Dreamer
Oil on canvas

Dynamic Symmetry
Oil on canvas

Geisha Doll
Oil on canvas

Japanese Fan
Oil on canvas

Lombard Poplars
Oil on canvas

Man with a Cape
Oil on canvas

Morning Haze
Oil on canvas

Portrait of E. O'Brien
Oil on canvas

Portrait of Libbie
Oil on canvas, 24 x 20″
Collection: Sue Rosenberg Wieser

Portrait of Milton Weiss
Pencil on paper, 17 x 13″
Collection: Carnegie Museum of Art, Pittsburgh, Pa.; Gift of Murray Z. Rosenberg, 78.27.1.425

Portrait of Rose
Oil on canvas

Portrait of Sari
Oil on canvas

Reflected Light
Oil on canvas

Silhouette
Oil on canvas

The Spirit of the Settlement
Oil on canvas
Mural for the former Irene Kaufmann Settlement; location unknown

Study in Rose and Green
Oil on canvas

Vagabond
Oil on canvas

Windswept
Oil on canvas

Youth
Oil on canvas

1923

Fantine
Oil on canvas

Green and Gold
Oil on canvas

Oil sketch for mural
Oil on board, 12 x 16″

Portrait of Libbie in Gypsy Shawl
Oil on board, 20 x 15″
Collection: Sue Rosenberg Wieser

Repose No. 2
Oil on canvas

Self-Portrait with Palette
Oil on board, 19 x 15″
Collection: Arline Rosenberg (Mrs. Murray)

1924

Fantasy No. 1
Oil on canvas

Portrait of Dean Daniel Carhart
Oil on canvas, 36 x 30″
Collection: University Art Gallery, University of Pittsburgh, Pittsburgh, Pa.

1925

Head of Girl in White, c. 1925
Oil on canvas, 20 x 16″

Helga
Oil on canvas, 40 x 40″
Collection: Jerome J. Segal, Dormont Manufacturing Company

Marta
Oil on wood, 24 x 18″
Collection: Virginia Kaufman

Portrait of Bennie
Oil on canvas

Portrait of Joseph Levin No. 1
Oil on canvas, 64 x 40″
Collection: Arline Rosenberg (Mrs. Murray)

Portrait of Libbie with Velázquez
Oil on canvas, 28 x 22″
Collection: Arline Rosenberg (Mrs. Murray)

Portrait of Pearl and Murray Zale
Oil on canvas

Portrait of Sara
Pencil on paper, 20½ x 16½″
Collection: Sara Berlin

Self-Portrait, c. 1925
Oil on canvas, 12 x 9″
Collection: College of Fine Arts, Carnegie Mellon University, Pittsburgh, Pa.

1926

Carnegie Tech Beanery
Oil on canvas

First Halloween
Oil and tempera on masonite, 30 x 36″
Collection: Sue Rosenberg Wieser

Gramps and Grandson (Joseph Levin)
Etching, 10 x 7″
Collection: Arline Rosenberg (Mrs. Murray)

Grandfather No. 1
Oil on canvas

Head of a Man
Oil on canvas

Portrait of Dr. Max Schoen
Oil on canvas, 40 x 36″
Collection: Carnegie Mellon University

Portrait of Erik with *Portrait of Gertrude Coleman*, 1923, verso
Oil on canvas, 36 x 30″
Collection: Westmoreland Museum of American Art, Greensburg, Pa.; Gift of Murray Z. Rosenberg, 1977.50

Portrait of Libbie in White Sweater
Oil on canvas, 36 x 30″
Collection: Arline Rosenberg (Mrs. Murray)

Portrait of Murray in Red Hat (The Artist)
Oil on fiber board, 19 x 15″
Collection: Arline Rosenberg (Mrs. Murray)

Portrait of Vincent Sollom
Oil on canvas

Model Resting, 1926
Oil on canvas

1927

Bread No. 1
Oil on canvas

The Critic
Oil on canvas

Portrait of Verner
Oil on canvas

The Thinker

Oil on canvas

1928

Around the Corner (Derelict)

Oil on canvas, 36 x 30″

Painting destroyed

Portrait of Dr. Dearth and Three Board Members

Oil on canvas

Portrait of Joseph Levin No. 2

Oil on canvas

Portrait of Rev. McMullen

Oil on canvas

Portrait of S. Garrison

Oil on canvas

Self-Portrait in Sweater

Oil on canvas, 24 x 19″

Collection: Jay Avner

1929

Portrait of Bernice (Seder)

Oil on canvas, 15 x 12″

Collection: Mark and Jo Beth Ravitz

Portrait of Dr. E. J. McCague

Oil on canvas

Portrait of Dr. Herbert Burnham Davis

Oil on canvas

Portrait of Dr. Robertson

Oil on canvas

Portrait of H. J. Parker

Oil on canvas

Portrait of Isaac Seder No. 1

Oil on canvas

Portrait of Isaac Seder No. 2

Oil on canvas

Portrait of M. and Rahl Smith

Oil on canvas

Portrait of Marcus Rauh

Oil on canvas

Portrait of a Young Girl

Pencil on paper, 8 x 5″

Collection: Sheryl and Bruce Wolf

1930

The Gold Gown

Oil on canvas, 38 x 28″

Collection: Arline Rosenberg (Mrs. Murray)

Interior No. 2

Oil on canvas

Murray Against Green

Oil on canvas, 16 x 20″

Collection: Dot and Joel Rosenberg

Portrait of Abraham Seder

Oil on canvas

Collection: Mildred Seder Levy

Portrait of Dr. Earhart

Oil on canvas

Portrait of Frank Thomson

Oil on canvas

Portrait of Howard Baer

Oil on canvas, 40 x 36″

Private collection

Portrait of Judge W. H. Seward Thomson

Oil on canvas

Portrait of Murray in Black Sweater

Oil on masonite, 20 x 16″

Collection: Arline Rosenberg (Mrs. Murray)

Portrait of Selma Ruttenberg

Watercolor on paper, 29 x 21″

Collection: Sue Rosenberg Wieser

Vacation Days No. 1

Oil on masonite, 19 x 23½″

Collection: Dot and Joel Rosenberg

Yoder Hotel, Forbes Street

Oil and tempera on masonite, 20 x 18″

Collection: Sue Rosenberg Wieser

1931

Breadwinner (Bearded Man)

Oil on board, 20 x 16″

Collection: Joan and Bernie Sheffler

City Shadows, Pittsburgh

Oil on canvas, 25 x 28″

Collection: Joseph M. Katz Graduate School of Business, University of Pittsburgh, Gift of Michelle Madoff

Hill District

Oil on masonite, 30 x 27″

Collection: Jerome J. Segal, Dormont Manufacturing Company

My Friend Twiggs

Oil on canvas, 40 x 33″

Painting destroyed.

Wet Day
Oil on canvas

Young Woman
Oil on canvas

1932

Front Yard, Pittsburgh
Oil on canvas

Gloucester Fish Houses
Oil on canvas, 16 x 20″
Collection: Sandy and Don Schneider

Greenfield Hill (Gazzam's Hill)
Oil on canvas, 39 x 40½″
Collection: Carnegie Museum of Art, Pittsburgh, Pa.; Purchase: Patrons Art Fund, 1957.35

Greenfield Hill (preparatory study)
Crayon on paper, 10⅜″ x 7$^{15}/_{16}$″
Collection: Carnegie Museum of Art, Pittsburgh, Pa.; Gift of Mrs. Samuel Rosenberg, 1982.26

Meditation (Libbie)
Oil on masonite, 24 x 20″
Collection: Arline Rosenberg (Mrs. Murray)

My Son Murray, Woodstock
Oil on masonite, 9 x 12″
Collection: Dot and Joel Rosenberg

Old Pittsburgh House
Oil on canvas

Portrait of Mildred (Seder)
Oil on canvas
Collection: Mildred Seder Levy

Portrait of Rowena (Kostellow)
Watercolor on paper, 30 x 20″

Portrait of Solomon and Anna Rosenberg, c. 1932
Oil on canvas, 20 x 24″
Collection: Mr. and Mrs. Charles Rosenberg

Portrait of Solomon Rosenberg No. 1
Oil on masonite, 24 x 20″
Collection: Allen J. Samowich

Portrait of Solomon Rosenbloom
Oil on canvas
Collection: formerly Hebrew Institute

Proud Owner
Oil on canvas, 36 x 40″
Collection: Naomi and Jerry Weiner

Second Avenue (Man-Made Desert, Street by the Mill)
Oil on canvas, 38 x 42″
Collection: Carnegie Museum of Art, Pittsburgh, Pa.; Gift of Mr. and Mrs. Charles Dreifus, Jr., in memory of his father, 1962.28

Street in Soho
Oil on masonite, 20 x 24″

Webster Avenue House
Oil on canvas, 40 x 26″
Collection: Ellen Rabin

Windy Day at Shady, Woodstock
Oil on canvas, 36 x 40″
Collection: Arline Rosenberg (Mrs. Murray)

1933

Conversation
Oil on canvas, 26 x 22″

Eviction (preparatory study)
Conte crayon on paper, 20 x 12″
Collection: Westmoreland Museum of American Art, Greensburg, Pa.; Gift of the Women's Committee, 2002.5

Fruit Seller
Oil on canvas, 33 x 26″
Collection: Joan and Simeon Friedberg

Logan and Clark Streets
Oil on masonite, 20 x 16″
Collection: Ruth Westerman

Philosopher
Oil on canvas

Portrait of Dr. A. Berle
Oil on canvas
Collection: Carnegie Mellon University

Portrait of Fred Lissfelt Children
Oil on canvas, 36 x 36″
Private collection

Portrait of Murray
Oil on masonite, 22 x 18″
Collection: Sue Rosenberg Wieser

Sunshine on Tustin Street
Oil on canvas, 18 x 20″
Collection: William B. Salsbury

Vacation Days No. 2 (Murray)
Oil on canvas, 36 x 28″
Collection: Arline Rosenberg (Mrs. Murray)

Watermelon Market
Oil on canvas, 36 x 40″
Collection: Mr. and Mrs. Robert P. Lazar

Wood for Sale
Tempera on masonite, 16 x 11″

Woodstock Auction
Tempera on paper, 16 x 20″
Collection: Joan and Simeon Friedberg

Woodstock Barnyard
Oil on canvas, 22 x 28″

1934

Eviction (preparatory study)
Conte crayon on paper, 23 x 19″
Private collection

Eviction (preparatory study)
Pencil and colored pencil on paper, 8 x 7″
Private collection

Eviction (preparatory study)
Pencil on paper, 9 x 7″
Private collection

Farmer and His Wife
Oil on canvas

Gloucester Docks
Oil on canvas, 30 x 40″
Private collection

God's Chillun
Oil on canvas, 36 x 48″
Collection: Westmoreland Museum of American Art, Greensburg, Pa.; William A. Coulter Fund, 1974.67

Near Herron Hill
Oil on canvas, 32 x 38″
Private collection

Portrait of Joseph Levin
Pencil on paper, 10 x 8″
Collection: Arline Rosenberg (Mrs. Murray)

Settlement on the Hudson
Oil on canvas, 38 x 44″
Collection: Mrs. Mary Smillie

Soho
Oil on canvas, 40 x 50″
Collection: Arline Rosenberg (Mrs. Murray)

Street Scene
Oil on canvas, 25 x 30″

1935

Autumn in Pittsburgh (sketch)
Oil on canvas

Cat's Alley
Oil on canvas, 16 x 20″

Chair in Rockport Bedroom
Oil on paper, 12 x 9″

Eviction
Oil on canvas, 40 x 36″
Collection: James Ruttenberg

Gloucester Harbor
Oil on canvas, 15 x 18″
Painting destroyed 1977

House by the Shore, Gloucester
Oil on masonite, 14 x 17″

Lightning at Pigeon Cove
Oil on canvas

Little Church on the Hill
Oil on canvas

Mellon Institute Under Construction
Oil on canvas, 22 x 18″

Monday Morning (After the Night Shift)
Oil on canvas, 30 x 36″
Collection: Arline Rosenberg (Mrs. Murray)

Monday Morning No. 1
Oil on canvas, 20 x 23″
Collection: Florence Schneider

Portrait of Eddy
Oil on canvas

Portrait of Judge Norman T. Boose
Oil on canvas

Portrait of a Mountaineer, Somerset
Oil on canvas
Collection: Somerset High School

Schenley Oval
Oil on board, 20 x 24″
Private collection

Sideshow
Oil on canvas, 46 x 50″
Private collection

Summer in Woodstock
Oil on canvas

Three Girls on Stoop
Oil on masonite, 30 x 25″
Courtesy: Concept Art Gallery, Pittsburgh, Pa.

Window at Dusk (Pittsburgh)
Oil on masonite, 24 x 20″
Painting destroyed

1936

Autumn in Pittsburgh
Oil on canvas, 25 x 28″
Collection: Mr. and Mrs. Henry L. Hillman

Band Concert, Plymouth, N.H.
Oil on canvas board, 12 x 16″

Coming Home from School
Oil on canvas, 33 x 24″
Collection: Ruth Westerman

Forgotten Man
Oil on canvas

Gloucester Docks
Pencil on paper, 10 x 8″
Collection: Dot and Joel Rosenberg

Gloucester Fisherwomen
Oil on masonite, 20 x 24″
Collection: Mr. and Mrs. Stanley R. Gumberg

Gloucester Fisherwomen (preparatory study)
Oil on canvas board, 20 x 24″
Collection: Mr. and Mrs. Stanley R. Gumberg

Hill Street Scene
Oil on masonite, 28 x 25″

Houses on the Hill
Oil on canvas

Lower Fifth Avenue
Oil on masonite, 20 x 24″
Collection: Arline Rosenberg (Mrs. Murray)

Mountain Road
Watercolor on paper

Portrait of Rabbi Lippmann Mayer, c. 1936
Oil on canvas, 36 x 31″
Collection: Rodef Shalom Congregation, Pittsburgh, Pa.

Retaining Wall-Webster Ave.
Oil on masonite, 18 x 20″

Spring in Schenley Park
Oil on canvas, 25 x 30″
Collection: Diane Haber March

Summer Boarders
Watercolor on paper

The Sun Shines in Pittsburgh
Oil on masonite, 20 x 24″
Collection: Mrs. Laibe Kessler

Winter
Oil on canvas

Wood for Sale (preparatory study for *The Sun Shines in Pittsburgh*), c. 1936
Pencil on paper, 8 13/16 x 10 1/8″
Collection: Carnegie Museum of Art, Pittsburgh, Pa.; Gift of Murray Z. Rosenberg, 78.27.1.343

Wyandotte Street
Oil on masonite, 24 x 20″
Collection: Warren and Judy Levine

1937

Clark Street Window, c. 1937
Oil on canvas, 20 x 16″
Collection: Mr. and Mrs. Charles Rosenberg

Fruit Market
Oil and tempera on canvas, 30 x 36″
Collection: Mildred Seder Levy

Fruit Market, c. 1937
Charcoal on paper, 9 1/2 x 12 3/8″
Collection: Carnegie Museum of Art, Pittsburgh, Pa.; Gift of Murray Z. Rosenberg, 78.27.1.554

The Gossips
Oil on canvas, 24 x 33″
Collection: University of Pittsburgh

Logan Street
Oil on canvas, 29 x 36″

Old Tire Shop
Oil on canvas

Portrait of Solomon Rosenberg No. 2
Oil on masonite, 24 x 20″
Collection: Elaine B. Avner

Portrait of Solomon Rosenberg No. 3
Oil on masonite, 24 x 20″
Collection: Jill Schneider

Spring Planting
Oil on canvas

Street Scene, Wick Street
Oil on masonite, 12 x 16″

Sunday Morning
Oil on masonite, 56 x 46″
Collection: Arline Rosenberg (Mrs. Murray)

Sunday Morning (preparatory study), c. 1937
Pencil on paper, 8 x 10″
Collection: Arline Rosenberg (Mrs. Murray)

1938

Doorways, Soho Street
Oil on canvas, 36 x 30″
Collection: Marcella L. Finegold

Evening Glow
Oil and tempera on masonite, 20 x 24″

Fifth Avenue Garden
Oil and tempera on canvas, 23 x 25″

Flowers in a White Bowl
Oil on canvas, 16 x 20″

Fruit Market (oil sketch)
Oil on masonite, 14 x 17″
Collection: Arline Rosenberg (Mrs. Murray)

Fruit and Logan Street
Oil and tempera on canvas, 54 x 48″
Collection: Mrs. Laibe Kessler

Job Lists
Oil and tempera on masonite, 20 x 24″
Collection: H. Wayne and Joice Ann Wiester

Keeping Warm No. 1
Oil and tempera on masonite, 20 x 24″

Logan Street Market
Oil on masonite, 14 x 17″

Rest
Oil and tempera on masonite, 44 x 38″
Collection: School District of Pittsburgh, Gift of 100 Friends of Art

Rest (preparatory study), c. 1938
Ink on card, 15 x 10″
Collection: Carnegie Museum of Art, Pittsburgh, Pa.; Gift of Murray Z. Rosenberg, 78.27.1.502

Second Avenue No. 2
Oil on canvas, 25 x 30″
Collection: Joan and Simeon Friedberg

1939

The Accordian Player (preparatory study for *The Dance*)
Oil on canvas board, 14 x 10″
Collection: Amy and Sy Kellman

Atwood Street Corner with *Dusk*, 1943, verso
Oil on masonite, 20 x 24″
Collection: Jerome J. Segal, Dormont Manufacturing Company

Before the Night
Oil on canvas

The Books Burn
Oil on canvas

The Dance
Oil on masonite, 42 x 48″
Collection: Arline Rosenberg (Mrs. Murray)

The Dance (preparatory study)
Pencil on paper, 10 x 12″
Collection: Arline Rosenberg (Mrs. Murray)

Demolition of a Church, Bouquet Street
Oil on masonite, 28 x 35″
Collection: H. Wayne and Joyce Ann Wiester

Excavation
Watercolor on paper, 16 x 20″

The Fall Game
Tempera on masonite, 36 x 40″

Hill District, c. 1930–39
Pencil on paper, 7⅞ x 11⅛″.
Collection: Carnegie Museum of Art, Pittsburgh; Gift of Murray Z. Rosenberg, 78.27.1.533

Keeping Warm No. 2
Oil on masonite, 18 x 22″
Collection: Jules and Elaine Levy

Mid-Morning Conversation
Oil on masonite, 25 x 30″
Collection: Rita and Edwin Langue

Near Stoyestown
Oil and tempera on masonite, 16 x 20″

Off Dinwiddie Street
Oil on canvas, 30 x 25″

Portrait of Dr. A. E. Maltby
Oil on canvas, 36 x 30″
Collection: Slippery Rock University

Portrait of J. A. Koch
Oil on canvas
Collection: Carnegie Mellon University

Portuguese Church in Gloucester
Oil on board, 24 x 30″
Collection: Arline Rosenberg (Mrs. Murray)

Sunday Afternoon, Lombard St.
Oil and tempera on masonite, 25 x 28″

Upper Colwell
Oil on canvas

The Work Is Done
Oil on canvas

1940

Backyards
Oil on masonite, 12 x 16″
Collection: Beatrice and James Litman

Bigelow Boulevard Under Construction
Oil and tempera on masonite, 36 x 40″
Collection: Arline Rosenberg (Mrs. Murray)

Bigelow Boulevard Under Construction, c. 1940
Pencil and colored pencil on paper, 10 x 12″
Collection: Arline Rosenberg (Mrs. Murray)

Bigelow Boulevard Under Construction (sketch)
Oil on canvas, 20 x 16″

The Bridge No. 2 (The Viaduct)
Oil on masonite, 25 x 30″
Collection: Ruth Westerman

Confluence, c. 1940
Oil on masonite, 20 x 24″
Collection: Allen J. Samowich

Corner of Walt's Place, Fort Hill
Oil on masonite, 18 x 20″
Collection: Edie Shapira and Mark Schmidhofer

Doorway on Devillier Street
Oil on canvas, 30 x 25″
Collection: Anthony P. Picadio

Dry Goods
Oil and tempera on masonite, 24 x 20″
Collection: Naomi and Jerry Weiner

Evening in Rockport
Oil on masonite, 20 x 24″

Farmers Market at Signal
Oil on masonite, 24 x 20″
Collection: Mildred Seder Levy

Geometric Composition
Oil on masonite, 20 x 18″
Collection: Anthony P. Picadio

Greenfield
Oil and tempera on masonite, 28 x 25″

House on the Hill
Watercolor on paper, 16 x 20″

Industrial Scene
Watercolor on paper, 10 x 14″
Collection: Westmoreland Museum of American Art, Greensburg, Pa.; Gift of Dr. Jacob Goldblum, 1984.340

Landscape, c. 1940
Oil on canvas, 12 x 14″
Collection: Linda Avner Bringman

Little Procession
Oil on canvas, 24 x 20″
Collection: Carnegie Museum of Art, Pittsburgh, Pa.; Gift of the Feldman family in memory of Joseph and Dorothy Feldman, 1996.84

Mother and Child
Tempera on masonite, 16 x 20″

Overhill Street
Oil and tempera on masonite, 20 x 24″

Overture with *Murray,* verso
Oil and tempera on masonite, 20 x 16″
Collection: Drs. Charles and Pamela Berlin

Portrait of Rebecca
Watercolor on paper, 30 x 20″

Roof Over Their Heads
Oil on masonite, 46 x 52″
Collection: Charles S. Fax

Roof Over Their Heads (preparatory study)
Pastel, oil, and ink on paper, 10 x 15″
Collection: Arline Rosenberg (Mrs. Murray)

Still Life No. 1
Oil and tempera on masonite, 27 x 24″
Collection: Drs. Charles and Pamela Berlin

Upper Soho
Oil on canvas, 46 x 52″

Veteran on Porch
Oil and tempera on masonite, 20 x 24″
Collection: Jerome J. Segal, Dormont Manufacturing Company

Walt's Place at Fort Hill
Oil on canvas, 42 x 48″
Collection: Mary Lane Salsbury

1941

Autumn in Schenley Park
Oil on masonite, 20 x 24″

Cook's Forest
Oil on masonite, 25 x 35″
Collection: Warren and Judy Levine

Evening Promenade
Oil on masonite, 24 x 30″
Collection: Ruth Westerman

Mexican Village
Pencil on paper, 9⁹⁄₁₆ x 11¹³⁄₁₆″
Collection: Carnegie Museum of Art, Pittsburgh, Pa.; Gift of Murray Z. Rosenberg, 1978.27.1.406

Procession, Mexico
Oil and tempera on masonite, 24 x 20″
Collection: Jerome J. Segal, Dormont Manufacturing Company

Rhythms
Oil on masonite, 20 x 24″
Courtesy: Concept Art Gallery, Pittsburgh, Pa.

Rockport
Watercolor on paper

Spring
Oil on canvas, 24 x 20″

A Street on the Hill
Oil on canvas

Student (Murray)
Oil and tempera on masonite, 30 x 25″
Collection: Sue Rosenberg Wieser

The Tavern
Oil on canvas

Tree in Patzcuaro, Mexico
Oil on canvas, 30 x 25″

Warm Broth
Oil on canvas, 25 x 30″

1942

Backyard Pattern
Oil and tempera on masonite, 25 x 30″
Collection: Jerome J. Segal, Dormont Manufacturing Company

Bread No. 1
Oil and tempera on masonite, 20 x 24″
Collection: Westmoreland Museum of American Art, Greensburg, Pa.; Gift of Murray Z. Rosenberg, 1977.77

Bread No. 2
Oil and tempera on canvas, 31 x 37″
Collection: Jennifer Harris Katry

Conspirators
Oil and tempera on masonite, 25 x 30″
Collection: Westmoreland Museum of American Art, Greensburg, Pa.; Gift of Murray Z. Rosenberg, 1977.79

Consultation
Oil and tempera on masonite, 16 x 20″
Collection: Westmoreland Museum of American Art, Greensburg, Pa.; Gift of Murray Z. Rosenberg, 1977.76

The Covenantor
Oil and tempera on masonite, 30 x 25″

Farrellton Store
Oil on masonite, 25 x 30″
Collection: Arline Rosenberg (Mrs. Murray)

The Lesson
Oil on masonite

The Lesson (preparatory study)
Ink and conte crayon on paper, 20 x 16″
Collection: Beatrice and James Litman

Libbie's Father (Joseph Levin)
Oil on masonite, 20 x 16″
Collection: Arline Rosenberg (Mrs. Murray)

Mayville
Oil on canvas, 26 x 31″

Moment in Memory
Oil on canvas

Portrait of Mrs. Sam Levinson
Oil on canvas

Some Can Drink
Oil on masonite, 20 x 24″

Steel Mill
Oil on canvas

1943

Conflict
Oil on masonite, 24 x 20″
Collection: Lawrence and Ina Gumberg

Discussion No. 1
Oil on canvas

Discussion No. 2
Oil and tempera on masonite, 20 x 24″

Dusk (preparatory study)
Pastel on paper, 8½ x 9¼
Collection: Dot and Joel Rosenberg

Implicitness
Oil on masonite, 30 x 25″
Collection: Dr. Milton and Lois Michaels

The Mirror
Oil on masonite, 30 x 25″
Collection: Arline Rosenberg (Mrs. Murray)

My Brother
Oil and tempera on masonite, 24 x 20″
Collection: Temple Sinai, Pittsburgh, Pa.

Of the Sea
Oil and tempera on masonite

Off the Highway
Oil on canvas

Out in the Night
Oil on masonite, 20 x 24″
Commissioned by Encyclopedia Brittanica, Chicago; location unknown

Schenley Park, Autumn Pattern
Oil on canvas, 24 x 28″
Collection: Sandy and Don Schneider

Some Have Meat
Oil and tempera on masonite, 24 x 20″
Collection: Westmoreland Museum of American Art, Greensburg, Pa., Gift of Charles Carpenter, 1960.771

Two Women with Table
Oil on masonite, 24 x 20″
Collection: Arline Rosenberg (Mrs. Murray)

Waiting Women
Oil and tempera on masonite, 25 x 30″
Collection: Arline Rosenberg (Mrs. Murray)

Whither? No. 1
Oil on masonite, 20 x 24″
Collection: Florence Schneider

Whither? No. 2
Oil on canvas, 40 x 48″

1944

Abundance
Oil and tempera on masonite, 25 x 30″
Collection: Carnegie Mellon University, Gift of Anita Morganstern

Asleep
Oil on masonite, 24 x 20″
Collection: Morton and Norma Sue Madden

Chaperone (Two Women)
Oil on paper

The Connoisseur (The Skull)
Oil and tempera on masonite, 25 x 30″
Collection: Joan and Jerry Apt

Eva Peron
Oil and tempera on masonite, 25 x 30″
Collection: Westmoreland Museum of American Art, Greensburg, Pa., Gift of Murray Z. Rosenberg, 1977.80

False Gods
Oil and tempera on masonite, 20 x 24″
Collection: Westmoreland Museum of American Art, Greensburg, Pa., Gift of Murray Z. Rosenberg, 1977.78

Fear
Oil and tempera on masonite, 24 x 20″
Collection: Jewish Community Center of Greater Pittsburgh, Pittsburgh, Pa.

Flight

Oil and tempera on masonite

Generalissimo (Man of Importance)

Oil on masonite, 20 x 16″

Collection: Westmoreland Museum of American Art, Greensburg, Pa.; Gift of Murray Z. Rosenberg, 1977.74

O, Mother

Oil and tempera on masonite, 24 x 20″

Patriarch

Oil and tempera on masonite, 24 x 20″

Collection: Butler Institute of American Art, Youngstown, Ohio

Pittsburgh Evening, Downtown

Oil on masonite, 24 x 20″

Collection: Jill Schneider

Protest

Oil and tempera on masonite

The Secret

Oil and tempera on masonite

Painting destroyed

The Stage

Oil on masonite

The Threshold

Oil and tempera on masonite, 24 x 20″

1945

Astrea (Esther)

Oil and tempera on masonite, 24 x 20″

Collection: Florence Z. Walk

Carnival No. 1 (Fantasy No. 1)

Oil and tempera on masonite, 25 x 30″

Chosen Land

Oil and tempera on masonite, 24 x 20″

Collection: Edie Shapira and Mark Schmidhofer

Clown

Oil on masonite, 30 x 25″

The Counselors

Oil and tempera on masonite, 29 x 23″

The Father

Oil and tempera on masonite, 30 x 25″

In the Garden No. 1

Oil and tempera on masonite, 20 x 16″

Collection: Brooke and Jamie Zimmerman

Israel

Oil on masonite, 30 x 25″

Collection: The Jewish Association on Aging, Pittsburgh, Pa.

Still Life with Cabbage

Oil on masonite, 25 x 30″

Collection: Arline Rosenberg (Mrs. Murray)

The Unknown

Oil on masonite

1946

The Beginning

Oil on masonite, 25 x 30″

Carnival No. 2

Oil on masonite, 25 x 30″

Private collection

The Child

Oil on masonite, 20 x 24″

Collection: Catherine and Mark Loevner

Family Portrait

Oil on masonite, 25 x 30″

Collection: Barbara and Stanley Spiegelman

Heritage

Oil on masonite

A King

Oil and tempera on masonite, 30 x 25″

Collection: Arline Rosenberg (Mrs. Murray)

Park Bench

Oil on canvas, 20 x 16″

Promise

Oil on canvas, 30 x 25″

When?

Oil and tempera on masonite

Painting destroyed

1947

The Balcony

Oil on canvas, 6 x 8″

Clowns

Oil and tempera on masonite

Missing, 1950, AAA Gallery, New York

Conformity

Oil on canvas

Dedication

Oil on canvas

Collection: Estate of Allen Funt

Easter Sunday

Oil on canvas

Emergence No. 1

Oil on canvas

Illusion

Oil and tempera on masonite

The Lamb

Oil and tempera on masonite, 20 x 30″

Collection: Morton and Norma Sue Madden

Long on the Way

Oil on masonite, 30 x 25″

Collection: University Museum, Indiana University of Pennsylvania, on extended loan to Mr. Frank Gorell

Portrait of Abe Litman

Charcoal on paper, 14 x 19″

Collection: Thomas and Sally Litman

Reminiscence

Oil on canvas

The Word

Oil on masonite, 30 x 25″

1948

Fantasy No. 2

Oil on board, 5 x 7″

Collection: David J. Vater

The Grandfather No. 2

Oil on masonite, 30 x 25″

Collection: Joseph Kalla

Head of a Man No. 2

Oil on masonite

Intermission

Oil on masonite, 25 x 30″

Collection: Phylis and Erwin Kalla

The Leaf

Oil on masonite, 20 x 16″

Collection: Ruth Westerman

Oft Told Tale

Oil and tempera on masonite

Portrait of Libbie

Oil on masonite, 19 x 16″

Collection: Ruth Westerman

Remembrances

Oil on masonite

A Rose

Oil on masonite

1949

Amos

Oil on canvas, 19 x 16″

Collection: Frederick N. Frank, Esq.

Awakening

Oil on canvas, 20 x 46″

Collection: Sara Berlin

Backstage

Oil on masonite, 24 x 30″

Collection: Murray and Claire Levine

The Book

Oil on canvas, 30 x 25″

Collection: Sara and Jack Gordon

Form and Shadow

Oil on masonite, 23 x 19″

Heir Apparent

Oil on canvas, 20 x 24″

Collection: Mark and Jo Beth Ravitz

The Present

Oil on canvas, 25 x 30″

Collection: Joseph Kalla

Untitled Composition 1949 No. 1

Oil on masonite, 10 x 12″

Collection: Westmoreland Museum of American Art, Greensburg, Pa.; Gift of Anita Morganstern, 1991.20

Untitled Composition 1949 No. 2

Oil on canvas, 16 x 14″

Untitled Composition 1949 No. 3

Oil on masonite, 20 x 24″

Collection: Natalie Meyers

Untitled Composition 1949 No. 4

Oil on masonite, 24 x 20″

Collection: Arline Rosenberg (Mrs. Murray)

Untitled Composition 1949 No. 5

Oil on canvas, 8 x 6″

Untitled Composition 1949 No. 6

Oil on masonite, 15 x 13″

Collection: Sara Berlin

Untitled Composition 1949 No. 7

Oil on masonite, 25 x 30″

Collection: Ronald A. Berlin

Untitled Composition 1949 No. 8

Oil on masonite, 30 x 25″

Collection: Arline Rosenberg (Mrs. Murray)

The Window
Oil on wood, 7 x 5″

1950

Adolescence
Oil on canvas on masonite, 24 x 18″
Collection: Arline Rosenberg (Mrs. Murray)

Balloon Man No. 1
Oil on canvas
Collection: Abbott Laboratories, Chicago

Balloon Man No. 2
Oil on canvas, 46 x 36″
Collection: Catherine and Mark Loevner

Brief Candle
Oil and tempera on masonite, 32 x 48″
Collection: Mr. and Mrs. Harvey F. Wimmer

Focus on Green
Oil on masonite, 24 x 20″
Collection: Sue Rosenberg Wieser

Focus on Red
Oil on masonite, 10 x 14″
Collection: Jerome J. Segal, Dormont Manufacturing Company

Gleam of Time
Oil on masonite, 20 x 24″
Collection: Beatrice and James Litman

Late Summer
Oil on masonite, 24 x 20″

Light Transcendent
Oil on masonite, 25 x 30″

Little Garden
Oil on canvas
Collection: Somerset Trust Company

Moment Implied
Oil on canvas

Recession: Pittsburgh
Oil on canvas, 36 x 45″
Collection: Sara and Jack Gordon

Woman in Lavender Dress
Oil on masonite, 30 x 25″
Collection: Arline Rosenberg (Mrs. Murray)

1952

Aquarium
Oil on masonite, 20 x 16″
Collection: Lisa and Peter Gordon

Christ Teaching (cartoon for mural)
Oil on masonite, 13½ x 41″
Collection: St. John Vianney Parish, St. Henry's Church, Pittsburgh, Pa.

Christ Teaching (cartoon for mural)
Pencil on tracing paper, 8 x 30″
Collection: St. John Vianney Parish, St. Henry's Church, Pittsburgh, Pa.

Christ Teaching (cartoon for mural)
Oil on masonite, 8 x 30″
Collection: St. John Vianney Parish, St. Henry's Church, Pittsburgh, Pa.

Christ Teaching (mural), 1951–52
Oil on canvas, 120 x 228″
Collection: St. John Vianney Parish, St. Henry's Church, Pittsburgh, Pa.

Christ Teaching (preparatory color pattern #1 for mural)
Oil on canvas, 6 x 22¼″
Collection: St. John Vianney Parish, St. Henry's Church, Pittsburgh, Pa.

Christ Teaching (preparatory color pattern #2 for mural)
Oil on canvas, 6 x 22″
Collection: St. John Vianney Parish, St. Henry's Church, Pittsburgh, Pa.

Christ Teaching (preparatory sketch for mural)
Pencil on paper, 10 x 30″
Collection: St. John Vianney Parish, St. Henry's Church, Pittsburgh, Pa.

Christ Teaching (sketch #2 in preparation for cartoon for mural)
Oil on canvas, 8 x 30″
Collection: St. John Vianney Parish, St. Henry's Church, Pittsburgh, Pa.

The Family
Oil on masonite, 30 x 24″
Collection:
Dr. and Mrs. Jack L. Paradise

Farmer's Market

Oil on canvas, 42 x 48″

Collection: Carnegie Museum of Art, Pittsburgh, Pa.; Gift of Mrs. Howard Felding in memory of Henry Boettcher, 1980.66.4

Light: Still and Moving

Oil on canvas, 29 x 35″

Madonna

Oil on unknown support, 24 x 20″

Collection: Ronald A. Berlin

Time Echoes

Oil on canvas, 72 x 36″

Collection: Carnegie Museum of Art, Pittsburgh, Pa.; Purchase: Patrons Art Fund, 1952.12

Uncertain Hour

Oil on canvas

1953

Composition

Oil on masonite, 25 x 18″

Collection: Arline Rosenberg (Mrs. Murray)

Emergence No. 2

Oil on canvas, 30 x 30″

Collection: Dr. and Mrs. Jack L. Paradise

Fantasy, c. 1953

Oil on masonite, 25 x 30″

Collection: Westmoreland Museum of American Art, Greensburg, Pa.; Gift of Mr. and Mrs. Sidney Lawrence, 1983.70

Nativity

Oil on unknown support

Collection: Abbott Laboratories, Chicago

Unstilled Earth

Oil on canvas, 45 x 30″

Collection: Dr. and Mrs. Richard Kalla

1954

Composition

Oil on canvas, 25 x 30″

Collection: Arline Rosenberg (Mrs. Murray)

Horizons

Oil on canvas, 36 x 40″

Collection: Rosella Broff (Mrs. Gilbert)

Maine, c. 1954

Oil on masonite, 12 x 12″

Private collection

Procession

Oil on canvas, 52 x 30″

To the Light No. 1

Oil on canvas

1955

Abstraction 1955 No. 3

Oil on canvas, 20 x 24″

Collection: Arline Rosenberg (Mrs. Murray)

At the Window No. 1

Oil on masonite, 24 x 20″

Private collection

Brown and Yellow

Oil on canvas

Falling Light

Oil on canvas, 30 x 10″

Fruit in Evening Light (April Sun)

Oil on canvas, 30 x 40″

Collection: Bernard M. Halpern

The Pool

Oil on canvas, 16 x 30″

Collection: Ruth Westerman

Red on Red

Oil on canvas

Reflections

Oil on canvas, 48 x 36″

The Rocket

Oil on canvas, 36 x 16″

Collection: Thomas and Sally Litman

Season's Turning

Oil on canvas, 42 x 48″

Collection: Karl and Jennifer Salatka

The Seed

Oil on canvas, 46 x 30″

Collection: Westmoreland Museum of American Art, Greensburg, Pa.; Gift of Mr. and Mrs. Sidney Lawrence, 1983.69

Time Resolved (Light on the Rock)

Oil on canvas, 36 x 18″

Collection: Arline Rosenberg (Mrs. Murray)

Untitled No. 17

Oil on canvas, 41 x 30″

Courtesy: Concept Art Gallery, Pittsburgh, Pa.

1956

Becoming

Oil on canvas, 71 x 46″

Collection: William H. Warner

Elusive Moment

Oil on canvas

Enveloping Light

Oil on canvas, 36 x 30″

The Glen

Oil on masonite, 36 x 18″

Collection: Kenneth A. Gardner

Incoming Tide

Oil on canvas, 36 x 50″

Painting destroyed in fire

The Light and the Rock

Oil on canvas, 54 x 36″

Low Tide

Oil on canvas, 30 x 40″

Renascence

Oil on canvas, 70 x 36″

Collection: Arline Rosenberg (Mrs. Murray)

Sunlit Rhythm

Oil on canvas, 40 x 30″

Collection: Mr. and Mrs. James Houston

To the Light No. 2

Oil on canvas, 44 x 36″

1957

Blue in Black

Oil on canvas, 60 x 45″

Composition

Oil on canvas, 40 x 50″

Collection: Arline Rosenberg (Mrs. Murray)

The Crag, Rockport

Oil on canvas, 48 x 36″

Ebb Tide

Oil on canvas, 30 x 36″

Green on Yellow, 1954–57

Oil on canvas, 54 x 46″

Interior No. 3

Oil on canvas, 60 x 72″

Collection: Washington County Museum of Fine Arts, Hagerstown, Md.; Gift of Dr. Winston Price, Baltimore, Md.

Light Translucent

Oil on canvas, 40 x 36″

Maine, 1957

Oil on canvas, 30 x 36″

Red on Grey

Oil on canvas

Yellow on White, 1955–57

Oil on canvas, 60 x 36″

Collection: Arline Rosenberg (Mrs. Murray)

1958

Composition in Blue and Red

Oil on canvas, 36 x 45″

Collection: Janet F. Lewis

Crescendo

Oil on canvas, 40 x 50″

Collection: Mr. and Mrs. Herbert Simon

Magic City

Oil on canvas, 40 x 50″

Orange and Black

Oil on canvas, 48 x 56″

Painting 1958 No. 2

Oil on canvas

Significant Shelter

Oil on canvas, 40 x 32″

1959

Blue Beyond Blue

Oil on canvas, 32 x 38″

Composition

Oil on canvas, 50 x 40″

Corridors

Oil on canvas, 40 x 50″

Embarkation

Oil on canvas, 64 x 50″

Painting 1959 No. 1

Oil on canvas

Perpetual Light No. 1

Oil on canvas, 50 x 40″

Collection: Dee Davis

Processional

Oil on canvas

Regeneration

Oil on canvas, 60 x 40″

Collection: Joseph Kalla

Tuscan Light

Oil on canvas, 36 x 28″

Collection: Kenneth A. Gardner

Variations (Untitled No. 7)
Oil on canvas, 25 x 30″
Collection: Anne and Neil Paylor

1960

Abstract Self-Portrait
Oil on board, 12 x 10″
Collection: Steven Mosites, Jr. and Cyndy Mosites

Branches, Yellow and Blue
Oil on canvas board, 25 x 17″
Collection: Arline Rosenberg (Mrs. Murray)

Still Life with Abstract Bottles
Oil/paper collage on masonite, 13 x 9″
Collection: Arline Rosenberg (Mrs. Murray)

Untitled Composition, c. 1960
Oil on canvas, 36 x 40″
Collection: Carnegie Museum of Art, Pittsburgh, Pa.; Gift of Mr. and Mrs. William P. Rogers in memory of Hugh Savage Clark, 1993.171.

Untitled Composition, c. 1960
Oil on canvas, 30 x 25″
Collection: Carnegie Museum of Art, Pittsburgh, Pa.; Gift of Helen Moore, through the Women's Committee, 2000.65.2

1961

Arrival
Oil on canvas, 46 x 42″
Collection: Bernard M. Halpern

The Bridge No. 3 (formerly *Light Burnished*), 1959–61
Oil on canvas, 30 x 40″

In the Beginning (Composition)
Oil on canvas, 56 x 93″
Collection: Temple Sinai, Pittsburgh, Pa.

Interior No. 4
Oil on canvas

Morning Light No. 1
Oil on canvas

Point Lobos No. 1
Oil on canvas, 40 x 50″
Collection: Greater Latrobe School District

Point Lobos No. 2
Oil on canvas

Transition
Oil on canvas, 52 x 45″

Wooded Silence
Oil on canvas, 62 x 42″
Collection: Florence Z. Walk

1962

Disappearing Image
Oil on canvas, 30 x 25″

Horizon No. 2
Oil on canvas, 36 x 40″
Collection: Dot and Joel Rosenberg

Portrait of Joel
Oil on canvas board, 20 x 16″
Collection: Arline Rosenberg (Mrs. Murray)

Red Beyond Red
Oil on canvas, 25 x 30″

1963

Arizona
Oil on canvas, 28 x 36″
Collection: Ruth Westerman

Ceremonial
Oil on canvas

The Fall
Oil on canvas, 50 x 40″

Revelation
Oil on canvas, 36 x 26″
Collection: Sue Rosenberg Wieser

1964

Afterglow, 1958–64
Oil on canvas, 26 x 36″
Collection: Jane and Ed Haskell

Composition (Untitled No. 6)
Oil on canvas, 30 x 25″
Collection: Sally and Fred Lehman

November (Homage to the Light)
Oil on canvas, 50 x 40″
Collection: Dr. and Mrs. Raymond Stept

Personages
Oil on canvas, 60 x 40″
Collection: Dot and Joel Rosenberg

Portent
Oil on canvas, 40 x 50″
Collection: Elaine and Jules Levy

A Presence
Oil on canvas, 50 x 40″

Through Eastern Windows
Oil on canvas, 52 x 72″
Collection: Rodef Shalom Congregation, Pittsburgh, Pa.

1965

Ascending Yellow
Oil on canvas, 51 x 56″

The Harbour
Oil on canvas, 40 x 50″
Collection: Carnegie Museum of Art, Pittsburgh, Pa.; Gift of Miriam M. Steinert, 2000.44

Man by the Sea No. 1
Oil on canvas, 48 x 40″
Collection: Mr. and Mrs. Henry L. Hillman

Portrait of Sue
Oil on canvas, 16 x 16″
Collection: Sue Rosenberg Wieser

Spring Light
Oil on canvas, 30 x 24″
Collection: Dot and Joel Rosenberg

1966

Echoes
Oil on canvas, 41 x 41″
Collection: Arline Rosenberg (Mrs. Murray)

On the Mountain
Oil on canvas, 54 x 40″
Collection: Philip and Anita Brostoff

Painting (Resolving Image)
Oil on canvas, 40 x 30″
Collection: Paul Ozimok

1967

On the Heights
Oil on canvas, 40 x 50″
Private collection

Painting, 1967
Oil on canvas, 66 x 42″
Collection: University Art Gallery, University of Pittsburgh, Pittsburgh, Pa.

Untitled (Red and Blue)
Acrylic on canvas, 30 x 40″
Collection: Arline Rosenberg (Mrs. Murray)

1968

Carnival No. 3
Acrylic on canvas, 25 x 30″
Collection: Sue Rosenberg Wieser

The Cave
Oil on canvas, 30 x 40″
Collection: Sandy and Don Schneider

Garden Motif
Oil on canvas board, 24 x 20″
Collection: Murray and Claire Levine

Untitled Composition No. 1
Acrylic on canvas, 30 x 40″
Collection: Lee and Myrna Silverman

1969

April No. 1
Oil on canvas, 32 x 45″
Collection: Arline Rosenberg (Mrs. Murray)

Clearstream No. 1
Oil on canvas, 36 x 40″
Collection: Joshua Whetzel

Encounter
Oil on canvas, 50 x 40″

The Edge
Oil on canvas, 48 x 36″

Fleeting Moment
Oil on canvas, 20 x 24″
Collection: Sandy and Don Schneider

Importance of Red
Oil on canvas, 48 x 35″
Collection: Amy and Sy Kellman

Light on the Mountain
Oil on canvas, 50 x 40″
Collection: Arline Rosenberg (Mrs. Murray)

Lilies: Red and Gold
Oil on masonite, 44 x 30″
Collection: Estate of Mr. and Mrs. Melvin Levine (Mary)

Painting 1969 No. 2
Oil on canvas, 25 x 30″
Collection: Barbara and Stanley Spiegelman

1970

April No. 2
Oil on canvas, 40 x 50″
Collection: Thomas and Sally Litman

Figure in Blue Light
Acrylic on canvas, 30 x 25″
Collection: Sewickley Academy, Sewickley, Pa.

Heart of the Rock

Oil on canvas, 40 x 40″

Collection: Dot and Joel Rosenberg

October Morning, 1969–1970

Oil on canvas, 42 x 52″

Private collection

Pivot

Oil on canvas, 50 x 40″

Collection: Westmoreland Museum of American Art, Greensburg, Pa.; Gift of Dr. and Mrs. Laibe Kessler, 1981.82

Portrait of Joel

Charcoal on paper, 16 x 14″

Collection: Dot and Joel Rosenberg

Studio Interior

Acrylic on canvas, 38 x 50″

Collection: Sue Rosenberg Wieser

Sue with Still Life

Oil on canvas, 22 x 27″

Collection: Arline Rosenberg (Mrs. Murray)

1971

Mountain Lake, 1965–71

Oil on canvas, 28 x 40″

Fleeting Substance, 1954–71

Oil on canvas, 50 x 42″

Collection: Allen H. Berkman

1972

At the Window No. 2, 1969–1972

Oil on canvas, 45 x 40″

Collection: Sam and Joan Kamin

Clearstream No. 2

Oil on canvas, 40 x 49″

Collection: Sue Rosenberg Wieser

Elusive Image

Oil on canvas, 30 x 25″

Collection: Florence Schneider

Interaction Blue and Red (formerly *Bright October Morning*), 1968–72

Oil on canvas, 38 x 48″

Collection: Ruth Westerman

Light and Image

Oil on canvas, 50 x 40″

Collection: Sandy and Don Schneider

Man by the Sea No. 2, 1968–72

Oil on canvas, 55 x 40″

Collection: Dot and Joel Rosenberg

Perpetual Light No. 2, 1964–72

Oil on canvas, 40 x 36″

Collection: Sue Rosenberg Wieser

Untitled Composition

Oil on canvas, 40 x 46″

Wedding in the Garden

Oil on canvas, 50 x 36″

Collection: Dot and Joel Rosenberg

NOTES

1. A short film of Rosenberg (three minutes and forty-seven seconds) was made in 1966 by Jean Connelly of WQED, the public television station in Pittsburgh, but no soundtrack was ever applied to it. It reveals Rosenberg's interest in his African sculptures as he shows them to Connelly, and shows the interior of his house and attached studio on Mount Royal Road, with all his paintings lined up on the floor.
2. Interview with Libbie Rosenberg by Elinore Mermelstein and Harold Kimball for the National Council of Jewish Women, Pittsburgh Section (13 November 1983), in the Archives of Industrial Society, University of Pittsburgh Library System Archives, Pittsburgh, Pa.
3. Unless otherwise noted, student information was gathered through telephone interviews conducted by author, and a Teaching Questionnaire that was mailed to 125 former students of Rosenberg's. The questionnaire asked about which classes they took with Rosenberg; where, specific aspects of Rosenberg's teaching methodology, as well as which painting techniques he demonstrated. Responses came from students who took classes with Rosenberg between 1938 and 1961. I am sincerely grateful to all of those students (and those who weren't his students) who responded to my questions: Bill Aiken, William Bean for Merry, Ken Beittel, Juleanne Addis Biehl, Rochelle Blumenfeld, Mel Bochner, David Byrne, Winifred Carr, Don Carter, Randolph Chalfant, Larry Cindrich, Robert Clements, Joan Cohen, Norman Daley, Ray DeFazio, Hilda Green Demsky, Arthur Elias, Eleanor Fax, Ann Fields, Elaine Fisher, Hugh Fitzgerald, Fran Grimes, Aaronel de Roy Gruber, Art Hansen, Jane Haskell, Milton Howarth, Katherine Kadish, Gloria Karn, Constantine Kermes, Len Kessler, Alan Kimmel, Robert Korn, Bernice Lehman, Dolly Lynch, Diane Haber March, Rita Marlier, Jay Matternes, Elizabeth McClain, George Nama, Sidney Navratil, Herb Olds, Philip Pearlstein, Bennard Perlman, Gloria Peterson, Hilda Pope, Mina Post, Lindsay Rosenberger, Eleanor Rushworth, Gretchen Schmertz, Mildred Schmertz, David Schnabel, Frances Scott, Phyllis Sloane, Dale Stein, Martha Sutherland, Beverly Wallace, and Elaine Wechsler.
4. Douglas Naylor, "Art for Life's Sake," *Pittsburgh Press* (27 July 1937).
5. Harry Salpeter, "A Human Sort of Artist," *Esquire* (March 1945), 83.
6. Sam Hood, "Samuel Rosenberg: Pittsburgh's Painter Laureate," *Pittsburgh Press* (3 November 1957), 33. Rosenberg thought this article to be the best of those written about him.
7. Jacob R. Coblens, letter to Rosenberg (31 August 1911), 3; Coblens, letter to Rosenberg (23 November 1911). Samuel Rosenberg Archives, Asheville, N.C.
8. Murray Z. Rosenberg, "Preparatory lecture notes" for slide presentation

(15 February 1981) during Samuel Rosenberg exhibition at University of Connecticut Library (25 January–6 March 1981). Samuel Rosenberg Archives.

9. Hood, "Samuel Rosenberg: Pittsburgh's Painter Laureate," 33.
10. Patrick J. Byrne was an interesting neighbor for Rosenberg. He had studied at the Cooper Union in New York, and at the Corcoran Art School in Washington, D.C. He worked on murals for Congressional library, was a decorator, court tipstaff, book collector, amateur scholar (he taught French and Italian), and father of thirteen. Byrne met the southwestern Pennsylvania painter, Arthur Sparks (1870–1919) at night classes at the Corcoran Art School around 1890. He went to Paris in 1900 for ten years and carried on a lively correspondence with Sparks. Byrne was responsible for Sparks's appointment in 1908 as first head of the Department of Painting and Design at Carnegie Tech. From card handwritten by Libbie Rosenberg in Samuel Rosenberg Archives; Hood, "Samuel Rosenberg: Pittsburgh's Painter Laureate," 33.
11. This was originally created as a three-quarter-length portrait with the artist holding a large palette in his right hand and paintbrush in his left, but Rosenberg cut it down because of damage to the canvas.
12. Rosenberg sent Coblens a self-portrait he had done, and when he wrote back with his critique, Coblens said it appeared that Rosenberg had acquired a Hapsburg jaw. Rosenberg wrote back to explain that he was studying Velázquez, and Velázquez was the court painter to Spain's King Philip IV, a Hapsburg.
13. This painting was the first piece of Rosenberg's work to be reproduced as a color gravure in the newspaper. *Pittsburgh Sun-Telegraph*, Sunday Edition, (5 October 1928).
14. Murray Z. Rosenberg, letter to Mickey Stern (24 April 1991) regarding the translation of the Matisse's letter to Henry Clifford in 1948. Jack Flam translated from Matisse's original letter, and it was a tertiary version that circulated among the art department faculty at Carnegie Tech in the 1950s. Copy of letter in Samuel Rosenberg Archives.
15. The interior setting, with its checkered floor and open doorway into the next room, recalls the Dutch paintings of the seventeenth century that Rosenberg so admired. Referring to the array of patterns, colors, and shapes, the art critic Penelope Redd called it "a charming concert." Rosenberg was one of eight Pittsburgh artists invited to exhibit in the Gulf Gallery exhibition at the Carnegie Institute. *First Halloween* was one of the three paintings he showed in that exhibition.
16. *Pittsburgh Sun-Telegraph* (24 October 1937) in which Murray is shown drawing a poster to be entered in the elementary school art show at the Community Fund's Exposition of Human Progress.
17. Ruth Westerman, under the direction of Sandy Schneider, organized two important Samuel Rosenberg exhibitions for the Jewish Community Center of Greater Pittsburgh: *Samuel Rosenberg: The Early Years* (5 June–29 June 1994) and *Samuel Rosenberg: The Transition Years* (30 May–8 July 1996).
18. Teresa Dalla Piccola Wood and Mary Brignano, *The Associated Artists of Pittsburgh: 1910–1985, The First Seventy-Five Years* (Pittsburgh, Pa., 1985), 25.
19. According to both Libbie and Murray Rosenberg, during his interview, Sam Hood mistakenly took literally what Rosenberg said in jest about his "lucrative career in portraits." Murray Z. Rosenberg, letter to Gail Stavitsky, Assistant Curator of Fine Arts, Museum of Art, Carnegie

Institute (26 July 1983). Samuel Rosenberg Archives.

20. Margaret Carlin, "At Home with Our Artists: A Place for Painting," *Pittsburgh Press* (17 March 1968).
21. Douglas Naylor, "Blind to Real Art," *Pittsburgh Press* (6 January 1935).
22. Naylor, "Blind to Real Art."
23. "Mr. Rosenberg Exhibits—Local Hill District is Theme," *The Arrow,* student publication of Pennsylvania College for Women (26 October 1938), Chatham College Archives.
24. By 1930, 85 percent of all professional artists were located in nine metropolitan areas including New York, Boston, Philadelphia, Detroit, Chicago, and San Francisco. Works Progress Administration Federal Art Project, *Frontiers of American Art* (San Francisco: M. H. deYoung Memorial Museum, 1939), 10.
25. Naylor, "Art for Life's Sake."
26. Robert Henri, *The Art Spirit* (New York: Harper & Row, Publishers, 1984), 116, 218.
27. Stefan Lorant, *Pittsburgh: The Story of An American City* (New York: Doubleday & Company, Inc., 1964), 340. Reproductions are found on pages 349–52; 482; 483; 489.
28. Lois Hollander, "Pen-Shots of Important People, Samuel Rosenberg," *Jewish Criterion* (15 February 1935), 9, 28.
29. Dorothy Kantner, *Pittsburgh Sun-Telegraph,* no title, no date. Scrapbook Volume I, p. 71. Samuel Rosenberg Archives.
30. Rich Gigler, "The Crash . . . 'No One Seemed To Know What Was Going On'," *Pittsburgh Press* (7 October 1979), 6.
31. William Faust, "Patrons Good Naturedly Talk Over Sleeping Places at Police Stations," *Pittsburgh Press* (19 March 1930). The agencies in Pittsburgh that offered relief included the Family Welfare Association of America; Pittsburgh Association for Improvement of Poor; the Salvation Army; and Goodwill Industries; "Family Relief Situation in Pittsburgh," *Greater Pittsburgh* (28 March 1931).
32. "City Ready to Begin Job Relief Program," *Pittsburgh Post-Gazette* (5 February 1931).
33. Bervard Nichols, "Pittsburgh Escapes Worst of Slump," *Greater Pittsburgh* (22 November 1930).
34. "Plants Here Get Millions in Contracts," *Pittsburgh Press* (12 July 1931).
35. "This is Shantytown, What Are You Going to Do About It?" *Bulletin Index* (24 September 1931).
36. "Call 5,000 Men Back into Jobs at Steel Mills," *Pittsburgh Post-Gazette* (10 June 1933); "Business Gain Creates 2,000 Jobs Here," *Pittsburgh Post-Gazette* (11 June 1933).
37. According to his wife, Libbie, Rosenberg changed the title of this painting from *Man-Made Desert* to *Street by the Mill* in response to John O'Connor's comment that "the Museum of Art board reacted negatively to his paintings of the poorer sections of Pittsburgh; they wanted him to paint the nicer parts." This painting was also incorrectly dated 1933 by the artist when he was asked to sign and date some of the paintings that were to be included in his 1960 retrospective exhibition at the Westmoreland County Museum of Art (now the Westmoreland Museum of American Art) in Greensburg, Pa. The painting was made in 1932 and was shown that year in the Associated Artists of Pittsburgh Thirty-second Annual Exhibition. Conversation with Libbie Rosenberg detailed in Museum of Art, Carnegie Institute/Memorandum to ACT, from Gail Stavitsky (7 July 1983) in Samuel Rosenberg file, Carnegie Museum of Art, Pittsburgh, Pa. The painting's title was changed again to its present title, *Second Avenue,* when it entered the collection of the Museum of Art, Carnegie Institute.
38. The title of the painting was changed in 1957 when it entered the collection of the

Museum of Art, Carnegie Institute. It is doubtful that this mystery can be solved because both areas no longer look anything like they did in the 1930s.

39. *New York Herald Tribune,* Sunday (4 March 1934), sec. VII.
40. Naylor, "Art for Life's Sake." Sam and Libbie spent several summer vacations in New England, so Sam had an opportunity to observe this difference in light.
41. Penelope Redd, *Pittsburgh Sun-Telegraph* (no date, 1933). Scrapbook Volume I, p. 12.
42. "Co-operation of Landlords is Necessary," *Pittsburgh Press* (14 April 1933). In the first four months of that year 69,533 families were already on relief.
43. Naylor, "Blind to Real Art."
44. Jeanette Jena, "Striking Art Put on Exhibit at Institute: Pittsburgh Vitality Is Shown in Work of Rosenberg," *Pittsburgh Post-Gazette* (25 March 1937).
45. "Rosenberg Gets Prize," *Pittsburgh Courier* (11 October 1947), regarding the Pepsi-Cola Company's *Paintings of the Year* exhibition. Scrapbook Volume II, p. 36.
46. Ralph Brem, "Artist Jams Life of Color into Exhibit," no paper identified, no date, but prior to the 15 March 1965 opening of the Samuel Rosenberg exhibition of nineteen paintings held at the Hewlett Gallery, 15 March–2 April 1965 in recognition of his retirement from teaching at Carnegie Tech in 1964 after forty years. Pittsburgh artists clipping file, Samuel Rosenberg. Carnegie Library, Art and Music Department, Pittsburgh, Pa.
47. Naylor, "Art for Life's Sake."
48. Edward M. Power, "Rediscovering Pittsburgh's Treasures: 17—Our Wonder of the Hill District," *Greater Pittsburgh* (February 1932), 25–26.
49. *Bulletin Index* (14 February 1935), title and author unknown. Scrapbook Volume I, p. 21.
50. Douglas Naylor, "Maybe You Will Call It Madness but Sober Painter of Tipsy Houses Calls Work 'Art'," *Pittsburgh Press* (26 February 1933). Interview with Douglas Naylor regarding paintings in the Associated Artists of Pittsburgh annual exhibition on February 25, 1933. This idea is similar to one put forth by Robert Lepper, a faculty colleague in Carnegie Tech's Fine Arts Department with Rosenberg. Called the "Oakland Project," Lepper gave his students a yearlong assignment to go out into the Oakland neighborhood, find a house, and from its architectural details and personal characteristics, describe the family that lived inside through drawings and paintings.
51. Naylor, "Art for Life's Sake."
52. Nearly thirty thousand Jews lived in Pittsburgh in 1910 and nearly all of them lived in the Hill District. Leonard Irvin Kuntz, *The Changing Pattern of the Distribution of the Jewish Population of Pittsburgh from Earliest Settlement to 1963.* (Ann Arbor, Michigan: University Microfilms, Inc., 1996), 42.
53. Franklin Toker, *Pittsburgh, An Urban Portrait* (State College, Pa.: Penn State University Press, 1986), 232–41.
54. Gilbert Love, *The Pittsburgh Press* (14 October 1938).
55. Love, "Applicants Near Starvation In Many Cases," *Pittsburgh Press* (14 October 1938).
56. Dorothy Kantner, "Pittsburghers Represented in Exhibit," *Pittsburgh Sun-Telegraph* (9 October 1938). The caption to the illustration read, "The Pittsburgh artist injects a biblical quality to his Pittsburgh scene and by doing so gives it an added depth and interest.")
57. Elmer Stephan, "Art Everyday," *Pittsburgh Press* (28 November 1938).
58. Jeanette Jena, "Annual Carnegie Show Proves Art Has No Frontiers," *Pittsburgh Post Gazette* (13 October 1938).
59. Charles Danver, "Street of Babel," *Pittsburgh Post-Gazette* (10 October 1938).

60. "Art, International's 36th," *Bulletin Index* (20 October 1938). The writer was suggesting a Rosenberg school of painting because of the admiration of his students and fellow artists for his work.
61. Grace Pagano, *Encyclopedia Britannica Collection of Contemporary American Painting* (Chicago: Encyclopedia Britannica, Inc., 1945), opposite plate 93.
62. Philip Klein, *A Social Study of Pittsburgh: Community Problems and Social Services of Allegheny County* (New York: Columbia University Press, 1938), Table 18. Table 19 reveals the contrast with Squirrel Hill where only 1.3 percent of the homes were without hot water, 1.8 percent with no indoor toilet facilities, and only 4.6% with no furnace-type heating.
63. Toker, 240.
64. Information on how Rosenberg made the painting came from Eleanor Fax, owner of the painting, in a letter to Rabbi Walter Jacob (20 February 1998), letter held by Ruth Westerman; Emily Genauer, "The Terrific Impact of the Moderns," *New York World-Telegram* (26 October 1940).
65. In preparation for building the Civic Arena, in 1961, more than fifteen hundred families were displaced from their homes in this area. Because the city had made no housing provisions for them, they ultimately crowded into other low income sections of the city such as East Liberty and Homewood-Brushton. "The Hill District: History," Carnegie Library, Pennsylvania Department; Joe William Trotter, Jr. and Eric Ledell Smith, eds., *African Americans in Pennsylvania: Shifting Historical Perspectives* (Harrisburg: The Pennsylvania Historical and Museum Commission and Pennsylvania State University Press, 1997), 425.
66. Hollander, "Pen-Shots of Important People, Samuel Rosenberg."
67. Matthew Baigell, *The American Scene: American Painting of the 1930s* (New York: Praeger Publishers, 1974), 18.
68. Unidentified author, *Pittsburgh Post-Gazette* (9 February 1935). Scrapbook Volume I, p. 17. Rosenberg held on to this painting for the Westmoreland County Museum of Art. Another one of his patrons, Harold Ruttenberg, who also owned *Eviction,* wanted to buy it. Rosenberg said the "two paintings do portray together a very meaningful part of our American culture." But he did not sell it to him because he wanted the painting to be in a museum collection. Information in letter from Samuel Rosenberg to Harold Ruttenberg (1 October 1968). Samuel Rosenberg Archives. The Whitney Museum of American Art was also interested in purchasing the painting after it was shown there in 1934, but they were without funds at the time to do so. Information from a letter in Samuel Rosenberg Artist File, Whitney Museum of American Art Library, New York.
69. Edward Alden Jewell, "Art in Review: Painting and Sculpture from 16 American Cities on Display at Museum of Modern Art," *New York Times* (12 December 1933), 28. The sixteen American cities that were selected to participate were: Atlanta, Baltimore, Boston, Buffalo, Chicago, Cleveland, Dallas, Detroit, Los Angeles, Minneapolis, Philadelphia, Pittsburgh, St. Louis, San Francisco, Santa Fe, and Seattle.
70. The WPA allowed artists to continue making art during the depression and war years and made that art accessible to a broad public; it was a major force in stimulating the public's interest in American art from its inception in 1935 until 1943.
71. Oliver Larkin, *Art and Life in America,* 2d ed. (New York: Holt, Rinehart and Winston, 1964), 416; "Art: U.S. Scene," *Time, The Weekly Newsmagazine* (24 December 1934),

24–27; Laurence E. Schmeckebier, *John Steuart Curry's Pageant of America* (New York: American Artists Group, 1943), 97.

72. Larkin, 429.
73. Larkin, 428.
74. Wood and Brignano, 30.
75. Naylor, "Art for Life's Sake."
76. "Steel Mills Hum at Boom Tempo to Meet Demand," *Pittsburgh Post Gazette,* (9 October 1939); Gilbert Love, "Black Skies Take District Out of the Red Once More," *Pittsburgh Press* (24 September 1939).
77. Toker, 240; *Pittsburgh Sun-Telegraph* (18 April 1939); "Now Where Will He Go?" *Pittsburgh Sun-Telegraph* (17 June 1940).
78. Larkin, 430.
79. Barbara Haskell, *The American Century: Art and Culture 1900–1950* (New York: Whitney Museum of American Art in association with W. W. Norton & Company, 1999), 337; Matlack Price, "2224 War Posters: A Review of the National Poster Competition," *American Artist* (December 1942), 4–11, 40; "America at War: One Hundred Contemporary Prints now on Exhibit in 26 American Museums and Galleries," *Magazine of Art* (October 1943), 225; Alfred M. Frankfurter, "Artists for Victory Exhibition: The Paintings," *Art News* (January 1943), 8–13, 31.
80. "Biography," *Bulletin Index* (16 March 1946), 18–20.
81. Salpeter, 149.
82. Brem, "Artist Jams Life of Color into Exhibit," Pittsburgh artist clipping files, Carnegie Library, Art and Music Department.
83. Pagano, *Encyclopedia Britannica Collection of Contemporary American Painting,* opposite plate 93.
84. Reference library, United States Holocaust Memorial Museum, Washington, D.C. Data obtained through telephone conversation as well as through the museum's Web site.
85. Penelope Redd Jones, "Noted Artists in Founders Day Show," *Pittsburgh Sun-Telegraph* (9 October 1944); Unidentified newspaper clipping. Scrapbook Volume II, p. 49; *New York Herald Tribune* (4 January 1948); Douglas Naylor, "Show Indicates That Most of Painters are Unaffected by War's Turmoil," *Pittsburgh Press* (12 October 1944).
86. An actual Torah is much larger than the one Rosenberg shows in his painting, and because of its size and weight, it is held straight up with both hands, so that the shoulder and upper body can help to support it.
87. "Blaze of Color Marks Show of Associated Artists Here," *Pittsburgh Sun-Telegraph* (15 February 1946), 10; Norwood MacGilvary, "Associated Artists Prize Winners," *Carnegie Magazine* (March 1946), 261.
88. Margaret Breuning, "The Radiant Color of Samuel Rosenberg," *Art Digest* (1 June 1944), 11.
89. David Schnabel, letter to the author (1 October 2001). Schnabel offered the Carnegie International exhibition as one option as to why Rosenberg made his stylistic and technical shift.
90. Randolph Chalfant, response to Teaching Questionnaire (14 July 2001).
91. While Rosenberg had occasionally used egg tempera in his work of the 1930s, the technique dominates in his work of the 1940s. Masonite offered a more rigid support and its absorption rate could be more controlled.
92. Dale Stein, response to Teaching Questionnaire (19 January 2002); David Schnabel, letters to the author (14 May and 16 May 2001).
93. Bill Aiken, response to Teaching Questionnaire (5 December 2001); Rochelle Blumenfeld, telephone interview by author (23 May 2000).
94. Philip Pearlstein, untitled paper presented at the Samuel Rosenberg Symposium,

Jewish Community Center of Greater Pittsburgh (5 October 1997).

95. Salpeter, "A Human Sort of Artist," 147. According to family members, Rosenberg often repeated that he disliked the comparison of his work and Abraham Rattner's. Nearly all of the New York critics who reviewed his two solo shows at Associated American Artists Gallery made this comparison.
96. Philip Pearlstein, letter to the author in response to questions regarding his experience at Carnegie Tech (7 December 2001).
97. Louise Bruner, "Carnegie Show Gives Panorama of America's Top Rank Painters," no paper identified, no date. Scrapbook Volume II, p. 11; *New York World Telegram* (3 June 1944).
98. *Israel* was reproduced in the city's newspapers and magazines, newspapers outside the state, and national periodicals at least fifteen different times over a four-month period, from October 1945 to January 1946, and again in May 1946; D.E.G., "Two Paintings Remain," *Carnegie Magazine* (January 1946), 207; John O'Connor, Jr. "Painting in the United States, 1945," *Carnegie Magazine* (November 1945), 142; Dorothy Grafly, "The Carnegie Institute's Annual Exhibition 'Painting in the United States' Shows Melting-Pot Leaven," *Christian Science Monitor* (13 October 1945).
99. *Bulletin Index* (12 January 1946), 13. Scrapbook Volume II, p. 26; painting was illustrated.
100. Mary M. Davis, "Three Portrait Studies in Museum Exhibit," *Toledo Sunday Times* (16 June 1946) re: exhibition of *Selected American Paintings,* Thirty-third Annual, at the Toledo Museum of Art. Painting illustrated.
101. Douglas Naylor, "Saint-Gaudens Asks 'Peace' with Foes of Abstract Art," *Pittsburgh Press,* no date. Scrapbook Volume II p. 26; Douglas Naylor, "Top Artists Put on Gloves, Defend Modern Art Show," *Pittsburgh Press* (8 December 1946).
102. *The Arrow* (25 October 1945).
103. Rosenberg, with his sense of humor, preceded the written statement with "Dear Miss Seneff: And I always thought you were my friend! Sincerely, Samuel Rosenberg." Typewritten letter to Jeannette F. Seneff, *Carnegie Magazine* (5 November 1948), in response to her letter to Rosenberg of 25 October 1948. Samuel Rosenberg Archives. The question was posed at the annual dinner given by the president of Carnegie Institute honoring the jury for the fall exhibition and the responses gathered were reprinted in "After All, What Is Art?" *Carnegie Magazine* (December 1948), 161.
104. Emily Genauer, "Balloon Vendors" ("What's New," company publication of Abbott Laboratories, North Chicago, Ill. Late Winter, 1957), cover, inside cover. Abbott Laboratories purchased the painting through the Associated American Artists Gallery in New York.
105. Typewritten description of the mural from Samuel Rosenberg to Father Gubanich, St. Henry's Church, no date. Samuel Rosenberg Archives.
106. Dorothy Kantner, "St. Henry's Church: Really an 'All Pittsburgh' Job," *Pittsburgh Sun-Telegraph* (23 November 1952); "Samuel Rosenberg Wins Honor for Church Mural," *YM&WHA Weekly* (28 November 1952).
107. Rita Marlier suggests that her father and his partner Ken Johnstone commissioned Rosenberg to create murals for several Catholic churches in Pittsburgh, but the comprehensive list of the artist's work does not confirm this. Rita Marlier, response to Teaching Questionnaire (26 September 2001).
108. They were however, paid attention to by the press, in an article that describes the dramatic placement of the pieces of

African sculpture in the Rosenberg home on Mt. Royal Road. Mary O'Hara, "African Sculpture Dramatic Décor," *Pittsburgh Press* (2 May 1956). Scrapbook Volume II, p. 100.

109. Unidentified author, *Haugh & Keenan Sentinel* (February 1950). Scrapbook Volume II, p. 64.
110. Hood, "Samuel Rosenberg: Pittsburgh's Painter Laureate," 33.
111. Douglas Naylor, "Painting Features 'Vanishing Act'," *Pittsburgh Press* (12 April 1956).
112. Brem, "Artist Jams Life of Color into Exhibit," Pittsburgh artist clipping files, Carnegie Library, Art and Music Department.
113. Samuel Rosenberg, letter to Arnold J. Auerbach, Director, YM&WHA, in which the artist declined a request to be involved in a fundraising campaign for the YM&WHA (9 February 1959). Samuel Rosenberg Archives.
114. Frederick S. Wight, *Hans Hofmann* (Los Angeles: University of California Press, 1957), 54; William Chapin Seitz, *Hans Hofmann* (New York: Museum of Modern Art. 1963), 27.
115. This jury of three New York artists selected only artists who represented the New York School in an abstract expressionist style. They did not make a conscious effort to select lesser-known artists, but in the end, that is who the exhibition included. In addition, since the jurors were not from the Pittsburgh region, they were not aware of who the well-known Pittsburgh artists were, and selected objectively. Jeanette Jena, "Associated Artists Show Opening Here Tonight," *Pittsburgh Post-Gazette* (9 March 1961).
116. Allen Berkman, telephone interview by author in whose collection the painting remains. He approved of Rosenberg's "reworking," as he said it improved the colors noticeably.
117. Of the mural he painted for the Irene Kaufmann Settlement, Rosenberg said: "The painting symbolizes the spirit of the Settlement. The central figure represents the Settlement as a Mother and Neighbor, opening her arms and heart to receive, assist, and protect those who come to Her for better and greater opportunities. These opportunities of Health, Education, Culture, Music, Drama, art, etc., are shown, ready to be of service to the Neighborhood."
118. Hull House in Chicago, and the Henry Street Settlement in New York City were two other such large settlements in the United States.
119. Seventeen different nationalities were served by the IKS Nursing Service as of 1916; memberships for the year 1916–1917 totaled 2,756. Sidney Teller, *Synopsis of Social Studies of the Neighborhood of the Irene Kaufmann Settlement, 1916–1917,* 5, 13. Jewish Community Center of Greater Pittsburgh Collection, Rauh Jewish Archives of the Historical Society of Western Pennsylvania, Pittsburgh, Pa.
120. *IKS Neighbors* (10 April 1927). Irene Kaufmann Settlement papers, Jewish Community Center of Greater Pittsburgh Collection, Rauh Jewish Archives of the Historical Society of Western Pennsylvania, Pittsburgh, Pa.
121. *IKS Neighbors* (29 January 1928). Irene Kaufmann Settlement papers, Jewish Community Center of Greater Pittsburgh Collection.
122. *IKS Neighbors* (1 March 1923; 1 May 1923. Irene Kaufmann Settlement papers, Jewish Community Center of Greater Pittsburgh Collection.
123. *IKS Neighbors* (1 May 1923). Irene Kaufmann Settlement papers, Jewish Community Center of Greater Pittsburgh Collection.
124. Leonard Kessler, response to Teaching Questionnaire (29 July 2001).

125. Chalfant, Questionnaire.
126. Chalfant, Questionnaire; Rosenberg was also generous with his time with students that weren't even in his classes when a few interior design students asked him if he would instruct them in a painting class. Information provided by Katherine Kadish in telephone interview by author (18 January 2002). She said that while Rosenberg was having a class upstairs in the Department of Fine Arts, he set her and a few fellow interior design students up in a classroom downstairs and periodically came down to review their work.
127. Videotaped interview with Libbie Rosenberg by Joel B. Rosenberg in multiple sessions (16 May 1983), 6. Samuel Rosenberg Archives.
128. Jeanette Jena, "They Practice What They Teach," *Carnegie Magazine* (June 1951), 189.
129. Excerpt from class notes "Night School 1931–1932," title in Libbie's handwriting. Samuel Rosenberg Archives. Twenty typed pages illustrated with pencil drawings as examples. The artist also kept a series of mimeographed papers containing the same text but printed without the illustrations. This was most likely a class handout or assignment of exercises to be completed by Rosenberg's students.
130. *Bulletin of the Carnegie Institute of Technology 1931–32*, Description of Courses and Subjects. Department of Architecture, 138–39. Carnegie Mellon University Archives.
131. *Bulletin of the Carnegie Institute of Technology 1931–32*, 141. Carnegie Mellon University Archives.
132. Drawing I, as outlined, was listed as a prerequisite for this course. *Bulletin of the Carnegie Institute of Technology*, 142. Carnegie Mellon University Archives.
133. *Bulletin of New Appointees, Carnegie Institute of Technology Personnel Directory, 1926–1966*, Carnegie Mellon University Archives.
134. Hugh Fitzgerald, response to Teaching Questionnaire (23 June 2001) and telephone interview by author (17 August 2001); Philip Pearlstein, letter to author (7 December 2001); Ray DeFazio, telephone interview by author, (9 January 2002).
135. Winifred Carr, response to Teaching Questionnaire (8 June 2001).
136. Kessler, Questionnaire (21, July 2001).
137. Henri, *The Art Spirit*, 16.
138. David Schnabel, letter to Ruth Westerman (15 March 1998).
139. Gloria Karn, response to Teaching Questionnaire (18 August 2001).
140. David Schnabel, letter to Ruth Westerman (10 February 1998).
141. Arthur Elias, response to Teaching Questionnaire (24 November 2001).
142. It would be inaccurate not to mention the small percentage of students to whom my questionnaire on Rosenberg's teaching was sent who responded negatively to their experience with him in the mid-1940s and early 1960s. Of the 125 questionnaires sent out, only three replied with such a response. They did not, it seems, agree with his independent and informal approach and felt they received nothing from him with regard to an art education. Some thought working in cubicles was claustrophobic, and felt it was demoralizing to have no instruction. A possible explanation for this contrast to the consensus of opinion, especially in the 1960s, was that Rosenberg was nearing his retirement after forty years of teaching, and perhaps he was weary of the demands put on him by students and was becoming less and less connected to the process. As to the experience of the mid-1940s, it was a period when classes were decimated by the war and he had very few students. It is conceivable that Rosenberg did not spend all the time he might have with them as he was preparing for his second exhibition in New York during that time. Perhaps it was neither of these reasons, but that he was

continuing to teach as he always had, as more of a guide, and not an instructor.

143. DeFazio, interview.

144. Wilfred A. Readio, "The Artist's Education at Carnegie," *Carnegie Magazine* (March 1951), 101.

145. Chalfant, Questionnaire.

146. Jay Matternes, response to Teaching Questionnaire (30 August 2001).

147. Chalfant, Questionnaire.

148. He referenced two books in particular on materials and techniques: Max Doerner's *The Materials of the Artist,* and Ralph Mayer's *The Artist's Handbook of Materials and Techniques,* which he considered the best resource in this regard.

149. The majority of his students who responded to my questionnaire repeated this statement.

150. While Rosenberg's classes offered unstructured learning, the curriculum for the first two years in the Department of Fine Arts at Carnegie Tech was highly structured with a heavy emphasis on drawing, figure drawing, color theory, and design. Students spent eight hours in class, five days a week, with very few choices in elective options open to them. David Schnabel, response to Teaching Questionnaire (14 May 2001).

151. David Schnabel, letter to Ruth Westerman (28 March 1998).

152. Robert Korn, response to Teaching Questionnaire (10 September 2001).

153. Elaine Wechsler, letter to Ruth Westerman (25 February 1998).

154. Sid Navratil, class of 1941 (31 August 2001); Constantine Kermes, class of 1946 (14 June 2001); Patrick Byrne, class of 1954 (27 August 2001); Bill Aiken, class of 1955 (5 December 2001).

155. DeFazio, interview.

156. Libbie Rosenberg, letter to Andy Warhol (3 March 1977). Samuel Rosenberg Archives.

157. Stein, Questionnaire.

158. DeFazio, interview; Jane Haskell, telephone interview by author (15 May 2000).

159. Stein, Questionnaire.

160. Paralleling the development of the IKS, sixteen young men, headed by Harry Applestein, formed the Young Men's Hebrew Association in 1910. In 1919, the group merged with the Young Women's Hebrew Association to form the YM&WHA. The Kaufmann family played a significant financial and directorial role in this association as well. (Edgar J. Kaufmann would become president after Applestein's retirement.) The Y was not just a social club or institution, they taught Bible classes and other activities but their principal goal was to be a social-cultural institution that was "decidedly Jewish in every aspect." Over the years, they offered a diverse experience and a comprehensive educational program of courses in music, art, drama, business, photography, English, French, history, public speaking, sports, economics, psychology, short story writing, sociology, and dancing, among a host of others. A canteen was opened on weekends for servicemen during World War II; seminars, workshops, and a film series were held on an ongoing basis. Music and art, however, were of primary importance, and the center invited prominent speakers to give lectures, internationally known musicians to perform, and noted artist/professors to teach their slate of art classes. *YM&WHA Weekly* (10 September 1926). Irene Kaufmann Settlement papers, Jewish Community Center of Greater Pittsburgh Collection.

161. *YM&WHA Weekly* (17 August 1928). Irene Kaufmann Settlement papers, Jewish Community Center of Greater Pittsburgh Collection.

162. *YM&WHA Weekly* (8 November 1929). Irene Kaufmann Settlement papers, Jewish

Community Center of Greater Pittsburgh Collection.

163. *YM&WHA Weekly* (15 September 1950), 3. Irene Kaufmann Settlement papers, Jewish Community Center of Greater Pittsburgh Collection.
164. *YM&WHA Weekly* (8 April 1927). Irene Kaufmann Settlement papers, Jewish Community Center of Greater Pittsburgh Collection.
165. *YM&WHA Weekly* (9 March 1934), 2. Irene Kaufmann Settlement papers, Jewish Community Center of Greater Pittsburgh Collection.
166. *YM&WHA Weekly* (4 May 1934). Irene Kaufmann Settlement papers, Jewish Community Center of Greater Pittsburgh Collection. In 1927, the fee structure was different: just $2.50 per semester for a one-hour course and $5.00 per semester for a two-hour course.
167. *YM&WHA Weekly* (20 May 1949), 3. Irene Kaufmann Settlement papers, Jewish Community Center of Greater Pittsburgh Collection..
168. *YM&WHA Weekly* (11 May 1945), 1. Irene Kaufmann Settlement papers, Jewish Community Center of Greater Pittsburgh Collection.
169. *YM&WHA Weekly* (23 January 1948); *YM&WHA Weekly* (7 May 1948). Irene Kaufmann Settlement papers, Jewish Community Center of Greater Pittsburgh Collection.
170. *YM&WHA Weekly* (21 May 1948). Irene Kaufmann Settlement papers, Jewish Community Center of Greater Pittsburgh Collection.
171. *YM&WHA Weekly* (13 January 1950), 2. Irene Kaufmann Settlement papers, Jewish Community Center of Greater Pittsburgh Collection.
172. *YM&WHA Weekly* (23 November 1951). Irene Kaufmann Settlement papers, Jewish Community Center of Greater Pittsburgh Collection.
173. *YM&WHA Weekly* (23 December 1956). Irene Kaufmann Settlement papers, Jewish Community Center of Greater Pittsburgh Collection.
174. Joan Cohen, student at both Carnegie Tech and the Y, response to Teaching Questionnaire (4 September 2001).
175. Eleanor Fax, response to Teaching Questionnaire (23 July 2001).
176. Even in illness, Rosenberg was still the teacher, and made this light-hearted comment to Jane Haskell and Lois Kaufman, two of his students from his Y Workshop in the 1950s, when they visited him in the hospital. Haskell, interview.
177. Fax, Questionnaire.
178. Elizabeth McClain, Morgantown, W. Va., response to Teaching Questionnaire (18 July 2001).
179. *YM&WHA Weekly* (20 May 1960). Irene Kaufmann Settlement papers, Jewish Community Center of Greater Pittsburgh Collection.
180. *YM&WHA Weekly* (2 October 1964). Irene Kaufmann Settlement papers, Jewish Community Center of Greater Pittsburgh Collection.
181. Harris W. Sacks, "Art Concepts Grow Worldwide Asserts Professor Samuel Rosenberg," *Jewish Chronicle,* no date, 22. Scrapbook Volume II, p. 112. The article indicated that Rosenberg would continue to teach advanced students on a part-time basis when he and Libbie weren't traveling, but that would not happen.
182. Morton Rosenbaum, letter to Advanced Art Workshop Students (15 September 1964), 2. Samuel Rosenberg Archives.
183. Samuel Rosenberg, letter to Arnold J. Auerbach, Director, Y-IKC (28 May 1964). Samuel Rosenberg Archives.
184. *The Arrow* (25 October 1945), 9.
185. Philip Pearlstein, letter to author. Philip and Murray became friends and Philip went home with him from time to time. It

was from Samuel Rosenberg that Philip learned to prepare masonite panels and how to make and use egg tempera and glazes.

186. John Scull was referred to as an "art-loving local banker" by Mildred Schmertz, who offered this information about the school in her response to my Teaching Questionnaire (21 April 2001). Her mother was a student there, and her father, Robert Schmertz, who taught Architecture at Carnegie Tech, taught a watercolor class there on weekends.

187. No records have been located that indicate when exactly the school was founded and first opened, but an undated article in Libbie's scrapbook that gives information about the school is included with a number of other clippings from 1937. "New Art School Opens in Somerset," Scrapbook Volume I, p. 65. Additional newspaper clippings noted that Rosenberg was missed at the school in the summer of 1938, and was referenced as again not on the faculty in a subsequent undated article. The latter was perhaps in 1941 since that is the summer he and Libbie traveled to Mexico. Scrapbook Volume I, p. 80.

188. Douglas Naylor, "Somerset: A Painting Spot Rivalling Famous Cape Cod," *Pittsburgh Press*, no date. Scrapbook Volume I, p. 80.

189. Sam and Libbie Rosenberg, letter to Murray Z. Rosenberg, August 1963. Samuel Rosenberg Archives. Rosenberg taught at USC from June 25 through August 3, 1962, and presumably during a similar time period the following summer when he was invited to return. Edward S. Peck, Acting Head, Department of Fine Arts, letter to Samuel Rosenberg, 10 November 1961. Samuel Rosenberg Archives.

190. An unidentified critic commented on the "decline of John Kane school and the rise of a Kostellow Era and Like Rosenberg Style" in the article "Pittsburgh Art on Exhibit, Sculpture, Crafts Shown," *Pittsburgh Sun-Telegraph* (8 February 1935). Scrapbook, Vol. I, p. 30. Three years later, an unidentified author in the article "Art, International's 36th" suggested that Carnegie Tech students "may henceforth be expected to fall into a Rosenberg school of painting." *Bulletin Index* (20 October 1938); another wrote that "Samuel Rosenberg stands miles above the 'Little Rosenbergs' scattered throughout" the Associated Artists of Pittsburgh exhibition. *Bulletin Index* (16 February 1939).

191. Leon Arkus, untitled lecture presented at the Samuel Rosenberg Symposium, Jewish Community Center of Greater Pittsburgh (5 October 1997).

192. Lectures, treatises, and notes held in Samuel Rosenberg Archives.

193. Samuel Rosenberg Archives. This lecture was most likely prepared for his night school students at Carnegie Tech, but because of the problems it deals with, could easily have been used for his Drawing and Painting classes at the Y as well.

194. "U.S. Tourists Invade Mexico, Teacher Says," unidentified newspaper clipping from 1941. Scrapbook Volume I, p. 84; Murray Z. Rosenberg, "Preparatory lecture notes" for slide presentation (15 February 1981) during Samuel Rosenberg exhibition at University of Connecticut Library (25 January–6 March 1981). Samuel Rosenberg Archives.

195. Dorothy Kantner, "Rosenberg's End Trip," *Pittsburgh Sun-Telegraph* (11 September 1938). In this article, Kantner reported that Sam didn't touch a brush the entire six weeks. He did make sketches, however, that referenced many of the sites he visited, now in the collection of Carnegie Museum of Art. On their trip to Colorado, Libbie kept a journal in which she transcribed her thoughts. In one entry in

particular, she wrote how angry she got with painters like Grant Wood: "It seemed to me the greatest audacity for men who are supposed to be our leading painters to give us tinny, hard, mechanical imitations of a glowing, vibrant, pulsing like expression. Under all the apparent quiet and peace of the country lies the force and the struggle, the push and the fight to live. I said to Sam that only Van Gogh had expressed that fight. But of course, that leaves out the quality of Corot, or Turner, or Constable. By afternoon, after seeing some three hundred miles of the country at a speed of fifty per, I got less angry with Grant Wood." Journal, which includes sketches by Rosenberg, in the collection of Carnegie Museum of Art, 78.27.1.210.

196. Sam and Libbie began spending time in Somerset County as early as 1925, as noted in an unidentified clipping, (21 June 1945). Scrapbook Volume II, p. 16, 17. They stayed with friends in Shanksville, and also Fort Hill, where they visited Walter Lissfelt's farm. Sam recorded his experiences to Fort Hill in two paintings of 1940, *Walt's Place* and *Corner Walt's Place.*

197. Dorothy Kantner, *Pittsburgh Sun-Telegraph,* (1958), no title or date. Scrapbook Volume II, p. 111.

198. Howard DeVree, "A Delayed First," *New York Times* (28 May 1944); Breuning, "The Radiant Color of Samuel Rosenberg"; Emily Genauer, "Samuel Rosenberg's Style," *New York World-Telegram* (3 June 1944); Unidentified author, "The Passing Shows 'Samuel Rosenberg'," Art News (30 June 1944), 22.

199. Margaret Bruening, "Fifty-Seventh Street in Review, Rosenberg in Pittsburgh," *Art Digest* (1 January 1948).

200. Sam Hunter, "Expressionism," *New York Times* (no date) with other clippings regarding same exhibition of January 1948, in Scrapbook Volume II, p. 49; Unidentified author, "Voice of World is Put on Canvas," New York City newspaper clipping, paper not identified (January 1948). Scrapbook Volume II, p. 49.

201. B. F. Dolbin, "Samuel Rosenberg," *Aufbau—Reconstruction* (9 January 1948), 9.

202. *Nativity* was reproduced in "What's New," (#180, 1953), 14, 15. Scrapbook Volume II, p. 90.

203. Grace Pagano was Director of Fine Arts for *Encyclopedia Britannica* and wrote the biographies of all the artists for the collection catalogue. Grace Pagano, "That's Why the Collection Was Born," *Carnegie Magazine* (January 1946), 201–5; Pagano, *Encyclopedia Britannica Collection of Contemporary American Painting* (Chicago, Ill.: Encyclopedia Britannica, Inc., 1945), plate 93; Walter Read Hovey, "Pittsburgh Is Given Wide Range of Art In Britannica Group," no newspaper identified. Scrapbook Volume II, p. 63.

204. Jeanette Jena, "Rosenberg Art Exhibition Draws Record Attendance," *Pittsburgh Post-Gazette* (9 January 1950).

205. Margie Carlin, "Rosenberg . . . In Memoriam," *Pittsburgh Press* (17 September 1972), 8; Hood, "Samuel Rosenberg: Pittsburgh's Painter Laureate," 33.

206. Samuel Rosenberg quoted in Carnegie International exhibition catalog, 1964.

SELECTED BIBLIOGRAPHY

Books and Catalogs

Baigell, Matthew. *The American Scene: American Painting of the 1930s.* New York: Praeger Publishers, 1974.

Bannard, Walter Darby. *Hans Hofmann: A Retrospective Exhibition.* Houston: The Museum of Fine Arts, 1976.

Barker, Virgil. *From Realism to Reality in Recent American Painting.* Lincoln, Neb.: University of Nebraska Press, 1959.

Berman, Greta, and Jeffrey Wechsler. *Realism and Realities: The Other Side of Painting, 1940–1960.* New Brunswick, N.J.: Rutgers University Art Gallery, 1982.

Baur, John H., Lloyd Goodrich, Dorothy C. Miller, James Thrall Soby, and Frederick S. Wight. *New Art in America: Fifty Painters of the 20th Century.* Greenwich, Conn.: York Graphic Society with Praeger, Inc., 1957.

Bodnar, John E. *The Ethnic Experience in Pennsylvania.* Lewisburg, Pa.: Bucknell University Press, 1973.

———. *Lives of their Own: Blacks, Italians, and Poles in Pittsburgh, 1900–1960.* Urbana, Ill.: University of Illinois Press, 1982.

Bolden, Frank, Eliza Smith Brown, and Laurence Glasco. *A Legacy in Bricks and Mortar: African-American Landmarks in Allegheny County.* Pittsburgh: Pittsburgh History and Landmarks Foundation, 1995.

Brown, Milton. *American Painting from the Armory Show to the Depression.* Princeton, N.J.: Princeton University Press, 1955.

Bustard, Bruce I. *A New Deal for the Arts.* Washington, D.C.: National Archives and Administration in association with University of Washington Press, 1997.

Cahill, Holger. *American Art Today, New York World's Fair.* New York: National Art Society, 1939.

———. *New Horizons in American Art.* New York: Museum of Modern Art, 1936.

Cheney, Sheldon. *Expressionism in Art.* New York: Liveright Publishing Corporation, 1934.

Contreras, Belisario R. *Tradition and Innovation in New Deal Art.* Lewisburg, Pa.: Bucknell University Press, 1983.

Coode, Thomas H., and John F. Bauman. *People, Poverty, and Politics.* Lewisburg, Pa.: Bucknell University Press, 1981.

Courthion, Pierre. *Georges Rouault.* New York: Harry N. Abrams, Inc., Publishers, 1977.

Curotto, Alberto. *Rouault.* New York: Harry N. Abrams, Inc., Publishers, 1997.

Darden, Joe T. *Afro-Americans in Pittsburgh: The Residential Segregation of a People.* Lexington, Mass: Lexington Books, 1973.

Davidson, Marshall B. *The Artists' America.* New York: The American Heritage Co., Inc., McGraw-Hill Book Co., 1973.

Doezema, Marianne. *George Bellows and Urban America.* New Haven, Conn.: Yale University Press, 1992.

Doss, Erika. *Benton, Pollock, and the Politics of Modernism: From Regionalism to Abstract Expressionism.* Chicago: University of Chicago Press, 1991.

Feldman, Jacob. *The Jewish Experience in Western Pennsylvania, A History 1755–1945.* Pittsburgh:

The Historical Society of Western Pennsylvania, 1986.

Goodman, Cynthia, Clement Greenberg, and Irving Sandler. *Hans Hofmann.* New York: Whitney Museum of American Art in association with Prestel-Verlag, 1990.

Haskell, Barbara. *The American Century: Art and Culture, 1900–1950.* New York: Whitney Museum of American Art in association with W. W. Norton and Company, 1999.

Henri, Robert. *The Art Spirit.* New York: Harper and Row, Publishers, 1951.

Hills, Patricia. *Social Concern and Urban Realism: American Painting of the 1930s.* Boston: Boston University Art Gallery, 1983.

Jewell, Edward Alden. *Have We an American Art?* New York: Longmans, Green and Co., 1939.

Joachimides, Christos M., and Norman Rosenthal. *American Art in the 20th Century: Painting and Sculpture 1913–1993.* Munich, Germany: Prestel-Verlag, 1993.

Klein, Philip: *A Social Study of Pittsburgh: Community Problems and Social Services of Allegheny County.* New York: Columbia University Press, 1938.

Kuntz, Leonard Irvin. *The Changing Pattern of the Distribution of the Jewish Population of Pittsburgh from Earliest Settlement to 1963.* Ann Arbor, Mich.: University Microfilms, Inc., 1996, 42.

Larkin, Oliver. *Art and Life in America.* 2d ed. New York: Holt, Rinehart and Winston, 1960.

Lorant, Stefan. *Pittsburgh: The Story of an American City.* Garden City, N.Y.: Doubleday and Company, Inc., 1964.

McKinzie, Richard D. *The New Deal for Artists.* Princeton, N.J.: Princeton University Press, 1973.

McLanathan, Richard. *The American Tradition in the Arts.* New York: Harcourt, Brace and World, Inc., 1968.

Morgan, Charles H. *George Bellows, Painter of America.* New York: Reynal and Company, 1965.

Morganstern, Anita. *Seventy-Five Years of Pittsburgh Art, Its Influences.* Pittsburgh: Carnegie Mellon University Art Gallery, 1985.

Museum of Modern Art. *Painting and Sculpture from 16 American Cities.* New York: Museum of Modern Art, 1933.

Neal, Kenneth. *A Wise Extravagance: The Founding of the Carnegie International Exhibitions, 1895–1901.* Pittsburgh: University of Pittsburgh Press, 1996.

O'Conner, Francis V. *The New Deal Art Projects, an Anthology of Memoirs.* Washington, D.C.: Smithsonian Institution Press, 1972.

Pagano, Grace. *Encyclopedia Britannica Collection of Contemporary American Painting.* Chicago: Encyclopedia Britannica, Inc., 1945.

Perlman, Bennard B. *The Immortal Eight: American Painting from Eakins to the Armory Show (1870–1913).* New York: Exposition Press, 1962.

———. *Robert Henri: His Life and Art.* New York: Dover Publications, Inc., 1991.

Quick, Michael. *The Paintings of George Bellows.* New York: Harry N. Abrams, Inc., 1992.

Sandler, Irving. *The New York School: The Painters and Sculptors of the Fifties.* New York: Harper and Row, Publishers, 1978.

Schmeckebier, Laurence E. *John Steuart Curry's Pageant of America.* New York: American Artists Group, 1943.

Seidenberg, Mel, and Roy Stryker. *A Pittsburgh Album: 1758–1958, Two Hundred Years of Memories in Pictures and Text.* Pittsburgh: *Pittsburgh Post-Gazette,* 1959.

Seitz, William Chapin. *Hans Hofmann.* New York, Museum of Modern Art, 1963.

Sweeney, James Gray. *Themes in American Painting.* Grand Rapids, Mich.: Grand Rapids Art Museum, 1977.

Toker, Franklin. *Pittsburgh, An Urban Portrait.* State College, Pa.: Penn State University Press, 1986.

Trotter, Joe William, Jr. and Eric Ledell Smith, eds. *African-Americans in Pennsylvania: Shifting Historical Perspectives.* Harrisburg: The Pennsylvania Historical and Museum Commission and Penn State University Press, 1997.

Watson, Forbes. *American Painting Today.* New York: American Federation of Arts, Oxford University Press, 1939.

Whiting, Cecile. *Anti-Facism in American Art.* New Haven, Conn.: Yale University Press, 1989.

Wight, Frederick S. *Hans Hofmann.* Berkeley, University of California Press, 1957.

Wilkins, David G. *Reflections and Realities: Selections from the Collection of Kitty and Harold Ruttenberg.* Pittsburgh: University Art Gallery, University of Pittsburgh, 1983.

Wood, Teresa Dalla Piccola, and Mary Brignano. *The Associated Artists of Pittsburgh: 1910–1985: The First Seventy-Five Years.* Pittsburgh: Associated Artists of Pittsburgh, 1985.

Works Progress Administration, Federal Art Project. *Frontiers of American Art.* San Francisco: M. H. deYoung Memorial Museum, 1939.

Youngner, Rita, and Emily Hetzel. *The Artist Looks at Industrial Pittsburgh: 1836–1993.* Pittsburgh: University Art Gallery, University of Pittsburgh, 1993.

Articles About and Including Rosenberg

"After All, What Is Art?" *Carnegie Magazine,* December 1948, 158–63.

"Associated Artists Annual." *Carnegie Magazine,* March 1954, 83–89.

———. "Samuel Rosenberg Paintings of Pittsburgh in the Thirties." *This Week in Pittsburgh: Pittsburgh's Civic Weekly,* 5 April 1963, 13, 15.

"Biography." *Bulletin Index,* 16 March 1946, 18–20.

"Blaze of Color Marks Show of Associated Artists Here." *Pittsburgh Sun-Telegraph,* 15 February 1946.

Breuning, Margaret. "Fifty-Seventh Street in Review, Rosenberg of Pittsburgh." *Art Digest,* 1 January 1948, 19.

———. "The Radiant Color of Samuel Rosenberg." *Art Digest,* 1 June 1944, 11.

Carlin, Margaret. "At Home with Our Artists: A Place for Painting." *Pittsburgh Press,* 17 March 1968.

———. "Rosenberg . . . In Memoriam," *Pittsburgh Press,* 17 September 1972, 8.

Danver, Charles. "Street of Babel." *Pittsburgh Post-Gazette,* 10 October 1938.

Davis, Mary M. "Three Portrait Studies in Museum Exhibit." *Toledo Sunday Times,* 16 June 1946.

DeVree, Howard. "A Delayed First." *New York Times,* 28 May 1944.

Dolbin, B. F. "Samuel Rosenberg." *Aufbau—Reconstruction,* 9 January 1948.

Genauer, Emily. "Balloon Vendors." "What's New," company publication of Abbott Laboratories, North Chicago, Ill., Late Winter, 1957.

———. "Samuel Rosenberg's Style." *New York World-Telegram,* 3 June 1944.

———. "The Terrific Impact of the Moderns." *New York World-Telegram,* 26 October 1940.

Grafly, Dorothy. "The Carnegie Institute's Annual Exhibition 'Painting in the United States' Shows Melting-Pot Leaven." *Christian Science Monitor,* 13 October 1945.

Hood, Sam. "Samuel Rosenberg: Pittsburgh's Painter Laureate." *Pittsburgh Press,* 3 November 1957, 32–33.

Hollander, Lois. "Pen-Shots of Important People, Samuel Rosenberg." *Jewish Criterion,* 15 February 1935, 9, 28.

Hovey, Walter Read. "The 1944 Carnegie from the Pittsburgh Point of View." *Art News,* 15–31 October 1944, 10–13.

———. "Survey of American Painting." *Art in America,* January 1941, 39–41.

Jena, Jeanette. "Annual Carnegie Show Proves Art Has No Frontiers." *Pittsburgh Post Gazette,* 13 October 1938.

———. "Associated Artists Show Opening Here Tonight." *Pittsburgh Post-Gazette,* 9 March 1961.

———. "Rosenberg Art Exhibition Draws Record Attendance." *Pittsburgh Post-Gazette,* 9 January 1950.

———. "Striking Art Put on Exhibit at Institute: Pittsburgh Vitality is Shown in Work of Rosenberg." *Pittsburgh Post-Gazette,* 25 March 1937.

———. "They Practice What They Teach." *Carnegie Magazine,* June 1951, 189–91.

Jensen, Claude. "Art, Artists, and the Thirty-Eighth Annual Exhibition." *Carnegie Magazine,* May 1948, 233–40.

Jones, Penelope Redd. "Noted Artists in Founders Day Show." *Pittsburgh Sun-Telegraph,* 9 October 1944.

Kantner, Dorothy. "Pittsburghers Represented in Exhibit." *Pittsburgh Sun-Telegraph,* 9 October 1938.

———. "Rosenberg's End Trip," *Pittsburgh Sun-Telegraph,* 11 September 1938.

———. "St. Henry's Church: Really an 'All Pittsburgh' Job." *Pittsburgh Sun-Telegraph,* 23 November 1952.

Kostellow, Alexander J. "The Art Outlook in Pittsburgh." *Carnegie Magazine,* February 1936, 259–67.

MacGilvary, Norwood. "Comments on the Exhibition of the Associated Artists of Pittsburgh." *Carnegie Magazine,* February 1941, 259–68.

———. "Associated Artists Prize Winners." *Carnegie Magazine,* March 1946, 259–66.

Naylor, Douglas. "Art for Life's Sake." *Pittsburgh Press,* 27 July 1937, 21.

———. "Blind to Real Art." *Pittsburgh Press,* 6 January 1935, 8.

———. "Maybe You Will Call It Madness but Sober Painter of Tipsy Houses Calls Work 'Art'," *Pittsburgh Press,* 26 February 1933.

———. "Painting Features 'Vanishing Act'." *Pittsburgh Press,* 12 April 1956.

———. "Show Indicates That Most of Painters are Unaffected by War's Turmoil." *Pittsburgh Press,* 12 October 1944.

———. "Top Artists Put on Gloves, Defend Modern Art Show," *Pittsburgh Press,* 8 December 1946.

O'Connor, John, Jr. "Samuel Rosenberg, Pittsburgh Artist." *Carnegie Magazine,* April 1937, 21–23.

———. "Thirty Pittsburgh Artists." *Carnegie Magazine,* June 1941, 76–77.

———. "Painting in the United States." *Carnegie Magazine,* November 1945, 139–46.

O'Hara, Mary. "African Sculpture Dramatic Décor." *Pittsburgh* Press, 2 May 1956.

"Optimism Keynote of 30th Annual by Pittsburgh Artists." *Art Digest,* 15 February 1940, 12.

"The Painter Laureate of Pittsburgh." *Jewish Criterion,* 20 January 1950, 8.

"Painting in Pittsburgh: The Carnegie Institute Presents Its Eleventh Summer Show." *Carnegie Magazine,* June 1944, 86–87.

"The Passing Shows 'Samuel Rosenberg'." *Art News,* 30 June 1944, 22.

Readio, Wilfred. "The Artist's Education at Carnegie." *Carnegie Magazine,* March 1951, 95–98, 101.

"Rosenberg's Rosenberg." *Bulletin Index,* 14 February 1935, 8–9.

Rosenberg, Samuel. "Painting with Egg Tempera: Notes on Materials and Methods of the Mixed Technic." *Art Instruction,* September 1939, 19–22, 36.

Salpeter, Harry. "A Human Sort of Artist." *Esquire,* March 1945, 83, 146–149.

"Samuel Rosenberg." *Art News,* January 1948.

"Samuel Rosenberg Wins Honor for Church Mural," *YM&WHA Weekly,* 28 November 1952.

Stephan, Elmer. "Art Everyday." *Pittsburgh Press,* 28 November 1938.

"Two Paintings Remain." *Carnegie Magazine,* January 1946, 206–8.

"Women Jurors Pick Pittsburgh's Most Successful Local Annual." *Arts Magazine,* 1 March 1941, 12.

Articles on General and Background Information

"America at War: One Hundred Contemporary Prints now on Exhibit in 26 American Museums and Galleries," *Magazine of Art,* October 1943.

"Art: U.S. Scene." *Time: The Weekly Newsmagazine,* 24 December 1934, 24–29.

"Artists of Pittsburgh, Amid War Production, Remain Artists." *Art Digest,* 1 March 1943, 10.

Bear, Donald. "For the New York World's Fair Contemporary Art Exhibition: Two Previews." *Parnassus,* March 1939, 14–18.

Benson, E. M. "The American Scene." *Magazine of Art,* February 1934, 53–66.

Bird, Paul. "Pointing the Way." *Art Digest,* 15 October 1939, 30.

Brennan, Francis E. "Note to American Artists." *Art News,* August–September 1942.

"Business Gain Creates 2,000 Jobs Here." *Pittsburgh Post-Gazette,* 11 June 1933.

Cahill, Holger. "New York World's Fair Solemnizes the Nuptials of Art and Commerce." *Art Digest,* 1 June 1939, 16–19.

"Call 5,000 Men Back into Jobs at Steel Mills." *Pittsburgh Post-Gazette,* 10 June 1933.

"Carnegie Institute Presents Great Survey of American Painting." *Art Digest,* 1 November 1940, 4–10.

"City Ready to Begin Job Relief Program." *Pittsburgh Post-Gazette,* 5 February 1931.

"Co-operation of Landlords is Necessary," *Pittsburgh Press,* 14 April 1933.

Cortissoz, Royal. "The Whitney Biennial and Other Episodes, American Art in the Mood of Today." *New York Herald Tribune,* 2 December 1934.

De Kooning, Elaine. "Hans Hofmann Paints a Picture." *Art News,* February 1950, 38–41; 58–59.

"Family Relief Situation in Pittsburgh." *Greater Pittsburgh,* 28 March 1931.

Faust, William. "Patrons Good Naturedly Talk Over Sleeping Places at Police Stations." *Pittsburgh Press,* 19 March 1930.

Flint, Ralph. "Whitney Museum Opens Its First Biennial Show." *Art News,* 26 November 1932, 1, 4.

Frankfurter, Alfred M. "Artists for Victory Exhibition: The Paintings." *Art News,* January 1943 8–13, 31.

Gigler, Rich. "The Crash . . . 'No One Seemed to Know What Was Going On'." *Pittsburgh Press,* 7 October 1979, 6.

Gilman, Roger. "American Tastes in Painting." *Parnassus* (November 1939): 4–7.

Goldwater, Robert. "A Symposium: The State of American Art." *Magazine of Art,* March 1949, 83–86, 90–92.

Grafly, Dorothy. "The Whitney Museum's Biennial." *American Magazine of Art,* January 1933, 5–12.

Gutheim, F. A. "American Art: A Geographic Interpretation." *Magazine of Art,* May 1935, 262–69.

Hine, Al. "Pittsburgh." *Holiday* (October 1949): 34–38, 50–51.

Hopkins, Kenneth R. "Some Factors in the Discontinuance of Participation of selected Junior-Age Negro Boys in the Program of Irene Kaufmann Settlement." Masters thesis, University of Pittsburgh, 1952.

Hovey, Walter Reed. "Exhibitions: Survey of American Painting." *Art in America,* January 1941, 39–41.

"Is Today's Artist with or against the Past?" *Art News,* Summer 1958, 26–31.

Jewell, Edward Alden. "Art in Review: Painting and Sculpture from 16 American Cities on Display at Museum of Modern Art." *New York Times,* 12 December 1933, 28.

———. "Government Takes a Hand—Work from Sixteen Cities at Modern Art Museum." *New York Times,* 17 December 1933, 12.

Kistler, Aline. "We Are What We Are—." *American Magazine of Art,* October 1935, 612–21.

Kovacic, Kristin. "Being Pittsburgh." *Pittsburgh Post-Gazette,* 24 March 1999, Op-Ed Page.

Landau, Ellen G. "'A Certain Rightness': Artists for Victory's 'America in the War' Exhibition of 1943." *Arts Magazine,* February 1986, 43–53.

Lane, James W. "This Year the Carnegie National: Pittsburgh's Brilliant Survey of 160 Years of U.S. Painting." *Art News,* Special Issue, 26 October 1940, 6–18.

Love, Gilbert. "Applicants Near Starvation in Many Cases." *Pittsburgh Press,* 14 October 1938.

———. "Black Skies Take District Out of the Red Once More." *Pittsburgh Press,* 24 September 1939.

Mangravite, Peppino. "The American Painter and His Environment." *American Magazine of Art,* April 1935, 198–203.

McCausland, Elizabeth. "Living American Art." *Parnassus,* May 1939, 16–25.

McKinney, Roland J. "American Art at San Francisco." *Magazine of Art,* March 1939, 152–61; 184–87.

Motherwell, Robert. "The Painter and the Audience." *Perspectives USA,* Autumn 1954, 107–13.

Nichols, Bervard. "Pittsburgh Escapes Worst of Slump." *Greater Pittsburgh,* 28 March 1931.

O'Conner, John, Jr. "Presenting the American Scene." *Carnegie Magazine,* February 1936, 274–78.

Ostendorf, Kristen. "Women Mine Memories from Life in a Coal Patch," *Pittsburgh Post-Gazette,* 19 August 1999.

Pagano, Grace. "That's Why the Collection Was Born." *Carnegie Magazine,* January 1946, 201–5.

Phillips, Duncan. "The Arts in Wartime." *Art News,* September 1942, 20, 23, 45.

"Plants Here Get Millions in Contracts." *Pittsburgh Press,* 12 July 1931.

Power, Edward M. "Rediscovering Pittsburgh's Treasures: 17—Our Wonder of the Hill District." *Greater Pittsburgh,* February 1932, 25–26.

Price, Matlack. "2224 War Posters: A Review of the National War Poster Competition." *American Artist,* December 1942, 4–11, 40.

"The Public Works of Art Project." *Carnegie Magazine,* January 1934, 245–46.

Readio, Wilfred A. "The Associated Artists of Pittsburgh." *Carnegie Magazine,* February 1931, 259–63.

Saint-Gaudens, Homer. "Exhibition of Paintings by Pittsburgh Artists." *Carnegie Magazine,* May–June 1933, 38–43.

Schofield, Paul. "Chicago Annual." *Parnassus,* December 1935, 24–25.

Schwartz, Jane. "Whitney Museum Is Now Holding Second Biennial." *Art News,* 1 December 1934, 6.

"Steel Mills Hum at Boom Tempo to Meet Demand." *Pittsburgh Post-Gazette,* 9 October 1939.

"Teaching the Student Artist." *Carnegie Magazine,* June 1933, 84–88.

"This is Shantytown, What Are You Going to Do About It?" *Bulletin Index,* 24 September 1931.

Venturi, Lionello. "Rouault." *Parnassus,* October 1939, 4–13.

Watson, Forbes. "The Land of the Free." *Magazine of Art,* November 1940, 610–23.

Wellman, Rita. "Pioneers and Contemporaries." *Parnassus,* January 1934, 11–13.

"'What Can I Do?" *Magazine of Art,* January 1942, 3.

Whiting, Philippa. "Speaking About Art." *American Magazine of Art,* March 1935, 106.

———. "Speaking About Art." *American Magazine of Art,* September 1935, 556–60.

"The Whitney's Second Biennial." *The American Magazine of Art,* January 1935, 44–48.

Wolfe, Jacqueline Welch. "The Changing Pattern of Residence of the Negro in Pittsburgh, Pennsylvania, with Emphasis on the Period 1930–1960." Masters thesis, University of Pittsburgh, 1964.

Unpublished Sources

Carnegie Library, Pittsburgh, Pa. Art and Music Department. Pittsburgh artist clipping files. Pennsylvania Department: Pittsburgh Depression, Hill District, Terrace Village, clipping and photographic files.

Carnegie Museum of Art, Pittsburgh, Pa. Samuel Rosenberg file.

Carnegie Mellon University Archives, Pittsburgh, Pa. University records of faculty, students, courses offered; *Bulletin of the Carnegie Institute of Technology.*

Chatham College Archives, Pittsburgh, Pa. Pennsylvania College for Women Bulletins and PCW Newsletters, *The Arrow*, 1937–1945.

Jewish Community Center of Greater Pittsburgh Collection, Rauh Jewish Archives of the Historical Society of Western Pennsylvania, Pittsburgh, Pa. Irene Kaufmann Settlement Papers. *IKS Neighbors*, 1920s. *YM&WHA Weekly*, 1920s–1960s.

Museum of Modern Art Library, New York, N.Y. Samuel Rosenberg Artist File.

Samuel Rosenberg Archives, Asheville, N.C. Scrapbooks of Libbie Rosenberg, volumes I and II. Videotaped interview with Libbie Rosenberg (16 May 1983) by Joel B. Rosenberg in multiple sessions. Letters of Murray Z. Rosenberg. Correspondence of Samuel Rosenberg and Libbie Rosenberg and miscellaneous, uncataloged papers.

University of Pittsburgh Library System Archives, Pittsburgh, Pennsylvania. Archives of Industrial Society. Oliver M. Kaufmann Photo Collection of the Irene Kaufmann Settlement, 1912–1969. Videotaped interview with Libbie Rosenberg (13 November 1983) for the National Council of Jewish Women.

United States Holocaust Memorial Museum Reference Library, Washington, D.C. Data obtained through telephone conversation as well as through the Museum's Web site.

Whitney Museum of American Art Library, New York, N.Y. Samuel Rosenberg Artist File.